Shelter

D0550332

Help with Housing Costs:

Universal Credit and Council Tax Rebates

2016-17

Sam Lister and Martin Ward

Help With Housing Costs: Guide to Universal Credit and Council Tax Rebates
Sam Lister and Martin Ward, 2014-17

Sam Lister is policy and practice officer at the Chartered Institute of Housing
(email: sam.lister@cih.org) and a founding director of Worcester
Citizens Advice Bureau and Whabac. He has specialised in
housing benefit and social security since 1993.

Martin Ward is an independent consultant and trainer on housing and
benefit related matters *(e-mail: mward@knowledgeflow.org.uk)*.
He has provided consultancy services and training for several
national organisations as well as many local authorities and large
and small housing providers across the UK since 1982.

Copyright © 2014-17
(for full details please contact the publishers)

The authors each assert the moral right to be
recognised as an author of this work

ISBN 978-0-9934984-0-4

Edited and typeset by Davies Communications
(www.daviescomms.com)

Printed by The Russell Press Ltd, Nottingham
(www.russellpress.com)

Chartered Institute of Housing

The Chartered Institute of Housing (CIH) is the independent voice for housing and the home of professional standards.

Our goal is simple – we want to provide everyone involved in housing with the advice, support and knowledge they need to be brilliant.

Chartered Institute of Housing
Octavia House
Westwood Way
Coventry
CV4 8JP

Telephone: 024 7685 1700
E-mail: *customer.services@cih.org*
Web site: *www.cih.org*

Shelter

Shelter helps over a million people a year struggling with bad housing or homelessness – and we campaign to prevent it in the first place.

We're here so no-one has to fight bad housing or homelessness on their own.

Please support us at *shelter.org.uk*

For more information about Shelter, please contact:

88 Old Street
London
EC1V 9HU

Tel: 0300 330 1234
shelter.org.uk

For help with your housing problems, phone Shelter's free housing advice helpline on 0808 800 4444 (open from 8am to 8pm on Mondays to Fridays and from 8am to 5pm on weekends: calls are free from UK landlines and main mobile networks) or visit *shelter.org.uk/advice*

Contents

Preface

This guide explains universal credit and council tax rebates, focusing on help with housing costs. It gives the rules which apply from 1st April 2016, using information available on 15th May 2016.

We welcome comments and criticisms on the contents of our guide and make every effort to ensure it is accurate. However, the only statement of the law is found in the relevant Acts, regulations, orders and rules (chapter 1).

This guide has been written with the help and encouragement of many other people. We wish to thank the following in particular:

Marion Conlon, Jonathan Reid, Martin Scott, Niki Walton, John Zebedee, Linda Davies and Peter Singer (editing and production) as well as staff from the Department for Work and Pensions and the Rent Service. Their help has been essential to the production of this guide.

Sam Lister and Martin Ward

May 2016

List of tables

Table		Page

Abbreviations

The principal abbreviations used in the guide are given below.

ADM	Advice for Decision Makers (DWP manual)
CTC	Child tax credit
CTR	Council tax rebate
DCLG	The Department for Communities and Local Government
DLA	Disability Living Allowance
DWP	The Department for Work and Pensions in Great Britain
ESA	Employment and support allowance
ESA(C)	Contributory employment and support allowance
ESA(IR)	Income-related employment and support allowance
GB	England, Scotland and Wales
HB	Housing benefit
HMRC	Her Majesty's Revenue and Customs
HMCTS	Her Majesty's Courts and Tribunals Service
IB	Incapacity benefit
IS	Income support
JSA	Jobseeker's allowance
JSA(C)	Contribution-based jobseeker's allowance
JSA(IB)	Income-based jobseeker's allowance
LCW	Limited capability for work
LCWRA	Limited capability for work and work-related activity
LHA	Local housing allowance
NISR	Northern Ireland Statutory Rules
PIP	Personal independence payment
SAR	Second adult rebate
SDA	Severe disablement allowance
SI	Statutory instrument
SMI	Support for Mortgage Interest
SPC	State pension credit
SSI	Scottish Statutory Instrument
UC	Universal credit
UK	England, Scotland, Wales and Northern Ireland
WTC	Working tax credit

Key to footnotes

For further information about footnotes see para 1.30.

AA	The Social Security Administration Act 1992
art	Article number
C&P	The Universal Credit, Personal Independence Payment, Jobseeker's Allowance and Employment and Support Allowance (Claims and Payments) Regulations 2013, SI No. 380
CTP	The Council Tax Reduction Schemes (Prescribed Requirements) (England) Regulations 2012, SI No. 2885
CTPW	The Council Tax Reduction Scheme and Prescribed Requirements (Wales) Regulations 2013, SI No. 3029
CTR	The Council Tax Reduction Schemes (Default Scheme) (England) Regulations 2012, SI No. 2886
CTRW	The Council Tax Reduction Schemes (Default Scheme) (Wales) Regulations 2013, SI No. 3035
CTS	The Council Tax (Scotland) Regulations 2012, SI No. 303
CTS60+	The Council Tax Reduction (State Pension Credit) (Scotland) Regulations 2012, SI No. 319
D&A	The Universal Credit, Personal Independence Payment, Jobseeker's Allowance and Employment and Support Allowance (Decisions and Appeals) Regulations 2013, SI No. 381
DDO	The Council Tax (Discount Disregards) Order 1992, SI 1992 No. 548
DDR	The Council Tax (Additional Provisions for Discount Disregards) Regulations 1992, SI 1992 No. 552
EEA	The Immigration (European Economic Area) Regulations 2006, SI No. 1003
FTPR	The Tribunal Procedure (First-tier Tribunal) (Social Entitlement Chamber) Rules 2008, SI No. 2685
LGFA	The Local Government Finance Act 1992
NIUC	The Universal Credit Regulations (Northern Ireland) 2016, NISR 2016 No. 216
NIWRO	The Welfare Reform (Northern Ireland) Order 2015, SI 2015 No. 2006 (NI1)
OP Regs	The Social Security (Overpayments and Recovery) Regulations 2013, SI No. 384
para	Paragraph number
POA	The Social Security (Payments on Account of Benefit) Regulations 2013, SI No. 383

reg	Regulation number
s	Section number
sch	Schedule number
SI	Statutory instrument [year and reference number]
SSA	Social Security Act 1998
TCEA	Tribunals, Courts and Enforcement Act 2007
UC	The Universal Credit Regulations 2013, SI No. 376
UCTP	The Universal Credit (Transitional Provisions) Regulations 2014, SI No. 1230
UTPR	The Tribunal Procedure (Upper Tribunal) Rules 2008, SI No. 2698
WRA	The Welfare Reform Act 2012

Chapter 1 **Introduction**

- Summary of universal credit: see paras 1.6-9.
- Summary of council tax rebate: see paras 1.10-12.
- The UC transitional rules and national expansion: see paras 1.13-25.
- Using this guide: see paras 1.26-30.
- Law and guidance: see paras 1.31-36.

1.1 Welcome to this guide, which explains the new system of getting help with your housing costs. The guide is for people claiming benefit, their landlords and mortgage lenders, advisers and those making decisions.

1.2 Universal credit (UC) helps you pay your rent, mortgage interest or similar payments. It also helps you with your basic living needs. It is being introduced in stages, so does not yet apply throughout the UK.

1.3 Council tax rebate (CTR) helps you pay your council tax. It applies throughout Great Britain but the details vary between England, Scotland and Wales and in England and Wales from one area to another.

1.4 If you live in an area where UC does not yet apply, you can get help with your rent (and/or rates in Northern Ireland) from housing benefit (HB). See the *Guide to Housing Benefit 2016-17*, which is the companion to this guide.

1.5 The rules in this guide apply from 11th April 2016. The next edition will give the rules from 10th April 2017. For basic definitions of the main terminology in this guide, see table 1.1.

Examples: Help with housing costs: UC and CTR

1. A single tenant

A single person rents her home. She claims UC and CTR and meets the conditions for them.

- She gets UC towards her living needs and her rent.
- She gets CTR towards her council tax.

2. A home owner couple

A couple are buying their home on a mortgage. They claim UC and CTR and meet the conditions for them.

- They get UC towards their living needs and their mortgage interest.
- They get CTR towards their council tax.

Table 1.1 **UC and CTR terminology**

Claimant (UC and CTR)

A claimant is someone who is making a claim (in CTR law called an 'application') for UC/CTR or someone who is getting UC/CTR.

Joint claimant (UC)

If you are claiming UC as a couple you are joint claimants. In CTR one of you is the claimant (in CTR law you are called the 'applicant'), but the claim covers you both.

Couple (UC and CTR)

You are a couple if you are two people who are married, in a civil partnership, or living together as a couple.

Single person (UC)

In UC you are a single person if you are not in a couple or not claiming as a couple (whether or not you have children or young persons).

Single claimant and lone parent (CTR)

In CTR you are a single claimant if you are not in a couple and have no children or young persons, or a lone parent if you are not in a couple and have one or more children or young persons.

Benefit unit (UC) and family (CTR)

In UC your benefit unit means the people you are claiming for. In CTR law this is called your family.

Child and young person (UC and CTR)

A child is someone aged under 16. A young person is someone aged 16 to 19 who is in or has recently left secondary education.

Working age and pension age (UC and CTR)

You are working age if you are under state pension credit (SPC) age. You are pension age if you have reached SPC age. During this benefit year (2016-17) SPC age is rising from 63 to 63¾.

Assessment period (UC)

UC is calculated on a monthly basis. Each monthly period is called an assessment period. Your first assessment period begins on the day your UC starts (this can be any date in the month) and the following ones start on the same date each month.

Benefit week (CTR)

CTR is calculated on a weekly basis. Each weekly period is called a benefit week (in CTR law it is called a 'reduction week'). Benefit weeks always begin on a Monday.

Maximum UC, allowances and elements (UC)

The calculation of your UC is based on your income and capital and your maximum UC. Your maximum UC is made up of a standard allowance and other elements you qualify for, including a housing costs element.

Maximum CTR, applicable amount, personal allowances, premiums and components (CTR)

The calculation of your CTR is based on your income and capital, your maximum CTR and your applicable amount. Your maximum CTR is the weekly amount of your council tax. Your applicable amount is made up of the personal allowances, premiums and components you qualify for.

Housing costs element (UC)

In UC the housing costs element is the part of your maximum UC which is for your housing costs. You can get a housing costs element whether you are a renter, owner-occupier or shared owner.

Eligible council tax (CTR)

In CTR your eligible council tax is the weekly amount of council tax you are liable to pay.

Housing cost contributions (UC) and non-dependant deductions (CTR)

If you have one or more non-dependants they may be expected to contribute towards your UC housing costs and/or your council tax. In UC this is called a housing cost contribution. In CTR it is called a non-dependant deduction.

Non-dependant (UC and CTR)

A non-dependant is an adult son, daughter, or other relative or friend who lives with you on a non-commercial basis.

Renter and tenant (UC and CTR)

Renter (mainly in UC) and tenant (mainly in CTR) both mean someone who is liable to pay rent (including for example a licensee).

Owner and shared owner (UC and CTR)

Owner means someone who owns or is buying their home. Shared owner means someone who is part renting and part buying their home.

DWP and Secretary of State (UC)

The DWP (Department for Work and Pensions) deals with claims for UC in Great Britain. The DFC (Department for Communities) will deal with claims for UC in Northern Ireland.

Authority (CTR)

An authority means any local council that issues bills for council tax and deals with claims for CTR.

The UC scheme

1.6   The key features of the UC scheme are as follows:

(a) UC is for working age claimants who meet the various conditions of entitlement: see chapter 2;

(b) it can help meet your living costs and housing costs: see paras 1.7-8;

(c) you claim UC from the DWP or DFC: see para 1.9;

(d) in the longer term it will apply throughout the UK;

(e) currently you must be in a particular area at the time of your UC claim: see paras 1.14-16;

(f) UC replaces several other social security benefits: see paras 1.18-20.

The amount of your UC

1.7   Depending on your financial and other circumstances, you can get UC towards:

(a) your basic living needs; and

(b) your housing costs.

The amount of your UC takes into account whether you have a partner and/or children or young persons who live with you. It also takes into account whether you have limited capability for work, are a carer, and/or have childcare costs. For further details see chapters 2, 9 and 10.

UC for housing costs

1.8   UC includes a 'housing costs element' which can help you pay any of the following:

(a) your rent (for exceptions see para 1.17);

(b) your mortgage interest or similar costs;

(c) your service charges.

In each case there are limits to how much you can get. Also the amount towards your rent can be reduced if you have one or more non-dependants living with you. And you cannot get help with your mortgage interest or similar costs if you have any kind of earned income. For further details see chapters 3 to 8.

How to get UC

1.9   To get UC, you make a claim to:

(a) the DWP (Department for Work and Pensions) in the areas of Great Britain where UC applies (para 1.14);

(b) the DFC (Department for Communities) in Northern Ireland once UC is introduced there (para 1.24).

If you are claiming UC as a couple you make a joint claim. UC is a monthly benefit based on 'assessment periods' which begin on the same day each month. It is paid to you at the end of each assessment period, or in some cases to your landlord or mortgage lender. If you are overpaid you may have to repay it. You can ask the DWP to reconsider your UC if you think it is wrong, and appeal to an independent tribunal. For further details see chapters 3 and 11 to 14.

The CTR scheme

1.10 The key features of the CTR scheme are as follows:

(a) CTR is for claimants of any age who meet the various conditions of entitlement: see chapters 15 and 16;

(b) it can help meet your council tax: see para 1.11;

(c) you claim CTR from your local authority: see para 1.12;

(d) it applies throughout Great Britain, but the details vary in England, Scotland and Wales, and in England and Wales from local authority area to area: see chapter 16;

(e) CTR was introduced on 1st April 2013, when it replaced council tax benefit.

The assessment of CTR

1.11 CTR can help you pay your council tax. How much you get depends on your financial and other circumstances:

(a) you get maximum CTR if you are on a passport benefit (JSA(IB), ESA(IR), IS or guarantee credit of SPC), and also if your only income is from UC;

(b) you can get CTR in other circumstances, for example if you receive other income as well as UC.

The amount you get can be reduced if you have one or more non-dependants living with you. For further details see chapters 17 and 18.

How to get CTR

1.12 To get CTR, you make a claim to the local authority that sends your council tax bill. If you are in a couple your claim covers both of you. CTR is a daily benefit, though most of the calculation rules are based on 'benefit weeks' (in the law called 'reduction weeks'). It is awarded as a credit to your council tax bill, so you have less council tax to pay. If you are overpaid you may have to repay it. You can ask your local authority to reconsider your CTR if you think it is wrong, and appeal to an independent tribunal. For further details see chapters 19 to 21.

The UC transitional rules in Great Britain

1.13 UC does not yet apply to all claimants in Great Britain who meet the basic conditions of entitlement. The rules about who can get UC now (the 'transitional rules'), and their key features are as follows:

(a) you must be in one of the prescribed postcodes and either meet the gateway conditions (para 1.16) when you claim (these postcodes are now called 'live service' areas) or be in one of the at present smaller number of postcodes where the 'UC full service' (former 'digital service') is in operation: see paras 1.14-16;

(b) you can get HB on specified supported accommodation while you are on UC: see para 1.17;

(c) but you cannot get HB in other cases, or in some cases other social security benefits: see paras 1.18-20.

To get UC you must also meet the basic conditions of entitlement described in chapter 2. Table 1.2 identifies the number of claimants getting UC between May 2013 and April 2016.

Table 1.2 **Numbers on UC (May 2013-April 2016)**

	Number of people on UC
May 2013	100
December 2013	3,780
May 2014	6,570
December 2014	26,940
May 2015	64,938
December 2015	175,505
April 2016	247,801

■ Source: DWP, Universal credit – experimental statistics [www].

Introduction and roll out of UC

1.14   UC is being introduced in stages. During the first year (from 29th April 2013) the 'pathfinder' conditions applied to all claims. The pathfinder conditions restricted who could apply to a group of claimants (mainly single people actively looking for work) who lived in specific postcodes (pathfinder areas). From June 2014 'gateway' conditions began to be used to control entitlement to UC in new postcodes. These were similar to the original pathfinder conditions but have been changed over time to allow claims from couples and people with children in some areas. Also, in response to the IT challenge involved in the introduction of the benefit, from November 2014 the DWP began to experiment with a 'twin track' method of administration. 'Live services' continue using the original IT systems and procedures but a limited number of 'digital service' areas (now known as 'full service' areas) were introduced to test new IT and aspects of administration. In these areas the gateway conditions do not apply and your on-going contact with the DWP should be online/electronic rather than in writing. Some of the main rules of the UC scheme are different in these 'full service' areas from those that apply in the 'live service' areas (Memo ADM 26/14).

1.15.   As of 1st May 2016 every Jobcentre Plus office in Great Britain is 'UC live' for single people looking for work. In a number of Jobcentre Plus offices UC is also live for new claims by couples and families [www]. As at April 2016 the UC 'full service' was in operation in specified postcodes in Sutton, Croydon, London Bridge, Hounslow, Musselburgh, Purley, Thornton Heath and Great Yarmouth [www]. The postcodes included in the 'full service' are due to increase from May 2016 onwards incrementally expanding to cover Great Britain over a two year period and replacing the 'live services' for existing claimants.

T1.2   www.gov.uk/government/collections/universal-credit-statistics

1.14   SI 2014/2887

1.15   www.gov.uk/guidance/jobcentres-where-you-can-claim-universal-credit
         www.gov.uk/apply-universal-credit

The gateway conditions

1.16 The gateway conditions can vary from one 'live service' area to another. In most cases (at the time of writing), the main gateway conditions are that you – and your partner if you are claiming UC as a couple – must:

(a) be aged 18 or more but not over 60½;

(b) have a bank (or credit union) account;

(c) have a national insurance number;

(d) be fit for work;

(e) not have earned income over £338 (£525 for a couple) per month;

(f) not have capital over £6,000;

(g) not be on ESA, JSA, IS, IB, SDA, DLA or PIP;

(h) not be self-employed or a company director;

(i) not be a carer, a student or a recent migrant;

(j) not be in supported accommodation, or homeless;

(k) not (in most areas) be an owner-occupier or shared owner;

(l) not (in some areas) have children or young persons, or be pregnant, or be a foster parent.

These conditions are expected to change, making UC available to more people. In some pathfinder areas, more detailed information is available online [www].

Housing benefit for specified supported accommodation

1.17 If you are entitled to UC, you can get HB if you live in 'specified supported accommodation'. Table 4.2 lists all the kinds of specified supported accommodation and further details are in paras 4.11-14. In these cases your UC is awarded only for your living costs. For HB in other cases see paras 1.18-20.

The replacement of existing benefits

1.18 In the longer term UC will completely replace the following social security benefits. They are called existing benefits in UC law:

(a) housing benefit (HB), but see para 1.17 for specified supported accommodation;

(b) income-based JSA (JSA(IB));

(c) income-related ESA (ESA(IR));

(d) income support (IS);

(e) child tax credit (CTC); and

(f) working tax credit (WTC).

While these continue to exist, the rules in paras 1.19-21 apply.

Claims for existing benefits

1.19 You cannot make a claim for any of the existing benefits (para 1.18) if you:

(a) are in a 'UC full service' area (para 1.13) – whether or not you have claimed UC; or

(b)   are in a 'UC live' area (para 1.16) and are on UC, or have claimed it and are waiting for a decision about it; or

(c)   were getting UC within the past six months, but did not qualify because you began to receive earned income or your earned income increased; or

(d)   claimed UC within the past six months, but did not qualify because of the level of your earned income.

This rule does not apply to HB for specified supported accommodation (para 1.17), but does apply to HB in other cases. (If (c) or (d) apply to you, see also paras 3.6-7.)

1.20   If you are already on an existing benefit, you can continue getting it as follows:

(a)   if you claim UC, until the day before your UC starts; or

(b)   if you become a couple with someone already on UC, until the end of your first UC assessment period as a couple; or

(c)   if earlier (in either of the above cases), until the existing benefit ends under the rules for that benefit.

This rule does not apply to HB for specified supported accommodation (para 1.17), but does apply to HB in other cases. (If (b) applies to you, see also para 3.5.)

If the right to claim UC is withdrawn

1.21   The DWP can withdraw the right to claim UC:

(a)   in any area of Great Britain; and/or

(b)   from any category of claimant,

in order to enable the efficient testing or administration of the UC scheme. If this applies to you, you can claim any of the existing benefits in para 1.18.

JSA(C)/ESA(C) and UC

1.22   Contributory JSA and contribution-based ESA continue as benefits separate from UC. You can get UC while you are on JSA(C) or ESA(C), but they count as income when your UC is calculated (table 10.3). In the longer term JSA(C) is renamed JSA and ESA(C) is renamed ESA. In the law they are also called 'new style' JSA and ESA.

State pension credit and UC

1.23   You can't get SPC and UC at the same time:

(a)   you can get UC if you are under SPC age (see para 2.10), or are in a couple and at least one of you is;

(b)   you can get SPC if you are over SPC age, or are in a couple and at least one of you is;

(c)   so if you are in a 'mixed age' couple (one under SPC age, one over it) you can choose between claiming UC or SPC – but while you are on UC you can't claim SPC.

1.21   UCTP 4, 5(1)

1.22   UCTP 2(1) definitions

1.23   WRA 34, sch 4; SI 2015/1529; NIWRO 40, sch 4

If you are an owner your SPC helps meet your housing costs. If you are a renter you can get HB as well as SPC. In the longer term, the government plans to include a new 'housing credit' in SPC that will help meet the housing costs of both owners and renters. This is expected to be similar to the UC housing costs element.

Introduction of UC in Northern Ireland

1.24 The government plans to introduce UC in Northern Ireland in 2017. The law governing the UC scheme in Northern Ireland is the Welfare Reform (Northern Ireland) Order SI 2015/2006, which is made using powers under the Northern Ireland (Welfare Reform) Act 2015. But (at the time of writing) further statutory rules are needed giving the details relating to housing costs and other matters.

1.25 Most of the rules described in the rest of this guide are expected to apply in the same way in Northern Ireland – including the abolition of HB and other existing benefits over a period of time – but the transitional rules may differ.

Using this guide

1.26 The UC and CTR rules in this guide apply from April 2016. For UC changes during 2013 to 2016, see table 1.3.

UC and CTR benefit figures

1.27 The UC figures in this guide apply from 11th April 2016 (the first Monday in the tax year) and the CTR figures apply from 1st April 2016. Most of the figures aren't increased this year. In UC the only increase is to the childcare costs element (para 9.37 and table 9.2) and the work allowance is for many claimants reduced or abolished (para 10.15 and table 10.1). The government plans to freeze most working age benefit rates for a further three years until April 2020 (Summer Budget 2015).

UC and CTR terminology

1.28 Table 1.1 summarises the main terms used in this guide, and shows the similarities and the differences between those used in UC and in CTR.

Abbreviations and footnotes

1.29 The tables at the front of this guide give:

  (a) a list of abbreviations used in the text; and

  (b) a key to the abbreviations used in the footnotes.

1.30 The footnotes throughout this guide refer to UC and CTR law (see paras 1.31 and 1.33). All the references are to the law as amended. CTR law is different in England, Scotland and Wales – the footnotes give the law for England (except where the paragraph relates only to Scotland or Wales). The equivalent footnotes for the law in Scotland and Wales are in appendix 4.

Table 1.3 **UC introduction and changes: key dates**

29 Apr 2013 SI 2013/376 SI 2013/983	The 'first stage of the transition to UC' begins with UC limited to single people. The first UC area is Ashton-under-Lyne, with more following later (para 1.14).
28 Oct 2013 SI 2013/2070	The benefit cap begins to apply in UC (para 9.57).
4 Dec 2013 SI 2013/2827 SI 2013/2828	Changes to UC size criteria to allow a bedroom for a disabled child who cannot share one (para 7.24).
28 Apr 2014 SI 2014/597	Changes to the UC bereavement run-on so that it applies following the death of a non-dependant (see para 11.36).
16 Jun 2014 SI 2014/1230	The 'second stage of the transition to UC' begins.
28 Jul 2014 SI 2014/1661 SI 2014/1923	UC is extended to couples in some areas. All UC claimants must meet the gateway conditions (paras 1.15-16).
3 Nov 2014 SI 2014/771 SI 2014/1626	Changes so that people in all types of specified supported accommodation (table 4.2) can get HB for their housing costs, and UC for their living costs only.
26 Nov 2014 SI 2014/2887	Amended main UC rules in 'digital service' (now 'full service') areas relating to claims from new and former couples, assessment periods, childcare costs and unearned income.
26 Nov 2014 SI 2014/2888	The amount of UC that can be paid to a landlord increases (para 12.33). Other miscellaneous changes.
8 Jan 2015 SI 2014/3126	The national maximum LHA amounts increase affecting individual claimants from 6th April 2015 (table 6.1 and para 6.18).
16 Feb 2015 SI 2015/101	The 'first phase of the national expansion of UC' begins for single people.
2 Mar 2015 SI 2015/32	UC is extended to people with children in some areas.
10 Jun 2015 SI 2015/546	EEA nationals whose only right to reside is as a jobseeker are no longer entitled to UC (para 2.34).
3 Aug 2015 SI 2015/1362	Waiting days are introduced so that many claimants don't get UC for the first seven days (paras 3.33-36).
2 Nov 2015 SI 2015/1753	LHA figures are frozen at April 2015 levels for four years (Summer Budget 2015). But if in any year the rent officer calculates that a lower figure applies, it affects individual claimants from the first Monday in the tax year (para 6.18).

4 Nov 2015 SI 2015/1754	Waiting days stop applying to former care-leavers aged under 22 (para 3.27). Changes ensure only one person can get the carer element (and/or carer's allowance) for caring for the same person (para 9.28). The earned income thresholds change from monthly to weekly amounts (paras 9.22, 10.80 etc).
16 Nov 2015 SI 2015/1780	People can no longer get 'existing benefits' if they claimed or received UC with earned income in the last six months (para 1.20).
1 Apr 2016 SI 2015/1647	The qualifying period for getting UC towards owner-occupier payments increases from three to nine monthly assessment periods, except for periods that began before 1st April 2016 (para 8.18).
11 Apr 2016 SI 2015/1649	The work allowance is restricted to people with children/young persons and/or with limited capability for work, and in many cases also reduced (paras 10.13-15 and table 10.1).
11 Apr 2016 SI 2015/1754	The childcare element increases. The percentage of costs it meets rises from 70% to 85% and the maximum amount rises (para 9.37 and table 9.2).

Planned changes

- During 2016, all areas of Great Britain and some areas in Northern Ireland become UC live areas. In these UC live areas the gateway conditions apply and only certain groups of claimant can claim UC. Starting in May 2016, some 'live service' areas in Great Britain become 'full service' areas – where anyone can claim UC (see paras 1.14-16).

- During 2016-18, the gradual conversion of all areas in Great Britain to full service areas.

- From autumn 2016, exempting everyone on carer's allowance, the carer element of UC or guardian's allowance from the benefit cap (table 9.7).

- During 2016-17, the phasing in of a reduced benefit cap (para 9.58).

- From April 2017 for new UC claims only: the removal of many 18-21 year olds' entitlement to a housing costs element (para 4.84); the restriction of the child element to two children/young persons and reduction of the 'first child' rate (para 9.15); and the reduction of the LCW element to nil (para 9.19).

- From 2017, the extension of the UC scheme to Northern Ireland (paras 1.24-25).

- From April 2018, making payments towards owner-occupiers' housing costs as a loan rather than an award of benefit (para 8.7).

- During 2018-21, the gradual transfer of claimants on existing benefits to UC (para 1.18), with transitional protection of some kind.

- From April 2018, making payments towards owner-occupiers' housing costs a loan rather than an award of benefit (para 8.7).

- At some future time, the extension of the UC scheme to include housing costs of those in specified accommodation (table 4.2), or the replacement of HB in these cases by a separate local authority scheme.

- Eventually, UC completely replacing HB, JSA(IB), ESA(IR), IS, CTC and WTC (and possibly also replacing CTR).

Law and guidance

UC law

1.31   The Act of Parliament governing the UC scheme in Great Britain is the Welfare Reform Act 2012. The regulations and orders giving the details of the scheme are listed in appendix 1. These are called statutory instruments (SIs). The main ones are the Universal Credit Regulations 2013 and the Universal Credit (Transitional Provisions) Regulations 2014. (For Northern Ireland see para 1.24.)

UC guidance

1.32   Government guidance on the UC scheme in Great Britain is the responsibility of the DWP and is contained in its Advice for Decision Makers (ADM).

CTR law

1.33   The Act of Parliament governing the CTR schemes is the Local Government Finance Act 1992 (as amended by the Local Government Finance Act 2012). The regulations and orders giving the details of the schemes are listed in appendix 1. They are called statutory instruments (SIs). The main ones are the six Council Tax Reduction Regulations listed there.

CTR guidance

1.34   Government guidance on the CTR scheme is the responsibility of the DCLG (Department of Communities and Local Government) in England, and of the Scottish and Welsh Governments.

Obtaining the law and guidance

1.35   The Acts, regulations, orders and government guidance are available online [www].

Case law

1.36   'Case law' means decisions of courts and Upper Tribunals which interpret the law. These set a precedent and are binding on DWP, DFC and local authority decision makers, and First-tier Tribunals. There is little case law about UC or CTR themselves. The cases referred to in this guide are usually about HB or other benefit law, and are relevant because of similarities with UC or CTR law. Most Upper Tribunal decisions are available online [www]. For further details about how decisions should be made, see chapter 1 of the *Guide to Housing Benefit*.

1.35   UC regulations with amendments: www.gov.uk/government/policies/simplifying-the-welfare-system-and-making-sure-work-pays/
         supporting-pages/welfare-reform-act-2012-regulations
         All other UC and CTR legislation: www.legislation.gov.uk
         UC guidance: www.gov.uk/government/publications/advice-for-decision-making-staff-guide
         CTR guidance (England): www.gov.uk/government/collections/localising-council-tax-support

1.36   www.osscsc.gov.uk/aspx/default.aspx

Chapter 2 **Who can get UC**

- General rules: see paras 2.1-4.
- Entitlement to UC: see paras 2.5-8.
- Age limits: see paras 2.9-17.
- Students: see paras 2.18-25.
- Presence in Great Britain: see paras 2.26-32.
- Migrants, prisoners, hospital detainees and religious orders: see paras 2.33-39.
- The claimant commitment: see paras 2.40-44.
- Your benefit unit: see paras 2.45-68.
- Non-dependants: see paras 2.69-76.

General rules

2.1 This chapter is about whether you can get UC, and who is included in your claim (your 'benefit unit').

Basic conditions

2.2 The basic conditions for getting UC relate to your personal circumstances. The details are in this chapter: see table 2.1 for the main rules.

Financial conditions

2.3 The financial conditions for getting UC are:

(a) your capital must not be over £16,000; and

(b) your income must be low enough for you to qualify.

The details are in chapter 9.

Transitional conditions

2.4 While UC is being introduced you must be in a pathfinder area to get it and there are other transitional conditions. In general terms:

(a) anyone in a UC 'full service' area can claim UC;

(b) only some people in a 'UC live' area can claim UC;

(c) but once you are on UC you can usually continue to get it even if you move, etc.

The details are in paras 1.13-25.

Table 2.1 **Basic conditions for UC**

If you are single	You must meet all the basic conditions:
	(a) you must be under state pension credit age
	(b) you must be aged 16 or more
	(c) if you are aged 16 or 17 you must be in an eligible group (see table 2.2)
	(d) if you are a student you must be in an eligible group (see table 2.3)
	(e) you must in most cases be in Great Britain
	(f) if you are a migrant you must meet special conditions (see para 2.34)
	(g) you must not be a prisoner, hospital detainee or member of a religious order (but for single prisoners' housing costs see paras 4.80-81)
	(h) you must accept a claimant commitment if required to do so
If you are in a couple	You can get UC as a couple if:
	■ you both meet all the basic conditions or
	■ you both meet them all except that (only) one of you does not meet condition (a) or (d)
	You can get UC as a single person if:
	■ you meet all the basic conditions and
	■ your partner meets them all apart from condition (c), (e), (f) or (g)

Entitlement to UC

2.5   You can get UC as a single person or as a couple. Table 2.1 summarises the rules. For whether you count as a 'single person' or a 'couple' see paras 2.46-58. For polygamous marriages see paras 2.59-60.

UC for single people

2.6   To get UC as a single person you must meet all the basic and financial conditions (see table 2.1 and chapter 9). You count as single if you are the only person in your benefit unit or if you are a lone parent (paras 2.46-47).

T2.1   WRA 4; UC 3(2),(3), Part 2; NIWRO 9; NIUC 3(1),(2), Part 2

2.5   WRA 1(1),(2); NIWRO 6(1),(2)

2.6   WRA 2(1)(a), 3(1); NIWRO 7(1)(a), 8(1)

UC for couples

2.7 To get UC as a couple (or 'joint claimants') you must:

(a) both meet all the basic conditions (see table 2.1); or

(b) both meet all those conditions except that (only) one of you is:

- over state pension credit age, or
- a student who is not in an eligible group.

And you must jointly meet the financial conditions (see chapter 9).

In a couple but claiming UC as a single person

2.8 If you are in a couple you can get UC as a single person if:

(a) you both meet all the basic conditions; except that

(b) your partner (but not you) is:

- a 16/17 year old who is not in an eligible group, or
- not in Great Britain, or
- a migrant who is not in an eligible group, or
- a prisoner, hospital detainee or member of a religious order.

And you must jointly meet the financial conditions (see chapter 9).

Age limits

2.9 This section gives the UC basic conditions relating to age, including the maximum age, minimum age and the rules for 16/17 year olds. (For planned changes to 18-21 year olds' housing costs, see para 4.84.)

Maximum age

2.10 To get UC you must be under state pension credit age ('SPC age') or if you are in a couple at least one of you must be under SPC age. During the year from 6th March 2016 to 6th March 2017, SPC age is gradually rising from 63 to 63¾. Appendix 3 gives the precise date you reach SPC age.

2.11 If you are over SPC age (or are in a couple and at least one of you is) you can get SPC instead of UC (para 1.23).

Minimum age

2.12 To get UC you must have reached the minimum age. This means you must be:

(a) aged 18 or more; or

(b) aged 16 or 17 and in an eligible group (see para 2.14).

2.7   WRA 2(1)(b), 3(2); UC 3(2); NIWRO 7(1)(b), 8(2); NIUC 3(1)

2.8   WRA 2(2), 3(1); UC 3(3); NIWRO 7(2), 8(1); NIUC 3(2)

2.10   WRA 4(1)(b),(4); UC 3(2)(a); NIWRO 9(1)(b),(4); NIUC 3(1)(a)

2.12   WRA 4(1)(a),(3); NIWRO 9(1)(a),(3)

2.13   If you are in a couple you can get UC if at least one of you meets condition (a) or (b) in para 2.12. If you meet condition (a) or (b) but your partner is a 16/17 year old who is not in an eligible group, you can get UC as a single person (see para 2.8).

16/17 year olds

2.14   If you are aged 16 or 17, you can get UC if you fall within one (or more) of the eligible groups in table 2.2.

Table 2.2 **16/17 year olds: the UC eligible groups**

All 16/17 year olds including care leavers	(a) You have a 'limited capability for work' (see para 9.19), or are waiting for an assessment about this and a registered medical practitioner has stated you are not fit for work
	(b) You are responsible for a child, or your partner (if you are in a couple) is responsible for a child or young person
Only 16/17 year olds who are not care leavers	(c) You are pregnant and it is no more than 11 weeks before your expected date of confinement, or you were pregnant and it is no more than 15 weeks after your baby's birth (including a still-birth after 24 weeks of pregnancy)
	(d) You meet the conditions for a carer element, or would do so except that you share your caring responsibilities with someone who gets the carer element instead of you (see para 9.28)
	(e) You are without parental support and are not being looked after by a local authority

Care leavers

2.15   You count as a 'care leaver' if you used to be looked after by a local authority and responsibility for supporting you continues to belong to them. If you are a 16/17 year old care leaver you can get UC if you fall within group (a) or (b) in table 2.2 (but you cannot get a UC housing costs elements towards your rent until you are 18: see para 4.83).

Looked after by a local authority

2.16   You count as being 'looked after by a local authority' if you are in local authority care.

2.13   UC 3(3)(a); NIUC 3(2)(a)

2.14   UC 8; NIUC 8

T2.2   UC 8, 30; NIUC 8, 31

2.15   UC 8(2),(4); NIUC 8(2),(4)

2.16   UC 2 definition: 'looked after by a local authority'; NIUC 2

Without parental support

2.17   You count as being 'without parental support' if you:

(a) have no parent or guardian (i.e. someone acting in the place of your parent); or

(b) cannot live with them because:

- you are estranged from them, or

- there is a serious risk to your physical or mental health or of significant harm to you if you did; or

(c) are living away from them, and they cannot support you financially because they:

- have a physical or mental impairment, or

- are detained in custody, or

- are prohibited from entering or re-entering Great Britain.

If you are without parental support you can get UC even if you are a 16/17 year old or a student in non-advanced education (see tables 2.2 and 2.3).

Students

2.18   This section gives the UC basic conditions for students. The law refers to people who are 'receiving education' but in this guide we use 'students' to mean the same thing.

Who is a student

2.19   You are a student if you are undertaking:

(a) non-advanced education (or have recently left): see paras 2.20-21; or

(b) full-time advanced or funded education: see paras 2.22-23; or

(c) any other course which is not compatible with your claimant commitment: see para 2.24.

For whether you can get UC as a student, see para 2.25.

Non-advanced education

2.20   This means education or training which:

(a) you have been enrolled or accepted on; and

(b) is not above GCE A level or equivalent (national standard level 3) [www]; and

(c) is provided at a school or college, or elsewhere if approved by the DWP; and

(d) takes up more than 12 hours per week on average during term-time of tuition, practical work, supervised study or taking examinations; and

(e) is not provided under a contract of employment; and

(f) in the case of training, is approved by the DWP. But this does not include government-sponsored work-preparation traineeships lasting up to six months which you began before you reached 25.

2.17   UC 8(1)(g),(3),(4); NIUC 8(1)(g),(3),(4)

2.19   UC 12(1),(1A),(2); NIUC 12(1),(2)

2.20   UC 5(1)(b),(2)-(4), 12(1A),(1B); NIUC 6(1)(b),(2)-(4); https://www.gov.uk/what-different-qualification-levels-mean

2.21   You count as being in non-advanced education:

(a) until the 31st August following your 16th birthday (whether or not you have in fact left education); and

(b) from then until the 31st August following your 19th birthday, but:

- only while you remain in the education, and

- if you are 19, only if you were enrolled or accepted on your course before you were 19.

Full-time advanced or funded education

2.22   This means:

(a) a full-time course of advanced education. It is advanced if it leads to a first or postgraduate degree or comparable qualification, a diploma of higher education or a higher national diploma; or is any other course above GCE A level, advanced GNVQ or higher or advanced Scottish national qualification; or

(b) any other full-time course of study or training at an educational establishment, for which you get a student loan, grant or award for your maintenance.

2.23   You count as being in this education from the day you start the course to the day it ends or you abandon it or are dismissed from it, including any vacations during that period. The same applies to a full-time module within a modular course, and in this case also includes any vacation after the full-time module but before the end of the course, and any time taken to complete the full-time module or re-take exams relating to it.

Incompatible courses

2.24   This means a course of study that is not compatible with any work-related requirement included in your UC claimant commitment (see para 2.43). You count as being on the course for the period described in para 2.23.

Which students can get UC

2.25   The rules are as follows:

(a) if you are a single person and you are a student, you cannot get UC unless you fall within one (or more) of the eligible groups in table 2.3;

(b) if you are in a couple and only one of you is a student, you can get UC (whether or not the student is in an eligible group);

(c) if you are in a couple and both of you are students, you cannot get UC unless at least one of you falls within one (or more) of the eligible groups in table 2.3.

2.21   UC 5(1),(2); NIUC 6(1),(2)

2.22   UC 12(2),(3), 68(7); NIUC 12(2),(3), 68(7)

2.23   UC 13(1)-(3); NIUC 13(1)-(3)

2.24   UC 12(4); NIUC 12(4)

2.25   WRA4(1)(d),(6); UC 3(2)(b), 13(4), 14; NIWRO 9(1)(d),(6); NIUC 3(1)(b), 13(4), 14

Table 2.3 **Students: the eligible groups**

(a) You are:

- in non-advanced education (see para 2.20), and

- without parental support (see para 2.17), and

- aged under 21, or aged 21 and reached that age while on your course.

(b) You:

- are on disability living allowance, personal independence payment or attendance allowance, and

- have 'limited capability for work' (see para 9.19).

(c) You or your partner are responsible for a child or young person.

(d) You or your partner are a foster parent and have a child placed with you.

(e) You or your partner have reached state pension credit age.

(f) You took time out of your course with the consent of your educational establishment because you were ill or caring for someone, and have now recovered or are no longer providing the care, but you have not resumed your course and are not eligible for a student loan or grant.

Presence in Great Britain

2.26 This section gives the UC basic conditions about being in Great Britain. This means England, Wales or Scotland (but not Northern Ireland, the Republic of Ireland, the Channel Islands or the Isle of Man).

2.27 To get UC you must be in Great Britain. This means you must be physically present here. If you are in a couple, and you are in Great Britain but your partner is not, you can get UC as a single person (see para 2.8). Exceptions to this rule are in paras 2.28-32. See also the rules for migrants in para 2.34.

Crown servants and HM Forces

2.28 You do not have to be in Great Britain to get UC if you are absent for the following reasons, nor does your partner if they are accompanying you:

(a) you are a Crown servant or member of HM Forces; and

(b) you are posted overseas to perform your duties; and

(c) immediately before you were posted overseas you were habitually resident in the UK.

T2.3   UC 2 definition: 'foster parent', 13(4), 14; NIUC 2, 13(4), 14

2.27   WRA 4(1)(c); UC 3(3)(b); NIWRO 9(1)(c); NIUC 3(2)(b)

2.28   UC 10; NIUC 10

Temporary absence from Great Britain: first month

2.29   If you are on UC, you can continue to get UC during a temporary absence from GB of up to one month (so long as it is not expected to exceed one month) whatever the reason for your absence – for example you could be on holiday.

Temporary absence from Great Britain: a death in the family

2.30   You can then continue to get UC for up to one further month during a temporary absence from GB, if your absence is in connection with the death of:

(a) your partner; or

(b) a child or young person you or your partner are responsible for; or

(c) a close relative (see para 4.45) of you or one of the above.

But this applies only if the DWP considers it would be unreasonable to expect you to return within the first month.

Temporary absence from Great Britain: medical treatment etc

2.31   If you are on UC, you can continue to get UC during a temporary absence from Great Britain of up to six months (so long as it is not expected to exceed six months) if your absence is solely in connection with you:

(a) being treated by (or under the supervision of) a qualified practitioner for an illness or physical or mental impairment; or

(b) undergoing convalescence or care which results from treatment for an illness or physical or mental impairment which you had before you left Great Britain; or

(c) accompanying your partner or a child or young person you are responsible for, if their absence is for one of the above reasons.

Temporary absences from Great Britain: mariners etc

2.32   If you are on UC, you can continue to get UC during a temporary absence from Great Britain of up to six months (so long as it is not expected to exceed six months) if you are:

(a) a mariner with a UK contract of employment; or

(b) a continental shelf worker in UK, EU or Norwegian waters.

2.29   UC 11(1)(a),(b)(i); NIUC 11(1)(a),(b)(i)

2.30   UC 11(2); NIUC 11(2)

2.31   UC 11(1)(a),(b)(ii),(3),(5); NIUC 11(1)(a),(b)(ii),(3),(5)

2.32   UC 11(1)(a),(b)(ii),(4),(5); NIUC 11(1)(a),(b)(ii),(4),(5)

Special groups

2.33 This section is about the UC basic conditions for migrants, prisoners, hospital detainees and members of religious orders.

Migrants

2.34 To get UC you must meet one of the following conditions:

(a) If you are a national of the Common Travel Area (CTA) (see para 2.36) you must

- be habitually resident in the CTA, or

- be present in the UK as result of your deportation, removal or expulsion from another country;

(b) If you are a national of any other country in the European Economic Area (EEA) (see para 2.36) and you:

- are a worker (i.e. in paid employment) or self employed in the UK,

- have retained worker or self employed status while temporarily unable to work due to sickness,

- have retained worker status while temporarily unemployed (which lasts for six months or longer if you have worked in the UK for at least one year), or

- are the family member of any of the above, or

- have worked in the UK but have retired due to old age or permanent incapacity and as a result have acquired a permanent right to reside [www], or

- have lived in the UK for at least five years under one of the rights above and you are habitually resident in the CTA, or

- have some other right to reside (e.g. as a student) other than as a jobseeker or a derivative right [www] and you are habitually resident in the CTA;

(c) if you are a national of any other country you must have been granted:

- refugee status, humanitarian protection or discretionary leave following an application you made for asylum, or

- leave under the 'Destitution Domestic Violence Concession' [www], or

- leave of any kind if you are national of Macedonia or Turkey and also be habitually resident in the CTA, or

- leave which allows you to have recourse to public funds and also be habitually resident in the CTA, or

- leave as a sponsored immigrant, be habitually resident in the CTA and also meet the additional condition in para 2.35.

If you are a couple and one of you meets these conditions but your partner does not, you can get UC as a single person (see para 2.8).

2.34   WRA 4(1)(c),(5); UC 3(3)(b),(e), 9; SI 2000/636 reg 2(1A), sch para 4; NIWRO 9(1)(c),(5); NIUC 3(2)(b),(e), 9; NISR 2000/71 reg 2, sch para 4
        http://www.housing-rights.info/EEA-workers-retired-and-self-employed.php
        https://www.gov.uk/government/publications/derivative-rights-of-residence
        https://www.gov.uk/government/publications/application-for-benefits-for-visa-holder-domestic-violence

2.35   If you have leave as a sponsored immigrant you are only entitled if you have been resident in the UK for at least five years or less than five years if the person (or every sponsor if there is more than one) who signed the undertaking to support you has died. In either case the five year period starts from the date of your entry to the UK or the date the maintenance undertaking was signed by your sponsor, whichever is the later.

2.36   The CTA means the UK (England, Wales, Scotland and Northern Ireland), the Republic of Ireland, the Channel Islands and the Isle of Man. The EEA means (apart from countries in the CTA) Austria, Belgium, Bulgaria, Croatia (but in this case the rules are stricter), Cyprus, Czech Republic, Denmark, Estonia, Finland, France, Germany, Greece, Hungary, Iceland, Italy, Latvia, Lichtenstein, Lithuania, Luxembourg, Malta, Netherlands, Norway, Poland, Portugal, Romania, Slovakia, Slovenia, Spain, Sweden and (for these purposes) Switzerland. For further details of the rules for migrants see paras 16.31-44 and the *Guide to Housing Benefit*.

Prisoners and hospital detainees

2.37   You are a prisoner if you are detained in custody or on temporary release, unless you are serving a sentence of imprisonment detained in hospital, in which case you are a hospital detainee.

2.38   You cannot get UC if you are a prisoner or a hospital detainee. The only exception is if you are single and a prisoner you may be able to get UC for your housing costs for up to six months: see para 4.80. If your partner is a prisoner or a hospital detainee and you are not you may be able to get UC as a single person (see para 2.8).

Members of religious orders

2.39   You cannot get UC if you are a member of a religious order and are fully maintained by them. If this applies to your partner but not you, you can get UC as a single person (see para 2.8).

The claimant commitment

2.40   Accepting a claimant commitment is one of the UC basic conditions. This section gives a summary of the rules about this. You can get further details of the rules online [www].

Who must accept a claimant commitment

2.41   To get UC you must accept a claimant commitment, or if you are in a couple you both must, unless the DWP considers that:

(a)   you lack the capacity to do so; or

(b)   there are exceptional circumstances which make it unreasonable to expect you to do so.

2.35   SI 2000/636 reg 2(1A), sch paras 2,3; NISR 2000/71 reg 2, sch paras 2,3

2.38   WRA 6(1)(a); UC 2 definition: 'prisoner', 3(3)(c),(d), 19(1)(b),(c),(4); NIWRO 11(1)(a); NIUC 2, 3(2)(c),(d), 19(1)(b),(c),(4)

2.39   WRA 6(1)(a); UC 3(3)(d), 19(1)(a); NIWRO 11(1)(a); NIUC 3(2)(d), 19(1)(a)

2.40   www.gov.uk/government/publications/universal-credit-and-your-claimant-commitment-quick-guide

2.41   WRA 4(1)(e),(7); UC 16; NIWRO 9(1)(e),(7); NIUC 16

What a claimant commitment contains

2.42   Your claimant commitment includes your duties in relation to your UC claim (for example to notify changes in your circumstances) and which work-related requirements (if any) you are expected to carry out.

Work-related requirements

2.43   You may be required to carry out one or more of the following 'work-related requirements':

   (a)   a work-focused interview requirement;

   (b)   a work preparation requirement;

   (c)   a work search requirement;

   (d)   a work availability requirement.

If you fail to carry out a requirement you may be subject to a sanction and you may or may not be able to get UC hardship payments: see paras 9.68-76.

No work search or work availability requirement

2.44   You do not have to carry out any work search or work availability requirement if you fall within one (or more) of the exempt groups in table 2.4. If you are claiming UC as a couple, table 2.4 applies separately to each of you.

Table 2.4 **Work-related requirements: the UC exempt groups**

Earnings level, work capability, work preparation, unfit to work	(a) You and/or your partner have earned income (paras 10.7-8) whose monthly amount is equivalent to at least the national minimum wage for your actual or expected hours or (if this is lower and you aren't in the DWP's In Work Pilot Scheme) £78.10 pw (single people) or £124.85 pw (couples)
	(b) You have a limited capability for work and work-related activity (see para 9.19)
	(c) You are carrying out required or voluntary work preparation and the DWP agrees
	(d) You are unfit for work. This applies for up to two periods of up to 14 days in any 12 months, or for more periods and/or days if the DWP agrees

---

2.42   WRA 14(1),(4); UC Part 8; NIWRO 19(1),(4); NIUC Part 8

2.43   WRA 14; UC Part 8; NIWRO 19; NIUC Part 8

2.44   See table 2.4

T2.4   (a)   UC 6(1A),90, 99(6),(6A); SI 2015/89; NIUC 7(2), 89, 97(14),(15)   (b)   WRA 19(2)(a); NIWRO 24(2)(a)
         (c)   UC 99(5)(a); NIUC 97(11)(a)   (d)   UC 99(4),(5)(c); NIUC 97(11)(c)

Children, fostering, adoption, pregnancy	(e)	You and/or your partner are responsible for a child under one year old. If you are in a couple this applies to only one of you; you jointly choose which of you this is
	(f)	You are the foster parent of a child under one year old. If you are in a couple who are both foster parents this applies to only one of you; you jointly choose which of you this is
	(g)	You have adopted a child and it is within 12 months of the date of adoption (or the date 14 days before the expected date of placement if you request the 12 months to begin then), but this does not apply if you are the child's close relative (see para 4.45) or foster parent
	(h)	You are pregnant and it is no more than 11 weeks before your expected date of confinement, or you were pregnant and it is no more than 15 weeks after your baby's birth (including a still-birth after 24 weeks of pregnancy)
Pension age, carers, students, domestic violence	(i)	You have reached state pension credit age
	(j)	You meet the conditions for a UC carer element, or would do so except that you share your caring responsibilities with someone who gets the carer element instead of you (see para 9.28), or you do not do so but the DWP agrees you have similar caring responsibilities
	(k)	You are a student and you fall within eligible group (a) in table 2.3, or you have a student loan, grant or award and fall within any of the other groups in that table
	(l)	You have been a victim of actual or threatened domestic violence within the past six months from a partner, former partner, or family member you are not (or no longer) living with. A 'family member' includes any close relative (see para 4.45). It also includes a grandparent, grandchild, step-brother/sister or brother/sister-in-law, or if any of them are in a couple, their partner. This applies for 13 weeks from when you notify the DWP about it, but only if it has not applied to you during the previous 12 months. It can apply for a further 13 weeks if you are responsible for a child

T2.4   (e)   WRA 19(2)(c),(6); UC 86; NIWRO 24(2)(c),(6); NIUC 85   (f)   UC 2,85,86, 89(1)(f); NIUC 2,84,85, 88(1)(f)

(g)   UC 89(1)(d),(3); NIUC 88(1)(d),(3)   (h)   UC 89(1)(c); NIUC 88(1)(c)

(i)   UC 89(1)(a); NIUC 88(1)(a)   (j)   WRA 19(2)(b); UC 30, 89(1)(b),(2); NIWRO 24(2)(b); NIUC 31, 88(1)(b),(2)

(k)   UC 68(7), 89(1)(e); NIUC 68(7), 88(1)(e)   (l)   UC 98; NIUC 96

Treatment abroad, drug/alcohol programmes, emergencies etc, death in the family	(m) You are temporarily absent from GB in connection with treatment, convalescence or care for you, your partner or a child or young person, and you meet the conditions in para 2.31
	(n) You are in an alcohol or drug dependency treatment programme and have been for no more than six months
	(o) You temporarily have new or increased child care responsibilities (including when a child is affected by death or violence) or are dealing with a domestic emergency, funeral arrangements etc, and the DWP agrees
	(p) Your partner, or a child or young person you or your partner are responsible for, or a child of yours (even if not included in your benefit unit) has died within the past six months
Prisoners, court proceedings, police protection, public duties	(q) You are a prisoner claiming UC for housing costs
	(r) You are attending a court or tribunal as a party to proceedings or witness
	(s) You are receiving police protection and have been for no more than six months
	(t) You are engaged in activities which the DWP agrees amount to a public duty

Your benefit unit

2.45 This section explains who is included in your 'benefit unit'. Your entitlement to UC is based on this (see para 9.4)

Single people

2.46 For UC purposes you are a 'single person' if you are not in a couple.

2.47 If you are a single person, your benefit unit is:

(a) you; and

(b) any children or young persons you are responsible for.

T2.4 (m) UC 99(3)(c); NIUC 97(6)(c)   (n) UC 99(3)(e); NIUC 97(6)(e)
(o) UC 99(4A)-(4C),(5)(b),(5A); NIUC 97(8)-(10),(11)(b),(12)   (p) UC 99(3)(d); NIUC 97(6)(d)
(q) UC 99(3)(b); NIUC 97(6)(b)   (r) UC 99(3)(a); NIUC 97(6)(a)
(s) UC 99(3)(f); NIUC 97(6)(f)   (t) UC 99(3)(g); NIUC 97(6)(g)
2.46 WRA 40; NIWRO 46
2.47 WRA 1(2)(a), 9(1)(a), 10(1); NIWRO 6(2)(a), 14(1)(a), 15(1)

Couples

2.48   For UC purposes you are a 'couple' if you are two people who are members of the same household (see para 2.51) and are:

    (a)   a married couple (of opposite sexes or the same sex) or civil partners (of the same sex); or

    (b)   living together as a married couple or civil partners (see para 2.53).

2.49   If you are in a couple and are claiming UC as a couple (see para 2.7), your benefit unit is:

    (a)   both of you; and

    (b)   any children or young persons either (or both) of you are responsible for.

2.50   If you are in a couple but claiming UC as a single person (see para 2.8), your benefit unit is:

    (a)   you; and

    (b)   any children or young persons you are responsible for.

Members of the same household

2.51   You are only a couple for UC purposes if you are members of the same household. (This applies to married couples and civil partners as well as couples who are living together: [2014] UKUT 186 (AAC).) You are not a couple if you:

    (a)   live in different dwellings and maintain them as separate homes (R(SB) 4/83); or

    (b)   live in the same dwelling but lead separate lives rather than living as one household (CIS/072/1994).

And you cannot be a member of two (or more) households at the same time (R(SB) 8/85).

2.52   A 'household' generally means a domestic arrangement involving two or more people who live together as a unit (R(IS) 1/99), even when they have a reasonable level of independence and self-sufficiency (R(SB) 8/85). It requires a settled course of daily living rather than visits from time to time (R(F) 2/81). So if you keep your eating, cooking, food storage, finances (including paying your housing costs), living space and family life separate you are unlikely to be members of the same household.

Living together

2.53   If you are not married or in a civil partnership you are only a couple for UC purposes if you are living together as though you were. This means considering:

    (a)   your purpose in living together (Crake and Butterworth v the Supplementary Benefit Commission); and

    (b)   if your purpose is unclear, your relationship and living arrangements.

2.48   WRA 39, 40; UC 2 definition: 'partner'; NIWRO 45, 46; NIUC 2

2.49   WRA 1(2)(b), 9(1)(b), 10(1); NIWRO 6(2)(b), 14(1)(b), 15(1)

2.50   WRA 1(2)(a), 2(2), 9(1)(a), 10(1); NIWRO 6(2)(a), 2(2), 14(1)(a), 15(1)

2.51   WRA 39(1)(a),(c); NIWRO 45(1)(a),(c)

2.53   WRA 39(1)(b),(d),(2); NIWRO 45(1)(b),(d),(2); Crake and Butterworth v SBC 21/07/80 QBD 1982 1 ALL ER 498

2.54 What matters is your relationship as a whole (R(SB) 17/81) taking account of the following factors (Crake case and [2013] UKUT 505 (AAC)):

(a) whether you share the same household;

(b) the stability of your relationship;

(c) your financial arrangement;

(d) whether you have a sexual relationship;

(e) whether you share responsibility for a child;

(f) whether you publicly acknowledge you are a couple;

(g) the emotional element of your relationship.

The last two points were emphasised in [2014] UKUT 17 (AAC), which held that 'a committed loving relationship must be established and publicly acknowledged'.

2.55 There are many reasons why two people might live in the same household or same dwelling. They might be a couple. But they might be landlord/lady and lodger, house sharers, etc. Even living together for reasons of 'care, companionship and mutual convenience' does not by itself mean you are a couple (R(SB) 35/85).

Ending a relationship

2.56 If you were a couple but your relationship has ended, your shared understanding that it has ended and your actual living arrangement are more important than any shared responsibilities and financial arrangements you still have (CIS/72/1994). But if you remain married or in a civil partnership, a shared understanding may not be enough by itself to show you are no longer a couple (CIS/2900/1998).

If your partner is temporarily absent

2.57 If your partner is temporarily absent from your household you continue to count as a couple, unless their absence exceeds or is expected to exceed six months.

2.58 This means you stop counting as a couple if and when your partner:

(a) decides not to return or decides to be absent for more than six months (whether they decide this at the beginning of the absence or during it); or

(b) has been absent for six months

For absences outside Great Britain see paras 2.28-32.

Polygamous marriages

2.59 For UC purposes you are in a 'polygamous marriage' if you or your husband or wife are married to more than one person under the laws of a country which permits polygamy.

2.57   UC 3(6); NIUC 3(5)

2.59   UC 3(5); NIUC 3(4)

2.60   The members of the polygamous marriage who live in your household can get UC as follows:

  (a) the two who were married earliest count as a couple;

  (b) each other person in the marriage counts as a single person.

The earlier rules about entitlement to UC and the benefit unit then apply: see paras 2.6-8 and 2.45-50.

Children and young persons

2.61   Your benefit unit includes the children and young persons:

  (a) you are responsible for, if you are:

  ▪   a single person, or

  ▪   in a couple but claiming UC as a single person;

  (b) you or your partner are responsible for, if you are:

  ▪   in a couple and claiming UC as a couple.

2.62   A 'child' means someone under the age of 16.

2.63   A 'young person' means someone aged 16 or more but under 20 (other than your partner) who:

  (a) is in or has recently left non-advanced education (see paras 2.20-21); and

  (b) is not on UC, ESA, JSA, HB, CTC or WTC.

Responsibility for a child or young person

2.64   For UC purposes you are responsible for a child or young person if he or she:

  (a) normally lives with you (see paras 2.65-66); and

  (b) is not being looked after by a local authority (see para 2.67); and

  (c) is not a prisoner (see para 4.79).

2.65   Whether a child or young person 'normally lives with you' is a question of fact and is usually straightforward. For example they could be your son or daughter, adopted by you, a step-child, a grandchild or any other child or young person (whether related to you or not), so long as they normally live with you.

2.60   UC 3(4); NIUC 3(3)

2.61   WRA 10(1); NIWRO 15(1)

2.62   WRA 40; NIWRO 46

2.63   WRA 10(5); UC 4(3), 5(1),(5); UCTP 28; NIWRO 15(5); NIUC 4(3), 5(1),(5)

2.64   UC 4(1),(2),(6); NIUC 4(1),(2),(6)

2.66 A child or young person can only be the responsibility of one single person or couple at any one time. If they normally live with two or more single persons or couples, they are the responsibility of the single person or couple with the main responsibility. You can choose ('nominate') who this is to be. But the DWP makes the choice instead if:

(a) you do not choose or cannot agree; or

(b) your choice does not reflect the arrangements between you.

If a child or young person is in local authority care

2.67 A child or young person is not included in your benefit unit if they are being 'looked after by a local authority' (this means in local authority care) unless this is for a planned short-term break to give you time off from caring for them, or one of a series of such breaks.

If a child or young person is temporarily absent

2.68 If a child or young person you are responsible for is temporarily absent from your household they continue to be included in your benefit unit, unless their absence exceeds or is expected to exceed:

(a) six months if they remain in Great Britain during the absence;

(b) one month if they are outside Great Britain;

(c) one further month if they remain outside Great Britain and this is in connection with the death of their close relative (see para 4.45) and it would be unreasonable for them to be expected to return within the first month;

(d) six months if they are outside Great Britain in connection with treatment, convalescence or care which meets the conditions in para 2.31.

Non-dependants

2.69 This section explains who counts as a non-dependant. If you are a renter and have one or more non-dependants living with you, this can affect the amount of UC you get for your housing costs: see paras 7.8 and 9.51.

Who is a non-dependant

2.70 A 'non-dependant' is anyone who:

(a) normally lives in the accommodation with you; and

(b) is not in any of the groups in table 2.5.

For example, a non-dependant is usually an adult son, daughter, other relative or friend who lives with you on a non-commercial basis, whether they are single or in a couple.

2.66   UC 4(4),(5); NIUC 4(4),(5)

2.67   UC 2 definition: 'looked after by a local authority', 4(6), 4A; NIUC 2, 4(6), 5

2.68   UC 4(7); NIUC 4(7)

2.70   UC sch 4 paras 3, 9(1),(2); NIUC sch 4 paras 3, 8(1),(2)

Table 2.5 **People who are not non-dependants**

(a) You and your partner, whether you are claiming UC as a couple or as a single person.

(b) Any child or young person (see para 2.72).

(c) A foster child placed with you or your partner.

(d) A resident landlord/landlady and members of their household.

(e) Anyone who is liable to make payments on a commercial basis on the accommodation including:

   ■ a lodger of yours (see paras 2.73-74)

   ■ a joint tenant of yours (if you rent your accommodation jointly) (see para 2.75)

   ■ a separate tenant of your landlord's (if your accommodation is rented out in separate lettings).

(f) A non-dependant of anyone described in (e) above (see para 2.76).

'Normally living in the accommodation with you'

2.71   To count as a non-dependant a person must 'normally live in the accommodation with you'. For example:

(a) someone who shares essential living accommodation with you, even if you each have your own bedroom, is likely to count as 'living with you' (CH/542/2006, CH/3656/2005, though the HB regulations in these cases have a different wording); but

(b) a short-term visitor does not count as 'normally' living with you. Nor does someone you take in temporarily because they have nowhere else to go (CH/4004/2004), though this may change as time goes by (CH/3935/2007).

Non-dependants and children/young persons

2.72   A child or young person (see paras 2.62-63) never counts as a non-dependant, whether you, your partner, anyone else or no-one is responsible for them. The only exception is that a child or young person of a non-dependant counts as a non-dependant (and this can be relevant to the size criteria: see para 7.14).

Non-dependants and lodgers

2.73   If you have a lodger who pays you rent on a commercial basis, the lodger does not count as a non-dependant.

T2.5   UC sch 4 paras 3, 9; NIUC sch 4 paras 3, 8

2.72   UC sch 4 para 9(1)(b),(2)(a),(c),(g); NIUC sch 4 para 8(1)(b),(2)(a),(c),(g)

2.73   UC sch 4 para 9(2)(d); NIUC sch 4 para 8(2)(d)

2.74 The difference between a lodger and a non-dependant is as follows:

(a) a lodger is someone who makes payments to you on a commercial basis (see table 4.4(a));

(b) a non-dependant may or may not pay their way. If they do pay you, it is on a non-commercial basis.

Non-dependants and joint tenants

2.75 If you rent your accommodation jointly, your joint tenants are not your non-dependants. For example, if two sisters, a father and son, three friends (and so on) are joint tenants, they are not non-dependants of each other.

2.76 If you jointly rent your accommodation and there is also a non-dependant living there, the non-dependant is included in the UC claim of only one of the joint tenants, as follows:

(a) the non-dependant may normally live with only one of the joint tenants. In that case, they are included in the UC claim of only that joint tenant;

(b) the non-dependant may normally live with more than one of the joint tenants. In that case, once they have been included in the UC claim of one joint tenant they are not included in the UC claim of any of the others.

2.75   UC sch 4 para 9(2)(d); NIUC sch 4 para 8(2)(d)

2.76   UC sch 4 para 9(2)(f); NIUC sch 4 para 8(2)(f)

Chapter 3 **UC claims**

- Making a claim: see paras 3.1-11.
- How to claim: see paras 3.12-18.
- Information and evidence: see paras 3.19-26.
- When your UC starts: see paras 3.27-36.
- Decisions, awards and assessment periods: see paras 3.37-43.
- Backdating: see paras 3.44-48.

Making a claim

3.1   You can only get UC if:

(a) you make a claim for it (see paras 3.2-3); or

(b) you are treated as having claimed it (see paras 3.4-7); or

(c) someone claims it on your behalf (see paras 3.8-11).

In each case you (or the person claiming on your behalf) must provide appropriate information and evidence.

Claiming as a single person

3.2   You make your claim yourself if:

(a) you are a single person (see paras 2.6 and 2.46-47); or

(b) you are in a couple or polygamous marriage and are eligible for UC as a single person (see paras 2.8 and 2.60).

Claiming as a couple (joint claimants)

3.3   You make your claim jointly with your partner if:

(a) you are a couple (see para 2.7); or

(b) you are in a polygamous marriage and are eligible for UC as a couple (see para 2.60).

The law also calls you 'joint claimants'.

3.1   AA 1,5; NIAA 1,5

3.2   WRA 2(1)(a),(2); UC 3(3),(4); NIWRO 7(1)(a),(2); NIUC 3(2),(3)

3.3   WRA 2(1)(b),(2); UC 3(4); NIWRO 7(1)(b),(2); NIUC 3(3)

If you should have claimed as a couple or as a single person

3.4　　The DWP:

(a)　can treat you as having claimed UC as a couple if:

- ■　you each made a claim as a single person, but

- ■　the DWP decides you are a couple;

(b)　must treat you as having claimed UC as a single person if:

- ■　you made a claim as a couple, but

- ■　you are only eligible for UC as a single person (paras 2.8 and 2.60).

If you become a couple or a single person

3.5　　If you are not in a UC 'full service' area (para 1.14) the DWP must treat you as having claimed UC if:

(a)　you have been getting UC as a single person but are now a couple (whether or not your new partner was previously getting UC);

(b)　you have been getting UC as a couple but your partner has died;

(c)　you have been getting UC as a couple but you are no longer a couple, and:

- ■　your partner first notified the DWP of that fact, and so carried on getting that UC award; but

- ■　you are no longer included in that UC award.

In these cases your UC continues based on your new circumstances (para 3.42).

If you previously claimed UC with earned income

3.6　　If you are not in a UC 'full service' area (para 1.14) the DWP must treat you as having claimed UC if:

(a)　you claimed UC within the past six months, but did not qualify because of the level of your earned income; or

(b)　you were getting UC within the past six months, but it ended because you began to receive earned income or your earned income increased;

(c)　and (in either case) the DWP receives information about your income from you or HMRC (para 3.26) showing you now qualify for UC.

In these cases your UC starts (or starts again) as described in para 3.42. The example illustrates this.

3.7　　The above rule applies when your earned income reduces or stops, or when some other change in your circumstances means you now qualify for UC (even if your earned income hasn't changed). Earned income means any kind of actual or notional earnings (paras 10.7-8 and 10.74 onwards). The rule can apply any number of times, so long as your UC doesn't stop for more than six months. This six months is sometimes called the 'UC re-award period'.

3.4　　C&P 9(1)-(4)

3.5　　UC 21(3),(4) saved by SI 2014/2887 reg.5; C&P 9(6) saved by SI 2014/2887 reg.5, 9(10)

3.6-7　　UC 21(1),(3) saved by SI 2014/2887 reg.5; 52, C&P 6 saved by SI 2014/2887 reg.53.8

Example: UC claims and earned income

Leslie claims UC on 3rd June. She has employed earnings which vary, and the DWP uses information from HMRC to assess these (para 10.22).

To begin with her earnings are low enough for her to qualify. So she is awarded UC from 3rd June and her UC assessment periods begin on the 3rd of each month (para 3.41).

In her assessment period beginning on 3rd August, her earnings become too high for her to qualify. So her UC stops from 3rd August (para 11.9).

But in her assessment period beginning on 3rd December, her earnings become low enough for her to qualify again. So she is treated as having claimed (para 3.6) and her UC starts from 3rd December (para 3.42).

The same would apply if Leslie was self-employed, but she would have to provide the DWP with information about her earnings (para 10.30).

If you are unable to act: attorneys etc

3.8   The following may act on your behalf in connection with your UC:

(a) a person who has power of attorney for you;

(b) a deputy appointed for you by the Court of Protection;

(c) a receiver appointed for you;

(d) in Scotland, a judicial factor or any guardian acting or appointed for you.

3.9   The DWP can appoint someone to act on your behalf in connection with your UC (known as an 'appointee') if:

(a) they apply in writing to do so (for example in a letter or online); and

(b) unless they are a firm or organisation, they are over 18 years old; and

(c) you do not have an attorney etc (see para 3.8).

They can be someone who already acts on your behalf in connection with HB or a social security benefit.

3.10   Your appointee has all the rights you have in connection with UC, including making a claim, receiving payments, and requesting a reconsideration or appeal. They continue to act on your behalf until:

(a) they resign their appointment. They must give the DWP one month's written notice of this; or

(b) the DWP ends their appointment; or

(c) the DWP is notified that you now have an attorney etc (see para 3.8).

3.8   General law about incapacity etc

3.9   C&P 2(1) definition: 'writing', 57(1)-(3),(6); UCTP 16

3.10   C&P 57(4),(5),(7),(8)

If your partner is unable to act

3.11   If you are claiming UC as a couple and your partner is unable to claim jointly with you, you can make the UC claim yourself on behalf of both of you.

How to claim

3.12   You can make your claim for UC:

(a) online; or

(b) by telephone if the DWP agrees to this.

Once you have submitted a claim you may subsequently be asked to provide evidence to confirm information you have given [www], to attend an interview, and to agree to conditions set out in a claimant commitment: see paras 2.40-44.

Online claims

3.13   Online claims are made to the DWP [www]. The website tells you what information you should have before you start the claim process. The DWP says that 'you need to allow up to 40 minutes for your online application because you must complete it in one session' [www]. Depending on your circumstances the DWP can provide you with assistance to do this in a DWP office or in your home. Your local council may also be able to help you with claiming UC.

Telephone claims

3.14   The DWP can agree to accept a telephone claim from particular groups of claimants or in individual cases. If you are not able to go online yourself you can contact an adviser on 0845 6000 723 or text phone 0845 6000 743 between 8am and 6pm, Monday to Friday (closed on bank and public holidays). Note that this call is not free and if it 'ends suddenly it is up to you to call back' [www].

Properly completed claims

3.15   Your claim for UC must be 'properly completed'. If it is an online claim, this means it must be in the approved form and completed in accordance with the instructions. You may also be required to provide appropriate authentication of your identity and other information, and maintain records of your claim. If it is a telephone claim, it is properly completed if you provided all the information during the call needed to decide your claim. See also paras 3.16-17.

3.11   C&P 9(5)

3.12   C&P 8(1),(2), 35
         https://about.universalcredit.service.gov.uk/kms/Pages/What_you_need_to_provide_evidence_of.pdf

3.13   C&P 8(1), sch 2
         www.gov.uk/apply-universal-credit
         http://about.universalcredit.service.gov.uk/kms/Pages/Making_an_online_claim.htm

3.14   C&P 8(2)
         http://about.universalcredit.service.gov.uk/kms/Pages/Contacting_Universal_Credit_Overview.htm

3.15   C&P 8(1),(4), sch 2 para 2

Defective claims

3.16   A claim which does not meet the conditions in para 3.15 is called 'defective'. If this applies to you, the DWP must tell you how you can properly complete your claim and what the time limits are for doing so (see para 3.17).

Properly completing a defective claim

3.17   You can properly complete a defective claim as follows:

(a) if it is an online claim, you re-submit the claim with the missing information, etc, now included;

(b) if it is a telephone claim, you need only provide the information, etc, that was missing.

If you do this within one month of when you were first informed that your claim was defective, or longer if the DWP considers it reasonable, your claim counts as having been made on the date you originally made it.

Amending or withdrawing a claim

3.18   Before the DWP decides your claim you can:

(a) amend it: the DWP then decides your claim on the amended basis; or

(b) withdraw it: the DWP then takes no further action on your claim.

You can amend or withdraw a claim by writing to the DWP (online or in a letter, etc), by telephoning them, or in any other way they agreed to.

Information and evidence

From you

3.19   The DWP can require you to provide information and evidence in order for it to decide:

(a) whether you are entitled to UC;

(b) whether your entitlement to UC should be changed;

(c) who your UC should be paid to.

If you're in a couple this applies to both of you, even if you are claiming UC as a single person. If you are claiming UC as a couple, information you have given to the DWP can be passed on to your partner.

3.20   The DWP must tell you what information and evidence it requires, and whether you should provide it online, by telephone, by personally attending a DWP office, or in some other way. It must also tell you when you should provide it by. If it is required for a UC claim, the time limit is one month from when the DWP first requested it, or longer if the DWP considers it reasonable.

3.16   C&P 8(3)-(5)

3.17   C&P 8(6)

3.18   C&P 2(1) definition: 'writing', 30, 31

3.19   C&P 37(1),(2),(4),(5),(8),(9), 38(1),(2),(6)

3.20   C&P 35, 37(3), 38(3)

3.21   UC law does not list what information or evidence you can be asked to provide (except as described in paras 3.23-26). Examples include details about yourself, your partner, your children/young persons, your housing costs, your non-dependants, and your and your partner's income, capital and entitlement to the various UC elements.

From third parties

3.22   The DWP can require:

(a)   your landlord to provide information and evidence about your rent;

(b)   your childcare provider to provide information and evidence relating to the UC childcare costs element (see para 9.36);

(c)   a person you are caring for to confirm information relating to the UC carer element (see paras 9.27-28);

(d)   a pension fund holder to provide information: see para 3.24;

(e)   a rent officer to provide information: see para 3.25.

They have one month to do this, or longer if the DWP considers it reasonable.

National Insurance numbers

3.23   You must provide your NI number and, if you are claiming UC as a couple, your partner's NI number. If you do not know it, you must provide information enabling the DWP to find it out. If you do not have one, you must apply for one.

Pension fund holders

3.24   If you or your partner:

(a)   have a personal or occupational pension scheme; and

(b)   are aged 60 or over; and

(c)   are not claiming personal independence payment,

the DWP can require you to provide information about the pension scheme, including the name and address of the holder and the policy or reference number. The DWP can then require the pension fund holder to provide information about how much is being paid or could be paid (for example if you have deferred your pension).

Rent officers

3.25   If you are a social sector renter, the DWP can refer your rent and/or service charges to the rent officer if these are unreasonably high (see paras 5.21-26). The DWP tells the rent officer your and your landlord's name and address, your rent and/or service charge details, and the number of bedrooms you have. The rent officer can require your landlord to provide information and evidence not obtainable from the DWP.

3.22   C&P 37(6),(7), 38(7),(8)

3.23   AA 1(1A); NIAA 1(1A); C&P 5

3.24   C&P 41

3.25   C&P 40

Income and capital

3.26 You should provide information about your:

(a) earnings from employment – but only if the DWP can't get the details from HMRC (paras 10.22);

(b) earnings from self-employment (paras 10.30);

(c) unearned income – but not usually social security benefits (table 10.3);

(d) capital (para 10.53).

If you are in a couple you should provide this information for both of you – even if you are claiming UC as a single person (para 10.3).

When your UC starts

Your first day of entitlement

3.27 Your UC starts:

(a) on your date of claim (paras 3.28-32); or

(b) seven days later if waiting days apply to you (paras 3.33-36).

Different rules apply if you are treated as having claimed UC (para 3.42) or qualify for backdating (para 3.44).

3.28 Your date of claim is the day your UC claim is received (online or by telephone) by the DWP. This includes the day a defective claim is received if you then properly complete it within the time limit (see para 3.17). Paras 3.29-32 give further rules.

If you receive assistance making an online claim

3.29 If you receive assistance making an online claim (see para 3.13), your date of claim is the date you first notified the DWP of your need for assistance.

If the DWP cannot take your telephone claim

3.30 If you telephone the DWP to make a claim but they cannot take your telephone claim until a later date, your date of claim is the day of your first telephone call if the later date is within one month of that.

Advance claims

3.31 If you do not qualify for UC when you claim it but will do so within one month, the date of claim is the day you first qualify. The DWP can agree to apply this rule for particular groups of claimants or in individual cases.

3.26 UC 54, 61; NIUC 53, 62

3.27 UC 19A(1); C&P 26(1); NIUC 20(1)

3.28 C&P 10(1)(a),(c), (2)

3.29 C&P 2(1) definition: 'appropriate office', 10(1)(b)

3.30 C&P 10(1)(d)

3.31 C&P 32

3.32 You can also choose to claim UC from a date in the future, for example if you claim in advance of losing a job or some other event. In this case, your date of claim is the day you are claiming from.

Waiting days

3.33 Waiting days mean you don't get UC for the first seven days beginning with your date of claim. Para 3.34 explains who they apply to and paras 3.35-36 give the exceptions.

Who waiting days apply to

3.34 Waiting days only apply if, on your date of claim, you:

(a) have to meet all the UC work-related requirements (para 2.43); or

(b) have (or might have) limited capability for work or for work and work-related activity (para 9.19) and apart from that you would have to meet all those requirements.

If you are claiming UC as a couple, waiting days apply if at least one of you falls within (a) or (b).

Waiting days exceptions

3.35 But waiting days don't apply if, on your date of claim, you:

(a) are a care leaver (para 2.15);

(b) are aged under 22 and were a care leaver before you reached 18 and are claiming UC for the first time;

(c) are aged 16 or 17 and without parental support (para 2.17);

(d) have been a victim of actual or threatened domestic violence within the past six months;

(e) have been a prisoner (para 2.36) within the past one month;

(f) are terminally ill (para 9.20);

(g) were entitled to JSA(C) or ESA(C) within the past three months;

(h) were entitled to JSA(IB), ESA(IR) or IS within the past three months and stopped qualifying for it because you started paid work (paras 10.7-8); or

(i) were entitled to JSA(IB), ESA(IR), IS, CTC, WTC or HB within the past one month.

If you are claiming UC as a couple, waiting days don't apply if at least one of you falls within the above exceptions.

3.36 Waiting days also don't apply if:

(a) you are treated as having claimed UC for any of the reasons in paras 3.5-7; or

(b) your date of claim was before 3rd August 2015.

3.32   C&P 10(1)

3.33   UC 19A(1), 20A; NIUC 20(1), 21

3.34   UC 19A(1),(2),(4); NIUC 20(1),(2),(4)

3.35-36 UC 2 definitions: 'employment support allowance', jobseeker's allowance', 'paid work', 19A(3), 98(2),(4); NIUC 2, 20(3), 96(3),(5)
         UCTP 2(1) definition: 'existing benefit', 16A; reg 1 of SI 2015/1362 – commencement date

Decisions, awards and assessment periods

Decisions about your UC

3.37 The DWP makes a decision about your UC:

(a) when you claim – about whether you are entitled and (if you are) how much you qualify for and how it will be paid;

(b) when your circumstances change while you are on UC (para 11.5); and

(c) when it changes a wrong decision (para 11.41).

Chapter 11 explains how you can ask for a decision to be changed and chapter 14 explains how you can then go on (in most cases) to make an appeal.

The DWP's notification to you

3.38 The DWP tells you about decisions relating to your UC claim and about any changes it makes to your UC. The law requires this if you have the right of appeal, but in practice the DWP notifies all decisions. It normally notifies you via your online account (para 3.13) but can also do so by telephone (para 3.14) or by post. The time limit that can apply when you ask for a decision to be changed (para 11.53) starts from when the decision is notified. For online notifications, this is said to mean the day the decision becomes available to view.

3.39 The DWP also notifies:

(a) your partner if you are claiming UC as a couple. It does this even if the notification is about sanctions or fraud, but has said it intends to protect sensitive information about your health and similar matters;

(b) your landlord etc if it decides to pay UC to them (para 12.11). It normally does this by post, saying how much they will receive but not what your personal or financial details are.

Awards of UC

3.40 There is no fixed time limit for an award of UC. It continues for each of your assessment periods until you stop being entitled to it. For the rules about when UC changes or ends, see chapter 11.

Assessment periods

3.41 Your UC is calculated and awarded for each 'assessment period'. An assessment period is one month:

(a) your first assessment period begins on the day your UC starts (in other words, your date of claim or seven days later: para 3.27);

(b) after that, your assessment periods begin on the same day of each following month, except as shown in table 3.1.

3.37 SSA 8, 10

3.38 D&A 4,51; C&P 38(6), sch 22
ssac.independent.gov.uk/pdf/uc-pip-decisions-appeals-draft-regs-2012-memorandum.pdf – see annex 2 para 5(b)-(d)

3.40 C&P 36(1)

3.41 WRA 7: UC 21(1),(1A),(2); NIWRO 12: NIUC 22(1)-(3)

3.42   Your assessment periods continue with the same start date each month when you are treated as having claimed UC for any of the reasons in paras 3.5-7. But if you have become a couple and both of you were previously getting UC (unless you are subject to the 'full service' rules (para 1.14)) you can chose whose assessment periods will continue. If you don't choose, the DWP chooses for you. If you are subject to the 'full service' rules the assessment period begins on the same day of each month as the assessment period for whichever of the previous awards ended earlier.

The amount of your UC in each assessment period

3.43   The amount of your UC in each assessment period is based on your personal, financial and other circumstances in that assessment period (chapter 9). If your circumstances change, your UC usually changes from the beginning of the assessment period in which the charge occurs (chapter 11).

Table 3.1 **UC assessment periods**

If your first assessment period starts on the day of the month in column 1, your following assessment periods start on the day of the month in column 2 (a), (b) or (c). For backdating see para 3.47.

1 – Start of first assessment period	2 – Start of following assessment periods		
	(a) Except February	(b) February not in a leap year	(c) February in a leap year
1st to 28th	Same as 1	Same as 1	Same as 1
29th	29th	27th	28th
30th	30th	27th	28th
31st	Last day (30th or 31st)	28th	29th

Examples: UC assessment periods

1. When waiting days apply

Liz makes a claim on 11th May and is awarded UC. Waiting days apply to her, so her UC starts on 18th May and her assessment periods begin on the 18th of each month.

2. When waiting days don't apply

Graham makes a claim on 11th May and is awarded UC. Waiting days don't apply to him, so his UC starts on 11th May and his assessment periods begin on the 11th of each month.

3.42   UC 21(3),(4) saved by SI 2014/2887 reg 5 in the 'live service' areas

T3.1   UC 21(2); NIUC 22(2)

Backdating

3.44 You can get UC for a period before you claim it if you meet the qualifying conditions in para 3.43. The UC regulations say that the DWP must 'extend the time for claiming' UC if you meet these conditions. In this guide, the term 'backdating' is used to mean the same thing.

Qualifying for backdating

3.45 You qualify for backdating if:

(a) one or more of the circumstances in table 3.2 applies to you; and

(b) as a result, you 'could not reasonably have been expected to make the claim earlier'.

If you are claiming UC as a couple, one or more of the circumstances in the table must apply to each of you (and (b) above must apply).

The backdating time limit

3.46 The maximum period for which UC can be backdated is one month. For example, if you claim UC on 25th January, it cannot be backdated before 25th December.

3.47 For claimants not subject to 'full service' area rules (para 1.14), whether you qualify for backdating for a full month or less than a month, backdating does not affect when your first and following normal assessment periods start (see para 3.41).

The amount of your UC in a backdated period

3.48 For claimants not subject to 'full service' area rules (para 1.14), the amount of your UC in a backdated period is calculated as follows:

(a) work out how much UC you would qualify for if the backdated period was an assessment period of one month (see para 3.43);

(b) multiply the result by 12;

(c) then divide by 365;

(d) then multiply by the number of days in your backdated period.

Table 3.2 **Backdating UC: qualifying circumstances**

To qualify for backdating one or more of the following must have meant you could not reasonably have claimed UC earlier.

(a) You were previously on JSA(IB), JSA(C), ESA(IR), ESA(C), IS, HB, CTC or WTC, and you were not told about the ending of that benefit until after it had ended.

(b) You have a disability.

3.44   C&P 26(2)

3.45   C&P 26(2)(a),(b),(4)

3.46   C&P 26(2)

3.47   UC 21(5), revoked by SI 2014/2887 3(1)(c) except in 'live service' areas see reg 5; NIUC 22(5)

3.48   UC 21(6), revoked by SI 2014/2887 3(1)(c) except in 'live service' areas see reg 5; NIUC 22(6)

(c)   You had an illness that prevented you from making a claim and you have given the DWP medical evidence that confirms this.

(d)   You were unable to make a claim on-line because the official computer system wasn't working.

(e)   You had a joint claim for UC but this ended because you stopped being a couple, you were the first to tell the DWP and you make a further claim for UC as a single person. (Not applicable to claimants who are subject to 'full service' area rules (para 1.14) – ADM 26/14).

(f)   The DWP decided not to award UC to you and your partner, or your UC award ended, because your partner did not accept the claimant commitment, but you are no longer a couple and you have made a further claim for UC as a single person.

Example: Backdating UC

A single person gets a letter from her local council on Tuesday 9th February saying her HB will end on Sunday 14th February. She is blind, and the friend who normally reads her letters to her is away on holiday from 7th to 21st February. He reads the letter to her on Monday 22nd February. She makes an online claim for UC that day and qualifies for UC. She asks the DWP to backdate her UC.

The DWP's decision

The DWP agrees that from 9th February she meets the conditions for qualifying for backdated UC (see para 3.45) as follows.

Qualifying circumstances

Her circumstances do not fall within (a) in table 3.2, because the council notified her before her HB ended. But they do fall within (b) in the table, because she has a disability.

Ability to claim earlier

Her blindness, and the unavailability of her friend, meant she could not reasonably have been expected to claim UC earlier.

Backdated period

Her first normal UC assessment period starts on 22nd February (when she made her online claim). So her backdated period is the 13 days from 9th to 21st February inclusive.

T3.2(a)   C&P 26(3)(a), (aa); UCTP 2(1) definition: 'existing benefits', 15(2)

T3.2(b)-(d) and (f)   C&P 26(3)(b)-(d) and (f)-(g) respectively

T3.2 (e)   C&P 26(3)(e) revoked by SI 2014/2887 3(2)(c)(i) subject to saving specified in SI 2014/2887 reg 5

Chapter 4 **UC for housing costs**

- The housing costs UC can meet: see paras 4.5-32.
- Liability for housing costs: see paras 4.33-36.
- People who are treated as liable or not liable: see paras 4.37-58.
- Occupying a dwelling as a home: see paras 4.59-62.
- Moving home, having two homes and temporary absences: see paras 4.63-78.
- Prisoners, care leavers and 18-21 year olds: see paras 4.79-84.

General rules

4.1   This chapter explains whether you can get UC towards your housing costs. This is called a UC 'housing costs element'. The three main conditions are in paras 4.2-4. For prisoners, care leavers and 18-21 year olds, see also paras 4.79-84. If you qualify for a UC housing costs element, it is included in the calculation of your UC. The result of the calculation may be that you get all, some or none of your housing costs met by UC (chapter 9).

The payment condition

4.2   You may be able to get UC towards:

(a) your rent payments;

(b) your owner-occupier payments;

(c) your service charge payments.

The rules are in table 4.1 and paras 4.5-32. Chapters 5-8 explain how much of these payments UC can meet.

The liability condition

4.3   You must be 'liable' to make the above payments to qualify for UC towards them. In some cases you can count as liable even if you are not, or count as not liable even though you are. The rules are in paras 4.33-58.

The occupation condition

4.4   You can get a UC housing costs element towards the dwelling you occupy as your home. In some cases you can get UC on two homes or during a temporary absence. The rules are in paras 4.59-78.

Table 4.1 **The housing costs UC can meet**

Rent payments

Renters and shared owners can get help with:

- rent under a tenancy
- rent under a licence or permission to occupy
- houseboat mooring charges
- caravan or mobile home site charges
- payments to charitable almshouses

Owner-occupier payments

Owner-occupiers and shared owners can get help with:

- loan interest payments
- alternative finance payments

Service charge payments

Renters, owner-occupiers and shared owners can get help with service charge payments.

Housing costs UC cannot meet

UC cannot help with payments for:

- a bail or probation hostel
- specified supported accommodation where HB can be paid instead
- a care home
- a tent or its site
- ground rent

Rent payments

4.5   If you are a renter you can get UC towards your rent and service charge payments. This section describes which payments count as 'rent payments'. For service charges, see paras 4.23-32.

Tenancies, licences, etc

4.6   Rent, licence payments and payments for permission to occupy all count as rent payments in UC. For example, this includes most social and private rented housing, whether self-contained or shared, and also bed and breakfast, co-operative and Crown lettings.

T4.1   UC 26, sch 1 paras 1-7; NIUC 27, sch 1 paras 1-8

4.5   UC 25(2)(a),(c); NIUC 26(2)(a),(c)

4.6   UC sch 1 para 2(a),(b); NIUC sch 1 para 2(a),(b)

Houseboats, caravans and mobile homes

4.7 If you live in a houseboat (including a canal narrow boat: CH/4250/2007), caravan or mobile home you can get UC towards your rent payments. Both the following count as rent payments in UC:

(a) the mooring or site charges (whether you rent or own it);

(b) the rent (if you rent it).

Charitable almshouses

4.8 If you live in an almshouse provided by a housing association (table 5.1 and para 6.3) which is a registered charity or exempt from registration, you can get UC towards your maintenance contributions there. But different rules apply if your landlord also provides you with support (paras 4.11-14).

Bail, probation and other hostels

4.9 If you live in a bail or probation hostel (also called 'approved premises') you cannot get UC towards your rent or service charge payments there.

4.10 If you live in any other kind of hostel you can get UC towards your housing costs (see para 4.6) unless it is specified supported accommodation.

Specified supported accommodation

4.11 If you live in 'specified supported accommodation' (called 'specified accommodation' in the law) you cannot get UC towards your rent or service charge payments there. Table 4.2 lists all the types of specified supported accommodation.

4.12 In these cases you can get HB towards your rent and certain service charges as allowed under the HB scheme (see *Guide to Housing Benefit* for details).

4.13 The advantage of being on HB is that:

(a) the HB benefit cap rules apply but you are unlikely to be affected by it because your rent is not counted;

(b) the HB rules about payment of your housing costs apply so any help with your rent can be paid straight to your landlord if you wish.

4.14 Whether your home counts as specified supported accommodation can be straightforward (e.g. in some hostel accommodation) or complicated (e.g. when the arrangements for support are not clear). For further details see the *Guide to Housing Benefit*.

4.7 UC sch 1 para 2(c),(d); NIUC sch 1 para 2(c),(d)

4.8 UC sch 1 para 2(e); NIUC sch 1 para 2(e)

4.9 UC sch 1 paras 1,3(c), 7(3)(b)(ii); NIUC sch 1 paras 1,3(c), 8(3)(b)(ii)

4.10 UC sch 1 para 2(a),(b); NIUC sch 1 para 2(a),(b)

4.11 UC sch 1 para 1 definition: 'exempt accommodation', 3(h), 3A, 7(3)(b)(iv); UCTP 2(1) definition: 'specified accommodation', 5(1)(b), (2)(a); NIUC sch 1 para 1, 3(e), 4, 8(3)(b)(iv)

Table 4.2 **Supported accommodation types**

This table lists the types of 'specified supported accommodation' (see para 4.11). In this table 'CSS' means care, support or supervision.

(a) Exempt accommodation[1]

Accommodation provider:[2]

- a housing association, registered or unregistered; or
- a registered charity; or
- a not for profit voluntary organisation; or
- an English non-metropolitan county council.

Condition:

- the accommodation provider, or someone on its behalf, provides the claimant with CSS.

(b) General supported accommodation[3]

Accommodation provider:[2]

- a housing association, registered or unregistered; or
- a registered charity; or
- a not for profit voluntary organisation; or
- an English county council which has a district council for each part of its area.

Conditions:

- the claimant receives CSS from the accommodation provider or someone else; and
- the claimant was admitted into the accommodation in order to meet a need for CSS.

(c) Domestic violence refuges

Accommodation provider:[2]

- a housing association, registered or unregistered; or
- a registered charity; or
- a not for profit voluntary organisation; or
- an English county council which has a district council for each part of its area; or
- an authority which administers HB.

Conditions:

- the building (or relevant part of it) is wholly or mainly used as non-permanent accommodation for people who have left their home as a result of domestic violence;[4] and
- the accommodation is provided to the claimant for that reason.

(d) Local authority hostels

Accommodation owner/manager:

- the building must be owned or managed by an authority which administers HB.

Conditions:

- the claimant receives CSS from the accommodation provider or someone else; and
- the building provides non-self-contained domestic accommodation with meals or adequate food-preparation facilities (and is not a care home or independent hospital).

Notes

1. *Exempt accommodation:* This also includes resettlement places where the provider was previously getting a grant for the provision or maintenance of such accommodation under s30 of the Jobseekers Act 1995.

2. *Accommodation provider:* In exempt accommodation this must be the tenant's immediate landlord, and this is likely to be the case in types (b) and (c).

3. *General supported accommodation:* This differs from exempt accommodation in two main ways:

    - the CSS can be provided or commissioned independently of the landlord;
    - the claimant must have been 'admitted' into the accommodation in order to receive CSS.

4. *Domestic violence:* This is defined as including controlling or coercive behaviour, violence, or psychological, physical, sexual, emotional, financial or other abuse, regardless of the gender or sexuality of the victim.

Care homes etc

4.15   If you live in a care home (in Scotland a care home service) or independent hospital you cannot get UC towards your rent or service charge payments there.

Tents

4.16   If you live in a tent or similar moveable structure you cannot get UC towards your rent or service charge payments for the tent or its site.

Crofts and croft land

4.17   If you live in a croft in Scotland you can get UC towards your housing costs on the croft and also on any associated croft land. This applies to rent, service charge and also owner occupier payments.

T4.2   As para 4.11

4.15   UC sch 1 paras 1, 3(d), 7(3)(b)(iii); NIUC sch 1 paras 1, 3(d), 8(3)(b)(iii)

4.16   UC sch 1 paras 1, 3(b), 7(3)(b)(i); NIUC sch 1 paras 1, 3(b), 8(3)(b)(i)

4.17   UC sch 3 para 2

Owner-occupier payments

4.18 If you are an owner-occupier you can get UC towards your owner-occupier and service charge payments. This section describes which payments count as 'owner-occupier payments' (see also para 4.17 for crofts). For service charges, see paras 4.23-32.

Loan interest payments

4.19 You can get UC towards the interest payments on a loan secured on your home. This could be a mortgage or similar loan from a bank or building society or any other organisation or individual. Only the interest payments are included. You cannot get UC towards any capital repayments you may be making. See paras 8.23-28 for further details.

Alternative finance payments

4.20 You can get UC towards payments under 'alternative finance arrangements' you entered into to acquire an interest in your home. These are defined in Part 10A of the Income Tax Act 2007 and are typically schemes designed for religious or other purposes to avoid the payment of interest. See paras 8.29-33 and table 8.1 for further details.

Shared owners

4.21 If you are part-buying and part-renting your home in a shared ownership scheme (also called equity sharing) you can get UC towards your rent, owner-occupier and service charge payments (chapters 5 and 8).

Ground rent

4.22 You cannot get UC towards any ground rent you pay on your home.

Service charge payments

4.23 This section describes which payments count as 'service charge payments' in UC. It applies whether you are a renter, owner-occupier or shared owner. It also applies if you only pay service charges.

Definition

4.24 For UC purposes:

(a) services means 'services or facilities for the use or benefit of persons occupying accommodation'; and

---

4.18   UC 25(2)(b),(c); NIUC 26(2)(b),(c)

4.19   UC sch 1 paras 4(1)(a), 5; NIUC sch 1 paras 5(1)(a), 6

4.20   UC sch 1 paras 4(1)(b), 6; NIUC sch 1 paras 5(1)(b), 7

4.21   UC 26(4)-(6); NIUC 27(4)-(6)

4.22   UC sch 1 para 3(a); NIUC sch 1 para 3(a)

4.24   UC sch 1 para 7(1)(a),(b),(2); NIUC sch 1 para 8(1)(a),(b),(2)

(b) 'service charge payments' means:

■ payments for all or part of the costs or charges relating to services or facilities, or

■ amounts which are fairly attributable to the costs or charges relating to available services or facilities.

4.25 Payments which meet the above definition are service charge payments whether they are:

(a) named in an agreement or not;

(b) paid in with the other payments you make on your home or separately;

(c) paid under the agreement under which you occupy your home or under a separate agreement.

Service charges and renters

4.26 If you are a renter you can get UC towards your service charge payments as well as your rent payments. But you cannot get help with these if you live in a bail or probation hostel, specified supported accommodation, care home or tent (see paras 4.9-16).

4.27 If you are renting social housing the distinction between rent and service charge payments is important as not all service charge payments can be included in your eligible rent (see paras 5.11 and 5.27). It is the law which decides whether a particular payment you make is rent or service charge, not your landlord or your letting agreement ([2009] UKUT 28 AAC, CH/3528/2006). For example, a landlord's normal overheads (such as maintenance, insurance, management costs, council tax and charges for voids in certain types of accommodation) count as rent, not services.

4.28 If you are renting private housing, your rent and service charge payments are combined together in the calculation of your eligible rent, so the distinction between them is less important (see para 6.10).

Service charges and owner-occupiers

4.29 If you are an owner-occupier you can get UC towards your service charge payments as well as your owner-occupier payments (see paras 5.27 and 8.10). The distinction between them is important as not all service charge payments can be included in your eligible housing costs (see paras 5.27 and 8.10).

4.30 If you have taken out a loan for your service charge payments, the interest on the loan counts as an owner-occupier payment (see para 4.19), not a service charge payment.

4.25   UC sch 1 para 7(4) ; NIUC sch 1 para 8(4)

4.26   UC 26(2)(b), sch 1 para 7(3)(b), sch 4 para 3; NIUC 27(2)(b), sch 1 para 8(3)(b), sch 4 para 3

4.27   UC sch 1 para 3(g), 8(7), sch 4 paras 3,31; NIUC sch 1 para 3(g), 9(7), sch 4 paras 3,30

4.28   UC sch 1 para 3(g), sch 4 para 3; NIUC sch 1 para 3(g), sch 4 para 3

4.29   UC 26(3)(b)(i), sch 1 paras 4(2), 7(1)(c), 8(7), sch 5 para 3; NIUC 27(3)(b)(i), sch 1 paras 5(2), 8(1)(c), 9(7), sch 5 para 3

4.30   UC sch 1 para 7(3)(a); NIUC sch 1 para 8(3)(a)

Service charges and shared owners

4.31   If you are a shared owner you can get UC towards your service charge payments (see para 5.27) as well as your rent and owner-occupier payments.

Service charges only cases

4.32   You can get UC towards your service charge payments (see para 5.27) even if you are not liable for owner-occupier or rent payments. This could apply if you own your home outright, live in a charitable almshouse where only service charges are payable, etc.

Liability for housing costs

4.33   To get UC for your housing costs you must be liable for rent, owner-occupier or service charge payments:

(a) if you are single, you yourself must be liable for them;

(b) if you are in a couple, either of you or both of you jointly must be liable.

4.34   You are 'liable' for rent, owner-occupier or service charge payments if you are:

(a) actually liable to pay them on a commercial basis (see paras 4.35-36); or

(b) 'treated as liable' to pay them (see paras 4.37-42).

But you cannot get UC for housing costs if you are 'treated as not liable' to pay them (see paras 4.43-58).

Liability

4.35   You are liable to make payments if you have a legal obligation or duty to pay them, whether you are:

(a) solely liable for them; or

(b) jointly liable with your partner; or

(c) jointly liable with others.

If you are an owner-occupier this should be in your loan and/or service charge agreement and is usually straightforward. If you are a renter, see table 4.3.

4.31   UC 26(4),(5), sch 4 para 3; NIUC 27(4),(5), sch 4 para 3

4.32   UC 26(3)(b)(ii), sch 5 para 3; NIUC 27(3)(b)(ii), sch 5 para 3

4.33   UC 25(3); NIUC 26(3)

Table 4.3 **Liability of renters**

(a) *Your letting agreement:* Although letting agreements are often in writing, an agreement by word of mouth can be sufficient to create a liability (R v Poole BC ex parte Ross).

(b) *Your landlord's circumstances:* To grant a letting and create a liability your landlord must have a sufficient legal interest in the dwelling (e.g. as an owner or tenant), but there can be exceptions (CH/2959/2006).

(c) *Your circumstances:* If you already have the right to occupy your home (e.g. as a joint owner) no-one can grant you a letting on it (e.g. another joint owner) so you cannot be liable.

(d) *If you are under 18 or unable to act:* If you have someone appointed to act for you they can enter a letting for you thus making you liable. If you do not and you are incapable of understanding an agreement you entered, the agreement may be void under Scottish law ([2011] UKHT 354 AAC) but not English and Welsh law (CH/2121/2006, ([2012] UKUT 12 AAC). If it is void, you are not liable.

(e) *Arrears, etc:* If you have arrears (even large arrears) or are paying less rent than your agreement says (whether or not your landlord has agreed to this), this does not by itself mean you are not liable ([2010] UKUT 43 AAC). But very large arrears would normally lead a landlord to end a letting, so they may suggest you are not liable (CH/1849/2007).

(f) *If your letting breaks your landlord's occupation agreement:* If by granting your letting your landlord has broken their own occupation agreement on your dwelling (e.g. because it says they must not rent it out), your own letting agreement is still valid so you are liable (Governors of Peabody Donation Fund v Higgins) until and unless your landlord's right to occupy is terminated.

(g) *If your landlord breaks the law:* If by granting your letting your landlord has committed a criminal offence (e.g. because a Housing Act prohibition order bans them from renting out your home), your letting agreement is unlikely to be valid and you are unlikely to be liable.

Commerciality

4.36 Whether your liability is on a commercial basis is a question of fact and judgment based on your individual circumstances. If you are an owner-occupier this is usually straight-forward. If you are a renter see table 4.4.

T4.3   R v Poole BC ex parte Ross 05/05/95 QBD 28 HLR 351

Table 4.4 **Commerciality and renters**

(a) *What makes a letting commercial:* Not only the financial arrangements between you and your landlord but all the terms of your agreement should be taken into account (R v Sutton LBC ex parte Partridge). Each case must be considered on its individual facts and is a matter of judgment (R(H) 1/03). The arrangements between you should be 'arms length' (R v Sheffield HBRB ex part Smith). It is their true factual basis which matters. If these show your letting is 'truly personal' it is not commercial regardless of what is written in your letting agreement (CH/3282/2006).

(b) *Personal and religious considerations:* If your letting is in fact commercial, friendliness and kindness between you and your landlord does not make it non-commercial (R v Poole BC ex parte Ross, CH/4854/2003, [2009] UKUT 13 AAC). If your letting is non-commercial, the fact that it was drawn up in a way that meets your religious beliefs does not make it commercial (R(H) 8/04).

(c) *Lettings between family members:* A letting between family members may or may not be commercial. The family arrangement is not decisive by itself. If the letting enables a disabled family member to be cared for more easily, this is not decisive by itself. Each case depends on its individual circumstances (CH/296/2004, CH/1096/2008, CH/2491/2007).

(d) *If the circumstances of your letting change:* If your letting was commercial when it began, it can become non-commercial if there is an identifiable reason for this (CH/3497/2005).

Treated as liable

4.37   If you are treated as liable to make rent, owner-occupier or service charge payments, you can get UC towards them in the same way as if you were actually liable. This section gives the rules about this.

If a partner, child or young person is liable

4.38   You are treated as liable if:

(a) you are in a couple but claiming UC as a single person (see para 2.8) and your partner (not you) is liable (for other couple cases see para 4.33); or

(b) you are single or in a couple and a child or young person is liable. This means a child or young person you are responsible for or your partner (even if they are not included in your UC claim) is responsible for.

This rule does not apply if you are in a polygamous marriage.

T4.4   R v Sutton LBC ex p Partridge 04/11/94 QBD 28 HLR 315; R v Sheffield HBRB ex p Smith 08/12/94 QBD 28 HLR 36; R (Ross) v Poole BC see footnote T4.3

4.37   UC 25(3)(a)(ii); NIUC 26(3)(a)(ii)

4.38   UC sch 2 para 1; NIUC sch 2 para 1

When the liable person is not paying

4.39 You are treated as liable if:

(a) the person who is actually liable is not making the payments (whether they are an individual, a company or some other body: R(H) 5/05); and

(b) you have to make the payments in order to continue occupying your home; and

(c) it would be unreasonable in the circumstances to expect you to make other arrangements; and

(d) it is reasonable in all the circumstances to treat you as liable. In the case of owner-occupier payments, what is 'reasonable' can be affected by the fact that the liable person may benefit if their housing costs are paid.

4.40 If you meet the above conditions, this rule may help you if (for example) your partner was liable to make the payments and has died, left you, or is absent for too long to get UC for them (see paras 4.74-81). But if the liable person cannot pay because they have been treated as not liable for the housing costs (see paras 4.43-58) it may not be 'reasonable' for you to be treated as liable (CH/606/2005).

When payments are waived in return for repair works

4.41 You are treated as liable for payments if the person they are due to has allowed you not to pay them as reasonable compensation for reasonable repairs or redecorations you have done (and which otherwise they would or should have done).

Rent free periods

4.42 If you are a renter, you are treated as liable for rent and/or service charge payments during any rent free periods allowed under your letting agreement (see para 9.49 for how this is calculated).

Treated as not liable

4.43 If you are treated as not liable to make rent, owner-occupier or service charge payments, you cannot get UC towards them. This section gives the rules about this.

Related to you

4.44 Some of the following rules refer to people who are related to you. This means:

(a) your partner, whether you are claiming UC with them or as a single person; or

(b) a child you or your partner are responsible for; or

4.39   UC sch 2 para 2; NIUC sch 2 para 2

4.41   UC sch 2 para 3; NIUC sch 2 para 3

4.42   UC sch 2 para 4, sch 4 para 7(4); NIUC sch 2 para 4, sch 4 para 6(5)

4.43   UC 25(3)(b); NIUC 26(3)(b)

4.44   UC sch 2 paras 5(1), 6(1), 7(1); NIUC sch 2 paras 5(1), 6(1), 7(1)

    (c) a young person you or your partner are responsible for; or

    (d) a close relative (see para 4.45) of you, or of any of the above, who lives in the accommodation with you (see para 4.46).

Close relative

4.45   A close relative means:

    (a) a parent, step-parent or parent-in-law; or

    (b) a brother or sister, including a half-brother or half-sister (R(SB) 22/87) but not a step-brother or step-sister; or

    (c) a daughter, son, step-daughter, step-son, daughter-in-law or son-in-law; or

    (d) if any of the above is in a couple, their partner.

Living in the accommodation with you

4.46   Some of the rules in this section refer to a person who 'lives in the accommodation' with you. This is likely to include any arrangement in which they share some essential living accommodation with you, even if you each have your own bedroom (CH/542/2006, CH/3656/2004, though the HB regulations in these cases had a different wording).

Renters with a resident landlord who is related to you

4.47   You are treated as not liable to make rent payments (and so cannot get UC towards them) if they are due to a landlord who:

    (a) is related to you (see para 4.44); and

    (b) lives in the accommodation with you (see para 4.46).

If this applies to you, you are also treated as not liable to make service charge payments due to that landlord.

Renters whose landlord is a company connected with you

4.48   You are treated as not liable to make rent payments (and so cannot get UC towards them) if they are due to a company and:

    (a) you are an owner or director of the company; or

    (b) at least one of its owners or directors is related to you (see para 4.44 (a), (c) and (d)).

If this applies to you, you are also treated as not liable to make service charge payments due to that company or another company which meets the above conditions.

4.49   This rule is likely to apply only to registered companies. Details of these and their directors can be checked online with Companies House [www].

4.45   UC 2 definition: 'close relative'; NIUC 2

4.47   UC sch 2 para 5; NIUC sch 2 para 5

4.48   UC sch 2 para 6(1),(2); NIUC sch 2 para 6(1),(2)

4.49   www.companies-house.gov.uk

4.50   An 'owner' of a company is defined in detailed terms based on company law. In broad terms it means someone who has at least 10% of the shares in, or otherwise has significant control of, the company or a parent company, whether alone or with or through associates.

Renters whose landlord is a trust connected with you

4.51   You are treated as not liable to make rent payments (and so cannot get UC towards them) if they are due to a trustee of a trust and:

(a)   you are a trustee or beneficiary of the trust; or

(b)   at least one of its trustees or beneficiaries is related to you (see para 4.44)

If this applies to you, you are also treated as not liable to make service charge payments due to a trustee of that trust or another trust which meets the above conditions.

4.52   A trust is an arrangement whereby the legal ownership of property, money, etc, is separated from its benefits (such as the right to live in it or receive income). Ownership (title) is held by the 'trustees' who ensure that its benefits are delivered for use by someone else, the 'beneficiary'.

Owners etc whose liability is to a household member

4.53   You are treated as not liable to make owner-occupier payments (and so cannot get UC towards them) if they are due to someone who lives in your household. If this applies to you, you are also treated as not liable to make service charge payments due to that person.

4.54   If you are liable for service charge payments only (see para 4.32), you are treated as not liable if they are due to someone who lives in your household.

4.55   A 'household' generally means a domestic arrangement involving two or more people who live together as a unit (R(IS) 1/99), even when they have a reasonable level of independence and self-sufficiency (R(SB) 8/85). It requires a settled course of daily living rather than visits from time to time (R(F) 2/81).

Renters, owners, etc: increases to recover arrears

4.56   If your rent, owner-occupier or service charge payments have been increased in order to recover arrears or other charges on your current or former home, you are treated as not liable for the amount of that increase (and so cannot get UC towards it). This applies only to increases to recover your own arrears or charges, not when increases are imposed across-the-board to recover arrears and charges generally.

4.50   UC sch 2 para 6(3)-(8); NIUC sch 2 para 6(3)-(8)

4.51   UC sch 2 para 7; NIUC sch 2 para 7

4.53   UC sch 2 para 8(1),(2); NIUC sch 2 para 8(1),(2)

4.54   UC sch 2 para 8(3); NIUC sch 2 para 8(3)

4.56   UC sch 2 para 9; NIUC sch 2 para 9

Renters, owners, etc: contrived liability

4.57   You are treated as not liable to make rent, owner-occupier or service charge payments (and so cannot get UC towards them) if the DWP is satisfied that your liability 'was contrived in order to secure the inclusion of the housing costs element in an award of universal credit or to increase the amount of that element' (but only when the other rules in this section do not apply).

4.58   This can only apply if there is evidence that you and/or someone else (such as your landlord or mortgage lender) have 'contrived' your liability as a way of gaining UC. This is different from saying you are not 'liable' for housing costs (see para 4.35), though in practice the two things can be hard to distinguish. If you are a renter, see table 4.5.

Table 4.5 **Contrived liability and renters**

(a)   *What makes a letting contrived:* You must be liable for rent but the liability must have been contrived as a way of gaining UC. The word 'contrived' implies abuse of the UC scheme (CH/39/2007). There must be evidence of this (R v Solihull HBRB ex parte Simpson), and the circumstances and intentions of both you and your landlord should be taken into account (R v Sutton HBRB ex parte Keegan).

(b)   *No liability vs contrived liability:* These are separate considerations and should not be confused (CSHB/718/2002). If your landlord is unlikely to evict you if you do not pay, this can be evidence that you are not liable (see table 4.3(e)) or that your liability is contrived (Solihull case).

(c)   *Lettings between family members:* If your landlord is a relation of yours (e.g. your parent) this does not by itself mean your letting is contrived (Solihull case). But see para 4.47 and table 4.4(c) for other rules which may affect you.

(d)   *Lettings to people on low incomes:* If you cannot afford your rent, this is not evidence that your letting is contrived (Solihull case). And there is no objection to landlords letting to people on low incomes in order to make a profit unless their charges and profits show abuse (CH/39/2007, R v Manchester CC ex parte Baragrove Properties).

Occupying a dwelling as your home

4.59   You can get a UC housing costs element towards the dwelling you normally occupy as your home: see paras 4.60-62.

4.57   UC sch 2 para 10; NIUC sch 2 para 10

T4.5   R (Simpson) v Solihull HBRB 03/12/93 QBD 26 HLR 370; R (Keegan) v Sutton HBRB 15/05/92 QBD 27 HLR 92; R (Baragrove Properties) v Manchester CC 15/03/91 QBD 23 HLR 337

4.59   UC 25(4), sch 3 para 1; NIUC 26(4), sch 3 para 1

A dwelling

4.60   A 'dwelling' has the same meaning as in council tax law (para 15.4). It can be a house, flat, etc, or a houseboat or mobile home used for domestic purposes. It must be in Great Britain.

Normally occupied as your home

4.61   Whether you 'normally occupy' a dwelling as your 'home' is a question of fact which is decided in your individual circumstances, and is not restricted to where your 'centre of interests' is (CH/1786/2005). It usually means more than simply being liable for housing costs: it means being physically present – though exceptions can arise (R(H) 9/05). However, accommodation you occupy only for a holiday cannot be a home and is not included.

4.62   If you occupy more than one dwelling, the question of which one you normally occupy as your home is decided by having regard to 'all the circumstances… including (among other things) any persons with whom [you occupy] each dwelling'. For example, if you are a couple and one of you occupies one home with children at school nearby, and the other is temporarily occupying another home to be near work, the first is likely to be your normal home.

Moving home and having two homes

4.63   Your UC usually changes from the beginning of the assessment period in which you move home (paras 11.23-24). This section explains the further rules that can apply when you move home and when you have two homes.

Fear of violence

4.64   The rules in paras 4.65-66 apply to you if:

(a) you have left your normal home and are occupying other accommodation; and

(b) it is unreasonable to expect you to return to your normal home because you have a reasonable fear of violence in your normal home or from a former partner, whether that violence would be towards yourself, your partner, or a child or young person you are responsible for (see para 4.67); but

(c) you intend to return to your normal home (see para 4.68).

4.65   If you meet the conditions in para 4.64, and are liable to make payments (as a renter or owner-occupier) on both your normal home and the other accommodation, you can – if it is reasonable – get a UC housing costs element covering both dwellings for a maximum of 12 months. For the amount, see table 4.6. If one of the addresses is in 'specified supported accommodation' (see paras 4.11-12), a similar rule allows you to get HB for that address while you are getting a UC housing costs element for the other one.

4.60   WRA 11(2); UC sch 3 para 1(4); NIWRO 16(2); NIUC sch 3 para 1(4)

4.61   UC sch 3 para 1(1); NIUC sch 3 para 1(1)

4.62   UC sch 3 para 1(3); NIUC sch 3 para 1(3)

4.64   UC sch 3 para 6(1); NIUC sch 3 para 6(1)

4.65   UC sch 3 paras 6(2),(4), 9(3); reg 7(6)(a)(i) of SI 2006/213 The Housing Benefit Regulations 2006; NIUC sch 3 paras 5(2),(4), 8(3)

4.66   If you meet the conditions in para 4.64, and are liable to make payments (as a renter or owner-occupier) on only one dwelling (whether this is your normal home or the other accommodation), you can – if it is reasonable – get a UC housing costs element for only that one, unless your absence exceeds or is expected to exceed 12 months: see paras 4.74-78.

4.67   You do not need to have suffered actual violence for the rules in paras 4.64-66 to apply. You need only have a reasonable fear that it may occur. If the fear is of violence in your normal home, it could be from anyone whether or not they are related to you. If the fear is of violence outside your normal home, it must be from a former partner. You do not need to have formally ended the relationship with them, but they must no longer count as your 'partner' for UC purposes (see para 2.48). In each case, the fear of violence must be such that it is unreasonable to expect you to return to your normal home.

4.68   However, you must have an intention to return to your normal home. This can include an intention to return when it becomes safe to do so. If at any point you decide not to return, you can from that point get a UC housing costs element only on what is now your normal home – which is likely to be the dwelling you are currently occupying.

Waiting for adaptations for a disability

4.69   You can get a UC housing costs element for a maximum of one month before you move into a new home if:

(a) you, your partner, or a child or young person you are responsible for is getting:

- the middle or highest rate of the care component of DLA, or
- attendance allowance, or
- the daily living component of PIP; and

(b) the delay in moving was necessary to enable your new home to be adapted to meet that person's disablement needs, and was reasonable; and

(c) you were liable to make payments on your new home (as a renter or owner-occupier) during that period.

The adaptations can include furnishing, carpeting or decorating as well as structural changes, provided that the change makes it more suitable for the needs of the disabled person: R (Mahmoudi) v Lewisham LBC.

4.70   If you meet the conditions in para 4.69, and were also getting a UC housing costs element (as a renter or owner-occupier) on your old home, you can get a UC housing costs element covering both dwellings for a maximum of one month. For the amount, see table 4.6.

Leaving hospital or a care home

4.71   You can get a UC housing costs element on a new home for a maximum of one month before you move into it if:

(a) you have now moved in; and

4.66   UC sch 3 para 6(3); NIUC sch 3 para 5(3)

4.69   UC sch 3 para 7; NIUC sch 3 para 6; R (Mahmoudi) v Lewisham CA (2014) www.bailii.org/ew/cases/EWCA/Civ/2014/284.html

4.70   UC sch 3 para 5; NIUC sch 3 para 4

4.71   UC sch 3 para 8; NIUC sch 3 para 7

(b) you were liable to make payments on it (as a renter or owner-occupier) during that period; and

(c) you were in a hospital (or similar institution) or a care home when the liability to make those payments arose. If you are in a couple, this must apply to both of you.

Moving out for repairs to be done

4.72 If you are required to leave your normal home because essential repairs are being done to it, and you intend to return there afterwards, you can get a UC housing costs element towards only one dwelling:

(a) if you are liable to make payments (as a renter or owner-occupier) on only one dwelling (whether this is your normal home or the other accommodation), you can get a UC housing costs element for only that one;

(b) if you are liable to make payments (as a renter or owner-occupier) on both dwellings, you can get a UC housing costs element only for your normal home.

Large families housed in two dwellings

4.73 You can get a UC housing costs element covering two dwellings (with no time limit) if:

(a) you were housed in them both by a social housing provider (see para 5.4) because of the number of children and young persons living with you; and

(b) you normally occupy both dwellings with children or young persons; and

(c) you are liable to make rent payments on both dwellings.

For the amount, see table 4.6.

Table 4.6 **Calculating a UC housing costs element for two homes**

Fear of violence and waiting for adaptations (see paras 4.65 and 4.70)

(a) Calculate the UC housing costs element separately for each dwelling in the normal way (see chapter 9), making any deductions for housing costs contributions applicable in each case.

(b) Add the two amounts together.

(c) If deductions for housing costs contributions were made for both dwellings, add back to figure (b) the deductions made for:

- the accommodation which is not your normal home, in fear of violence cases;

- your new home, in waiting for adaptations cases.

4.72   UC sch 3 para 3; NIUC sch 3 para 2

4.73   UC sch 3 para 4; NIUC sch 3 para 3

T4.6   UC sch 4 paras 17-19, 25(3),(4); NIUC sch 4 paras 16-18, 24(3),(4)

4.74   UC sch 3 para 9(1),(3); NIUC sch 3 para 8(1),(3)

> **Large families housed in two dwellings** (see para 4.73)
>
> (a) Calculate the UC housing costs element as if the two dwellings were one dwelling by:
>
>   ▪ adding together the two eligible rents;
>
>   ▪ adding together the two lots of bedrooms;
>
>   ▪ making any deductions for housing cost contributions only once.
>
> (b) If the rent on both dwellings is due to a social housing provider (see para 5.4), and neither is temporary accommodation (see para 5.5), make the calculations in (a) using the rules in chapter 5.
>
> (c) In all other cases, make the calculations in (a) using the rules in chapter 6.

Temporary absences

4.74   You can get a UC housing costs element during a temporary absence from your normal home, unless your absence exceeds or is expected to exceed:

(a) 12 months if the absence is because of fear of violence: see para 4.66;

(b) six months if the absence is for any other reason. For example, this could be on holiday, to work or look for work, in hospital, trying out a care home, going to care for (or be cared for by) a friend or relative, and so on. For exceptions, see para 4.76.

4.75   The six months rule (see para 4.74(b)) also applies if you are temporarily absent from accommodation which is not your normal home but which you are occupying because of fear of violence (see para 4.64)

4.76   The rules in paras 4.74-75 do not apply if you are absent for repairs to be done: in that case, see para 4.72. For prisoners, see paras 4.79-81. For absences from Great Britain, see paras 2.26-32.

When is an absence 'temporary'?

4.77   Whether your absence is 'temporary' is a question of fact. For example, it cannot be temporary if you do not intend to return – nor if it is objectively impossible for you to do so (CSHB/405/2005).

The length of absence

4.78   When you begin a temporary absence, the question is whether it is 'expected to exceed' the time limit (six months or 12 months: see para 4.74). If it is, no UC housing costs element can be awarded. The question is reconsidered as and when your situation changes. If, during your absence, it becomes clear that it will exceed the time limit, your UC housing costs element stops. It also stops when your absence reaches the time limit. See paras 4.39-40 for whether someone else may be able to claim a UC housing costs element during your absence.

4.75   UC sch 3 para 9(1); NIUC sch 3 para 8(1)

4.76   UC sch 3 para 9(2); NIUC sch 3 para 8(2)

4.79   UC 2 definition: 'prisoner'; NIUC 2

Prisoners

Who is a 'prisoner'

4.79   For UC purposes, you count as a 'prisoner' if you are:

(a) detained in custody – whether pending trial, pending sentence, on conviction, or sentenced by a court; or

(b) on temporary release (also called home leave or ROTL – release on temporary licence).

But you do not count as a 'prisoner' if you are detained in hospital: see para 2.36.

Eligibility for a UC housing costs element

4.80   You can get a UC housing costs element for the first six months that you are a prisoner if:

(a) you were entitled to UC as a single person immediately before you became a prisoner (whether you were actually single, or in a couple but claiming UC as a single person: see para 2.8); and

(b) the calculation of that award of UC included a UC housing costs element; and

(c) you have not been sentenced, or have been sentenced to a term that is not expected to extend beyond six months.

But you cannot get UC for anything else while you are a prisoner: see para 2.37.

4.81   The rule in para 4.80 means that you cannot get UC at all if you claim it after you become a prisoner. You can get a UC housing costs element only if you claimed it before you became a prisoner:

(a) if you have not been sentenced, you can get this for a maximum of six months (regardless of the possible length of any sentence you may get);

(b) once you are sentenced, the test is whether your term in prison is expected to exceed six months. If it is, your UC housing costs element stops. In considering this any remission you could get must be allowed for. So if your sentence is no longer than one year you are likely to qualify (and your sentence can be longer than this if you are eligible for Home Detention Curfew).

See paras 2.37 and 4.39-40 for whether someone else may be able to claim a UC housing costs element during your absence.

4.80   UC 19(1)-(3); NIUC 19(1)-(3)

Care leavers

Who is a care leaver

4.82 You count as a 'care leaver' if you used to be in local authority care and responsibility for supporting you continues to belong to them.

Eligibility for a UC housing costs element

4.83 The following rules apply if you are a care leaver:

(a) if you are aged 16 or 17 and you are liable for rent (see paras 4.33-34):

- you cannot get a UC housing costs element towards your rent or service charge payments,

- but you can get UC (apart from the housing costs element) if you are in group (a) or (b) in table 2.2;

(b) if you are aged 16 or 17 and you are liable for service charges but not rent:

- you can get UC including a housing costs element towards your service charge payments (see para 4.32) if you are in group (a) or (b) in table 2.2;

(c) if you are aged 18 or more:

- you can get UC including a housing costs element towards your rent, owner-occupier and/or service charge payments.

See paras 2.12-16 for further details, including the rules for couples.

18-21 year olds

Planned changes

4.84 The government plans to stop 18-21 year olds getting a UC housing costs element from April 2017, unless they are:

(a) working or have recently left work;

(b) responsible for at least one child or young person;

(c) in certain 'vulnerable groups' (possibly similar to the excepted groups in table 6.2); or

(d) already getting a UC housing costs element before then.

Eighteen-21 year olds who fall within (a) to (d) should still be able to get UC with a housing costs element from April 2017. Otherwise, for new UC claims from April 2017, 18-21 year olds will only be able to get UC without a housing costs element. (Summer Budget 2015.) No further details were available at the time of writing.

4.82   UC 2 definition: 'looked after by a local authority'; NIUC 2

4.83   UC 8(2),(4), 26(3)(b)(ii), sch 4 para 4; NIUC 8(2),(4), 27(3)(b)(ii), sch 4 para 4

Chapter 5 **Eligible rent: social sector**

- Social sector renters: see paras 5.1-8.
- The amount of your eligible rent: see paras 5.9-15.
- Reductions for under-occupation: see paras 5.16-20.
- Unreasonably high rents etc: see paras 5.21-26.
- Service charges (for social sector renters and owner-occupiers): see paras 5.27-33.
- Changes to social sector rents: see paras 5.34-35.

Social sector renters

5.1 This chapter explains how your UC housing costs element is worked out if you are a social sector renter. For renters, the housing costs element is also called your eligible rent.

5.2 To qualify for a housing costs element you must meet the conditions in chapter 4 as well as this chapter. Chapter 9 explains how your housing costs element affects the amount of your UC, and how it can be reduced if you have one or more non-dependants.

Who is a social sector renter

5.3 You are a social sector renter if you are:

(a) liable to pay rent (with or without service charges) to a social housing provider; and

(b) not in temporary accommodation (see para 5.5).

Social housing providers

5.4 All local authorities and most housing associations and housing trusts are social housing providers. The full list is in table 5.1.

Temporary accommodation

5.5 'Temporary accommodation' means accommodation provided to you because you were homeless or threatened with homelessness, and which you rent from:

(a) a local authority; or

(b) any other social housing provider following an arrangement with a local authority.

5.6 If you are renting temporary accommodation you fall within the rules relating to private sector renters (chapter 6).

5.3   UC sch 4 para 30; NIUC sch 4 para 29

5.4   UC 2 definition: 'local authority', sch 4 para 2; NIUC sch 4 para 2

5.5   UC sch 4 para 21; NIUC sch 4 para 20

5.6   UC sch 4 para 20(1)(b); NIUC sch 4 para 19(1)(b)

Table 5.1 **Social housing providers**

All the following are social housing providers. If you rent your home from any of them (unless it is temporary accommodation) this chapter applies to you.

(a) Local authorities

- in England: county, district and parish councils, London boroughs, the City of London and the council of the Isles of Scilly

- in Wales: county, county borough and community councils

- in Scotland: the council that issues your council tax bill

(b) Housing associations, trusts, etc

- in England: registered providers of social housing (i.e. any landlord who is registered with the Homes and Communities Agency: but see note)

- in Wales and Scotland: registered social landlords, i.e. any landlord that is registered with the Scottish or Welsh Government

Note:

Registered providers of social housing can be profit making or non-profit making. If they are profit making:

- their social housing falls within the rules in this chapter. This means housing let below a market rent (such as part of the Affordable Rent Programme) and shared ownership tenancies;

- their other housing is commercial, and falls within the rules in chapter 6.

If they are non-profit making, all their housing falls within the rules in this chapter.

Exceptions: supported accommodation

5.7   You cannot get UC towards rent or service charges for 'specified supported accommodation', but you may be able to get HB instead. For the details, see paras 4.11-14.

Exceptions: 16/17 year old care leavers

5.8   You cannot get UC towards your rent or service charges if you are aged 16 or 17 and are a care leaver. For further details, see paras 4.82-83.

T5.1   UC 2 – definition of 'local authority', sch 4 para 2; NIUC sch 4 para 2

5.8   UC sch 4 para 4; NIUC sch 4 para 4

The amount of your eligible rent

5.9   The rest of this chapter explains how to work out your eligible rent. The rules are summarised in table 5.2. (For information about general changes to social sector rents, see paras 5.34-35.)

Table 5.2 **Eligible rent: social sector renters**

Step 1: Rent and eligible service charges (see paras 5.10-12)

Your eligible rent is the monthly total of your:

- rent payments; and
- eligible service charge payments (if any).

But this is reduced if any of the following steps apply to you.

Step 2: Certain joint tenancies (see paras 5.13-15)

If you are in a joint tenancy (for example a house-share) and at least one joint tenant is not in your benefit unit, the eligible rent is split between you and the other joint tenant(s).

Step 3: Reductions for under-occupation (see paras 5.16-20)

If your home has more bedrooms than the UC rules say you are entitled to, your eligible rent is reduced by:

- 14% if you have one extra bedroom;
- 25% if you have two or more extra bedrooms.

But this does not apply if Step 2 applies to you.

Step 4: Reductions for high rents (see paras 5.21-26)

If the amounts in Step 1 are unreasonably high, they can be referred to the rent officer, and this may mean your eligible rent is reduced. If this applies to you, this reduction is made before Step 2 or 3.

5.10   The amount of your eligible rent depends on whether you are:

(a) a sole tenant – in other words, you are the only person liable for rent on your home; or

(b) a joint tenant with only your partner and/or a child or young person you are responsible for – in other words, you are all in the same benefit unit; or

(c) a joint tenant with at least one person who is neither your partner nor a child or young person you are responsible for – in other words, you are in different benefit units.

If (a) or (b) applies to you, see the general rule in paras 5.11-12. If (c) applies to you, see paras 5.13-15. (For more on who is in your benefit unit, see paras 2.45 onwards.)

T5.2   UC sch 4 paras 3,5,6,31,34,35; NIUC sch 4 paras 3,5,30,33,34

Eligible rent: the general rule

5.11   The general rule is that your eligible rent is the monthly total of:

(a) your rent payments; and

(b) your eligible service charge payments (if any).

See chapter 4 for which rent and service charge payments count, and paras 5.27-33 for which service charges are eligible. For how to convert payments to a monthly figure, see para 9.47.

5.12   But your eligible rent is reduced if you are under-occupying (see paras 5.16-20). It may also be reduced if your rent or service charge payments are unreasonably high (see paras 5.21-26).

Eligible rent: joint tenants not in the same benefit unit

5.13   If you have at least one joint tenant who is not in your benefit unit, the general rule in paras 5.11-12 applies to you, with two differences:

(a) your eligible rent is your share of the monthly total of rent and eligible service charge payments;

(b) the rules about under-occupation do not apply to you.

5.14   Your share is worked out as follows:

(a) start with the monthly total of the rent and eligible service charge payments on your dwelling;

(b) divide this by the total number of joint tenants (including yourself);

(c) multiply the result by the number of joint tenants (including yourself) who are in your benefit unit.

The last step is only needed in the kind of situation illustrated in example 4.

5.15   But if the above would produce an unreasonable result, the DWP can agree to split the eligible rent in some other way, taking account of all the circumstances, including how many joint tenants there are and how you actually split your rent and eligible service charges. See example 5.

Examples: the amount of eligible rent

In all these examples, the eligible rent for the dwelling (including eligible service charges) is £600 per month, the tenants are not under-occupying, and the rent is not unreasonably high.

1. **A sole tenant**
    - The tenant's eligible rent is simply £600 per month.

2. **A couple who are the only joint tenants**
    - Their eligible rent is simply £600 per month.

5.11   UC sch 4 paras 3,5,6,34,35; NIUC sch 4 paras 3,5,33,34

5.13   UC sch 4 para 35(1),(2),(4); NIUC sch 4 para 34(1),(2),(4)

5.14   UC sch 4 paras 2 definition:'listed persons', 35(4); NIUC sch 4 paras 2, 34(4)

5.15   UC sch 4 para 35(5); NIUC sch 4 para 34(5)

3. **Three joint tenants who are not related**

 ■ Each one's eligible rent is £200 per month.

4. **Three joint tenants two of whom are a couple**

 ■ The couple's eligible rent is £400 per month (two-thirds of £600).
 ■ The single person's eligible rent is £200 per month (a third of £600).

5. **A different split of the eligible rent**

 ■ The couple in example 4 have one bedroom and have always paid half the rent. The same applies to the single person. The DWP agrees it is reasonable to split the eligible rent the same way.
 ■ So the couple's eligible rent is £300 per month, and so is the single person's.

Reductions for under-occupation

5.16 Your eligible rent is reduced if you are under-occupying your home. You count as under-occupying if you have more bedrooms in your home than the UC rules say you are entitled to. Other rooms (such as living rooms) are not taken into account.

Exceptions

5.17 The rules about under-occupation do not apply to you if:

(a) you have a joint tenant who is not in your benefit unit (see para 5.13); or

(b) you are a shared owner (see para 4.21).

How many bedrooms you are entitled to

5.18 You qualify for one bedroom for each of the following occupiers of your home: a couple, a single person over 16, two children under 16 if they are of the same sex, or under 10 if they are of opposite sexes, and each other child. You may also qualify for an additional bedroom if you are a foster parent, or require overnight care, or have a disabled child who needs their own room. See chapter 7 for the full rules. See also paras 11.34-35 for the 'bereavement run-on', which can mean you continue to qualify for a bedroom for up to three months for a member of your household who has died.

The amount of the reduction

5.19 Your eligible rent is reduced by:

(a) 14% if you have one bedroom more than you are entitled to;

(b) 25% if you have two or more bedrooms more than you are entitled to.

See the following examples.

5.16   UC sch 4 para 36(1); NIUC sch 4 para 35(1)

5.17   UC sch 4 paras 35(4), 36(5); NIUC sch 4 paras 34(4), 35(5)

5.18   UC sch 4 paras 8-12; NIUC sch 4 paras 7-11

5.19   UC sch 4 para 36(2)-(4); NIUC sch 4 para 36(2)-(4)

Examples: reductions for under-occupation

1. **One extra bedroom.**
   A couple have two children under 10. They rent a three bedroom house and no-one else lives with them. The eligible rent for the dwelling is £1,000 per month.

   They qualify for two bedrooms, one for themselves and one for the children. Because their home has one bedroom more than this, their eligible rent is reduced by 14% (£140) to £860 per month.

2. **Two extra bedrooms.**
   A single person rents a three-bedroom house and no-one else lives with her. The eligible rent for the dwelling is £1,000 per month.

   She qualifies for one bedroom. Because her home has two bedrooms more than this, her eligible rent is reduced by 25% (£250) to £750 per month.

For further examples, see chapter 7.

Reductions and discretionary housing payments (DHPs)

5.20   If your eligible rent is reduced because you are under-occupying (para 5.19), or because your rent is unreasonably high (para 5.26), you may be able to get a DHP from your local council. For details of the DHP scheme, see chapter 25 of the *Guide to Housing Benefit*.

Reductions for unreasonably high rents

5.21   This section explains how your eligible rent could be reduced if the rent officer makes a 'housing payment determination' saying that your rent and/or service charge payments are unreasonably high. The rent officer can only do this if the DWP requests it. This in practice is rare.

5.22   Rent officers are independent of the DWP. They are government employees in the Rent Service (in England), the Rent Officer Service (in Wales) or the Rent Registration Service (in Scotland).

Housing payment determinations

5.23   The DWP can request a housing payment determination if it considers that your:

(a) rent payments; and/or

(b) eligible service charge payments (see table 5.3),

are 'greater than it is reasonable to meet by way of the [UC] housing costs element'. DWP guidance (ADM F3253) says this could happen if your rent is higher than the LHA figure that would apply if you were a private sector renter, but also says that any special circumstances should be taken into account.

5.23   UC sch 4 paras 3, 32(1),(2); NIUC sch 4 paras 3,31

5.24   When making a housing payment determination, the rent officer:

(a) bases this on the whole of your accommodation (even if you are a joint tenant);

(b) looks separately at each rent and/or service charge payment the DWP has asked them to consider;

(c) decides whether the amount is reasonable (see para 5.25); and

(d) if it is not, tells the DWP what amount is reasonable.

If your home is in the Affordable Rent Programme, the rent officer must agree that your rent payments (but not necessarily your service charge payments) are reasonable.

5.25   The rent officer takes account of the level of rent and/or service charge payments which a landlord could 'reasonably be expected to obtain' on accommodation which:

(a) has the same number of bedrooms as yours;

(b) has the same kind of landlord as yours (see table 5.1(a) or (b));

(c) is in a similar reasonable state of repair to yours; and

(d) is in the same council area as yours. If this area doesn't have enough meeting these conditions, the rent officer includes accommodation in an adjoining council area (or areas).

The rent officer excludes the cost of care, support or supervision and other excluded services (see table 5.3).

How the reduction applies

5.26   if the rent officer decides your rent and/or service charge payments are unreasonably high, the DWP:

(a) uses the amount the rent officer says is reasonable (rather than the amount you actually pay) to work out your eligible rent; but

(b) can agree not to do this if it wouldn't be 'appropriate'.

And if the rules about joint tenants or under-occupying your home (see paras 5.13-19) also apply to you, they apply after this rule (see table 5.2).

Service charges

5.27   This section is about service charges. It applies to the assessment of:

(a) your eligible rent if you are a social sector renter (see para 5.4);

(b) your eligible housing costs if you are an owner-occupier (see para 8.3);

(c) your eligible housing costs if you are a shared owner (see para 4.31) in a scheme run by a social sector landlord (see para 5.3);

(d) your eligible housing costs if you are only liable for service charges (see para 4.32).

If you are a private sector renter, or shared owner in a scheme run by a private sector landlord, different rules apply: see paras 6.9-10.

5.24-25 art 5 and sch 2 of SI 2013/382;

5.26   UC sch 4 para 35(3),(4); NIUC sch 4 para 34(3),(4)

Which service charges are eligible for UC

5.28   A service charge is eligible for UC if it meets all the following conditions:

(a) it is for an eligible kind of service, not an excluded kind (see paras 5.29-30);

(b) you have to pay it in order to occupy your home (see para 5.31); and

(c) the service and amount are reasonable (see paras 5.32-33).

Eligible and excluded services

5.29   Table 5.3 lists the kinds of service charges which are eligible for UC, and those which are excluded from UC.

5.30   If a service charge is:

(a) 'eligible', this means it is included in your eligible rent (if you are a social sector renter) or eligible housing costs (if you are an owner-occupier, shared owner, or only liable for service charges);

(b) 'excluded', this means you cannot get UC for it. See also para 4.27 about distinguishing eligible and excluded services from rent.

A condition of occupying your home

5.31   To be eligible for UC, a service charge must be one you have to pay in order to have the right to occupy your home (see para 4.35). This does not need to have applied since you moved in so long as, when you agreed to pay it, the alternative was that you could lose your home.

Table 5.3 **Service charges**

Eligible service charges

Categories A to D are listed in the law as being eligible for UC.

Maintaining the general standard of accommodation (Category A)

- External window cleaning on upper floors.
- For owner-occupiers and shared owners only, separately identifiable payments for maintenance and/or repairs.

General upkeep of communal areas (Category B)

- Ongoing maintenance and/or cleaning of communal areas.
- Supply of water, fuel or other commodities to communal areas.

'Communal areas' include internal areas, external areas and areas for reasonable facilities such as laundry rooms and children's play areas. DWP guidance (ADM para F2072) says that ground maintenance (e.g. lawn mowing, litter removal and lighting for access areas) and tenant parking (excluding security costs) should be included.

5.28   UC sch 1 para 8(2)-(6); NIUC sch 1 para 9(2)-(6)

5.29   UC sch 1 paras 8(4),(6); NIUC sch 1 paras 9(4),(6)

5.31   UC sch 1 para 8(3); NIUC sch 1 para 9(3)

Basic communal services (Category C)

- Provision of basic communal services.

- Ongoing maintenance, cleaning and/or repair in connection with basic communal services.

'Basic communal services' are those available to everyone in the accommodation, such as refuse collection, communal lifts, secure building access and/or TV/wireless aerials for receiving a free service. DWP guidance (ADM paras F2073-74) says that communal telephones (but not call costs) should be included, as should a fair proportion of the staff management and administration costs of providing communal services.

Accommodation-specific charges (Category D)

- Use of essential items in your own accommodation, such as furniture and domestic appliances.

Excluded service charges

The first two items are listed in the law as being excluded from UC. The others are excluded from UC because they do not fall within categories A to D, and are based on DWP guidance (ADM para F2077).

- Food of any kind.

- Medical or personal services of any kind, including personal care.

- Nursing care, emergency alarm systems or individual personal alarms.

- Equipment or adaptations relating to disability or infirmity.

- Counselling, support or intensive housing management.

- Fuel, water or sewerage charges for your own accommodation.

- Living expenses such as heating, lighting or hot water.

- Cleaning your own accommodation or having your laundry done.

- Gardening your own garden.

- Recreational facilities or subscription/fee-based TV.

- Transport, permits, licences or maintenance of unadopted roads.

- Any other service or facility not included in categories A to D.

Special cases

The following are listed in the law as being excluded from UC, even if they are for items falling within categories A to D.

- Services or facilities that could be met by public funds (e.g. Supporting People) even if you do not yourself qualify for such help.

- Payments which result in an asset changing hands (e.g. if you pay for furniture but after a period it will become yours).

See also paras 5.31-33.

T5.3   UC sch 1 para 8(4),(6); NIUC sch 1 para 9(4),(6)

Examples: Eligible housing costs and service charges

In these examples, the basic communal services are eligible for UC (table 5.3).

1. **A social sector renter**

   A social sector renter (who is not under-occupying) pays rent of £500 per month, plus service charges of £40 per month for basic communal services. So his eligible rent is £540 per month.

2. **An owner-occupier**

   An owner-occupier pays interest on her mortgage and is eligible for £300 per month for this (chapter 8). She also pays £20 per month on her lease for basic communal services. So her eligible housing costs are £320 per month.

Unreasonable kinds of service charges

5.32　　A service charge can be excluded from UC if the services or facilities are of a kind which it is not 'reasonable to provide'. Although the rules about which service charges are eligible are already strict (table 5.3), this rule could, for example, apply to maintenance and/or repairs, and DWP guidance (ADM para F2065) gives the example of maintaining a luxury item such as a swimming pool.

Unreasonably high service charges

5.33　　A service charge can be excluded from UC if the costs and charges relating to it are not of a 'reasonable amount'. But:

(a) if you are a social sector renter or shared owner, the service charge must be referred to the rent officer for a determination (paras 5.21-26). DWP guidance (ADM para F2068) confirms that this means the reasonable part of the amount for the service charge is eligible for UC (and only the unreasonable part is excluded);

(b) if you are an owner-occupier, DWP guidance (ADM para F2066) is that service charges should not be excluded from UC under this rule.

Changes to social sector rents

5.34　　The government plans that social sector rents in England will:

(a) reduce by 1% in April 2016 and in each of the next three Aprils; but

(b) increase for higher income tenants in April 2017 to make them equivalent or nearer to private sector market rent levels.

(Summer Budget 2015.)

5.35　　If you are on UC, your eligible rent should reduce or increase by the same amount, and so should your UC (see paras 11.23-24) unless your other circumstances change. So you shouldn't be better or worse off as a result of the change.

5.32　　UC sch 1 para 8(5); NIUC sch 1 para 9(5)

5.33　　UC sch 1 para 8(5); NIUC sch 1 para 9(5)

Chapter 6 **Eligible rent: private sector**

- Private sector renters: see paras 6.1-6.
- The amount of your eligible rent: see paras 6.7-14.
- The local housing allowance (LHA) figures: see paras 6.15-21.
- The size of accommodation you qualify for: see paras 6.22-27.

Private sector renters

6.1   This chapter explains how your UC housing costs element is worked out if you are a private sector renter. For renters, the housing costs element is also called your eligible rent.

6.2   To qualify for a housing costs element you must meet the conditions in chapter 4 as well as this chapter. Chapter 9 explains how your housing costs element affects the amount of your UC, and how it can be reduced if you have one or more non-dependants.

Who is a private sector renter

6.3   You are a private sector renter if you are liable to pay rent (with or without service charges) to anyone other than a social housing provider. For example, they could be a private landlord, a lettings agency or a company; or a registered charity or other not-for-profit organisation which is not a social housing provider. (For who counts as a social housing provider, see table 5.1.)

Temporary accommodation

6.4   You are also assessed under the rules for private sector renters if you are in temporary accommodation. See para 5.5 for what counts as temporary accommodation.

Exceptions: supported accommodation

6.5   You cannot get UC towards your rent or service charges for 'specified supported accommodation', but you may be able to get HB instead. For the details, see paras 4.11-14.

Exceptions: 16/17 year old care leavers

6.6   You cannot get UC towards your rent or service charges if you are aged 16 or 17 and are a care leaver. For further details, see paras 4.82-83.

6.3   UC sch 4 para 20; NIUC sch 4 para 19

6.4   UC sch 4 para 20(1)(b), 21; NIUC sch 4 para 19(1)(b), 20

6.6   UC sch 4 para 4; NIUC sch 4 para 4

The amount of your eligible rent

6.7   The rest of this chapter explains how to work out your eligible rent.

6.8   The amount of your eligible rent depends on whether you are:

  (a)   a sole tenant – in other words you are the only person liable for rent on your home; or

  (b)   a joint tenant with only your partner and/or a child or young person you are responsible for – in other words, you are all in the same benefit unit; or

  (c)   a joint tenant with at least one person who is neither your partner nor a child or young person you are responsible for – in other words, you are in different benefit units.

If (a) or (b) applies to you, see the general rule in paras 6.9-10. If (c) applies to you, see paras 6.11-13. (For more on who is in your benefit unit, see paras 2.45 onwards.)

Eligible rent: the general rule

6.9   The general rule is that your eligible rent equals:

  (a)   your actual monthly rent (see para 6.10); or

  (b)   if it is lower, the local housing allowance (LHA) figure which applies to you (see para 6.17).

Actual monthly rent

6.10   Your actual monthly rent is the monthly total of your:

  (a)   rent payments; and

  (b)   service charge payments (if any).

See chapter 4 for which rent and service charge payments count. Unlike the rules for social sector renters, no service charges are excluded. For how to convert payments to a monthly figure, see para 9.47.

Eligible rent: joint tenants not in the same benefit unit

6.11   If you have at least one joint tenant who is not in your benefit unit, the actual monthly rent (see paragraph 6.10) is split between you and the other joint tenant(s). Your eligible rent equals:

  (a)   your share of the actual monthly rent; or

  (b)   if it is lower, the LHA figure which applies to you.

6.12   Your share is worked out as follows:

  (a)   start with the actual monthly rent on your dwelling;

  (b)   divide this by the total number of joint tenants (including yourself);

  (c)   multiply the result by the number of joint tenants (including yourself) who are in your benefit unit.

The last step is only needed in the kind of situation illustrated in example 4.

6.9   UC sch 4 para 22; NIUC sch 4 para 21

6.10   UC sch 4 paras 3,5,6,23,24; NIUC sch 4 paras 3,5,22,23

6.11   UC sch 4 para 24(1),(2),(4); NIUC sch 4 para 23(1),(2),(4)

6.12   UC sch 4 paras 2 definition: 'listed persons', 24(4); NIUC sch 4 paras 2, 23(4)

6.13　　But if the above would produce an unreasonable result, the DWP can agree to split the actual monthly rent in some other way, taking account of all the circumstances including how many joint tenants there are and how you actually split your rent and eligible service charges. See example 5.

Legal terminology: 'core rent' and 'cap rent'

6.14　　UC law and guidance uses these terms:

(a)　'core rent' means your actual monthly rent (or share of it);

(b)　'cap rent' means the LHA figure which applies to you.

Examples: Actual monthly rent and eligible rent

1. A sole tenant

- A sole tenant's actual monthly rent is £900.
- If her LHA figure is £800, her eligible rent is £800.

2. A couple who are the only joint tenants

- Their actual monthly rent is £700.
- If their LHA figure is £800, their eligible rent is £700.

3. Three joint tenants who are not related

- The actually monthly rent for their dwelling is £1,200.
- So each one's share of it is £400 (⅓ of £1,200).
- If the LHA figure (for each of them) is £350, each one's eligible rent is £350.

4. Three joint tenants, two of whom are a couple

- The couple are claiming UC, but the single person is not.
- The actual monthly rent for the dwelling is £1,200.
- So the couple's share is £800 (⅔ of £1,200).
- If their LHA figure is £1,000, their eligible rent is £800.

5. A different split of the actual monthly rent

- The couple in example 4 have the use of three of the four bedrooms (they have children) and have always paid ¾ of the rent. The DWP agrees it is reasonable to split the actual monthly rent the same way.
- So their share is now £900 (¾ of £1,200).
- If their LHA figure is £1,000, their eligible rent is £900.

6.13　　UC sch 4 para 24(5); NIUC sch 4 para 23(5)

The local housing allowance (LHA) figures

6.15   LHA figures are used in deciding your eligible rent (see paras 6.9 and 6.11). They are monthly figures set by the rent officer, and are available for the whole of Great Britain online [www].

6.16   Rent officers are independent of the DWP. They are government employees in the Rent Service (in England), the Rent Officer Service (in Wales) or Rent Registration Service (in Scotland).

Which LHA figure applies to you

6.17   The LHA figure which applies to you is the one for:

(a)   the size of accommodation the UC rules say you are entitled to (see paras 6.23-27); and

(b)   the area your home is in. In the law this is called a 'broad rental market area' (BRMA).

Your LHA figure changes whenever you become entitled to a different size of accommodation (e.g. when someone moves in or out) or move to an area with different LHA figures. See paras 11.14-23 for the date your UC changes.

6.18   Each year the rent officer sets LHA figures for the sizes of accommodation listed in table 6.1. These vary from area to area but can never be greater than the national maximum amounts shown in the table. The rent officer sets the figures on the last working day in January, and you can view them online from then (para 6.15). But they take effect:

(a)   on the first Monday in the tax year (11th April in 2016); or

(b)   if you are already on UC, from the first day of your assessment period beginning on or after that date.

6.19   In the year from 11th April 2016, each LHA figure is either:

(a)   the same as April 2015's figure; or

(b)   if this is lower, the rent at the 30th percentile (see para 6.20).

The government plans that LHA figures won't increase until April 2020. (Summer Budget 2015.)

6.20   The rent at the 30th percentile means the highest rent within the bottom 30% of rents in the rent officer's data. This data is taken from actual rents (including service charges) payable during the year ending on the preceding 30th September, on accommodation which:

(a)   is rented on an assured tenancy;

(b)   is in a reasonable state of repair;

(c)   is the correct size and in the correct area (see para 6.17). If that area doesn't have enough accommodation of that size, the rent officer can include accommodation from a comparable area (or areas).

6.15   https://lha-direct.voa.gov.uk/search.aspx
            http://www.nihe.gov.uk/index/benefits/lha/current_lha_rates.htm

6.17   UC sch 4 para 25(1),(2),(5); NIUC sch 4 para 24(1),(2),(5)

6.18-20 arts 3,4 and sch 1 of SI 2013/382;arts 3,4 and sch 1 of NISR 2016/222

The rent officer excludes rents paid by people on UC or HB (this is to avoid the effect UC/HB could have on rent levels) and very high or very low rents (rents which a landlord couldn't 'reasonably be expected to obtain'). The UC rules are slightly different from those used in HB (see chapter 8 of the *Guide to Housing Benefit*) but the LHA figures for UC and HB are usually the same.

Table 6.1 **LHA figures: sizes of accommodation and maximum amounts**

Size of accommodation	National monthly maximum
(a) one-bedroom shared accommodation	£1129.42
(b) one-bedroom self-contained accommodation	£1129.42
(c) two-bedroom dwellings	£1310.13
(d) three-bedroom dwellings	£1536.01
(e) four-bedroom dwellings	£1807.07

Notes:

In practice actual LHAs for (a) are lower than those for (b) (though the national maximums are the same).

For which size of accommodation applies to you, see paras 6.23-27.

LHAs and discretionary housing payments (DHPs)

6.21   If your LHA figure is lower than your actual monthly rent you may be able to get a DHP from your local council. For details of the DHP scheme, see chapter 25 of the *Guide to Housing Benefit*.

T6.1   SI 2013/382 sch 1 para 4, SI 2014/3126;

The size of accommodation you qualify for

6.22   This section explains what size of accommodation you are entitled to if you are a private sector renter. This affects which LHA figure is used in assessing your eligible rent (see para 6.17).

Examples: LHAs and size of accommodation

1. A single person aged 24

- Unless she is in an excepted group (see table 6.2), she qualifies for the LHA for one-bedroom shared accommodation.

2. A single person aged 58

- He qualifies for the LHA for one-bedroom self-contained accommodation.

3. A couple

- They qualify for the LHA for one-bedroom self-contained accommodation.

4. A couple with a son aged 9 and a daughter aged 7

- The couple qualify for the LHA for a two-bedroom dwelling.

5. The son in example 4 reaches the age of 10

- Because the children are no longer expected to share a bedroom (see para 6.25), the couple qualify for the LHA for a three-bedroom dwelling.

6. Three joint tenants who are not related

- They are all under 35 and none of them is in an excepted group (see table 6.2). So each one qualifies for the LHA for one-bedroom shared accommodation.

7. Two brothers who are joint tenants

- They are in their 40s, and the daughter of one of them lives with him.
  So that brother qualifies for the LHA for a two-bedroom dwelling.
  The other brother qualifies for the LHA for one-bedroom self-contained accommodation.

For further examples about size of accommodation, see chapter 7.

Sizes of accommodation

6.23   The sizes of accommodation are given in table 6.1. The size you qualify for is worked out as follows:

(a)   you qualify for accommodation with the appropriate number of bedrooms for the occupiers of your home: see para 6.25. Other rooms (such as living rooms) are not taken into account;

(b)   but the maximum number of bedrooms is always four;

(c)   and if you are a single person under 35, you may qualify for one-bedroom shared accommodation (rather than self-contained): see para 6.26.

Joint tenants not in the same benefit unit

6.24   If you have at least one joint tenant who is not in your benefit unit, the size of accommodation you qualify for is worked out separately for each single joint tenant or joint tenant couple. See the earlier examples 6 and 7.

How many bedrooms you are entitled to

6.25   You qualify for one bedroom for each of the following occupiers of your home: a couple, a single person over 16, two children under 16 if they are of the same sex, or under 10 if they are of opposite sexes, and each other child. You may also qualify for an additional bedroom if you are a foster parent, or require overnight care, or have a disabled child that needs their own room. See chapter 7 for the full rules. See also paras 11.34-35 for the 'bereavement run-on' which can mean you continue to qualify for a bedroom for up to three months for a member of your household who has died. But (unlike social sector tenants) the maximum number of bedrooms for private sector tenants is always four.

Single people under 35

6.26   You qualify for one-bedroom shared accommodation (rather than self-contained) if you are:

(a)   a single person, or in a couple but claiming UC as a single person (see paras 2.6 and 2.8); and

(b)   under 35 years old; and

(c)   not in any of the excepted groups in table 6.2.

This rule never applies to you if you are claiming UC as a couple.

6.23   UC sch 4 paras 8-12, 26-29; NIUC sch 4 paras 7-11, 25-28

6.24   UC sch 4 paras 8,9; NIUC sch 4 paras 7,8

6.25   UC sch 4 paras 8-12, 26; NIUC sch 4 paras 7-11, 25

6.26   UC sch 4 paras 27, 28(1),(2); NIUC sch 4 paras 26, 27(1),(2)

Table 6.2 **Single people under 35: the UC excepted groups**

If you are single and are in any of these groups, you qualify for one-bedroom self-contained accommodation (para 6.26).

(a) You are responsible for one or more children or young persons (see paras 2.61-68).

(b) You have one or more non-dependants (see paras 2.69-76).

(c) You are in receipt of:

■ the middle or highest rate of the care component of disability living allowance, or

■ the daily living component of personal independence payment, or

■ a benefit equivalent to attendance allowance (see para 10.37).

(d) You are aged 18 or over but under 22, and on your 16th birthday you were living in accommodation provided by social services because you were in their care.

(e) You are aged 25 or over, and are an ex-offender managed under a multi-agency (MAPPA) agreement because you pose a serious risk of harm to the public.

(f) You are aged 25 or over, and:

■ you have occupied one or more hostels for homeless people (see para 6.27) for at least three months. This does not need to have been a continuous three months, and it does not need to have been recent; and

■ while you were there, you were offered and you accepted support with rehabilitation or resettlement within the community.

Hostels for homeless people

6.27　A hostel for homeless people (see table 6.2(f)) means a building which meets all the following conditions:

(a) it provides non-self-contained domestic accommodation, together with meals or adequate food-preparation facilities;

(b) its main purpose is to provide accommodation together with care, support or supervision, in order to assist homeless people to be rehabilitated or resettled in the community;

(c) it is:

■ managed or owned by a social housing provider other than a local authority (see table 5.1), or

■ run on a non-commercial basis, and wholly or partly funded by a government department or agency or local authority, or

■ managed by a registered charity or non-profit-making voluntary organisation;

(d) it is not a care home (see para 4.15).

T6.2　UC 2 definition: 'attendance allowance', sch 4 paras 28(3),(4), 29; NIUC 2, sch 4 paras 27(3),(4), 28

6.27　UC 2 definition: 'local authority', sch 4 para 29(10); NIUC sch 4 para 28(6)

Chapter 7 **The size criteria**

- ■ The size criteria and your eligible rent: see paras 7.1-4.
- ■ The number of bedrooms you qualify for: see paras 7.5-7.
- ■ Which occupiers are included: see paras 7.8-18.
- ■ Qualifying for an additional bedroom: see paras 7.19-26.

The size criteria and eligible rent

7.1 This chapter explains how many bedrooms you qualify for in the calculation of your UC if you rent your home. The rules about this are known as the size criteria. Opponents of the rules say they are a 'bedroom tax'; supporters say they prevent a 'spare room subsidy'.

How the number of bedrooms affects your UC

7.2 If you rent your home, the housing costs element of your UC depends on the amount of your eligible rent (see paras 9.39-49). This in turn depends on how many bedrooms you qualify for, as follows:

(a) if you are a social sector renter:
- ■ the UC size criteria say how many bedrooms you qualify for (see para 7.5 onwards),
- ■ your eligible rent is reduced if you have more bedrooms than you qualify for (see paras 5.16-20),
- ■ whether a particular room is a bedroom can therefore be important (see paras 7.6-7);

(b) if you are a private sector renter:
- ■ the UC size criteria say how many bedrooms you qualify for (see para 7.5 onwards),
- ■ your eligible rent is limited to the local housing allowance figure which applies to you (see paras 6.9-27),
- ■ whether a particular room is a bedroom is not relevant, because your LHA figure is based on how many bedrooms you qualify for, not how many there are in your home.

If you are a shared owner the rules in (a) or (b) apply (depending on whether your shared ownership scheme is run by a social or private sector landlord), but only to your eligible rent, not to your owner-occupier payments (see para 8.11). The size criteria do not apply if you are an owner occupier.

7.3 If the size criteria mean your eligible rent is lower than your actual rent, you may be able to get a discretionary housing payment from your local council (see paras 5.20 and 6.21).

7.4 The Court of Appeal has recently decided the HB size criteria unlawfully discriminate against severely disabled children who require overnight care and their parents/carers, and also against women living in sanctuary schemes as a result of domestic violence: (R(Rutherford) v SSWP). This is an HB case but it is likely to apply similarly to UC. In earlier cases, courts and Upper Tribunals decided that the size criteria do not unlawfully discriminate against disabled people or separated parents with shared care of a child. The Supreme Court is expected to decide many of these cases in 2016. The court might (or might not) decide that an additional bedroom should be allowed in one or more of the above situations.

The number of bedrooms you qualify for

7.5　　Table 7.1 shows how to work out the number of bedrooms you qualify for. If you are a private sector renter, the maximum number is four. (This limit does not apply if you are a social renter.)

Table 7.1 **The UC size criteria**

General rules (see paras 7.8-18)

One bedroom is allowed for each of the following occupiers of your home:

- yourself, or yourself and your partner if you are claiming UC as a couple;
- each young person aged 16 or over;
- each non-dependant aged 16 or over;
- two children under 16 of the same sex;
- two children under 10 of the same or opposite sex;
- any other child aged under 16.

Children are expected to share bedrooms in whatever way results in the smallest number of bedrooms. See examples 5 and 6.

Additional bedrooms (see paras 7.19-26)

One or more additional bedrooms can be allowed for:

- a foster parent;
- an overnight carer;
- a disabled child who needs their own bedroom.

What counts as a bedroom

7.6　　Whether a particular room in your home is a bedroom (rather than a living room, storage room, etc) can be important if you are a social sector renter (see para 7.2). Neither UC law nor DWP guidance (ADM paras F3110-38) define what a bedroom is (but see para 7.7). In practice, the DWP is likely to follow your landlord's description of whether a room is a bedroom (for example in your letting agreement), but you can ask the DWP to reconsider this and appeal to a tribunal if you disagree (see chapter 14).

7.4　　R (Rutherford) v SSWP CA (2016) www.bailii.org/ew/cases/EWCA/Civ/2016/29.html

7.5　　UC sch 4 paras 8,10; NIUC sch 4 paras 7,9

T7.1　　WRA 40 definition: 'child'; UC sch 4 paras 10,12; NIWRO 46; NIUC sch 4 paras 9,11

Examples: How many bedrooms you qualify for

1. A single person who is the only occupier

She qualifies for one bedroom. If she is a private renter under 35, see para 6.26 for whether she qualifies for shared or self-contained accommodation.

2. A couple who are the only occupiers

They qualify for one bedroom.

3. A single person with three children

He has sons aged 15 and 8 and a daughter aged 13. The sons are expected to share a bedroom. So the household qualifies for three bedrooms.

4. The older son in example 3 reaches 16

Now none of the children are expected to share a bedroom. So the household qualifies for four bedrooms.

5. A couple with four children

They have daughters aged 13 and 4 and sons aged 14 and 8. The children are expected to share bedrooms in the way that results in the smallest number of bedrooms. So the daughters are expected to share, and so are the sons. The household qualifies for three bedrooms.

6. The couple in example 5 have a baby

The couple now qualify for four bedrooms. No way of sharing bedrooms can result in a lower number.

7. A single person with two non-dependants

The household qualifies for three bedrooms. This is the case even if the non-dependants are a couple: see para 7.14.

Examples including additional bedrooms are later in this chapter.

7.7 The following points are based on the Upper Tribunal's decisions in [2014] UKUT 525 (AAC) and [2016] UKUT 164 (AAC). Because a 'bedroom' is not defined, it has its ordinary or familiar meaning. Practical factors that should be considered include '(a) size, configuration and overall dimensions, (b) access, (c) natural and electric lighting, (d) ventilation, and (e) privacy', taking into account the individual circumstances of the occupiers (see paras 7.8-15 and 7.19-26). For example it should be possible to get into bed from within the room, and there should be somewhere to put clothes and a glass of water. How you actually use a particular room and/or your landlord's description of it are less likely to be relevant than whether it could be used as a bedroom by any of the occupiers. But in [2015] UKUT 282 (AAC) the Upper Tribunal decided that a bedroom can stop counting as a bedroom if exceptional circumstances relating to physical or mental disability mean it is now used as a living room.

Which occupiers are included

7.8   The following occupiers of your home are taken into account in deciding how many bedrooms you qualify for:

(a) the people in your benefit unit (see paras 7.10-13); and

(b) non-dependants (see paras 7.14-16).

In the law these are called the members of your 'extended benefit unit'. See also paras 11.34-35 for the 'bereavement run-on' which can mean you continue to qualify for a bedroom for up to three months for a member of your extended benefit unit who has died.

7.9   The DWP decides which occupiers to include, not (for example) the rent officer. Decisions about this are appealable to a tribunal: [2010] UKUT 79 AAC.

People in your benefit unit

7.10   Your benefit unit is yourself, your partner if you are claiming UC as a couple, and any children or young persons you are responsible for. For more on who is in your benefit unit, see paras 2.45-68. Table 7.1 shows how many bedrooms you qualify for.

7.11   A child or young person who spends time in more than one home (for example with each parent) can only be included as an occupier in one of these (para 2.66).

If you or your partner are temporarily absent

7.12   If you and/or your partner are temporarily absent, you are included as an occupier during:

(a) an absence from Great Britain which meets the conditions in paras 2.29-32; or

(b) the first six months that you are a prisoner if you meet the conditions in para 4.80.

If a child or young person is temporarily absent

7.13   A child or young person who is temporarily absent is included as an occupier during:

(a) any period they are included in your benefit unit (see para 2.68);

(b) the first six months they are in local authority care (see para 2.67); or

(c) the first six months they are a prisoner (see para 4.79).

But (b) and (c) only apply if they were included in your benefit unit immediately before their absence, and you then qualified for the housing costs element in your award of UC.

Non-dependants

7.14   Non-dependants are normally adult sons, daughters or other relatives or friends who live with you on a non-commercial basis. For more on who is a non-dependant, see paras 2.69-76. If you have one or more non-dependants the rules are as follows:

7.8   UC sch 4 para 9(1); NIUC sch 4 para 8(1)

7.10   UC sch 4 para 10(1)(a),(b),(d)-(f); NIUC sch 4 para 9(1)(a),(b),(d)-(f)

7.12   UC sch 4 para 11(1),(3); NIUC sch 4 para 10(1),(3)

7.13   UC sch 4 para 11(1),(2); NIUC sch 4 para 10(1),(2)

(a)   you are allowed one bedroom for each non-dependant over 16 (see table 7.1). This
      means two bedrooms for two non-dependants over 16 even if they are a couple – but
      each of them may be expected to make a housing costs contribution (see para 9.51);

(b)   one bedroom is allowed for each young person over 16 who is the responsibility of a
      non-dependant (rather than of you or your partner) – because they also count as a
      non-dependant (see para 2.72);

(c)   no bedroom is allowed for a child under 16 who is the responsibility of a non-
      dependant (rather than of you or your partner) – but if the child is under 5 the
      non-dependant is not expected to make a housing costs contribution (see table 9.5).

If a non-dependant is temporarily absent

7.15   A non-dependant who is temporarily absent is included as an occupier during:

(a)   an absence from Great Britain which meets the conditions in paras 2.39-32; or

(b)   the first six months that they are a prisoner if they meet the conditions in para 4.79; or

(c)   the first six months in any other circumstances so long as their absence is not expected
      to exceed six months. (For example they could be away studying.)

But these only apply if they were your non-dependant or included in your benefit unit
immediately before their absence, and you then qualified for the housing costs element in
your UC.

Non-dependants in the armed forces

7.16   A non-dependant who is temporarily absent is included as an occupier if they are:

(a)   your or your partner's son, daughter, step-son, or step-daughter; and

(b)   a member of the armed forces who is away on operations (para 2.28).

There is no time limit to this rule so long as they intend to return. But it only applies if they
were your non-dependant or included in your benefit unit immediately before their absence
(whether or not you then qualified for the housing costs element in your UC).

Other people in your home

7.17   Bedrooms are not allowed for anyone other than those described above (paras 7.8-16).
For example they are not allowed for:

(a)   your partner if you are in a couple but claiming UC as a single person (see para 2.8);

(b)   your husbands and wives in a polygamous marriage, other than the one you are
      claiming UC with (see para 2.60);

(c)   lodgers of yours;

(d)   separate tenants of your landlord (if your accommodation is rented out in separate
      lettings);

(e)   a resident landlord/landlady;

7.14   WRA 40 definition: 'child'; UC sch 4 para 10(1)(c); NIWRO 46; NIUC sch 4 para 9(1)(c)

7.15   UC sch 4 para 11(1),(4),(5)(a)-(c),(6); NIUC sch 4 para 10(1),(4),(5)(a)-(c),(6)

7.16   UC sch 4 paras 2 definition: 'member of the armed forces', 11(1),(4),(5)(d); NIUC sch 4 paras 2, 10(1),(4),(5)(d)

(f)   joint tenants who are not in your benefit unit (see para 7.18);

(g)   non-dependants of any of the above (but see para 2.76 for non-dependants of joint tenants);

(h)   children and young persons for whom any of the above are responsible;

(i)   children for whom a non-dependant of yours is responsible (see para 7.14);

(j)   foster children (but see para 7.21 for when an additional bedroom is allowed for a foster parent).

Joint tenants not in the same benefit unit

7.18   The following rules apply if you are in a joint tenancy (for example a house share) and at least one joint tenant is not in your benefit unit:

(a)   if you are a private sector renter, the size criteria apply separately to each single joint tenant or joint tenant couple: see para 6.24;

(b)   if you are a social sector renter, the size criteria do not apply to you at all: see para 5.17.

Additional bedrooms

7.19   This section explains when an additional bedroom is allowed for:

(a)   a foster parent with or without a placed child (see para 7.21);

(b)   an overnight non-resident carer (see paras 7.22-23);

(c)   a disabled child who needs their own room (see paras 7.24-26).

7.20   The maximum number of bedrooms you could qualify for (if you met all the necessary conditions) is:

(a)   one if you or your partner are a foster parent (or you both are); plus

(b)   one if you or your partner require overnight care (or you both do); plus

(c)   one for each disabled child who needs their own room; plus

(d)   the appropriate number of bedrooms for the occupiers in your home (other than in (c)) following the general rules in table 7.1.

But if you are a private sector renter, the maximum number is four. (This limit does not apply if you are a social sector renter.) For social and private sector renters, see also para 7.4 for possible changes to the rules.

Fostering/kinship and pre-adoption

7.21   You qualify for one additional bedroom if you, or your partner if you are claiming UC as a couple:

(a)   are a foster parent (in Scotland a kinship carer) who has a child placed with you; or

(b)   are waiting for a foster placement and have been approved for one, but in this case only for 12 months; or

---

7.20   UC sch 4 paras 12(1),(2),(7)-(9), 26; NIUC sch 4 paras 11(1),(2),(7)-(9), 25

7.21   UC 2 definition: 'foster parent', 89(3)(a), sch 4 para 12(1)(b),(4),(5),(7); NIUC 2, 88(3)(a), sch 4 para 11(1)(b),(4),(5),(7)

(c) have a child placed with you prior to adoption (unless you are the child's close relative: see para 4.45).

If you are claiming UC as a couple you qualify for one additional bedroom, not two, even if you both meet the above condition.

> **Example: A foster parent**
>
> A couple are foster parents. They have two sons of their own aged 13 and 11, and two foster daughters aged 12 and 9.
>
> The couple qualify for one bedroom for themselves, and one for their two sons. Although they do not qualify for a bedroom for the foster daughters under the general rules (table 7.1), they qualify for one additional bedroom as foster parents. So they qualify for three bedrooms in all.

Overnight carers

7.22   You qualify for one additional bedroom if you, or your partner if you are claiming UC as a couple:

(a) are in receipt of

- the middle or highest care component of disability living allowance; or
- the daily living component of personal independence payment; or
- a benefit equivalent to attendance allowance (see para 10.37); and

(b) are provided with overnight care on a regular basis by one or more people who stay in your home and are engaged for this purpose, but who do not live with you.

If you are claiming UC as a couple, you qualify for one additional bedroom, not two, even if you both meet the above condition.

7.23   It is not necessary for an actual bedroom to be available for your overnight carer(s). And the care does not have to be every night or on the majority of nights; but must be provided regularly – which means 'habitually', 'customarily' or 'commonly', not just 'on occasion' or 'when needed': [2014] UKUT 325 (AAC).

> **Example: Overnight carers**
>
> A husband and wife live alone. The husband receives the daily living component of personal independence payment, and a rota of carers stay every night of the week to care for him. At the weekend his wife provides overnight care for him.
>
> The couple qualify for one bedroom under the general rules (table 7.1), and one additional bedroom because the carers provide regular overnight care. So they qualify for two bedrooms in all.

7.22   UC sch 4 para 12(3); NIUC sch 4 para 11(3)

Disabled children who need their own bedroom

7.24   You qualify for one additional bedroom for each child who:

(a) is in receipt of the middle or highest rate of the care component of disability living allowance; and

(b) due to their disability is 'not reasonably able to share a room with another child'.

But an additional bedroom is allowed only if this is necessary to ensure the child has their own bedroom.

7.25   The rule applies only to a child under 16 for whom you, or your partner if you are claiming UC as a couple, are responsible.

7.26   DWP guidance (ADM para F5135) gives examples of a child who 'disrupts the sleep of and may pose a risk to' or 'would significantly disturb the sleep of' another child; but this does not suggest these are the only situations in which an additional bedroom can be allowed.

Examples: Disabled children who need their own bedroom

In these examples the disabled children meet the conditions in para 7.24.

1. A couple with one disabled child

They have no other children. Under the general rules they qualify for two bedrooms. So no additional bedroom is needed or allowed.

2. A couple with two disabled children under 10

They have no other children. Under the general rules they qualify for two bedrooms (table 7.1). An additional bedroom is needed and allowed. So they qualify for three bedrooms.

3. A single person with three children, two of whom are disabled

The disabled children are girls aged 9 and 7. The other child is a boy aged 13. Under the general rules they qualify for three bedrooms. An additional bedroom is needed and allowed. So they qualify for four bedrooms.

7.24   UC sch 4 para 12(6),(8); NIUC sch 4 para 11(6),(8)

7.25   UC sch 4 para 12(6); NIUC sch 4 para 11(6)

Chapter 8 **Eligible housing costs: owner-occupiers**

- General rules: see paras 8.1-7.
- The amount of your housing costs element: see paras 8.8-16.
- The qualifying period: see paras 8.17-22.
- Loan interest payments: see paras 8.23-28.
- Alternative finance payments: see paras 8.29-33.
- The standard rate of interest: see paras 8.34-37.

General rules

8.1 This chapter explains how your UC housing costs element is worked out if you are an owner-occupier or shared owner. The housing costs element is also called your eligible housing costs.

8.2 To qualify for a housing costs element you must meet the conditions in chapter 4 as well as this chapter. Chapter 9 explains how your housing costs element affects the amount of your UC.

Owner occupiers

8.3 You are an owner occupier if you are buying your home or you own it outright, but not if you are a shared owner.

Shared owners

8.4 You are a shared owner if you are liable for both rent payments and owner occupier payments. In England and Wales 'shared owner' means you own a percentage of the value of your home (typically 25%, 50% or 75%) on a shared ownership lease. In Scotland it means you jointly own your home with your landlord and have the right to purchase their share.

UC or JSA/ESA/IS

8.5 The UC housing costs element for owner-occupiers and shared owners replaces support for mortgage interest (SMI) currently payable as part of your claim for JSA(IB), ESA(IR) or IS (see chapter 24 of the *Guide to Housing Benefit*). Although there are many similarities between the two schemes (e.g. the standard interest rate) there are also some important differences such as the rules about non-dependants, earned income, and home improvement loans (paras 8.10-11, 8.14 and 8.26).

8.3   UC sch 5 para 1(2); NIUC sch 5 para 1(2)

8.4   UC 26(6); sch 5 para 1(2); NIUC 27(6); sch 5 para 1(2)

8.5-6   UCPT 2(1) definition: 'existing benefit', 5(1)

8.6 You cannot receive both SMI and a UC housing costs element at the same time. In practice, during the introduction of UC most owner-occupiers and shared owners continue to get JSA/ESA/IS rather than UC, and if you are told you can't claim UC you can claim JSA/ESA/IS instead (paras 1.15-16 and 1.21).

8.7 The government plans to change the rules about SMI payments (and presumably also UC owner-occupier payments) so that from April 2018 they will be repayable interest-bearing loans secured against your home. (Summer Budget 2015.)

The amount of your housing costs element

8.8 The rest of this chapter explains how to work out your housing costs element (your eligible housing costs).

Owner occupier payments

8.9 'Owner occupier payments' (for both owner occupiers and shared owners) are:

(a) eligible loan interest payments (para 8.24); or

(b) alternative finance payments (para 8.29).

Housing costs element for owner occupiers

8.10 If you are an owner occupier, your housing costs element is the total of:

(a) your owner occupier payments; and

(b) your eligible service charges (if any): see para 5.27.

For exceptions see para 8.13. Unlike the housing costs element for renters, no deduction is made for non-dependants.

Housing costs element for shared owners

8.11 If you are a shared owner, your housing costs element is the total of:

(a) your owner-occupier payments; and

(b) your eligible rent including eligible service charges: see chapters 5 and 6.

For exceptions see para 8.13. Deductions can be made from your eligible rent for non-dependants (para 9.51) but not from your owner-occupier payments.

8.9 UC sch 1 para 4; NIUC sch 1 para 5

8.10 UC 26(3), sch 5 paras 2,3,8,9; NIUC 27(3), sch 5 paras 2,3,8,9

8.11 UC 26(4),(5), sch 5 paras 2,3,8,9; NIUC 27(4),(5), sch 5 paras 2,3,8,9

Joint owner-occupiers and joint shared owners

8.12 If you are jointly liable for owner occupier payments with someone else (other than your partner if you are claiming UC as a couple: para 2.7):

(a) the payments can be wholly included in the housing costs element of one of you, or split between the housing costs element of each of you;

(b) but the law and the DWP guidance (ADM para F4072) don't give any further details about how this is decided.

If you are an owner-occupier, the same applies to service charges you are jointly liable for. But if you are a shared owner, see paras 5.13-15 and 6.11-13 for rent and service charges you are jointly liable for.

Exceptions

8.13 You can't get a housing costs element towards your owner occupier payments if:

(a) you or your partner have earned income (para 8.14); or

(b) you haven't yet completed your qualifying period (para 8.17).

If you are an owner-occupier the same applies to service charges. See also chapter 4 for other exceptions.

Earned income

8.14 You can't get UC towards your owner-occupier payments (para 8.9), or service charges if you are an owner-occupier, during any assessment period in which you have earned income. In any assessment period in which you have earned income your housing costs element is:

(a) nil if you are an owner-occupier;

(b) made up of only your eligible rent and service charges if you are a shared owner.

When your earned income stops, this continues to apply until you have completed a new qualifying period (para 8.17).

8.15 There are no exceptions to this rule. It applies to any kind of income you or your partner have (paras 10.3 and 10.7), irrespective of the nature of the work, its duration or the level of earnings. Working for only one day, or for just one hour a week disqualifies you.

8.16 Since even low earnings disqualify you, it is possible to be worse off if you start work. This is known as the employment trap (see the example).

8.12   UC sch 5 paras 2,8(3); NIUC sch 5 paras 2,8(3)

8.14-15 UC sch 5 para 4; NIUC sch 5 para 4

Example: Loss of housing costs element: starting work

Zara is a single 35 year old who is on UC (and CTR) and is buying her home. She has completed the initial qualifying period and gets a UC housing costs element of £260 towards her mortgage interest payments (see para 8.25 and the example there). Then she gets a part-time job for two months. Her earned income is £380 (too low for tax and national insurance, and she doesn't qualify for a UC work allowance: para 10.13). All the figures are monthly (monthly equivalent for CTR).

1. Before she starts work

UC calculation

■ standard allowance (table 9.2)	£317.82
■ housing costs element	£260.00
■ amount of UC	£577.82

Total income (UC only)   **£577.82**

Her council tax payments are nil (see note).

2. While she is working

UC calculation

■ standard allowance	£317.82
■ no housing costs element (para 8.14)	
■ earned income deduction (£380 x 65%)	− £247.00
■ amount of UC	£70.82

Total income (earnings £511 plus UC £57.82)   **£450.82**

Her council tax payments are £26.60
(see note), reducing this to £424.22.

3. After she stops working

UC calculation

The figures are for the first nine assessment periods.

■ standard allowance	£317.82
■ no housing costs element (para 8.14)	
■ amount of UC	£317.82

Total income (UC only)   **£317.82**

Her council tax payments are nil (see note).

Note: council tax and CTR

In periods 1 and 3, her only income is from UC, so her CTR equals the amount of her council tax (paras 17.9-10). In period 2, the calculation is as follows:

- income (para 18.6) = DWP's figure (£380) plus UC (£70.82) £450.82
- applicable amount (para 17.48) = UC maximum award £317.82
- excess income £133.00
- council tax payments after CTR (£133 x 20%) £26.60

The qualifying period

8.17   You can't get UC towards your owner occupier payments (para 8.9), or service charges if you are an owner-occupier, until you have completed a qualifying period. During your qualifying period your housing costs element is:

(a) nil if you are an owner-occupier ;

(b) made up only of your eligible rent and service charges if you are a shared owner.

The length of the qualifying period and conditions during it

8.18   The qualifying period is nine consecutive assessment periods in each of which you must meet the following conditions:

(a) you receive UC;

(b) you don't have any earned income (paras 8.14-15); and

(c) you are liable to make owner-occupier payments if you are an owner-occupier, on your home (chapter 4).

But if your qualifying period began before 1st April 2016, it is three consecutive qualifying periods in each of which you must meet these conditions.

The start of the qualifying period

8.19   The first assessment period to count towards your qualifying period is the one in which you begin to meet the conditions in para 8.18. For example, this could be the one in which your UC starts, or the one in which you stop receiving earned income (see examples).

8.17   UC sch 5 para 5(1); NIUC sch 5 para 5(1)

8.18   UC sch 5 para 5(2); reg 8 of SI 2015/1647; NIUC sch 5 para 5(2)

8.19   UC sch 5 para 5(1),(2); NIUC sch 5 para 5(1),(2)

Examples: The qualifying period

An owner-occupier who claims UC

An owner-occupier claims UC and is awarded it from 10th September (his assessment periods begin on the 10th of each month). He is liable for loan interest payments and eligible service charges on his home, and doesn't have any earned income.

- His qualifying period runs from 10th September to 9th June.
- So his housing costs element (for the loan interest and service charge payments) starts on 10th June.

A shared owner who stops work while on UC

A shared owner claims UC and is awarded it from 10th September (her assessment periods begin on the 10th of each month). She is liable for loan interest payments, rent and eligible service charges on her home. To begin with she has earned income, but this stops on 27th November.

- She is awarded a housing costs element towards just her rent and service charges from 10th September.
- Her qualifying period runs from 10th November to 9th August.
- So her housing costs element increases to include her loan interest payments (as well as her rent and service charges) from 10th August (ADM para F4050).

Interruptions in the qualifying period

8.20　If you stop meeting one or more of the conditions in para 8.18, your qualifying period stops running. And if you then start to meet the conditions again, you have to start and complete a new qualifying period.

Serving the qualifying period while on JSA, ESA or IS

8.21　If you receive JSA, ESA or IS immediately before the start of your UC award, the days you receive JSA/ESA/IS count towards your qualifying period as shown in the example.

Example: Days on JSA and qualifying period

A claimant lives alone. He claims JSA and is awarded it from 10th September. On 17th October his girlfriend moves in and they claim UC as a couple. They are awarded UC from 17th October (their assessment periods begin on the 17th of each month). He is liable for loan interest payments, and neither of them have any earned income.

- The qualifying period runs from 10th September to 9th June.
- Because it ends part way through their assessment period beginning on 17th May, the housing costs element begins on 17th May.

8.20   UC sch 5 para 5(3); NIUC sch 5 para 5(3)

8.21   UC sch 5 para 6; UCTP 29; NIUC sch 5 para 6

Qualifying period for joint owners who cease to be a couple

8.22   This rule applies if your UC award is ended because you have ceased to be part of a couple and a further award is made for the same home. In any further award that follows, the whole or part of any assessment period that would have counted in your previous award is carried forward and taken into account in your further award.

Loan interest payments

Qualifying loan interest payments

8.23   Your total loan interest payments form all or part of your housing costs element (paras 8.9-11). Your loan interest payments are only eligible for help while you occupy the dwelling as your home (chapter 4). You can never get UC towards any capital repayments you make.

What are loan interest payments

8.24   Your loan interest payments are payments of interest on a loan that is secured against the dwelling. Any loan that is secured against the dwelling counts – even if it was taken out to purchase items other than the home itself (e.g. a car loan or for home improvements). If there is more than one loan secured against the property these can be added together (up to the limit: para 8.25).

The calculation and capital limit: loan interest payments

8.25   The amount of your loan interest payments is calculated as follows:

(a) find the amount of capital owed for each eligible loan (para 8.23) and add them together;

(b) multiply the lower of:

- the total from (a), or
- £200,000,

by the standard rate of interest (para 8.34);

(c) divide the result from (b) by 12.

The result is the amount that is included as your loan interest payments. £200,000 is the capital limit. But see para 8.26 if the total capital owed includes a loan to pay for adaptations to the home to meet the needs of a disabled family member.

8.22   UC sch 5 para 7; NIUC sch 5 para 7

8.23   UC sch 5 paras 8(1),10(1); NIUC sch 5 paras 8(1),10(1)

8.24   UC sch 1 para 5, sch 5 para 10(1); NIUC sch 1 para 6, sch 5 para 10(1)

8.25   UC sch 5 para 10(2); NIUC sch 5 para 10(2)

Example: Calculating loan interest payments

A single claimant is an unemployed home owner who meets the claimant commitment and qualifies for UC.

She purchased her home for £140,000 with a £120,000 repayment mortgage from her bank. The term of the loan is 25 years. At the time of her claim she has repaid £20,000 of the outstanding capital. The interest rate currently charged by her bank on her mortgage is 4.00%. Her current mortgage payments are £640.12 per month (including capital and interest).

She has completed her initial qualifying period (para 8.17) and her UC now includes the housing costs element to help with her mortgage. On the date she completes her qualifying period the standard rate of interest is 3.12%.

Her loan interest payments (which make up her housing costs element) are calculated as follows:

Total outstanding capital (£120,000 – £20,000)	£100,000
Standard rate of interest	3.12%
Annual housing costs (3.12% x £100,000)	£3,120
Loan interest payments (£3,120 divided by 12)	£260
Housing costs element (she has no service charge payments)	£260

Adjustment in capital limit for disability adaptations

8.26   The following applies to you if:

(a) you, your partner, or a child or young person you are responsible for is getting:

- the middle or highest rate of the care component of DLA, or
- attendance allowance, or
- the daily living component of PIP; and

(b) you have a loan which was for necessary adaptations to meet the person's disablement needs; and

(c) that loan means that the total capital owed on all your loans is greater than £200,000.

In this case, all the other loans are added together in the usual way (subject to the £200,000 limit) and then the loan for adaptations is added to it. And it is this (higher) figure that is multiplied by the standard rate of interest (and divided by 12).

8.26   UC sch 5 para 10(3); NIUC sch 5 para 10(3)

Changes in capital owed on loans included in housing costs element

8.27 If you have been awarded a housing costs element, any change in the capital owed on a loan already included in that element is not taken into account until:

(a) the first anniversary of the date your housing costs element was first included in your UC award; or

(b) if the change occurs after the first anniversary, the next anniversary.

This rule applies regardless of whether the capital owed has gone up or down. But it does not apply to any new loans taken out after a housing costs element has been included in your award (para 8.28).

Taking out a new loan after a housing costs element award

8.28 If you have been awarded a housing costs element and the amount of capital outstanding has increased because you have taken out a new loan, this is treated as a change of circumstances in the usual way (chapter 11). The change is taken into account from the first day of the assessment period in which the loan was taken out. Any subsequent changes in the capital owed on the new loan are taken into account on the housing costs element anniversary date (para 8.27).

Alternative finance payments

Qualifying alternative finance payments

8.29 Your alternative finance payments form all or part of your housing costs element (paras 8.9-11). To qualify, alternative finance payments must arise from a financial arrangement recognised by UK law that was undertaken for home purchase (either full ownership or shared ownership). Alternative finance payments are only eligible for UC while you occupy the dwelling as your home (chapter 4).

What are alternative finance payments

8.30 Alternative finance payments are payments made under finance products recognised in UK law (known as 'alternative finance arrangements') that have been structured so that they do not involve the payment or receipt of interest. They were designed for Islamic and other religious purposes but can be used by anyone.

8.31 Although alternative finance arrangements are structured differently to conventional finance products, the lender's return is economically equal to the finance costs of borrowing. There many different types of product that are recognised in UK law: the most common examples are in table 8.1.

8.27   UC sch 5 para 10(4),(5); NIUC sch 5 para 10(4),(5)

8.28   D&A 23(1), 34, 35(4);

8.29   UC sch 5 paras 8(1),11(1); NIUC sch 5 paras 8(1),11(1)

8.30   Part 10A Income Tax Act 2007; UC sch 1 para 6; NIUC sch 1 para 7

The calculation and capital limit: alternative finance payments

8.32   The amount of your alternative finance payments is calculated as follows:

(a) find the purchase price of the home (para 8.33) to which the alternative finance payments relate;

(b) multiply the lower of

- the total from (a), or

- £200,000,

by the standard rate of interest (para 8.34);

(c) divide the result from (b) by 12.

The result is the amount that is included in your housing costs element as your alternative finance payments. £200,000 is the capital limit.

8.33   The purchase price is the amount paid by the finance institution to acquire an interest in the property, less the amount of any initial payment (e.g. a deposit) made by you: in other words, the net sum paid by your lender rather than the purchase price of the property itself.

Table 8.1 **Examples of alternative finance arrangements**

Purchase and resale (Murabaha)

The finance provider buys the home and immediately re-sells it to the home-owner at an agreed higher price, payable either in instalments or in one lump sum at a later date.

Diminishing shared ownership (Musharaka)

This is a partnership contract used to purchase a property. The bank and a customer usually both acquire beneficial interests in the asset. The home owner may pay a fee for the use of the asset, while also making payments in stages to gradually acquire an increasing share in, and ultimately all, the ownership of the home.

Profit share agency (Mudaraba/Wakala)

The customer deposits money with a finance institution (usually a bank) and either allows the bank to use it or appoints them as their agent to invest it. Any profits made are shared by the bank and the customer as agreed. The customer may pay a fee to the bank for its services.

Investment bonds (Sukuk)

These are similar to corporate bonds or a collective investment scheme. The finance institution provides the money to the customer to acquire the home in return for a share certificate in the ownership of the property. The property is used and managed by the home owner on behalf of the certificate holders.

8.32   UC sch 5 para 11(2); NIUC sch 5 para 11(2)

8.33   UC sch 5 para 11(3); NIUC sch 5 para 11(3)

The standard rate of interest

8.34 The amount included in your housing costs element for loan interest payments or alternative finance payments is based on the standard rate of interest, rather than the actual interest or alternative finance charges you pay.

8.35 The standard rate of interest is based on the average mortgage rate published by the Bank of England [www]. The standard rate of interest on 1st April 2016 was 3.12%.

8.36 The standard rate of interest is only changed when the Bank of England publishes an average mortgage rate that differs from it by 0.5% or more. The Secretary of State then sets a date on which the revised rate is applied to all claims.

8.37 At least seven days before the new rate comes into effect it must be published on a publicly accessible website, together with the date the new rate will apply from for the calculation of the housing costs element.

8.34-37 UC sch 5 para 12; NIUC sch 5 para 12

8.35 www.bankofengland.co.uk/statistics/bankstats/index.htm see table G1.4 column headed HSDE

Chapter 9 **Calculating UC**

- The amount of your UC: see paras 9.1-11.
- The standard allowance: see paras 9.12-16.
- The work capability elements: see paras 9.17-26.
- The carer and child care costs elements: see paras 9.27-38.
- The housing costs element: see paras 9.39-49.
- Housing cost contributions from non-dependants: see paras 9.50-56.
- The benefit cap: see paras 9.57-67.
- Hardship payments if a sanction applies to you: see paras 9.68-76.

The amount of your UC

9.1 This chapter explains how your UC is calculated and how your housing costs are taken into account.

9.2 UC is a monthly benefit. Your entitlement is assessed for each monthly assessment period of your award. For the rules about assessment periods, and when UC starts, changes and ends, see chapters 3 and 11.

The calculation

9.3 The following steps (see paras 9.4-11) give the calculation of UC. Table 9.1 summarises the rules.

Your maximum UC

9.4 Your 'maximum UC' is the total of:

(a) a standard allowance for your basic living needs, or for both of you if you are claiming UC as a couple;

(b) additional amounts (called 'elements') for children and young persons, work capability, carers and childcare costs; and

(c) a housing costs element towards your rent or owner-occupier costs.

These are explained in paras 9.12-56.

Your income and capital

9.5 The amount of UC you qualify for depends on your income and capital. If you are in a couple, your partner's income and capital are included with yours. This is done even if you are in a couple but claiming UC as a single person (see para 2.8).

9.4   WRA 1(3), 8(2); NIWRO 6(3), 13(2)
9.5   WRA 5; UC 3(3), 18(2), 22(3); NIWRO 10; NIUC 3(2), 18(2), 23(3)

Table 9.1 **Amount of UC**

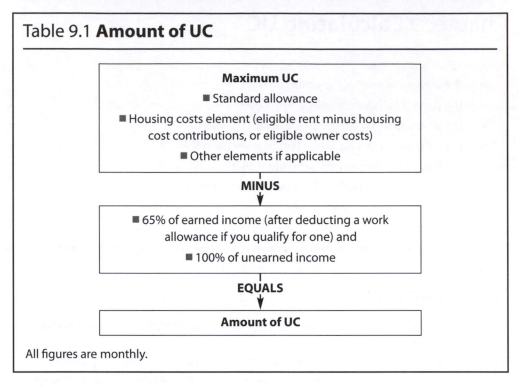

Maximum UC
- Standard allowance
- Housing costs element (eligible rent minus housing cost contributions, or eligible owner costs)
- Other elements if applicable

MINUS

- 65% of earned income (after deducting a work allowance if you qualify for one) and
- 100% of unearned income

EQUALS

Amount of UC

All figures are monthly.

Capital and the capital limit

9.6   If your capital is over £16,000 you do not qualify for UC. See chapter 10 for how your (and your partner's) capital is assessed and which kinds of capital are counted or ignored.

Income and the amount of UC

9.7   If you have no income, you qualify for maximum UC (see para 9.4).

9.8   If you have income, you qualify for maximum UC minus:

(a)   65% of your earned income (after a work allowance has been deducted if you qualify for one); and

(b)   the whole of your unearned income.

See chapter 10 for how your (and your partner's) income is assessed, the work allowance, and which kinds of income are counted or ignored.

Minimum UC

9.9   If the above calculation results in a figure of at least one penny a month you are awarded UC.

T9.1   WRA 5(1)(b),(2)(b), 8(1),(3),(4); UC 22(1), (3); NIWRO 10(1)(b),(2)(b), 13(1),(3),(4); NIUC 23(1), (3)

9.6   WRA 5(1)(a),(2)(a); UC 18(1); NIWRO 10(1)(a),(2)(a); NIUC 18(1)

9.7   WRA 5(1)(b),(2)(b), 8(1)(a); NIWRO 10(1)(b),(2)(b), 13(1)(a)

9.8   WRA 5(1)(b),(2)(b), 8(1),(3),(4); UC 22(1), (3); NIWRO 10(1)(b),(2)(b), 13(1),(3),(4); NIUC 23(1), (3)

9.9   UC 17; NIUC 17

Rounding

9.10 Amounts used in the calculation of UC are rounded to the nearest penny, with halfpennies being rounded upwards.

Other calculation rules

9.11 Your UC can be reduced if:

(a) the 'benefit cap' applies to you (see paras 9.57-67);

(b) a sanction applies to you, but in this case you may qualify for a hardship payment (see paras 9.68-76);

(c) part of your UC is paid to a third party, for example because of rent, mortgage, utility, child support or other debts (see para 12.26); or

(d) an overpayment of UC (or related administrative penalty) is being recovered (see para 13.27).

Examples: Amount of UC

All figures are monthly. None of the claimants have capital. Only the claimant in example 1 is under 25.

1. Single renter under 25, no income

His eligible rent is £400.

Maximum UC

■ standard allowance	£251.77
■ housing costs element (eligible rent)	£400.00
■ total	£651.77
Amount of UC	£651.77

2. Couple, owners, two children, unearned income only

Their eligible owner costs are £250. Their unearned income is £300 maintenance received by one partner.

Maximum UC

■ standard allowance	£498.89
■ two child elements (£277.08 + £231.67)	£508.75
■ housing costs element (eligible owner costs)	£250.00
■ total	£1257.64

Income deduction

■ unearned income £300 x 100%	– £300.00
Amount of UC	£957.64

9.10   UC 6(1); NIUC 7(1)

3. Couple, renters, no children, earned income only

Their eligible rent is £1300. Their earned income is £2500.

Maximum UC

- standard allowance   £498.89
- housing costs element (eligible rent)   £1300.00
- total   £1798.89

Income deduction

- earned income £2500 x 65%   – £1625.00

Amount of UC   £173.89

(They don't qualify for a work allowance: see paras 10.13-15 and the examples there.)

Allowances and elements

9.12   This section explains which UC allowances and elements you qualify for. The ones you qualify for are added together to give your maximum UC (see para 9.4).

9.13   Table 9.2 summarises all the allowances and elements and gives their amounts.

Standard allowance

9.14   Everyone qualifies for a standard allowance. You get:

(a) the single rate if you are a single person, or in a couple but claiming UC as a single person (see para 2.8). A lower figure applies if you are under 25;

(b) the couple rate if you are claiming UC as a couple. A lower figure applies if you are both under 25.

Child element

9.15   You qualify for a child element for each child or young person you are responsible for (see paras 2.61-68):

(a) if you have one child/young person, you get the 'first child' rate;

(b) if you have more than one, you get the 'first child' rate for one of them, and the 'other child' rate for each of the others.

The government plans to limit the child element to two children/young persons for new UC claims made on or after 6th April 2017, and to reduce the 'first child' rate to the amount of the 'other child' rate for first children born on or after that date. (Summer Budget 2015.)

Disabled child addition

9.16   You qualify for the disabled child addition (as well as the child element) for each child or young person who meets one of the following conditions:

9.14   WRA 9; UC 36(1), (3); NIWRO 14; NIUC 38(1), (3)

9.15   WRA 10; UC 24(1), 36(1); NIWRO 15; NIUC 25(1), 38(1)

9.16   WRA 10; UC 2 definition: 'blind', 24(2), 36(1); NIWRO 15; NIUC 2, 25(2), 38(1)

(a) you get the higher rate for each child/young person who is:

- entitled to the highest rate of the care component of disability living allowance, or

- entitled to the enhanced rate of the daily living component of personal independence payment, or

- certified as blind or severely sight-impaired by a consultant ophthalmologist;

(b) you get the lower rate for each child/young person who is:

- entitled to the middle or lowest rate of the care component of disability living allowance, or

- entitled to the standard rate of the daily living component of personal independence payment.

Table 9.2 **UC allowances and elements (2016-17)**

	Monthly amount
Standard allowance	
■ single under 25	£251.77
■ single aged 25 or over	£317.82
■ couple both under 25	£395.20
■ couple at least one aged 25 or over	£498.89
Child element	
■ first child	£277.08
■ each other child	£231.67
Disabled child addition	
■ higher rate	£367.92
■ lower rate	£126.11
Work capability elements	
■ LCW element	£126.11
■ LCWRA element	£315.60
Carer element	£150.39
Childcare costs element	
■ maximum for one child	£646.35
■ maximum for two or more children	£1108.04
Housing costs element	
■ equals eligible rent minus housing cost contributions, or eligible owner-occupier costs	

T9.2   UC 36(1); NIUC 38(1)

Examples: Standard allowance, child element and disabled child addition

The claimants may qualify for other elements, so these examples are not totalled.

1. Single person under 25, one child, not disabled

▪ standard allowance	£251.77
▪ child element (first child)	£277.08

2. Couple over 25, two children, one certified as blind

▪ standard allowance	£498.89
▪ child element (first child)	£277.08
▪ child element (other child)	£231.67
▪ disabled child addition (higher rate)	£367.92

The figures are the same whether the older or younger child is blind.

Work capability elements

9.17   There are two work capability elements, called the 'LCW' and 'LCWRA' elements. You qualify for:

(a) the LCW element if you have limited capability for work; or

(b) the LCWRA element if you have limited capability for work and work-related activity.

The amounts are in table 9.2 and further rules are in paras 9.18-26. The government plans to reduce the LCW element to nil for new UC claims made on or after 6th April 2017. (Summer Budget 2015.)

9.18   You cannot get the LCW and LCWRA elements at the same time:

(a) if you are a single person (or claiming UC as a single person) you get whichever one you qualify for;

(b) if you are claiming UC as a couple, you get:

▪ one LCWRA element if at least one of you qualifies for it, or

▪ one LCW element if at least one of you qualifies for it (and neither of you qualifies for the LCWRA element).

See para 9.29 for further rules which apply if you also qualify for the carer element.

Who has limited capability for work/work-related activity

9.19   Whether you have:

(a) 'limited capability for work' (the LCW condition); or

(b) 'limited capability for work and work-related activity' (the LCWRA condition),

is assessed by the DWP and this decision is appealable to a tribunal (see chapter 14). The

---

9.17   WRA 12; UC 27(1),(2), 36(1); NIWRO 17; NIUC 28(1),(2), 38(1)

9.18   UC 27(4); NIUC 28(4)

9.19   UC 27(3), 38-44, schs 6, 7; NIUC 28(3), 40-45, schs 6, 7

assessment is based on the extent (if any) to which you can carry out a fixed list of activities, and can include a medical examination. The main exceptions to this are in paras 9.20-22.

9.20　　In some circumstances you are accepted as meeting the above conditions without an assessment. For example, you meet the LCW condition if you are in hospital, and meet the LCWRA condition if you are terminally ill. Being terminally ill means suffering a progressive disease which is likely to lead to death within six months. If you are terminally ill you can choose whether or not to tell the DWP. If and when you do, you are awarded the LCWRA element back to when you became terminally ill (para 11.30).

9.21　　You are automatically accepted as meeting the LCW or LCWRA condition in your UC claim if you meet the equivalent condition in a claim for ESA (employment and support allowance), IB, SDA or IS. In ESA, the LCW element is called the 'work-related activity component' and the LCWRA element is called the 'support component'.

9.22　　If you have earned income (paras 10.7-8), the assessment in para 9.19 is not made (so you do not meet the LCW or LCWRA condition) unless:

(a)　its monthly amount is less than what you would get for working 16 hours a week at the national minimum wage; or

(b)　you are on disability living allowance, personal independence payment or attendance allowance or an equivalent benefit (see para 10.37).

The LCW/LCWRA waiting period

9.23　　You cannot get an LCW or LCWRA element until you have completed a waiting period:

(a)　you have to wait three months beginning with:

- the first day you provide medical evidence about your limited capability for work, or

- if you have earned income and para 9.22 applies to you, the day you claim UC or first ask for the LCW/LCWRA component to be included in it;

(b)　your LCW/LCWRA element is awarded from the beginning of the assessment period following the day those three months end.

So because assessment periods are one month, the waiting period can be up to four months. See the example (and for exceptions see para 9.24).

9.20　　UC 2 definition: 'terminally ill', 39(1)(b),(6), 40(1)(b),(5), schs 8,9; NIUC 2, 40(1)(b),(6), 41(1)(b),(5), schs 8,9

9.21　　UC 39(1)(a), 40(1)(a)(ii); UCTP 19-27; NIUC 40(1)(a), 41(1)(a)(ii)

9.22　　UC 41(2),(3); NIUC 42(2),(3)

9.23　　UC 28(1),(2); NIUC 29(1),(2)

Example: The LCW/LCWRA waiting period

A claimant is awarded UC for the first time from 4th July (she was not previously on ESA, IB, SDA or IS). On 17th July she provides medical evidence that she qualifies for the LCW element, and in due course this is accepted.

Her waiting period lasts for three months from 17th July to 16th October, and then until the first day of her next assessment period, which is 4th November. So her LCW element is awarded from 4th November.

Exceptions to the waiting period

9.24   The waiting period does not apply to you if:

(a) you are entitled to ESA and it includes the work-related activity component or support component (see para 9.21) – or this applied on the day before your UC award started but your contributory ESA has now run out; or

(b) you meet similar conditions in relation to a claim for IB, SDA or IS; or

(c) you are terminally ill (see para 9.20); or

(d) you are transferring from the LCW element to the LCWRA element; or

(e) you were getting an LCW/LCWRA element in a previous award of UC which ended because:

- your income became too high. In this case, the gap between the two UC awards must be no longer than six months, or

- you became a couple or stopped being a couple. In this case there must be no gap between the two UC awards.

9.25   If you began a waiting period in a previous award of UC but did not complete it, and the award ended for either of the reasons in para 9.24(e), the waiting period ends on the day it would have ended had that award continued.

UC during a waiting period

9.26   During a waiting period, if the amount of your income means you:

(a) would qualify for UC with the LCW/LCWRA element; but

(b) would not qualify for UC without it,

you are awarded UC of one penny a month.

9.24   UC 28(3)(a),(4)-(6); UCTP 19-27; NIUC 29(3)(a),(4)-(6)

9.25   UC 28(3)(b); NIUC 29(3)(b)

9.26   UC 28(7); NIUC 29(7)

Carer element

9.27   You qualify for the carer element if:

(a) you are the carer of a severely disabled person aged 16 or more (they could be someone in your household, including your partner, or someone outside it) and;

(b) you don't receive any earned income for caring for them; and

(c) either

- you get carer's allowance for this; or

- you meet the conditions for carer's allowance, or you would do except that your earnings are too high. The main condition is that you are regularly and substantially caring for them for at least 35 hours per week.

The amount is in table 9.2. If you are claiming UC as a couple and you each meet the above conditions in relation to a different severely disabled person, you get two carer elements (one each). Further rules are in paras 9.28-29.

Shared care

9.28   Only one person can count as the carer for each severely disabled person. This applies to carer's allowance as well as the carer element. If two or more people meet the conditions for carer's allowance and/or the carer element, you choose who is to count as the carer, or if you do not the DWP chooses. So unless you agree to change who counts as the carer, you can't get the carer element if your partner or anyone else gets carer's allowance or the carer element for the severely disabled person.

9.27   WRA 12; UC 29(1)-(3), 30, 36(1); NIWRO 17; NIUC 30(1)-(3), 31, 38(1)

9.28   UC 29(1),(3); NIUC 30(1),(3)

Carer element and work capability elements

9.29   If you are a single person (or claiming UC as a single person) you cannot get a carer element and an LCW or LCWRA element at the same time. You get the element which is worth most. If you are claiming UC as a couple there are limits to getting these at the same time. You get the element (or combination of elements) that is worth most but without making you better off than two single people. Table 9.3 gives the rules about this.

Table 9.3 **Carer element and LCW/LCWRA elements**

This table explains which element(s) you get if you meet the LCW or LCWRA condition (paras 9.17-25) and the carer condition (paras 9.27-28) at the same time. UC law is not completely clear for couples, and other interpretations may be possible in some couple cases.

Single people who meet the LCWRA condition (para 9.18(a))	■ You get the LCWRA element (but not the carer element).
Single people who meet the LCW condition (para 9.18(a))	■ You get the carer element (but not the LCW element).

Couples who meet the LCWRA condition (para 9.18(b))	■ You get the LCWRA element.
	■ You also get one carer element (never two), but only if:
	  ■ both of you meet the LCWRA condition and one or both of you meet the carer condition, or
	  ■ one of you meets the LCWRA condition and the other one meets the carer condition.

Couples who meet the LCW condition (para 9.18(b))	■ You get two carer elements (but no LCW element) if both of you meet the carer condition. ■ You get one carer element if one of you meets the carer condition. You also get the LCW element, but only if the other one meets the LCW condition.

9.29   UC 29(4); NIUC 30(4)

T9.3   UC 29(4); NIUC 30(4)

Childcare costs element

9.30   You qualify for the childcare costs element if you meet:

(a) the work condition (see paras 9.31-33); and

(b) the childcare costs condition (see paras 9.34-36).

The amount is 85% of your childcare costs up to a fixed limit (see paras 9.37-38).

The work condition

9.31   If you are a single person you meet the work condition if you:

(a) are in paid work; or

(b) have an offer of paid work that is due to start before the end of your next assessment period; or

(c) ceased paid work in your current assessment period or up to one month before it began; or

(d) are receiving statutory sick, maternity, paternity or adoption pay or maternity allowance.

What counts as paid work is described in para 9.33. For assessment periods, see paras 3.41-43.

9.32   If you are in a couple (even if you are claiming UC as a single person):

(a) both of you must meet the work condition in para 9.31; or

(b) one of you must meet the work condition and the other one must be unable to provide childcare because they:

- have limited capability for work (or for work and work-related activity): see para 9.19, or

- meet the conditions for carer's allowance (whether or not they have claimed it), or would do so except that their earnings are too high (see para 9.27), or

- are temporarily absent from your household (see para 2.57).

Paid work

9.33   'Paid work' means work for which payment is made or expected. But it does not include work which is for a charitable or voluntary organisation or as a volunteer, and for which only expenses are paid or expected.

9.30   WRA 12; UC 31; NIWRO 17; NIUC 32

9.31   UC 31(1)(a),(2); NIUC 33(1)(a),(2)

9.32   UC 3(6), 32(1)(b),(2); NIUC 3(5), 33(1)(b),(2)

9.33   UC 2 definition: 'paid work'; NIUC 2

The childcare costs condition

9.34   You meet the childcare costs condition if you or your partner (if you are claiming UC as a couple) pay childcare charges for a child or young person you are responsible for. This means:

     (a)   a child under 16; or

     (b)   a young person aged 16, but only in the period before the first Monday in September following their 16th birthday.

9.35   Childcare charges only count for these purposes if they are to enable you to:

     (a)   continue in paid work; or

     (b)   take up paid work, in the situation in para 9.31(b); or

     (c)   maintain arrangements you had before you left paid work, in the situations in para 9.31(c) and (d).

9.36   In order to count for these purposes, the childcare charges must be paid to:

     (a)   a registered childminder, childcare agency or equivalent (including an approved childcare provider outside Great Britain); or

     (b)   an out-of-school-hours (or pre-school age) scheme provided by a school as part of its school activities.

Childcare provided by the child's 'close relative' (see para 4.45) in the child's home, or by the child's foster parent, is not included.

The amount of the childcare element

9.37   The amount of your childcare element is:

     (a)   85% of the monthly childcare charges you pay; or

     (b)   the maximum amount in table 9.2 (if that is lower than the 85%).

Before 11th April 2016, the childcare element was less generous. If you were already on UC then, the above percentage and the maximum amount in table 9.2 apply from your first assessment period beginning on or after that date.

9.38   Childcare charges you pay in any particular assessment period are only taken into account if you report them to the DWP before the end of your next assessment period. But any amount of your childcare charges is ignored which:

     (a)   the DWP considers excessive for the extent of your or your partner's paid work; or

     (b)   is met by an employer or any other person; or

     (c)   is met by government payments in connection with any work-related activity or training you are undertaking.

9.34   UC 33(1)(a), 35(9); NIUC 34(1)(a), 37(6)

9.35   UC 33(1)(b); NIUC 34(1)(b)

9.36   UC 35; NIUC 37

9.37   UC 34(1), 36(1); NIUC 35(1), 38(1)

9.38   UC 33(2), 34(2),(3); NIUC 34(2), 35(2),(3)

> **Example: Childcare element and amount of UC**
>
> Kate is 29 and has a child of 7. She works and pays a registered childminder £500 a month. Her eligible rent is £800 a month and she has no non-dependants. She has no capital, and her earnings (after deducting the work allowance) are £1500 a month.
>
> **Maximum UC**
>
> | | |
> |---|---|
> | ▪ Standard allowance | £317.82 |
> | ▪ Child element (first child) | £277.08 |
> | ▪ Childcare element (85% of £500) | £425.00 |
> | ▪ Housing costs element (eligible rent) | £800.00 |
> | ▪ Total | £1819.90 |
>
> **Amount of UC**
>
> | | |
> |---|---|
> | ▪ Maximum UC | £1819.90 |
> | ▪ Earned income deduction (65% of £1500) | – £975.00 |
> | ▪ Monthly amount of UC | £844.90 |

The housing costs element

9.39   You qualify for a housing costs element if you are liable to pay rent, owner-occupier and/or service charges on your home. This is explained in chapter 4. See paras 9.41-49 for how much you qualify for.

9.40   Your housing costs element is added to the standard allowance and other elements you qualify for to give the amount of your maximum UC: see para 9.4.

The amount of your housing costs element: owners

9.41   If you are an owner-occupier your housing costs element equals your monthly eligible owner costs (see para 8.4). Unlike the rules for renters, there is no deduction for housing cost contributions.

9.42   But if you are an owner-occupier you do not qualify for a housing costs element if you have any kind of earned income (paras 10.7-8). If you are in a couple (even if you are claiming UC as a single person) you do not qualify if either of you has earned income.

The amount of your housing costs element: shared owners

9.43   If you are a shared owner your housing costs element equals:

(a)   your monthly eligible owner costs (see para 9.41); plus

(b)   your monthly eligible rent minus any housing cost contributions (see paras 9.44-49).

But if you or your partner have any kind of earned income, only (b) applies to you.

9.39   WRA 11(1),(2); UC 25; NIWRO 16(1),(2); NIUC 26

9.41   UC 26(1),(3), sch 5 para 9; NIUC 27(1),(3), sch 5 para 9

9.42   UC sch 5 para 4(1),(2); NIUC sch 5 para 4(1),(2)

9.43   UC 26(1),(4)-(6), sch 5 para 4(3); NIUC 27(1),(4)-(6), sch 5 para 4(3)

The amount of your housing costs element: renters

9.44   If you are a renter your housing costs element equals:

(a) your monthly eligible rent (see paras 5.11 and 6.9);

(b) minus any housing cost contributions expected from non-dependants living with you (see paras 9.50-56).

9.45   If the housing cost contributions are greater than (or equal to) your monthly eligible rent, your housing costs element is nil. No part of the housing cost contributions is ever deducted from your standard allowance or from other elements you qualify for or (if you are a shared owner) your eligible owner costs.

A housing costs element for two homes

9.46   Chapter 3 describes when you can get a housing costs element for two homes. See table 3.1 for how the amount is worked out in double UC cases.

Converting rent and service charges to a monthly figure

9.47   Because UC is a monthly benefit, rent or service charge payments which are not monthly are converted to a monthly figure:

(a) multiply weekly payments by 52 then divide by 12;

(b) multiply two-weekly payments by 26 then divide by 12;

(c) multiply four-weekly payments by 13 then divide by 12;

(d) multiply three-monthly payments by 4 then divide by 12;

(e) divide annual payments by 12.

These rules apply to rent and service charges in all cases. They do not apply to mortgage interest etc (see paras 8.25 and 8.32 instead). The law gives no specific rule for daily payments. But these usually occur only in the types of accommodation where UC cannot be paid towards housing costs (see para 4.11).

Estimating housing costs

9.48   The DWP can agree to estimate the amount of your housing costs if it doesn't have all the information and evidence it needs about them.

Rent-free and service charge-free periods

9.49   If you have rent-free or service charge-free periods (periods during which rent or service charges are not payable), first calculate the annual figure as follows:

(a) if your payments are weekly, subtract the number of rent-free weeks from 52, and multiply your weekly payment by the result;

(b) if your payments are two-weekly, subtract the number of rent-free two-weeks from 26, and multiply your two-weekly payment by the result;

9.44   UC 26(1),(2), sch 4 paras 13,14(2), 22, 23; NIUC 27(1),(2), sch 4 paras 12, 13(2), 21,22

9.45   UC sch 4 para 14(3); NIUC sch 4 para 13(3)

9.47   UC sch 4 para 7(1),(2), sch 5 para 13(1),(3); NIUC sch 4 para 6(1),(2), sch 5 para 13(1),(3)

9.49   UC sch 4 para 7(2)(d),(3),(3A),(4), sch 5 para 13(4),(4A),(5); NIUC sch 4 para 6(2)(d),(3),(4),(5), sch 5 para 13(4),(5),(6)

(c) if your payments are four-weekly, subtract the number of rent-free four-weeks from 13, and multiply your four-weekly payment by the result;

(d) in any other case, add together all the payments you are liable to make over a 12 month period.

Then divide the result by 12.

Housing cost contributions

9.50 This section describes the housing cost contributions which are deducted from your eligible rent to obtain your housing costs element. This applies if you are a renter (see para 9.44) or a shared owner (see para 9.43). No housing cost contributions are deducted if you are an owner-occupier (see para 9.41).

Housing cost contributions and non-dependants

9.51 One housing cost contribution is deducted from your eligible rent for each non-dependant you have. If two non-dependants are a couple, this means two deductions (not one between them).

9.52 A non-dependant is usually an adult son, daughter, other relative or friend who lives with you on a non-commercial basis: for the details see paras 2.69-76. A housing cost contribution can be described as the amount they are expected to contribute towards your housing costs.

The amount of the contribution

9.53 In 2015-17 the monthly amount of the housing cost contribution is £69.37. This figure applies to each non-dependant, no matter what income they have. But see paras 9.55-56 for when no contribution applies at all.

9.54 The UC contribution of £69.37 per month contrasts with the HB figures (which are called non-dependant deductions). These vary with the non-dependant's income and range from £63.05 to £406.47 (monthly equivalents). If you have a non-dependant in well-paid full-time work, you could be more than £4,000 a year better off on UC than on HB.

When no contribution applies

9.55 No housing cost contribution applies for any of the non-dependants in your home if:

(a) you are a single person (or claiming UC as a single person) and you are in any of the groups in table 9.4; or

(b) you are a couple and at least one of you is in any of the groups in table 9.4.

9.56 No housing cost contribution applies for any particular non-dependant in your home who is in any of the groups in table 9.5.

9.51   UC sch 4 para 13; NIUC sch 4 para 12

9.53   UC sch 4 para 14(1); NIUC sch 4 para 13(1)

9.55   UC sch 4 para 15(1); NIUC sch 4 para 14(1)

9.56   UC sch 4 para 16(1); NIUC sch 4 para 15(1)

Table 9.4 **No housing cost contributions: your circumstances**

No housing cost contributions apply if you or your partner are:

(a) in receipt of:

- the middle or highest rate of the care component of disability living allowance, or

- the daily living component of personal independence payment, or

- attendance allowance or an equivalent benefit (see para 10.37);

(b) entitled to any of the above benefits, but not receiving it because of being in hospital; or

(c) certified as blind or severely sight-impaired by a consultant ophthalmologist.

Table 9.5 **No housing cost contributions: non-dependant's circumstances**

No housing cost contribution applies for any non-dependant who is:

(a) under 21 years old;

(b) responsible for a child under 5 years old;

(c) your son, daughter, step-son or step-daughter (or your partner's if you are claiming UC as a couple) and is a member of the armed forces who is away on operations;

(d) in receipt of:

- the middle or highest rate of the care component of disability living allowance, or

- the daily living component of personal independence payment, or

- attendance allowance or an equivalent benefit (see para 10.37);

(e) entitled to one of the above benefits, but not receiving it because of being in hospital;

(f) in receipt of state pension credit;

(g) in receipt of carer's allowance; or

(h) a prisoner (see para 2.36).

T9.4   UC 2 definition: 'blind', sch 4 para 15(2); NIUC 2, sch 4 para 14(2)

T9.5   UC sch 4 paras 2 definition: 'member of the armed forces', 16(2); NIUC sch 4 paras 2, 15(2)

Examples: Housing cost contributions

All figures are monthly. No-one in these examples (except the younger son in example 2) is in any of the groups in tables 9.4 or 9.5.

1. One non-dependant

Ewan's eligible rent is £600. He has one non-dependant, his daughter aged 30.

- Eligible rent   £600.00
- Housing cost contribution   – £69.37
- Housing costs element   £530.63

2. Two non-dependants

Rosie's eligible rent is £950. She has two non-dependants, her sons aged 20 and 24.

- Eligible rent   £950.00
- Housing cost contribution (older son only)   – £69.37
- Housing costs element   £880.63

3. Two non-dependants who are a couple

Hazel's eligible rent is £700. She has two non-dependants, her son and daughter-in-law.

- Eligible rent   £700.00
- Two housing cost contributions (2 x £69.37)   – £138.74
- Housing costs element   £561.26

The UC benefit cap

9.57   This section describes how the 'benefit cap' can reduce your UC so that the total of your UC and other welfare benefits does not exceed a fixed monthly figure. Exceptions are given in paras 9.61-67. If your UC is reduced because of the benefit cap, you may be able to get a discretionary housing payment from your local council (see the *Guide to Housing Benefit*).

The amount of the benefit cap

9.58   The monthly amount of the benefit cap is:

(a)   £1517 if you are a single person (or claiming UC as a single person) and are not responsible for any children or young persons;

(b)   £2167 if you are a single person and are responsible for at least one child or young person;

(c)   £2167 if you are a couple (with or without children/young persons).

This is equivalent to £18,200 and £26,000 per year. The government plans to phase in a reduction of these figures during 2016-17 to £15,410 and £23,000 per year in London, and £13,400 and £20,000 per year elsewhere. (Summer Budget 2015.)

9.58   UC 79(3); NIUC 79(3)

The amount of the UC reduction

9.59   Table 9.6 shows how the amount of the reduction (if any) is calculated.

Table 9.6 **Calculating UC benefit cap reductions**

For each assessment period of one month:

(a)   Add together your and your partner's entitlement to all the following welfare benefits in that month (see para 9.60):

- universal credit
- child benefit
- carer's allowance
- guardian's allowance
- jobseeker's allowance
- employment and support allowance
- maternity allowance
- bereavement allowance
- widow's pension
- widowed mother's allowance
- widowed parent's allowance

(b)   If you qualify for the UC childcare costs element in that month (see para 9.30), subtract its full amount (see para 9.37) from the above total. (Otherwise skip this step.)

(c)   If the result exceeds £1,517/£2,167 (see para 9.58) your UC for that month is reduced by the amount of this excess.

Note:

Step (b) 'protects' the childcare costs element from the UC benefit cap (even if the amount of your UC is less than your childcare costs element). It is described in a more complicated way in the law, but this table gives the correct result.

9.60 The calculation in table 9.6 takes account of the welfare benefits shown there, using the amounts before any reductions for sanctions, recoveries of overpayments and administrative penalties, or payments to third parties. But the following are not included:

(a) any amount of a welfare benefit you do not receive because of the rules about overlapping benefits;

(b) any ESA you are disqualified from receiving.

Benefits other than UC are calculated and converted to a monthly figure as described in para 10.33. Your partner's benefits are included if you are in a couple (even if you are claiming UC as a single person). But if you become a couple while you are on UC, and your new partner is on HB but not UC, their benefits are not included during the assessment period in which you become a couple.

Benefit cap exceptions

9.61 The benefit cap does not apply to you if:

(a) you have earned income of at least £430 a month: see para 9.62; or

(b) you qualify for a 'grace period' after leaving paid work or after a reduction in your earned income: see paras 9.63-66; or

(c) you qualify for certain benefits etc: see para 9.67.

If you have earned income

9.62 The benefit cap does not apply to you in any assessment period of one month in which you have earned income of at least £430 for that month. This means employed and/or self-employed earnings assessed as in chapter 10 (but not the kind of notional self-employed earnings in para 10.78). If you are in a couple, your partner's earned income is included (even if you are claiming UC as a single person).

If you qualify for a grace period

9.63 The benefit cap does not apply to you during a 'grace period'. You qualify for a grace period if you had earned income of at least £430 a month (see para 9.62) in each of the 12 months before your grace period begins, and:

(a) your earned income reduces below £430 a month (or ends) while you are on UC; or

(b) you or your partner (even if you are claiming UC as a single person) ceased paid work (see para 9.33) before your entitlement to UC began.

The rules in these cases are in paras 9.64-66.

9.60   UC 78(2), 80; UCTP 9; NIUC 78, 80

9.62   UC 82(1)(a),(4); NIUC 82(1)(a),(4)

9.63   WRA 40 definition: 'claimant'; UC 78(2), 82(1)(b),(2)-(4); NIWRO 46; NIUC 78(2), 82(1)(b),(2)-(4)

9.64   If your earned income reduces below £430 a month (or ends) while you are on UC (see para 9.63):

(a)   your grace period starts on the first day of the assessment period in which that happens;

(b)   it lasts for nine months (in other words, nine assessment periods).

See example 1.

9.65   If you or your partner ceased paid work before your entitlement to UC began (see para 9.63):

(a)   your grace period starts on the day after you or your partner ceased paid work (if this applies to both you and your partner, use the most recent of these days);

(b)   it lasts nine months – but the benefit cap does not apply to you until the assessment period following the one in which the grace period ends.

See example 2.

9.66   If your entitlement to UC ends before the end of the nine months, your grace period ends when your UC ends.

Examples: The UC benefit cap and the grace period

1. A reduction in earned income

A single person has been on UC for over 12 months. She has had earned income of at least £430 per month throughout that time, so no benefit cap has applied to her (see para 9.62). Her assessment periods start on the 23rd of each month. She loses her job on 31st March.

Her grace period (see para 9.64) begins on 23rd March and lasts nine months until 22nd December. The benefit cap applies to her from 23rd December.

2. Losing paid work then claiming UC

A single person has been working for many years with earned income of at least £430 a month. He loses paid work on 15th January. When he claims UC a few weeks later, he is awarded it from 26th February. So his assessment periods begin on the 26th of each month.

His grace period (see para 9.65) begins on 16th January and lasts nine months until 15th October. The benefit cap applies to him from the first day of his next assessment period, which is 26th October.

9.64   UC 82(2)(a); NIUC 82(2)(a)

9.65   UC 82(2)(b); NIUC 82(2)(b)

9.66   UC 82(2); NIUC 82(2)

If you qualify for certain benefits etc

9.67   The benefit cap does not apply to you in any assessment period in which you (or your partner if you are claiming UC as a couple) are in one or more of the excepted groups in table 9.7.

Table 9.7 **The UC benefit cap: excepted groups**

(a) You qualify for:
- the LCWRA element (see para 9.17), or
- the ESA support component (see para 9.21).

(b) You are in receipt of:
- disability living allowance,
- personal independence payment,
- attendance allowance or an equivalent benefit (see para 10.37),
- industrial injuries benefit,
- a war widow's, widower's, or surviving civil partner's pension,
- a war disablement pension,
- a payment under the Armed Forces and Reserve Forces compensation scheme, or
- a payment from a foreign government similar to any of the last three items;

or are entitled to any of these, but not receiving it because of being in hospital or a care home.

(c) You are responsible for a child or young person who is in receipt of:
- disability living allowance, or
- personal independence payment;

or is entitled to either of these, but not receiving it because of being in hospital or a care home.

Notes:

Couples: If you are claiming UC as a couple, references to 'you' also include your partner.

Carers: If you are caring for your partner (and claiming UC as a couple) or a child or young person, you are in an excepted group if (b) or (c) applies to them. If you get carer's allowance for caring for another relative who lives with you, a High Court decision says you also count as being in an excepted group from 26/11/2015 (Hurley and others v SSWP). From autumn 2016, the government plans to change the law so that everyone on carer's allowance, the carer element or guardian's allowance is in an excepted group (Budget, March 2016).

Other exceptions to the benefit cap: see paras 9.62-66.

9.67   UC 83; NIUC 83

T9.7   UC 83; NIUC 83; Hurley and others v SSWP EWHC (2015); http://www.bailii.org/ew/cases/EWHC/Admin/2015/3382.html

Hardship payments

9.68   This section describes the hardship payments you may be able to get if your UC is reduced due to a sanction.

Sanctions

9.69   In broad terms, a sanction can apply to you if:

(a) you fail to apply for a vacancy, take up an offer of work or meet another work-related requirement when you are on UC (see paras 2.40-44); or

(b) you lost work or pay voluntarily or for no good reason before claiming UC; or

(c) a sanction is transferred from your JSA or ESA to your UC.

There are detailed rules about how long a sanction lasts. The longest possible period is 1,095 days (three years) if you are aged 18 or over, or 28 days if you are aged 16 or 17.

9.70   The monthly amount of the sanction equals:

(a) the whole of your standard allowance (see table 9.2) if you are aged 18 or over; but

(b) 40% of your standard allowance if you:

- are aged 16 or 17, or

- do not have to carry out any work-related requirements because you fall within groups (e) to (h) in table 2.4 (for example because you have a child under one year old), or

- are required only to carry out a work-focused interview (this applies to certain foster parents and friend or family carers with a child under five years old); but

(c) nil if you have limited capacity for work and work-related activity (see para 9.19(b)).

This is deducted from your UC at a daily rate for each day a sanction applies to you. The daily rate is the monthly amount multiplied by 12 then divided by 365. If you are claiming UC as a couple, half the daily rate applies for each one of you a sanction applies to.

9.69   WRA 26, 27; UC 100-113, sch 11; NIWRO 31, 32; NIUC 98-110, sch 11

9.70   UC 90, 91, 111; NIUC 89, 90, 108

Who qualifies for a hardship payment

9.71 You qualify for a hardship payment if:

(a) you are aged 18 or over; and

(b) the amount of your sanction equals the whole of your standard allowance (see para 9.70(a)); and

(c) you make an application (see para 9.73); and

(d) you have met any work-related requirements applying to you during the seven days before your application is made; and

(e) the DWP accepts that you are 'in hardship' (see para 9.72).

If you meet all these conditions, the DWP must award you a hardship payment. See paras 9.74-75 for the period and amount.

What 'in hardship' means

9.72 You are accepted as being in hardship only if you (or you and your partner if you are claiming UC as a couple):

(a) cannot meet your 'most basic and essential needs' for accommodation, heating, food and/or hygiene, or those of a child or young person you are responsible for; and

(b) cannot do so solely because of the sanction; and

(c) have made 'every effort' to:

- access alternative support to meet or partially meet these needs, and

- stop incurring expenditure which does not relate to them.

Applying for a hardship payment

9.73 You can apply for a hardship payment on a form provided for this purpose or in any other manner accepted by the DWP. If you are claiming UC as a couple, either of you may apply. You must provide the information and evidence which is required, and accept that the hardship payment is recoverable (see para 9.76). A separate hardship application is needed for each period (see para 9.74).

The period of the hardship payment

9.74 Each hardship payment covers the period:

(a) from the date you applied (or if later, the date you provided the information and evidence required);

(b) to the day before your next normal monthly payment of UC is due (or if that is seven days or less, to the day before the next but one payment is due).

9.71   WRA 28, UC 116(1); NIWRO 33, NIUC 111(1)

9.72   UC 116(2),(3); NIUC 116(2),(3)

9.73   UC 116(1)(c)-(e); NIUC 111(1)(c)-(e)

9.74   UC 117; NIUC 112

The amount of the hardship payment

9.75   The amount of your hardship payment is calculated as follows:

(a) start with the amount of UC you lost (as a result of the sanction) in the assessment period before the one in which you made your application;

(b) multiply this by 60%;

(c) multiply the result by 12;

(d) then divide by 365;

(e) then multiply by the number of days in the period your hardship payment covers (see para 9.74).

For sanctions lasting longer than a couple of months or so, the effect of this roundabout calculation is approximately the same as if your sanction was 40% of your standard allowance.

Repaying hardship payments

9.76   Hardship payments are 'recoverable'. This means you are expected to repay them by receiving less UC in the future. But you do not have to repay them during any assessment period in which your earnings (including your partner's if you are claiming UC as a couple) are equal to or higher than the minimum wage for your actual or expected hours of work. And once you have had this level of earnings for 26 weeks since a sanction last applied to you, they stop being recoverable altogether.

9.75   UC 118; NIUC 113

9.76   UC 119; NIUC 114

Chapter 10 **Income and capital for UC**

- General rules about income and capital: see paras 10.1-6.
- Earned income and the work allowance: see paras 10.7-15.
- Employed earnings: see paras 10.16-22.
- Self-employed earnings: see paras 10.23-30.
- Unearned income: see paras 10.31-52.
- Capital: see paras 10.53-72.
- Notional income and capital: see paras 10.73-89.

General rules

10.1   This chapter explains how your income and capital are assessed for UC purposes. It describes which kinds of income and capital are counted and which are 'disregarded' (which means ignored).

10.2   If you have capital over £16,000 you cannot get UC: see para 10.55. Otherwise your income (including assumed income from capital) affects how much UC you get: see paras 10.9 and 10.32. For the UC calculations, see paras 9.3-10.

Whose income and capital are taken into account

10.3   The assessment of your UC takes into account:

(a) your income and capital if you are a single person;

(b) your and your partner's income and capital if you are in a couple.

Your partner's income and capital are included with yours even if you are claiming UC as a single person (see para 2.8). In this chapter, 'your' income and capital includes the income and capital of your partner.

Distinguishing capital from income

10.4   The UC regulations do not provide a definition of income or capital, but the distinction is usually straightforward. For example:

(a) capital includes savings, investments and property, but some capital is disregarded;

(b) income includes earnings, maintenance and benefits, but some income is disregarded.

The rest of this chapter gives the rules for all of these.

10.5   A particular payment you receive might be capital (for example an inheritance) or income (for example earnings). This depends on 'the true characteristics of the payment in the hands of the recipient', not what the payment is called by the person paying it: Minter v Hull City Council.

10.3   UC 18, 22(1),(3); NIUC 18, 23(1),(3)

10.5   Minter v Hull CC 13/10/11 CA (2011) www.bailii.org/ew/cases/EWCA/Civ/2011/1155.html

10.6 However, a payment of income can turn into capital. For example, if you receive wages, benefits etc monthly, what you have not spent by the end of the month becomes part of your capital: CH/1561/2005.

Earned income

10.7 Your earned income means your income from:

(a) employment: see paras 10.16-22;

(b) self-employment: see paras 10.23-30; and

(c) any other paid work: see para 10.8.

It can also include notional earnings (see paras 10.74 onwards), but not rent you receive (see paras 10.51 and 10.71-72). For DWP guidance see ADM chapter H3.

10.8 'Any other paid work' means any other work for which payment is made or expected – for example if you are neither employed nor self-employed but someone pays you for a one-off job. It does not include work which is for a charitable or voluntary organisation or as a volunteer, and for which only expenses are paid or expected.

Why earned income is assessed

10.9 Your earned income is taken into account as follows:

(a) if you qualify for a work allowance (paras 10.13-15):

■ first the work allowance is deducted from your earned income,

■ then your 'maximum UC' is reduced by 65% of the remainder (paras 9.7-8);

(b) if you don't qualify for a work allowance:

■ your maximum UC is reduced by 65% of your earned income;

(c) but if you have earned income (no matter how much or how little) you cannot get UC towards any owner-occupier payments (see paras 9.42-43).

The examples illustrate this.

10.10 The UC reduction of 65% of earned income is more generous than the reduction in JSA, ESA and IS, which is 100%. This is designed to encourage people to take up employment or become self-employed or increase their earnings.

Assessment periods and monthly amounts

10.11 The amount of your earned income in any UC assessment period of one month is based on what you actually receive in that month. But if your employment or self-employment has ended in that month the DWP can disregard your earned income from it (though it doesn't have to: [2015] UKUT 696 (AAC)). See also paras 10.22 and 10.30.

10.7   UC 52; NIUC 51

10.8   UC 2 definition: 'paid work', 52(a)(iii); NIUC 2 definition: 'paid work', 51(a)(iii)

10.9   UC 22(1),(3); NIUC 23(1),(3)

10.11   UC 54(1),(6); NIUC 53(1)

10.12   The DWP can estimate the earned income you receive or are expected to receive in:

(a) the first assessment period following your UC claim; and/or

(b) any assessment period for which you do not provide information.

Examples: Earned income, work allowance and housing costs element

In both these examples the claimants are single, over 25 and responsible for one child (but don't qualify for any UC elements apart from that). All figures are monthly..

1. A renter

Penny's monthly eligible rent is £400. Her earned income is £1,°000. Deducting her work allowance of £192 gives £808.

Maximum UC:

■ standard allowance	£317.82
■ child element	£277.08
■ housing costs element (eligible rent)	£400.00
■ total	£994.90
Deduction for earned income: £808 x 65%	– £525.20
Amount of UC	£469.70

2. An owner-occupier

Bob's eligible owner costs are £400. His earned income is £1000. Deducting his work allowance of £397 gives £603.

Maximum UC:

■ standard allowance	£317.82
■ child element	£277.08
■ no housing costs element (because he has earned income)	£0.00
■ total	£594.90
Deduction for earned income: £603 x 65%	– £391.95
Amount of UC	£202.95

The work allowance

10.13   You qualify for a work allowance if you or your partner:

(a) are responsible for at least one child or young person (paras 2.61-64); and/or

(b) have limited capability for work or for work and work-related activity (para 9.19).

10.14   The UC work allowance is deducted from your monthly earned income (from employment, self-employment, etc: paras 10.7-8). It can be described as the monthly amount you are allowed to 'keep' before your earned income affects the amount of your UC.

10.12   UC 54(2); NIUC 53(2)

10.13-14   UC 22(1)(b),(3); NIUC 23(1)(b),(3)

The amount of the work allowance

10.15   The amounts of the work allowance are in table 10.1. These apply from 11th April 2016. They apply whether you are single or in a couple. If you are in a couple they apply to your combined earnings (even if you are claiming UC as a single person: para 2.8). Before 11th April 2016 the work allowance was in many cases more generous. If you were already on UC then, the amount in table 10.1 applies from your assessment period beginning on or after that date.

Table 10.1 **The UC work allowance**

	Monthly amount
Lower rate	£192
This applies if you are a renter or shared owner (in other words, when your UC includes an amount for rent)	
Higher rate	£397
This applies if you are an owner occupier or have no housing costs (in other words, when your UC doesn't include an amount for housing costs: for owners, see para 10.9)	
These amounts apply to all single people and couples who qualify: paras 10.13-15.	

Employed earnings

What are employed earnings

10.16   Your 'employed earnings' are your earnings from employment 'under a contract of service' (an employment contract) or 'in an office'. People employed in an office include directors of limited companies, local authority councillors and clergy.

The amount of your employed earnings

10.17   The amount of your employed earnings in an assessment period is:

(a) all the earnings you receive in that period which are subject to income tax (for exceptions see paras 10.18-20); and

(b) repayments and refunds of income tax and national insurance in that period; and

(c) any statutory sick, maternity, paternity or adoption pay you receive in that period;

(d) minus amounts for your income tax, national insurance, pension contributions and payroll giving in that period (see para 10.21).

See also paras 10.13-15 for the work allowance, and paras 10.74-76 for notional earnings.

10.15   UC 22(2); SI 2015/1649 reg 1; NIUC 23(2)

T10.1   UC 22; NIUC 23

10.16   UC 52(a)(i), 55(1); NIUC 51(a)(i), 55(1)

10.17   UC 55(1),(2),(4),(5); NIUC 55(1),(2),(4),(6)

Excluded earnings

10.18   Employee benefits, such as free use of your employer's facilities, are not included in your earnings whether you pay tax on them or not.

Expenses paid by your employer

10.19   If your employer pays you expenses, these are:

(a) included in your earnings if they are taxable (for example if your employer pays your travel costs between your home and work place);

(b) not included if they are not taxable (for example if your employer pays your travel costs between work places).

Expenses if you are in a service user group

10.20   Expenses you are paid for taking part in a service user group are not included in your earnings. This applies if you are a member of the service user group or the carer of a service user group member, for service user groups relating to health, social care, social housing, etc.

Deductions for tax etc

10.21   The following are deducted from your employed earnings:

(a) tax and class 1 national insurance contributions you pay in the assessment period;

(b) tax-deductible pension contributions you make in that period; and

(c) amounts you donate in that period under a PAYE 'payroll giving' scheme approved for tax purposes.

Information used to assess employed earnings

10.22   In most cases, the DWP uses information from HMRC to assess your employed earnings. This is because PAYE law requires most employers to provide details of employees' earnings to HMRC using its Real Time Information system. The DWP counts you as receiving the earnings when it gets this information. But the DWP makes its own decision if this information is likely to be unreliable, or your employer fails to provide it, or you disagree with it. If these arrangements are not in place for some reason, you should report your employed earnings to the DWP each month. The DWP should tell you when you have to do this, and if you fail to follow the reporting instructions your UC could be suspended (para 11.72). See also para 10.12 for when the DWP can estimate your employed earnings.

10.18   UC 55(2); NIUC 55(2)

10.19   UC 55(3)(a); NIUC 55(3)(a)

10.20   UC 53(2), 55(3)(b); NIUC 52(2), 55(3)(b)

10.21   UC 53(1), 55(4A),(5); NIUC 52(1), 55(5),(6)

10.22   AA 159D; UC 54,61;NIAA 159D; NIUC 53,62

Self-employed earnings

What are self-employed earnings

10.23   Your 'self-employed earnings' are your earnings (other than employed earnings) from any kind of business which is a 'trade, profession or vocation'. For example, this includes plumbers, private tutors and independent preachers, and applies whether you are a sole trader or in a partnership. For DWP guidance see ADM chapter H4.

The amount of your self-employed earnings

10.24   The amount of your self-employed earnings in an assessment period is:

(a) your business income in that period (see para 10.25);

(b) minus:

   ▪ your allowable business expenses in that period (see paras 10.26-28), and

   ▪ amounts for your income tax, national insurance and pension contributions in that period (see para 10.29).

But if this gives a low figure, you can be counted as having a higher amount of earnings: see paras 10.78-81. See also paras 10.13-15 for the work allowance.

Business income

10.25   Your business income is all the income actually received in relation to your business, including:

(a) money payments (cash, credit transfers, cheques, etc);

(b) payments in kind (this means in goods, not money);

(c) repayments and refunds of income tax, national insurance and VAT; and

(d) the value of assets you sell or stop using for your business (if you earlier claimed them as an allowable expense).

Money owed to you (for example if someone hasn't paid you yet) is not included. Nor are loans or capital payments into your business.

Allowable business expenses

10.26   Your business expenses are allowable only if they are:

(a) 'wholly and exclusively incurred' for the purposes of your business; and

(b) not 'incurred unreasonably'; and

(c) not excluded expenses (see para 10.28).

If you pay VAT, you may include this as an allowable business expense. Money you owe (for example if you haven't paid a bill yet) is not allowable. For DWP guidance see ADM paras H4197-4275.

10.23   UC 52(a)(ii), 57(1); NIUC 51(a)(ii), 57(1)

10.24   UC 57(2); NIUC 57(2)

10.25   UC 57(4)-(5); NIUC 57(3)-(4)

10.26   UC 58(1),(2); NIUC 59(1),(2)

Expenses for mixed purposes

10.27   If you have expenses which are partly for business and partly for private purposes, the identifiable business part is allowable if it meets the conditions in para 10.26. This is done by making a calculation of your business and personal use. But a flat rate allowance or adjustment can alternatively be made in the cases in table 10.2. The example illustrates both methods.

Table 10.2 **Self-employed expenses: flat rate allowances and adjustments**

The following are available as alternatives to making a calculation of actual business and personal use. All amounts are monthly.

(a) Allowance for business use of a motor vehicle

If you use a motor vehicle for both business and personal purposes, the flat rate allowance for business use depends on your business mileage in the month. It is:

- for a motorcycle, 24p per mile;
- for a car, van or other motor vehicle:
    - 45p per mile for the first 833 miles, plus
    - 25p per mile after that.

In the case of a car or motorcycle, no further expenses are allowed for it.

(b) Allowance for business use of your home

If you use your home for business purposes, the flat rate allowance for business use depends on the number of hours you spend there on 'income-generating activities' in the month. It is:

- £10 for at least 25 (but not more than 50) hours;
- £18 for more than 50 (but not more than 100) hours;
- £26 for more than 100 hours.

(c) Adjustment for personal use of business premises

This applies to premises you mainly use for business purposes but which you (or you and anyone else) also occupy for personal use. (For example, if your business is running a care home and you live there or stay there.) The flat rate amount is deducted from the total allowable expenses on the premises in the month. It is:

- £350 if one person (you) occupies the premises;
- £500 if two people (including you) do so;
- £650 if three or more people (including you) do so.

10.27   UC 58(1)(b),(4), 59(1); NIUC 59(1)(b),(5), 60(1)

T10.2   UC 53(1), 59(2)-(4); NIUC 52(1), 60(2)-(4)

Example: Allowable expenses for vehicle use

A self-employed plumber uses his car for both business and personal purposes. In a particular month he drives 2,000 miles, of which 1,500 are for business and 500 are for personal use. His total expenditure for this is £700.

Actual calculation of business use

Based on these mileages, his business use is ¾ of the total, so his allowable expenses are £525.

Flat rate allowance for business use

Based on his business mileage, his allowable expenses (see table 10.2(a)) are:

- 833 miles at 45p   £374.85
- 1,167 miles at 25p   £291.75
- Total   £666.60

Excluded expenses

10.28   The following expenses are not allowable:

(a)   any expenditure on non-depreciating assets, such as property, shares or investments;

(b)   losses incurred in relation to a previous assessment period;

(c)   any business entertainment;

(d)   repayments of capital on any loan;

(e)   interest payments on any loan beyond £41 per month.

The first £41 per month of interest you pay on loans is allowable.

Deductions for tax etc

10.29   The following are deducted from your self-employed earnings:

(a)   tax and class 2 and/or 4 national insurance contributions you pay to HMRC in the assessment period; and

(b)   tax-deductible pension contributions you make in that period (unless these have already been deducted from any employed earnings you have: see para 10.21).

10.28   UC 58(3),(3A); NIUC 59(3),(4)

10.29   UC 53(1), 57(2); NIUC 52(1), 57(2)

Information used to assess self-employed earnings

10.30   You should report your self-employed earnings to the DWP each month. The DWP usually expects you to do this between seven days before and 14 days after the end of each assessment period (para 3.41), giving information on:

(a) the business income you actually receive during that assessment period;

(b) the allowable expenses you actually pay out during that assessment period; and

(c) the tax, national insurance and pension contributions you actually pay out during that assessment period.

If you fail to follow the reporting instructions your UC could be suspended (para 11.72). See also para 10.12 for when the DWP can estimate your self-employed earnings.

Example: Assessing self-employed earnings

A self-employed plumber provides the following information for a particular month. She used her van wholly for business purposes. She used the flat rate allowance for use of her home (see table 10.2(b)). All her expenses are allowable. So her self-employed earnings are shown below.

Income received		£1,492
Use of van	£314	
Buying in stock for use in trade	£170	
Payment to sub-contractor	£80	
Telephone, postage, stationery	£76	
Advertising, subscriptions	£42	
Use of home	£18	
Tax/NI paid to HMRC	£68	
Total allowable expenses		£768
Self-employed earnings		£724

Unearned income

10.31   Only certain kinds of income count as your 'unearned income'. These are summarised in table 10.3 and further details are in paras 10.34-52. All other kinds of unearned income are disregarded: for some examples see para 10.36.

Table 10.3 **What counts as unearned income in UC**

     (a)   Retirement pension income (see para 10.34)

     (b)   The following social security benefits (see para 10.35):

- jobseeker's allowance (contribution-based);
- employment and support allowance (contributory);
- carer's allowance;
- bereavement allowance;
- maternity allowance;
- widow's pension;
- widowed mother's allowance;
- widowed partner's allowance;
- industrial injuries benefit;
- incapacity benefit;
- severe disablement allowance.

     (c)   Payments from a foreign government analogous to any of the above.

     (d)   Maintenance from your current or former spouse or civil partner (see para 10.38).

     (e)   Student income (see para 10.39).

     (f)   Training allowances (see para 10.44).

     (g)   Sports Council awards (see para 10.45).

     (h)   Some insurance payments (see para 10.47).

     (i)   Income from an annuity (see para 10.48).

     (j)   Income from a trust (see para 10.49).

     (k)   Assumed income from capital (see para 10.56).

     (l)   Capital treated as income (see paras 10.59-60).

     (m)   Some kinds of rental income and other taxable income (see paras 10.50-51).

In many cases there are further rules and/or disregards. See the paras shown above, and for notional unearned income see para 10.82.

10.31   UC 66; NIUC 66

T10.3   UC 66(1)(a)-(m); UCTP 25; NIUC 66(1)(a)-(m)

Why unearned income is assessed

10.32   Your 'maximum UC' is reduced by the whole amount of your unearned income (see paras 9.7-8).

Assessment periods and monthly amounts

10.33   The amount of your unearned income in any UC assessment period of one month is calculated as a monthly figure. Payments which are not monthly are converted to a monthly figure:

   (a)   multiply weekly payments by 52 then divide by 12;

   (b)   multiply four-weekly payments by 13 then divide by 12;

   (c)   multiply three-monthly payments by four then divide by 12;

   (d)   divide annual payments by 12.

If your unearned income fluctuates, the monthly amount is calculated over any identifiable cycle, or if there isn't one, over three months or whatever period would give a more accurate result. For student income see table 10.4.

Example: Unearned income and amount of UC

A couple in their 30s have one child. One partner has JSA(C) of £73.10 a week, which is £316.77 a month. The other has maintenance of £300 a month. So their monthly unearned income is £616.77. (Child benefit is disregarded.) They have no earnings or capital, and their eligible rent is £400.

Maximum UC:

■ standard allowance	£498.89
■ child element	£277.08
■ housing costs element (eligible rent)	£400.00
■ total	£1,175.97
Deduction for unearned income	– £616.77
Amount of UC	£559.20

Retirement pension income

10.34   Retirement pension income counts in full as unearned income. This means any kind of state, occupational or personal retirement pension, including any increase for a partner (but for state pension credit see para 10.36).

Social security benefits

10.35   Table 10.3(b) lists the social security benefits which count as unearned income. They count in full, except for any amount you do not receive because of the rules about overlapping benefits.

10.33   UC 73; NIUC 73

10.34   UC 66(1)(a), 67; NIUC 66(1)(a), 67

10.35   UC 66(1)(b); NIUC 66(1)(b)

Benefits which are disregarded

10.36   All other state benefits are disregarded. Examples of disregarded benefits and other payments are:

(a)   disability living allowance;

(b)   personal independence payment;

(c)   attendance allowance;

(d)   benefits equivalent to attendance allowance (see para 10.37);

(e)   child benefit;

(f)   guardian's allowance;

(g)   council tax rebate;

(h)   housing benefit;

(i)   working tax credit;

(j)   child tax credit;

(k)   state pension credit;

(l)   jobseeker's allowance (income-based);

(m) employment and support allowance (income-related);

(n)   income support;

(o)   war pensions;

(p)   fostering payments and all the local authority cash benefits in para 18.51.

In most cases, you cannot get the benefits listed in (h) to (n) at the same time as UC: see paras 1.17-20. Statutory sick, maternity, paternity and adoption pay count as employed earnings: see para 10.17.

10.37   The following benefits are equivalent to attendance allowance:

(a)   increases in industrial injuries benefit for constant attendance or exceptionally severe disablement;

(b)   increases in war disablement pension for attendance, constant attendance or exceptionally severe disablement;

(c)   payments for attendance under the Personal Injuries (Civilians) scheme.

Maintenance

10.38   Maintenance counts in full as unearned income if:

(a)   you receive it from your current or former husband, wife or civil partner; and

(b)   it is paid under a maintenance agreement or court order.

This is the case whether the maintenance is paid to you for yourself or for a child, young person or non-dependant.

10.37   UC 2 definitions: 'attendance allowance', 'war disablement pension'; NIUC 2

10.38   UC 66(1)(d); NIUC 66(1)(d)

Student income

10.39   You count as having student income if:

(a)   you are a student in full-time advanced or funded education (see paras 2.22-23); and

(b)   you receive:

- a student loan, or could receive one (see para 10.40), and/or
- a student grant (see paras 10.41-43).

This counts as unearned income. See table 10.4 for when it is taken into account and how to calculate the amount. Any other kinds of student income (for example education maintenance allowances, 16-19 bursary fund payments and hardship fund payments) are disregarded (but for training allowances see para 10.44).

Student loans

10.40   You are counted as having income from a student loan if:

(a)   you receive a student loan under a government scheme; or

(b)   you could obtain one by taking reasonable steps to do so.

In each case you are counted as having the maximum amount you could obtain (including increases for extra weeks) by taking reasonable steps to do so. And this applies even if your actual student loan has been reduced because you, your partner, your parent or anyone else is expected to contribute to it, or because you have a grant.

Student grants

10.41   You are counted as having income from a student grant if you receive any kind of educational grant or award (apart from one you are paid as an under 21-year-old in non-advanced education). This includes grants and awards from government and all other sources.

10.42   If you have income from both a grant and a student loan (see paras 10.40-41), only the following parts of the grant (if you receive them) are counted:

(a)   amounts for the maintenance of your partner, child, young person, non-dependant or anyone other than yourself; and

(b)   amounts specified in the grant as being towards your rent payments (but only if they are rent payments which can be met by UC: see paras 4.5-8 and 4.17).

In this case the rest of your grant (or all of it if you do not receive either of the above) is disregarded.

10.39   UC 66(1)(e), 68(1),(6); NIUC 66(1)(e), 68(1),(6)

10.40   UC 68(2),(5),(7), 69; NIUC 68(2),(5),(7), 69

10.41   UC 68(3),(4),(7); NIUC 68(3),(4),(7)

10.42   UC 68(3), sch 1 para 2; NIUC 68(3), sch 1 para 2

10.43   If you have income from a grant but not from a student loan (see paras 10.40-41), the whole of your grant is counted except for any amounts included in it for:

(a) tuition or examination fees;

(b) any kind of disability you have;

(c) term-time residential study away from your educational establishment;

(d) maintaining a home whose costs are not included in your housing costs element and which is not your term-time address;

(e) the maintenance of anyone not included in your or anyone else's UC award;

(f) books and equipment;

(g) travel expenses as a result of your attendance on the course;

(h) childcare costs.

Table 10.4 **The monthly amount of student income**

Your student income (from a student loan and/or grant: see paras 10.39-43) is calculated as follows:

■   it is averaged over the number of monthly assessment periods described below;

■   then £110 is disregarded in each of those assessment periods.

(a) One year or shorter courses

Average student income:

■   from the assessment period in which the course starts;

■   to the assessment period before the one in which the course ends.

(b) Two year or longer courses with long vacations

For each year, average student income:

■   from the assessment period in which:

■   the course starts (first year), or

■   the previous long vacation ends (other years);

■   to the assessment period before the one in which:

■   the following long vacation starts, or

■   the course ends (final year).

10.43   UC 70; NIUC 70

T10.4   UC 68(1),(7), 71; NIUC 68(1),(7), 71

(c) Two year or longer courses without long vacations

For each year, average student income:

- from the assessment period in which:
  - the course starts (first year), or
  - the year starts (other years);
- to the assessment period before the one in which:
  - the next year starts, or
  - the course ends (final year).

'Long vacation'

This means the longest vacation in any year, but if it is less than one month you do not count as having long vacations.

Training allowances

10.44 Training allowances count as unearned income only if:

(a) they are paid under a government work programme training scheme; and

(b) they are for your living expenses (see para 10.46) or are instead of UC.

Sports Council awards

10.45 Sports Council awards count as unearned income only if they are for your living expenses (see para 10.46).

'Living expenses'

10.46 For the above purpose (paras 10.44-45) living expenses mean the cost of food, ordinary clothing or footwear, household fuel, rent, council tax or other housing costs, for yourself, your partner and any child or young person you are responsible for.

Insurance payments

10.47 Insurance payments count as your unearned income only if they are paid under a policy you took out to insure yourself against:

(a) losing income due to illness, accident or redundancy; or

(b) being unable to maintain mortgage payments which are included in your housing costs element (see para 4.19 and chapter 8).

10.44   UC 66(1)(f); NIUC 66(1)(f)

10.45   UC 66(1)(g); NIUC 66(1)(g)

10.46   UC 66(2); NIUC 66(2)

10.47   UC 66(1)(h); NIUC 66(1)(h)

Income from an annuity

10.48   An annuity is an investment made with an insurance company which in return pays you a regular amount. This might be for your retirement or for other purposes. Payments from an annuity count as unearned income if they are:

(a)   payments of income; or

(b)   regular payments of capital which relate to a specific period (see para 10.60).

But if the annuity was purchased using a personal injury payment this income is disregarded; see para 10.65.

Income from a trust

10.49   If money is held for you in a trust, and the trustees pay you an income, this counts as unearned income. But payments from a trust are disregarded if the trust:

(a)   holds a personal injury payment (see para 10.65); or

(b)   is a government trust described in para 10.66.

Other taxable income

10.50   Other income you have counts as unearned income if:

(a)   it is taxable under income tax law (Part 5 of the Income Tax (Trading and Other Income) Act 2005); and

(b)   it is not earned income (see paras 10.7-30).

For example, this can include rental income (see paras 10.51 and 10.71), or royalties, copyright, patent and similar payments, unless these are part of your self-employed (or employed) earnings.

Rent received from a lodger in your home

10.51   The first £7,500 (£4,250 in 2015-16) per tax year of rent you receive from one or more lodgers in your home is disregarded. This is because HMRC's 'rent a room' scheme means it is not taxable (see para 10.50). It also (if you are renting your home) reflects the fact that lodgers are not included in deciding the size of accommodation you qualify for (see para 7.17). Any amount you receive over £7,500 per tax year is converted to a monthly figure and counts as your unearned income. See paras 10.71-72 if you receive rent on property other than your home.

Other unearned income

10.52   The following also count as unearned income:

(a)   assumed income from capital: see para 10.56;

(b)   some instalments or regular payments of capital: see paras 10.59-60; and

(c)   notional unearned income: see para 10.82.

10.48   UC 66(1)(i), 67(1); NIUC 66(1)(i), 67(1)

10.49   UC 66(1)(j); NIUC 66(1)(j)

10.50   UC 66(1)(m); NIUC 66(1)(m)

10.51   UC 66(1)(m); NIUC 66(1)(m)

Capital

10.53 All of your capital is taken into account unless it is disregarded. Table 10.5 lists all the kinds of disregarded capital. See paras 10.4-6 for how to distinguish capital from income. For DWP guidance on capital see ADM chapters H1 and H2.

10.54 For example your capital includes:

(a) savings (in cash or in a savings account etc);

(b) investments (shares etc);

(c) property (unless it is disregarded: see table 10.5); and

(d) lump sum payments you receive (for example an inheritance).

It can also include notional capital (see paras 10.83-88).

Why capital is assessed

10.55 Your capital (apart from disregarded capital) is taken into account as follows:

(a) if it is more than £16,000 you are not entitled to UC; otherwise

(b) the first £6,000 is ignored;

(c) the remainder up to £16,000 is counted as providing you with an assumed amount of income (see para 10.56).

Assumed income from capital

10.56 The assumed income from your capital is calculated as follows:

(a) from the total amount of your capital (apart from disregarded capital) deduct £6,000;

(b) then divide the remainder by 250;

(c) if the result is not an exact multiple of £4.35, round the result up to the next whole multiple of £4.35;

(d) this gives the monthly amount of your assumed income from capital. It is counted as your unearned income: see paras 10.31-32. (The law calls it the 'yield' from your capital.)

Capital in an annuity or trust is not included in step (a) if you count as having income from it (see paras 10.48-49). Apart from that, the above applies whether or not you have actual income from your capital (and for actual income from capital see paras 10.68-72).

10.53   UC 46(1); NIUC 46(1)

10.54   UC 72(1); NIUC 72(1)

10.55   UC 72(1); NIUC 72(1)

10.56   UC 66(1)(k), 72; NIUC 66(1)(k), 72

Example: Assumed income from capital

A UC claimant has capital, assessed under the rules in this chapter, of £12,085.93.

- The first £6,000 is ignored, leaving £6,085.93.
- Divide this by 250, giving (to the nearest penny) £24.34.
- Round this up to the next multiple of £4.35, which is £26.10.
- The claimant's assumed monthly income from capital is £26.10.

Table 10.5 **Disregarded capital**

Your home and other premises

In (a) to (e) only one dwelling can be a person's home at any one time. In (a) to (c) there is no time limit.

(a) Your home.

(b) The home of a 'close relative' (see para 4.45) who:

- has 'limited capability for work' (or for 'work and work-related activity'): see para 9.19; or
- has reached state pension credit age: see para 2.10.

(c) The home of your partner if:

- your relationship has not ended; but
- you are not claiming UC as a couple because your circumstances mean you live apart (for example, one of you is in residential care).

(d) A home you intend to occupy if:

- you acquired it within the past six months*; or
- you are taking steps to obtain possession of it, and first sought legal advice about this or began proceedings within the past six months*; or
- you are carrying out essential repairs or alterations to make it fit for occupation, and began doing so within the past six months*.

(e) Your former home if you ceased to occupy it because your relationship with your partner has ended, and:

- they are a lone parent and live in it as their home (in this case there is no time limit); or
- you ceased to occupy it within the past six months*.

(f) A home or any other premises you are taking reasonable steps to dispose of, and began doing so within the past six months*.

T10.5(a)-(s)   UC sch 10 paras 1 to 19 respectively, also para 1(2) for (a) to (e); NIUC sch 10 paras 1 to 19

Business assets

(g) Any assets which are wholly or mainly used for a business you are carrying on (see para 10.23).

(h) Any assets which were wholly or mainly used for a business you ceased within the past six months* if;

- you are taking reasonable steps to dispose of them; or

- you ceased business because of 'incapacity' and reasonably expect to begin again when you recover.

Money in a life insurance, pension or funeral plan scheme

(i) The value of a life insurance policy.

(j) The value of an occupational or personal pension scheme.

(k) The value of a funeral plan contract, if its only purpose is to provide a funeral.

Money held for particular purposes

(l) Money deposited with a housing association as a condition of occupying your home.

(m) Money you received within the past six months*, and which you intend to use to buy a home, if:

- it is the proceeds of the sale of your former home; or

- it is a grant made to you for the sole purpose of buying a home; or

- it was deposited with a housing association.

(n) Money you received under an insurance policy within the past six months* because of loss or damage to your home or personal possessions.

(o) Money you received within the past six months* which:

- is for making essential repairs or alterations to your home or former home: and

- was given to you (as a grant, loan, gift or otherwise) on condition that it is so used.

Benefits and local authority payments

(p) A social fund payment you received within the past 12 months.

(q) A payment you received from a local authority within the past 12 months, if it was paid:

- by social services to avoid taking a child into care or to a child or young person who is leaving or has left care; or

- to meet anyone's welfare needs relating to old age or disability (for example a community care or direct care payment) apart from any living expenses described in para 10.46.

(r) A payment you received within the past 12 months which was for arrears of (or compensation for late payment of):

  ■ UC; or

  ■ any benefit listed in para 10.36 (a) to (n); or

  ■ any other UK social security benefit which does not count as unearned income in UC.

Gallantry awards and personal possessions

(s) Any payment made to you as a holder of the Victoria Cross or George Cross. There is no time limit.

(t) Your personal possessions. This means any physical assets other than land, property or business assets: R(H) 7/08.

Extending the six-month disregards

* The DWP can extend any of the six-month disregards in this table if it is reasonable to do so in the circumstances.

Note: see paras 10.63-67 for further disregards relating to personal injury, compensation and independent living payments.

Valuing capital

10.57 Each item of your capital is calculated as follows:

(a) start with its current market or surrender value;

(b) then disregard 10% if selling it would involve costs;

(c) then disregard any debt or charge secured on it.

Jointly held capital

10.58 If you own a capital item jointly with one or more other people, you are assumed to own it in equal shares unless you provide evidence that it should be divided in some other way.

Example: Valuing capital

A couple own 1,000 shares in a company. Their sell price is currently 34p each.

  ■ Their market value is £340.

  ■ Deduct 10% from this for sale costs, giving £306.

  ■ No debt or charge is secured on them, so their capital value is £306.

If two brothers jointly owned the shares, the capital value of each one's share would be £153.

T10.5(t) UC 46(2); NIUC 46(2)

T10.5(*) UC 48(2); NIUC 48(2)

10.57 UC 49(1); NIUC 49(1)

10.58 UC 47; NIUC 47

Instalments of capital

10.59   If capital is payable to you in instalments, each instalment counts as capital. But any particular instalment which would take your total capital over £16,000 counts as unearned income (not capital).

Regular payments of capital

10.60   If you receive regular payments of capital which relate to a specific period (and para 10.59 does not apply) these count as unearned income (not capital). For example this applies to annuities (see para 10.48).

Capital held in a foreign currency

10.61   If you hold capital in a currency other than sterling, any charge or commission for converting it to sterling is disregarded from it.

Capital outside the UK

10.62   The following rules apply if you possess capital in a country outside the UK:

(a)   if there is no prohibition in that country against bringing the money to the UK, its market value is the market value in that country;

(b)   if there is such a prohibition, its market value is the amount it would raise if it was sold to a willing buyer in the UK.

The rules in paras 10.57 and 10.61 then apply.

Personal injury payments

10.63   A personal injury payment means money which was awarded to you, or which you (or someone on your behalf) agreed to, as a consequence of a personal injury you had.

10.64   Personal injury payments are disregarded in calculating your capital if they:

(a)   are held in a trust (and other capital in the trust deriving from them is also disregarded);

(b)   are administered by a court on your behalf, or can only be used under a court's direction; or

(c)   were paid to you within the past 12 months. This may allow time for them to be placed in a trust so that (a) then applies.

10.59   UC 46(1)(a),(4), 66(1)(l); NIUC 46(1)(a),(4), 66(1)(l)

10.60   UC 46(1)(a),(3), 66(1)(l); NIUC 46(1)(a),(3), 66(1)(l)

10.61   UC 49(3); NIUC 49(3)

10.62   UC 49(2); NIUC 49(2)

10.63   UC 75(1); NIUC 75(1)

10.64   UC 75(4)-(6); NIUC 75(4)-(6)

10.65   Personal injury payments are disregarded in calculating your unearned income if they are:

(a) income paid to you from a trust described in para 10.64(a); or

(b) income paid to you by a court or under a court's direction in the situation described in para 10.64(b); or

(c) regular payments to you under an agreement or court order; or

(d) payments to you from an annuity which was purchased using a personal injury payment.

Compensation and independent living payments

10.66   Payments from government schemes and trusts set up for the following purposes are disregarded in the calculation of both your capital and your income. This means any government scheme or trust which:

(a) compensates you for having been diagnosed with variant Creutzfeldt-Jacob disease (vCJD); or

(b) compensates you for having been infected with contaminated blood products (examples include the Macfarlane Trust, Eileen Trust and MFET Ltd); or

(c) compensates you because you were interned or suffered forced labour, injury, property loss or loss of a child in the Second World War; or

(d) compensates you for the London bombings on 7th July 2005; or

(e) supports you, if you have a disability, to live independently in your home (for example the Independent Living Funds).

10.67   If you are the parent, partner, son or daughter of a person in para 10.66 (a) or (b), payments from the trust or scheme to you, or passed on to you by that person (as a payment or inheritance), are disregarded in most circumstances.

Actual income from capital

10.68   'Actual income from capital' means:

(a) interest (on a savings account etc);

(b) dividends (on shares etc);

(c) rent (on property you rent out); and

(d) any other 'actual income derived from' your capital.

Paras 10.69-72 give the rules about this.

10.65   UC 75(2)-(5); NIUC 75(2)-(5)

10.66   UC 76(1),(2); NIUC 76(1),(2)

10.67   UC 76(3); NIUC 76(3)

10.68   UC 72(3); NIUC 72(3)

Income from disregarded capital

10.69 If the capital is disregarded in the assessment of UC (see table 10.5), actual income you receive on it counts as your income. It is usually unearned income (see para 10.50). But if you are self-employed, income you receive on your business assets is included in your self-employed earnings (see para 10.25). For rent see para 10.71.

Income from counted capital

10.70 If the capital is counted in the assessment of UC (see para 10.53), actual income you receive on it counts as your capital from the day it is due. For example this applies to interest you receive on (and leave in) a savings account. For rent see para 10.72.

Rent received on disregarded property

10.71 The rule in para 10.69 means that if you receive rent on a property which is disregarded (see table 10.5 (a) to (f)), the rent counts as your income. Since it is the taxable amount which is taken into account (see para 10.50) the expenses you incur on the property are deducted. For rent from a lodger in your home, see para 10.51.

Rent received on counted property

10.72 The rule in para 10.70 means that if you receive rent on a property which is not disregarded, the rent counts as your capital from the day it is due. But your capital goes down when you pay for expenses you incur on that property. See the example. (If you receive rent from a property business different rules apply: see paras 10.16, 10.23 and 10.87.)

Example: Rent received on a counted property

A single person owns a house he does not live in. He rents the rooms there to separate tenants through an agency. The house does not fall within any of the capital disregards, and because he has a large mortgage its capital value is not over £16,000 (see para 10.57).

His income from the rent is taken into account as capital (see para 10.72). Each month he receives rent of £900 from which he pays £800 for agency fees, council tax, utility bills and his mortgage. This means his capital goes up by £100 a month.

10.69   UC 52, 66(1)(m); NIUC 51, 66(1)(m)

10.70   UC 72(3); NIUC 72(3)

10.71   UC 66(1)(m); NIUC 66(1)(m)

10.72   UC 72(3); NIUC 72(3)

Notional income and capital

10.73   This section explains when you are counted as having income or capital you do not in fact have. This is called 'notional' income or capital.

Notional earnings: trade disputes

10.74   You are counted as having notional earnings if you withdraw your labour as part of a trade dispute (go on strike). In this case, the amount of your notional earnings is what you would receive if you hadn't done so.

Notional earnings: deprivation

10.75   You are counted as having notional earnings if:

(a) you have deprived yourself of earnings, or your employer has arranged for this; and

(b) the purpose of this was to make you entitled to UC or to more UC. This is assumed to apply to you if you actually became entitled to UC or more UC, and this was a foreseeable and intended consequence of what you or your employer did.

In this case, the amount of your notional earnings is the amount you have deprived yourself of.

Notional earnings: paid less than the going rate

10.76   You are counted as having notional earnings if:

(a) you provide services (see para 10.77) for another person who pays nothing for them, or pays less than would be paid for comparable services in the same location; and

(b) that person's means were sufficient to pay for those services, or pay more for them.

In this case, the amount of your notional earnings is what would be reasonable for the provision of the services.

10.77   The rule in para 10.76 does not apply to services you provide:

(a) to a charitable or voluntary organisation, if it is reasonable for you to be paid nothing for them, or less for them; or

(b) as a service user (see para 10.20); or

(c) under a government training or employment programme.

10.74   UC 2 definition: 'trade dispute', 56; NIUC 2, 56

10.75   UC 52(b), 60(1),(2); NIUC 51(b), 61(1),(2)

10.76   UC 52(b), 60(3); NIUC 51(b), 61(3)

10.77   UC 60(4) ; NIUC 61(4)

Notional earnings: gainful self-employment

10.78   You are counted as having notional earnings if:

(a) you are in 'gainful self-employment'. This means your business is your main employment and is 'organised, developed, regular and carried on in the expectation of profit'; and

(b) as a condition of getting UC you are required to carry out all the work requirements in para 2.43; and

(c) your own monthly earnings are below your own minimum income floor; and

(d) your combined monthly earnings (if you are in a couple) are below your combined minimum income floors; and

(e) you are not in a UC start-up period, nor in an assessment period containing the first or last day of a start-up period.

For the minimum income floor see para 10.80, and for UC start-up periods see para 10.81. In (c) and (d), monthly earnings mean earnings from this and any other employment or self-employment (after deductions for tax and national insurance). For DWP guidance see ADM paras H4020-57.

10.79   In this case, the amount of your notional earnings is:

(a) the difference between:

   ▪ your own monthly earnings, and

   ▪ your own minimum income floor; or

(b) if it is lower (and you are in a couple), the difference between:

   ▪ your combined monthly earnings, and

   ▪ your combined minimum income floors.

The overall effect is that the total of your actual and notional earnings is at least as much as your minimum income floor (or your combined minimum income floors if you are in a couple).

The minimum income floor

10.80   Your 'minimum income floor' is what you would earn in a month (after deductions for tax and national insurance) for working 35 hours a week at the national minimum wage. But a lower number of hours can apply to you if the DWP decides this is compatible with your caring responsibilities for a child, a foster child or a person who has a physical or mental impairment. If you are in a couple your partner's minimum income floor is the same, but only one of you can qualify for a lower number of hours for caring for your children.

10.78   UC 52(b), 62(1), (5), 64; NIUC 51(b), 63(1), (6), 65

10.79   UC 62(1)-(4); NIUC 63(1)-(4)

10.80   UC 62(2)-(4), 85, 88, 90(2)(b),(3); NIUC 63(2)-(4), 84, 87, 89(2)(b),(3)

The UC start-up period

10.81   You qualify for a UC start-up period if:

(a) you began the business which is your main employment within the past 12 months; and

(b) you are taking active steps to increase your earnings from it up to your minimum income floor (see para 10.80); and

(c) you have not begun a UC start-up period for a similar business within the past five years.

The start-up period lasts for 12 months starting from the beginning of the assessment period in which the DWP agrees you are in gainful self-employment (see para 10.78(a)). But it can be brought to an early end if you stop being in gainful self-employment or stop taking steps to increase your earnings.

Example: The UC start-up period

A single person's UC assessment periods start on the 26th of each month. She decides to try self-employment as an illustrator but earns nothing to begin with. She then starts selling work, and the DWP decides on 4th March 2016 that she is in gainful self-employment.

So a UC start-up period applies to her from 26th February 2016 for 12 months. During the 13 months from 26th February 2015 to 25th March 2017 (see para 10.78(e)), she is not counted as having notional earnings, and only her actual earnings are taken into account.

Notional unearned income: available on application

10.82   You are counted as having notional unearned income equal to any amount which:

(a) would be available to you if you applied for it; but

(b) you haven't applied for.

This rule applies to retirement pension income and any other kind of unearned income listed in table 10.3(c)-(m). But it does not apply to any UK social security benefit.

Notional capital: deprivation

10.83   You are counted as having notional capital if:

(a) you have deprived yourself of capital; and

(b) the purpose of this was to make you entitled to UC or to more UC.

In this case, the amount of your notional capital is the amount you have deprived yourself of. See paras 10.84-86 for further details.

10.81   UC 63; NIUC 64

10.82   UC 66(1), 74; NIUC 66(1), 74

10.83   UC 50(1); NIUC 50(1)

Notional capital: exceptions

10.84   The rule in para 10.83 does not apply when you spend capital to:

(a) pay off or reduce any debt you owe; or

(b) buy goods or services if this is reasonable in your circumstances.

What deprivation means

10.85   In deciding whether you have deprived yourself of capital, 'the test is one of purpose', and you can only have deprived yourself if obtaining UC formed 'a positive part' of your planning: [2011] UKUT 500 (AAC). If it is clear that you did not (or could not) appreciate what you were doing, or the consequences of it, you cannot count as having deprived yourself: R(H) 1/06. For further examples of how deprivation has been interpreted, see chapter 13 of the *Guide to Housing Benefit*. For DWP guidance see ADM paras H1795-1846.

How notional capital reduces

10.86   If you are counted as having notional capital (see para 10.82), the amount reduces as follows (whether you are on UC or not):

(a) if your notional capital is more than £16,000, it reduces each month by the amount of UC you would qualify for (if any) in that month without the notional capital;

(b) if your notional capital is more than £6,000 (but not more than £16,000), it reduces each month by the assumed amount of income it produces: see para 10.56.

Notional capital and earnings: companies

10.87   You are counted as having notional capital and earnings from a company if:

(a) your relationship to the company is analogous to that of a sole owner or partner; and

(b) the company carries on a trade or a property business; and

(c) the company is not an intermediary or managed service company paying you taxable earnings (under Chapter 8 or 9 of Part 2 of the Income Tax (Earnings and Pensions) Act 2003).

10.88   In this case, you are counted as having notional capital equal to the value of the company or your share in it. But the value of company assets used wholly and exclusively for trade purposes is disregarded, and your actual holding in the company is also disregarded. For DWP guidance, see ADM paras H1874-82.

10.89   And you are counted as having notional earnings equal to the income of the company or your share of it. This is calculated using the rules for self-employed earnings (see paras 10.24-30). If it is your main employment the rules about notional earnings from self-employment apply (see paras 10.78-80), but you do not qualify for a UC start-up period (see para 10.81).

10.84   UC 50(2); NIUC 50(2)

10.86   UC 50(3); NIUC 50(3)

10.87   UC 77(1),(5),(6); NIUC 77(1),(5),(6)

10.88   UC 77(2),(3)(a); NIUC 77(2),(3)(a)

10.89   UC 77(3)(b),(c),(4); NIUC 77(3)(b),(c),(4)

Chapter 11 **UC changes**

- Changes of circumstances: see paras 11.3-13.
- When changes of circumstances take effect: see paras 11.14-37.
- Changing wrong decisions: see paras 11.38-46.
- When changed decisions take effect: see paras 11.47-68.
- Suspending, restoring and terminating payments of UC: see paras 11.69-80.

11.1 Your UC can change:

(a) because of a change in your or someone else's circumstances; or

(b) because the DWP changes a decision that was wrong.

For example your UC could increase, reduce or end.

11.2 In the law, changes are also called revisions or supersessions. Table 11.1 explains these terms.

Table 11.1 **Decisions, revisions and supersessions**

Decisions

The DWP makes decisions:

(a) when you claim UC (chapter 3);

(b) when you report a change of circumstances, or the DWP is aware of a change without you reporting it (para 11.5); and

(c) when you ask for a decision to be changed because you think it is wrong, or the DWP realises it is wrong without you asking (para 11.41).

The kinds of decision in (b) and (c) are also called revisions and supersessions. Asking for a decision to be changed is often called 'requesting a reconsideration'.

Revisions

A revision is a decision which alters your UC from the same date (in most cases) as the decision it is altering. Revisions are mainly used when a wrong decision is changed. If they are advantageous to you they often have time limits (paras 11.47-53).

Supersessions

A supersession is a decision which alters your UC from a date later than the decision it is altering. Supersessions are mainly used for changes of circumstances, and sometimes when a wrong decision is changed. If they are advantageous to you they often have time limits (paras 11.14-21 and 11.47-53). A 'closed period supersession' is used when a change of circumstances took place in the past and has already come to an end. It means your UC is altered, but only for that past fixed period (CH/2595/2003).

Changes of circumstances

11.3   This section explains how your UC changes when there is a change in your or someone else's circumstances.

11.4   The DWP can change your UC:

(a) because you or someone else have told it about a change of circumstances (paras 11.7-8); or

(b) on its own initiative (because it is aware of a change of circumstances).

The DWP's decision about the change

11.5   The DWP makes a decision about the change of circumstances. This is also called a 'supersession' or (in a few cases) a 'revision' (table 11.1). But you don't have to use these terms. When you report a change the DWP should treat you as having requested whichever of these is appropriate.

11.6   The DWP's decision could:

(a) increase your UC;

(b) reduce or end your UC; or

(c) change how your UC is paid.

Paras 11.14 onwards give more information about this and explain when the change takes effect.

Duty to tell the DWP about changes

11.7   You have a duty to report any change of circumstances which you might reasonably be expected to know could affect:

(a) your continuing entitlement to UC;

(b) the amount of UC awarded; or

(c) the payment of UC.

These are sometimes called 'relevant changes'. You should tell the DWP as soon as reasonably practicable after the change occurs. If you delay reporting changes that increase your UC, you may end up getting less UC than you could have done (para 11.17).

11.4   D&A 23, sch 3 paras 21,29

11.5   SSA 9-10; D & A 12,20(1), 22,23,33(1)

11.7   C&P 38(1),(4), D & A 36(9)

11.8   If you are getting UC as a couple, the above duty applies to both of you. If you are in a couple but getting UC as a single person, it is your duty to report changes relating to both of you. The duty also applies to:

(a)   someone getting UC on your behalf (para 12.5);

(b)   a landlord etc getting UC payments (para 12.11); and

(c)   in appropriate cases, a childcare provider, someone you are caring for, or a pension fund holder (para 3.22).

Kinds of change you should report

11.9   The DWP should explain the kinds of change you need to tell it about. For example:

(a)   changes in your housing costs (see also para 11.23-24);

(b)   changes in your or your partner's income or capital (for earnings and DWP benefits see also paras 11.26 and 11.31);

(c)   other changes relating to you, your benefit unit, non-dependants, or someone you are caring for (chapter 9).

How to tell the DWP about changes

11.10   You should normally be able to tell the DWP about changes via your online account (para 3.13). If you are told not to use that method, you should be given a contact point you can telephone or write to about changes. You may also be able to report births and deaths by using the Tell Us Once service through the local register office or DWP Bereavement Service.

Information and evidence

11.11   The DWP can ask you for information and evidence about a change of circumstances. The rules are the same as when you made a claim (paras 3.19-20). If you fail to provide this the DWP could suspend payments of your UC (para 11.72).

The DWP's notification to you

11.12   The DWP tells you about decisions changing your UC: see paras 3.37-39. It usually tells you about changes in the amount of your UC at the end of each month (para 11.13) and about other changes when they occur (e.g. about how your UC is paid).

Assessment periods and the 'whole month' approach

11.13   Your UC is awarded for assessment periods of one month (para 3.41) and most changes take effect from the beginning of an assessment period (tables 11.2 and 11.3). This 'whole month' approach simplifies UC administration. It means the DWP doesn't have to pro-rata changes that take place part way through an assessment period. There are two ways it can affect you:

11.8   C&P 38(1),(4),(7),(8),41

11.10   C&P 2 definition: 'appropriate office', 38(5),39, sch 2

11.11   C&P 38(2),(3); D & A 33(2),(3)

(a) it can help you if a change that increases your UC takes place near the end of an assessment period, because the increased amount is paid from the beginning of the assessment period;

(b) it can cause you budgeting difficulties if a change that reduces (or ends) your UC takes place near the end of an assessment period, because the reduced amount (or no UC) is paid from the beginning of the assessment period.

The later examples illustrate this.

When changes of circumstances take effect

11.14   The date from which a change of circumstances alters your UC is called the 'effective date'. The rules about this are summarised in table 11.2. In this section, references to 'you' reporting a change also include when someone else reports it (para 11.8).

Table 11.2 **Changes of circumstances: effective date**

Type of change	Effective date of change
Advantageous changes (changes increasing UC: paras 11.15-17)	
(a) Reported or made within the time limit (the end of the assessment period or in some cases later: para 11.20)	The first day of the assessment period in which the change takes (or took) place
(b) Reported or made outside the time limit	The first day of the assessment period in which the change is reported, or the DWP first takes action to make it (if this is earlier)
Disadvantageous changes (changes reducing or ending UC: paras 11.18-19)	
(c) Whenever reported or made	The first day of the assessment period in which the change takes (or took) place

Notes

■   For exceptions see para 11.22.

■   In the law, (a) to (c) are all supersessions (table 11.1).

T11.2   D&A sch 1 paras 20,21,29

Advantageous changes

11.15 A change is advantageous if it increases your UC.

11.16 If you report the change, or the DWP makes the change, within the time limit (para 11.20), it takes effect from the first day of the assessment period in which the change takes (or took) place.

For exceptions see para 11.22.

11.17 Otherwise, the change takes effect from the first date of the assessment period in which:

(a) you report the change; or

(b) the DWP first takes action to make it (if this is earlier).

For exceptions see para 11.22.

Disadvantageous changes

11.18 A change is disadvantageous if it reduces or ends your UC.

11.19 Whenever you report the change, or whenever the DWP makes the change, it takes effect from the first day of the assessment period in which the change takes (or took) place. For exceptions see para 11.22.

Time limit for advantageous changes

11.20 An advantageous change is reported, or made by the DWP, within the time limit if:

(a) you report the change to the DWP within the assessment period in which it takes place; or

(b) you report the change to the DWP up to 13 months after it takes place, and the DWP agrees (para 11.21); or

(c) the DWP first takes action to make the change within the assessment period in which the change takes place.

11.21 When you report a change late (para 11.20(b)), the DWP can only agree to this if:

(a) there are special circumstances why it wasn't practicable for you to report the change earlier – for example if you, your partner or a child or young person were suffering a serious illness or postal services are disrupted (ADM para A4211); and

(b) it is reasonable to allow you extra time – the longer you take the more compelling your reasons have to be.

But the DWP can't take account of ignorance or misunderstanding of the law or the time limits, or of an Upper Tribunal or court interpreting the law in a new way.

11.16   D&A sch 1 para 20

11.17   D&A sch 1 para 21

11.19   D&A sch 1 paras 20,29

11.20-21   D&A 36

Exceptions

11.22 The following kinds of change have rules which are in some cases different from those in paras 11.15-21:

   (a) moves and changes in housing costs (paras 11.23-24);

   (b) changes in rent officer figures (paras 6.17-18 and 11.63-65);

   (c) changes in who your UC is paid to (para 11.25);

   (d) changes in earned income (paras 11.26-27);

   (e) changes in capability for work (paras 11.28-30);

   (f) changes in DWP benefits (paras 11.31-32);

   (g) reaching state pension credit age (para 11.33);

   (h) qualifying for bereavement run-on because someone has died (paras 11.34-35); and

   (i) changes in the law or case law (paras 11.36-37).

See also para 3.5 if you become a couple or a single person while you are on UC.

Examples: changes of circumstances: effective date

1. Starting to pay for childcare costs

Abigail is working and getting UC. Her assessment periods begin on the 26th of each month. She starts paying a childminder to look after her son on 6th June and qualifies for more UC because she is entitled to a childcare costs element. This is an advantageous change (paras 11.15-17) so:

■ if she reports this to the DWP on (or before) 25th June, she is within the time limit and her UC increases from 26th May;

■ if she reports this on 4th July and doesn't have special circumstances for her delay, her UC increases from 26th June.

2. An increase in capital

Barney is unemployed and getting UC. His assessment periods begin on the 26th of each month. His capital increases on 6th June and he qualifies for less UC. This is a disadvantageous change (paras 11.18-19) so:

■ whenever he reports this to the DWP, his UC reduces from 26th May;

■ if the increase in his capital is so great that he no longer qualifies for UC, his UC ends on 25th May.

3. A rent increase

Clodagh is getting UC and her assessment periods begin on the 21st of each month. Her rent increases on 1st October and she qualifies for more UC. This is an advantageous change so:

■ if she reports this to the DWP on (or before) 20th October, she is within the time limit and her UC increases from 21st September;

■ if she reports this on 4th December and doesn't have special circumstances for her delay, her UC increases from 21st November.

4. Size of accommodation needed

Desmond is getting UC and his assessment periods begin on the 21st of each month. His daughter moves out on 1st October and he qualifies for less UC because he is no longer entitled to a bedroom for her. This is a disadvantageous change so:

■ whenever he reports this to the DWP, his UC reduces from 21st September.

Moves and changes in housing costs

11.23 You should tell the DWP when you move home or when your housing costs change. You need to report changes in rent even if you are renting from a council or social landlord. But this may change in the future, because the DWP is looking at whether it can automatically gather rent details from councils and large registered providers of housing.

11.24 The rules in paras 11.15-21 apply to the above changes, but for changes in rent officer figures see instead paras 6.17-18 and 11.63-65. When a rent increase means you qualify for more UC, your UC increases from the first day of the assessment period in which your rent goes up, so long as you report this on time (para 11.20). But the DWP has wrongly advised some claimants that their UC will increase from the assessment period after that. If this happens to you, see para 11.43 for how to change the DWP's decision.

Changes in who your UC is paid to

11.25 Your UC can be paid to your landlord etc instead of you (para 12.11). If the DWP changes who it is paid to, the change is likely to take effect from the assessment period in which you request this or the DWP decides this. But there could be exceptions in appropriate cases.

Changes in earned income

11.26 You should tell the DWP when you or you or partner start or stop work. But the DWP should be able to take changes in your or your partner's earned income into account automatically – either because you have to provide information about it to the DWP each month, or because the DWP gets the information from HMRC (paras 10.22 and 10.30).

11.27 The rules in paras 11.15-21 apply when you or your partner start or stop work, or your or your partner's earned income increases. But when your or your partner's income reduces, the following applies instead:

(a) if you provide the DWP with any information it needs when required to, your UC increases from the first day of the assessment period in which that reduction takes place;

(b) otherwise the DWP can estimate the amount (para 10.12).

See also paras 3.6-7 if your or your partner's earned income reduces within six months of the DWP saying you don't qualify for UC.

11.25   D&A 10,21,25
11.27   D&A sch 1 para 22

Changes in capability for work

11.28   You should tell the DWP when your or your partner's capability for work changes in a way that affects your entitlement to an LCW or LCWRA element (paras 9.17-22).

11.29   The rules in paras 11.15-21 apply when your or your partner's capability for work changes. But if:

(a)   the change means you no longer qualify for an LCW/LCWRA element, and

(b)   you couldn't reasonably have been expected to know you should tell the DWP about the change;

your UC changes from the first day of the assessment period in which the DWP makes its decision. So you haven't been overpaid UC.

11.30   Different rules also apply if the DWP has made a decision not to award you an LCW/LCWRA element (the original decision), and then decides to award it because:

(a)   it has received new evidence from a healthcare professional etc; or

(b)   it has changed its mind about whether you or your partner need an assessment (para 9.20); or

(c)   you have told it you or your partner are terminally ill (para 9.20).

In cases (a) and (b) you are awarded the LCW/LCWRA element from when the original decision took effect (or should have). In case (c) you are awarded the LCWRA element from the first day of the assessment period in which you or your partner became terminally ill (or from when your UC began, if this is later). So in all these cases you are awarded arrears of UC.

Changes in DWP benefits

11.31   You shouldn't need to tell the DWP (because it knows already) about changes in your entitlement to any DWP benefit, including when your entitlement starts or stops. This also applies to changes in your partner's, child's or young person's entitlement to a DWP benefit.

11.32   In these cases the rules in paras 11.15-21 don't apply. Instead your UC changes:

(a)   from the first day of the assessment period in which the DWP benefit changes (or changed); or

(b)   from when your UC began, if this is later.

If this means your UC increases from a date in the past, you are awarded arrears of UC back to then. But if it means your UC reduces or ends from a date in the past, you have been overpaid back to then.

Reaching state pension credit age

11.33   When you or your partner reach SPC age (para 2.10) you can get SPC. You can make an advance claim for SPC at any time in the four months before reaching SPC age. If you do,

---

11.29   D&A sch 1 paras 23-25,28,30

11.30   D&A 5(2)(c),23(2),26(1),(3),35(9), sch 1 para 28

11.32   D&A 12,21, sch1 para 31

your UC continues until the day before you or your partner reach SPC age. It is awarded on a daily basis in your last UC assessment period. So if you then qualify for SPC there is no gap between your UC and SPC.

Bereavement run-on

11.34 The bereavement run-on delays the impact of a death on your UC. You qualify for a bereavement run-on if one of the following has died:

(a) your partner if you are claiming UC as a couple;

(b) a child or young person you were responsible for;

(c) a person you were caring for, if you qualified for the UC carer element for caring for them (see para 9.27); or

(d) a non-dependant.

11.35 When you qualify for a bereavement run-on, your maximum UC (see paras 9.12-49) is calculated as though the person had not died during:

(a) the assessment period containing the date of the death; and

(b) the next two assessment periods.

But changes in your financial and other circumstances are taken into account in the normal way. The examples illustrate how bereavement run-on works.

Examples: Bereavement run-on

1. Death of a partner

A home owner couple are on UC and their assessment periods start on the 13th of each month. Their maximum UC includes the LCW element for one of them (see para 9.17). The partner who qualifies for the LCW element dies on 3rd June.

Because of the bereavement run-on, the surviving partner continues to qualify for the LCW element up to and including 12th August. But the surviving partner's new financial circumstances are taken into account from 13th May.

2. Death of a non-dependant

A single person renting a housing association flat is on UC and his assessment periods begin on the last day of each month. His mother lives with him (she is his non-dependant) so he qualifies for two bedroom accommodation in calculating his housing costs element (see para 7.8) but his mother is expected to make a housing cost contribution (see para 9.51). His mother dies on 3rd June.

Because of the bereavement run-on, he continues to qualify for two bedroom accommodation until 31st August, and a housing cost contribution continues to be deducted until then.

11.33   D&A sch 1 para 26

11.34-35   UC 37

Changes in the law or case law

11.36   When there is a change in UC law, the Act or regulations making the change always say when it takes effect. For recent examples, see paras 9.37 and 10.15.

11.37   Different rules apply to new case law (para 1.36). When an Upper Tribunal or court makes a decision in someone else's case and this affects your own case, the DWP normally changes your UC from the date of that new decision. But there can be exceptions when there are a number of cases about similar matters, and one is used as a 'lead case' for other 'look-alike cases'.

Changing wrong decisions

11.38   This section explains how wrong decisions about your UC are changed, for example if they were based on incorrect facts or applied the law incorrectly.

11.39   When a decision is wrong, the DWP can change it:

    (a) because you or someone else have asked it to (paras 11.43-44); or

    (b) on its own initiative (because is realises the decision is wrong).

The DWP's original decision

11.40   The decision that is wrong is called the 'original decision'. It could be a decision the DWP made when you claimed UC or when there was a change in your or someone else's circumstances.

The DWP's new decision

11.41   The DWP makes a new decision to replace the original decision. The new decision is also called a 'revision' or 'supersession' (table 11.1). But you don't have to use these terms. When you ask for a decision to be changed the DWP should treat you as having requested whichever of these is appropriate.

11.42   The DWP's new decision could:

    (a) increase your UC, or award you UC if the original decision wrongly said you weren't entitled to it;

    (b) reduce or end your UC; or

    (c) change an overpayment of UC or how it is recovered.

Paras 11.47 onwards give more information about this and explain when the new decision takes effect.

11.36   D&A sch 1 paras 32,33

11.37   SSA98 s27; D & A 35(5)

11.39   D&A 5,8,22

11.41   SSA 9-10; D & A 5,8,20(1), 22,32,33(1)

Asking for a decision to be changed

11.43 You can ask for a decision to be changed by contacting the DWP via your online account (para 3.13) or by telephone or in writing. This is often called 'requesting a reconsideration', and if you wish you can first ask for a written statement of reasons (para 14.9). You should contact the DWP as soon as possible, otherwise you may end up getting less UC than you might have done (para 11.50).

11.44 If you are in a couple, either of you can ask for a decision to be changed. But if you only claimed as a single person, you (rather than your partner) should normally do this. Someone else who is affected by a decision can also ask for it to be changed. For example:

(a) someone claiming UC on your behalf (paras 3.8-10);

(b) a landlord etc if they think your UC should be paid to them (para 12.11); or

(c) someone who has been told an overpayment of UC is recoverable from them (paras 13.19-26).

Information and evidence

11.45 When you ask for a decision to be changed you should provide any information and evidence you want the DWP to consider. The DWP can also ask you for information and evidence, and you have one month to provide this or longer if the DWP allows. If you fail to do this within the time allowed, the DWP can just use whatever information and evidence it does have. It could also suspend payments of your UC (para 11.72).

The DWP's notification to you

11.46 The DWP tells you about decisions changing your UC: see paras 3.37-39. If you ask for a decision to be changed, it tells you the new decision or that it has decided not to change the original decision. If someone else asks for a decision to be changed, it tells you and them this. See chapter 14 for how and when you can go on to appeal to a tribunal.

When changed decisions take effect

11.47 When the DWP changes a wrong decision, the date from which its new decision takes effect is called the 'effective date'. The rules about this are summarised in table 11.3. In this section, references to 'you' requesting a change also include when someone else requests it (para 11.44).

11.43   D&A 2 definition: 'appropriate office', 5(1)(b)

11.44   D&A 5(1)(b)

11.45   C&P 38(2),(3); D&A 20(2),(3),33(2),(3)

Table 11.3 **Changing wrong decisions: effective date**

Type of change	Effective date of new decision
Advantageous changes (changes increasing or awarding UC: paras 11.48-50)	
(a) Requested or made within the time limit (one month or in some cases longer: para 11.53)	The date the original decision took effect (or should have)
(b) Requested or made outside the time limit	The first day of the assessment period in which the change is requested, or the DWP first takes action to make it (if this is earlier)
Disadvantageous changes (changes reducing or ending UC: paras 11.51-52)	
(c) Whenever requested or made	The date the original decision took effect (or should have)

Notes

■   For exceptions, see para 11.54.

■   In the law, (a) and (c) are revisions and (b) is a supersession (table 11.1).

Advantageous changes

11.48   A change is advantageous if the DWP's new decision means:

(a) you qualify for more UC; or

(b) you are entitled to UC (if the original decision said you weren't entitled).

11.49   If you request the change, or the DWP makes the change, within the time limit (para 11.53):

(a) the DWP's new decision takes effect from the date the original decision took effect (or should have);

(b) so you are awarded arrears of UC back to then.

11.50   Otherwise:

(a) the DWP's new decision takes effect from the first day of the assessment period in which:

■   you request the change, or

■   the DWP first takes action to make it (if this is earlier);

T11.3   D&A 5,9(b),21,24,35(2),(4)

11.49   D&A 5,21

11.50   D&A 24,35(2),(4)

(b) so you aren't awarded arrears of UC;

(c) but (a) and (b) only apply to increases in UC (para 11.48(a)); to be awarded UC you need to make a new claim (chapter 3).

For exceptions see para 11.54.

Disadvantageous changes

11.51 A change is disadvantageous if the DWP's new decision means:

(a) you qualify for less UC; or

(b) you are not entitled to UC.

11.52 Whenever you request the change, or whenever the DWP makes the change:

(a) the DWP's new decision takes effect from the date the original decision took effect (or should have);

(b) so you have been overpaid UC back to then.

For exceptions see para 11.54.

Time limit for advantageous changes

11.53 An advantageous change is requested, or made by the DWP, within the time limit if:

(a) you ask the DWP to change a decision within one month of being notified about it (para 3.38); or

(b) you ask for a written statement of reasons (para 14.9) within that month, and then ask the DWP to change the decision within 14 days of:

■ the end of that month, or

■ the DWP providing the written statement (if this is later); or

(c) you ask the DWP to change the decision up to 13 months later than (a) or (b) and the DWP agrees (paras 14.12-15); or

(d) the DWP first takes action to change the decision within one month of notifying you about it.

Exceptions

11.54 Changes to the following kinds of decision have rules which are different from those in paras 11.48-53:

(a) decisions that are wrong because of official error (paras 11.55-60);

(b) decisions about rent officer figures, the benefit cap, sanctions etc (paras 11.61-65);

(c) decisions about overpayments (para 11.66);

(d) decisions you have appealed (para 11.67); and

(e) decisions you can't appeal (paras 11.68).

11.52 D&A 9(b),21

11.53 D&A 2 definition: 'date of notification', 5(1),6,38(4)

Examples: Changing wrong decisions: effective date

1. Capital that should be disregarded

Eva has been getting UC since 9th January and her assessment periods begin on the 9th of each month. She realises she forgot to tell the DWP that some of her capital comes from an insurance payment in December for flood damage to her home. She asks the DWP to change her UC and the DWP agrees. This is an advantageous change (paras 11.48-50) so:

- ■ if she requests the change on (or before) 8th February, she is within the time limit and her UC increases from 9th January;
- ■ if she requests the change on 15th February and doesn't have special circumstances for her delay, her UC increases from 9th February.

2. Undeclared earnings

Frank has been getting UC since 9th January and his assessment periods begin on the 9th of each month. The DWP discovers he has been working since before he claimed UC and changes his UC. This is a disadvantageous change (paras 11.51-52) so:

- ■ whenever the DWP makes the change, his UC reduces from 9th January.

3. An official error

Gertrude claimed UC on 9th January. She is a full-time student with a low income. Although she told the DWP when she claimed that she was a foster parent and had a foster child placed with her, the DWP said she wasn't entitled to UC. She asks the DWP to change this decision and the DWP agrees it was wrong because of official error (para 11.57) so:

- ■ whenever she requests the change, she is awarded UC from 9th January.

Changing decisions that are wrong because of official error

11.55   The DWP should change any decision that is wrong because of official error (para 11.57).

11.56   Whenever you request the change, or whenever the DWP makes the change:

(a) the DWP's new decision takes effect from the date the original decision took effect (or should have);

(b) so if the change is advantageous (para 11.48) you are awarded arrears of UC back to then, but if it is disadvantageous (para 11.51) you have been overpaid back to then.

Official errors

11.57   An official error means:

(a) an error made by a DWP officer, or someone employed by and acting for the DWP, or someone providing services to the DWP (see paras 11.58-60 for examples);

(b) but not if you or anyone outside the DWP caused or materially contributed to it (e.g. if you didn't give the DWP correct information).

Paras 11.55-56 apply to (a), but paras 11.48-53 apply to (b).

11.56   D&A 9(a),21

11.57   D&A 2 definitions: 'official error', 'designated authority'

Mistakes of fact

11.58 There is a mistake of fact if the DWP makes a decision in ignorance of, or based on a mistake about, a material fact (a fact that affects your UC). Paras 11.55-56 apply if this is due to official error, otherwise paras 11.48-53 apply.

Errors of law

11.59 There is an error of law if:

(a) the DWP wrongly applies the law in making a decision;

(b) but not when it is shown to be an error of law only by an Upper Tribunal or court (e.g. when it interprets the law in a new way).

Paras 11.55-56 apply to (a), but paras 11.48-53 apply to (b).

Accidental errors

11.60 There is an accidental error if the DWP fails to record, or to put into action, its true intentions (e.g. by mis-entering data on a computer). The DWP can correct an accidental error in a decision, or in a record of a decision, at any time. It must notify you of the correction whether or not it alters your UC, and the correction must be treated as part of the decision or record. Paras 11.48-53 apply if the correction does alter your UC, but the time limit in para 11.53 ignores any period before you are notified of the correction.

Changing decisions about rent officer figures, the benefit cap, sanctions etc

11.61 The DWP should change any decision that:

(a) uses a rent officer figure when it shouldn't do, or uses the wrong figure or area (para 11.63);

(b) applies the benefit cap when it shouldn't do, or calculates it incorrectly (paras 9.57-67);

(c) applies a sanction when it shouldn't do, or calculates it incorrectly (paras 9.69-75); or

(d) wrongly reduces or ends your UC under the Fraud Act 2001.

This applies even if you contributed to the decision being wrong (e.g. if you didn't give the DWP correct information).

11.62 Whenever you request the change, or whenever the DWP makes the change:

(a) the DWP's new decision takes effect from the date the original decision took effect (or should have);

(b) so if the change is advantageous (para 11.48) you are awarded arrears of UC back to then, but if it is disadvantageous (para 11.51) you have been overpaid UC back to then.

11.58   D&A definition: 'official error', 9

11.59   D&A 2 definition: 'official error', 9(a)

11.60   D&A 9(a), 38

11.62   D&A 10,14,19,21

Rent officer figures

11.63   Rent officer figures are used in UC as follows:

(a) if you are a private sector renter, the DWP uses rent officer figures and areas (called LHA and BRMA determinations) to calculate your eligible rent (paras 6.15-20);

(b) if you are a social sector renter, the DWP can ask the rent officer for a figure (called a housing payment determination) and can choose whether or not to use it in calculating your eligible rent (paras 5.21-26).

Paras 11.59-60 apply if the DWP uses a rent officer figure when it shouldn't do, or uses the wrong figure or area. But see instead para 11.64 if the rent officer corrects a figure, or paras 6.17-18 if your LHA figure changes in April or because your circumstances change.

Corrections to rent officer figures

11.64   The rent officer can reconsider any figure or area used in UC and correct it if they consider it is wrong. This is called a redetermination. The DWP can ask them to do this, or they can do it on their own initiative. If you think the rent officer has got a figure or area wrong, you could try asking them to change it, or asking the DWP to ask them (the law doesn't say that you can or that you can't).

11.65   When a rent officer redetermination means a new figure applies to you:

(a) if it is higher, the DWP's new decision takes effect from when its original decision took effect (or should have) – so you get arrears of UC back to then;

(b) if it is lower, the DWP's new decision takes effect from the first day of the assessment period following the one in which the DWP receives the figure from the rent officer – so you haven't been overpaid UC.

Changing decisions about overpayments

11.66   The DWP can change a decision about:

(a) whether you have been overpaid UC (para 13.1);

(b) the amount of an overpayment (paras 13.7-11);

(c) who it should be recovered from (paras 13.19-26); or

(d) whether it shouldn't be recovered because of hardship etc (paras 13.5-6).

You can ask the DWP to do this at any time, or it can do this at any time on its own initiative. In cases (a) and (b) the DWP's new decision normally takes effect from the date of the decision that meant you were overpaid (paras 13.2-4) – so you should be repaid any amount that was wrongly recovered from you. In cases (c) and (d) the DWP's new decision is likely to take effect from the assessment period in which you request the change or the DWP makes it. But in all of these cases there can be exceptions.

11.65   D&A 19(2),21,30,35(14)

11.66   D&A 10,21,25,35(2),(4)

Changing decisions you have appealed

11.67 Chapter 14 explains the rules about appealing to an independent tribunal. Before you appeal you have to ask the DWP to reconsider the decision you want to appeal (paras 11.43-44 and 14.1).

When you appeal, the DWP:

(a) can change the decision before the appeal takes place (paras 14.16-17);

(b) should normally apply the tribunal's decision once the appeal has taken place (paras 14.57 and 14.63).

Changing decisions you can't appeal

11.68 If a decision is of a kind that can't be appealed (table 14.1), you can ask the DWP to change it at any time, or the DWP can change it at any time on its own initiative. The rules for some non-appealable decisions are in paras 11.25, 11.63-65 and 11.66(d). In other cases, the DWP's new decision is likely to take effect from the date the original decision took effect (or should have), or from the assessment period in which it makes the change – but there can be exceptions in appropriate cases.

Suspending, restoring and terminating UC

11.69 This section explains how the DWP can suspend, restore or terminate your UC. The general rules about this are in paras 11.70-76, and the rules for appeals cases are in paras 11.77-79.

Suspending UC

11.70 Suspending UC means that all or part of your UC payments is stopped for the time being. The DWP has told its decision-makers that they should always take account of whether hardship will result before doing this (ADM para A4317).

11.71 The DWP can suspend all or part of your UC when:

(a) it doubts whether you meet the conditions of entitlement for UC;

(b) it is considering whether to change a decision about your UC (paras 11.4 and 11.39);

(c) it considers there may be an overpayment of UC; or

(d) you don't appear to live at your last notified address.

The DWP can do this straightaway or first ask for information or evidence (para 11.72).

11.67   D&A 11,31,37

11.68   D&A 10,21,25,35(2),(4)

11.71   SSA 22; D&A 44(1),(2)(a)

Information and evidence

11.72　　When the DWP requires information or evidence, it must notify you of what it requires and how long you have to provide it. It must allow you at least 14 days and can allow longer. The DWP can then suspend all or part of your UC if you don't:

(a) provide the information or evidence within the time allowed; or

(b) satisfy the DWP within that time that it doesn't exist or is impossible to obtain.

Restoring UC

11.73　　The DWP must restore payments of your UC when it is satisfied that:

(a) UC is properly payable;

(b) there are no outstanding matters to be resolved; and

(c) you have provided any information or evidence it required, or it doesn't exist or is impossible to obtain.

11.74　　Restoring UC means paying the UC that was suspended. The payments should be at the same amount as before; but the rules in paras 11.3-68 apply if there has been a change of circumstances or a decision was wrong.

Terminating UC

11.75　　The DWP must terminate your UC if:

(a) it suspended payments of your UC in full;

(b) it required you to provide information or evidence;

(c) more than one month has passed since it required this; and

(d) you haven't provided the information or evidence or satisfied the DWP that it doesn't exist or is impossible to obtain.

The DWP can extend the time limit of one month if this is reasonable (ADM para A4338).

11.76　　Terminating UC means you don't get any more payments and your entitlement ends; but the rules in paras 11.3-68 apply if your UC should have stopped from an earlier date. The DWP should notify you when it terminates your UC.

Suspending and restoring UC in appeals cases

11.77　　The DWP can suspend all or part of your UC when an appeal is pending against:

(a) a decision of a First-tier Tribunal, Upper Tribunal or court in your own case; or

(b) a decision of an Upper Tribunal or court in another person's case, and it appears to the DWP that the outcome of the appeal could mean your UC should be changed.

11.72　　SSA 22; D & A 45

11.73　　D&A 46(a),(b)

11.75　　SSA 23; D & A 47

11.77　　SSA 21; D & A 44(1),(2)(b),(c)

11.78 An appeal counts as 'pending' if:

(a) the DWP has requested a statement of reasons from the First-tier Tribunal and is waiting for this; or

(b) the DWP is waiting for a decision from the Upper Tribunal or court; or

(c) the DWP has received the statement of reasons or decision and:

- is considering whether to apply for permission to appeal,

- has applied for permission to appeal and is waiting for a decision on this, or

- has received permission to appeal and is considering whether to appeal; or

(d) the DWP has made an appeal and it hasn't yet been decided; or

(e) you or the other person (para 11.77) have made an appeal and it hasn't yet been decided.

In cases (a) to (d) the DWP should keep you informed of its plans.

11.79 The DWP must restore payments of your UC when:

(a) it runs out of time to request a statement of reasons, apply for permission to appeal, or appeal; or

(b) it withdraws an application for permission to appeal, or an appeal; or

(c) it is refused permission to appeal and can't take any further steps to obtain it.

But if the DWP needs information or evidence, the rules in paras 11.72-76 apply.

Changing decisions about suspending, restoring or terminating UC

11.80 You can ask the DWP to reconsider a decision about suspending, restoring or terminating your UC (para 11.43). You can then appeal to a tribunal about a decision to terminate your UC or to alter it when it is restored, but not about a decision to suspend your UC or to restore it without altering it (para 14.8).

11.78   SSA 98 s.21(3); D&A 44(3)-(5)

11.79   D&A 46(c),(d)

11.80   D&A 10,21,25

Chapter 12 **UC payments**

- How, when and to whom UC payments are normally made: see paras 12.1-4.
- Payment of UC to someone else acting on your behalf: see paras 12.5-6.
- Budgeting and bill payment: see para 12.7.
- Alternative payment arrangements that allow more frequent payments and for the redirecting or splitting of payments between partners: see paras 12.8-10.
- Alternative payment arrangements under which UC managed payments may be paid directly to the landlord: see paras 12.11-18.
- Direct payments to qualifying lenders where UC includes help with the cost of owning the home: see paras 12.19-25.
- Deductions paid to a third party if you have housing cost, rent or service charge arrears, council tax arrears or certain other debts: see paras 12.26-37.
- Loss of the right to a UC payment if it is not collected and what happens to outstanding payments on the death of the claimant: see paras 12.38-39.
- Payments on account in the form of UC advance payments and budgeting advances: see paras 12.40-49.

How, when and to whom UC is normally paid

Method of payment

12.1   UC is usually paid by direct credit transfer into your bank, building society or other account in monthly payments. During the first stage of transition to UC and subsequent gateway requirements a necessary condition of entitlement was to have a bank, building society or Post Office account or a current account with a Credit Union. When you first claim UC you are asked for the details of the account you want it paid into. In limited circumstances, if you can't use an account, UC can be paid through the Simple Payment Service (ADM B1006 – 07). This enables you to collect your benefit by using a Simple Payment card at a paypoint outlet which displays the Simple Payment logo [www].

Example

Brian is entitled to a UC payment for the monthly assessment period from 5th June to 4th July. The payment is credited to his building society account in the seven days after 4th July and on the same day in each subsequent month.

12.1   C&P Regs, 47(1), 46(1), 47(2); SI 2013/386 12(e), SI 2013/983 sch 5 7(e)
         www.gov.uk/simple-payment

Date of payment

12.2   UC is paid in arrears normally up to seven days after the last day of your monthly assessment period or as soon as reasonably practicable after that. If you are subject to waiting days at the start of your claim you usually get the first payment one month and 14 days after you made your claim. If there are delays in deciding or paying your benefit and this is placing you in financial need, you may be able to get a payment on account in the form of a UC advance payment (see para 12.42). Also the DWP may change the frequency of payment if a single monthly amount causes you problems (see para 12.8).

12.3   The DWP can decide to make a particular credit transfer at other times if it appears appropriate for the purpose of:

  (a) paying arrears of benefit; or

  (b) making a payment at the end of an award or for any similar purpose.

Payment to couples

12.4   If you are in a couple and joint claimants, UC is normally only paid into one account. This can be an account in:

  (a) your name;

  (b) your partner's name; or

  (c) your joint names.

If you can't both decide which account the benefit should be paid into, the DWP can make the decision. This is not an appealable decision. If a single payment to your partner's account or a joint account causes you difficulties, the DWP may decide to split the payment between you (see para 12.9).

Payment to other people on your behalf

12.5   UC can be paid into a bank or other account in:

  (a) an appointee's name – i.e. the name of someone who has been appointed by the DWP to get and deal with your benefit payments – because you are unable for the time being to act – or the name of someone who had previously been appointed to deal with your HB payments by the council and who agrees to be an appointee for UC purposes;

  (b) the name of someone who has been authorised to act on your behalf under specific legislation, e.g. an attorney with general power or the power to receive benefit, a deputy appointed by the Court of Protection, a receiver appointed under the Mental Health Act 1983, or in Scotland a judicial factor or any guardian acting or appointed under the Adults with Incapacity (Scotland) Act 2000; or

  (c) the joint names of yourself and any of the above.

12.2   C&P Regs, 45, 47(2)

12.3   C&P Regs, 47(3)

12.4   C&P Regs, 46(1), 47(4)-(5),

12.5   C&P Regs, 46(1), 57

12.6 Someone who wants to be appointed to get and deal with your UC payments when you're unable to act must be over the age of 18. They should write to the DWP asking to be appointed. The appointment can be ended at any time by the DWP. If the appointee wants to give up the role they must give the DWP a month's written notice.

Budgeting and bill payment

12.7 A single monthly payment of UC which may include money for the rent can pose a significant budgeting and bill payment challenge. This is particularly so if your HB has previously been paid direct to the landlord. And your landlord may be concerned that you will get into rent arrears. The Government recognises these problems but says that it wants you to take personal responsibility for your finances and to budget on a monthly basis so that you find it easier to take up monthly paid employment [www]. You may, however, need help dealing with this change. The DWP aims to identify this (in conjunction with other agencies) either when you first become entitled to UC or once an award has been made. It can provide you with personal budgeting support in the form of:

(a) money advice – to help you manage your money and pay bills on time;

(b) alternative payment arrangements – such as more frequent payments, payments split between partners, and direct managed payments to your landlord.

Alternative payment arrangements

UC paid more often than once a month

12.8 The DWP can pay you more often than once a month if you are having problems budgeting and there is a risk of financial harm to you or you family. The DWP recommends two payments every month in these circumstances but, exceptionally, it may make four [www].

Re-directing and splitting payments between partners

12.9 The DWP can arrange for the UC payable for you and your partner to be paid:

(a) wholly to one of you; or

(b) split between you in such proportion as it thinks appropriate.

12.6   C&P Regs, 57(3)-(4),(8)

12.7   DWP UC Guidance on personal budgeting support and alternative payment arrangements (March 2015)
         www.gov.uk/government/uploads/system/uploads/attachment_data/file/418485/personal-budgeting-support-guidance.pdf

12.8   FN: C&P Regs, 47(1)
         DWP UC Guidance on personal budgeting support and alternative payment arrangements (March 2015)
         www.gov.uk/government/uploads/system/uploads/attachment_data/file/418485/personal-budgeting-support-guidance.pdf

12.9   C&P Regs, 47(6)

12.10   It only does this, however, if it is in the interests of:

(a) both of you;

(b) a child or young person for whom one or both of the you are responsible; or

(c) a severely disabled person – where your UC includes an amount because you have regular and substantial caring responsibilities for that person.

Such re-direction or splitting of payments should be considered in specific situations such as financial abuse where one of you is mismanaging the payments.

Payments of UC to your landlord or someone else

12.11   The DWP can decide to pay your UC either wholly or in part (for example the housing element) to someone else, such as your landlord. The DWP should only do this where it appears necessary to protect your interests or the interests the people identified in para 12.10. The DWP provides guidance on paying the UC housing element to your landlord (known as managed payments) in two documents: UC and rented housing – frequently asked questions (Jan 2016) [www] and UC Personal Budgeting Support and Alternative Payment Arrangements (March 2015) [www]. If an amount for rent is included in your UC and the DWP is considering alternative payment arrangements it says it gives top priority to paying the housing element direct to your landlord over other alternative arrangements.

12.12   A private landlord normally only knows if you claim UC if you tell them. If your landlord is a social landlord the DWP writes to tell them that you have claimed. The DWP asks landlords to say if individual tenants are likely to need support. Your landlord can contact the UC Service Centre by calling 0345 600 0723 to tell them about any concerns they have about your financial capability. If when you claim UC the DWP thinks that you need support with budgeting (after for example considering information and evidence supplied by you, your representative or your landlord) it may decide to put in place an alternative payment arrangement including managed payments to your landlord. But just because your HB was paid to your landlord does not necessarily mean that your UC housing element will be. The DWP says that it considers each case on its merits.

12.13   Key factors that the DWP considers in deciding if an alternative payment arrangement is appropriate are set out in the UC Guidance on Personal Budgeting Support. Alternative payment arrangements including managed payments of UC to your landlord (if appropriate) are described as highly likely if you:

(a)   have addiction problems (e.g. drug, alcohol or gambling);

(b)   have learning difficulties (including problems with reading/writing or numbers);

(c)   have severe or multiple debt problems;

(d)   live in temporary or supported accommodation;

(e)   are homeless;

12.10   C&P Regs, 47(6)

12.11   C&P Regs, 58(1)
         www.gov.uk/government/uploads/system/uploads/attachment_data/file/491047/uc-rented-housing-faq-Jan16.pdf

12.12   WRA s. 131 SI 2012/1483 5(1)(g), 5(3A)

(f)   suffer domestic violence or abuse;

(g)   have a mental health condition;

(h)   are in rent arrears or face eviction;

(i)   are aged 16 or 17; or

(j)   have multiple and complex needs.

Alternative payment arrangements are also possible in other circumstances.

Rent arrears and managed payments of UC to your landlord

12.14   If you, your representative or your landlord tell the DWP that you have rent arrears equal to the amount of one month's rent the DWP may decide to offer you budgeting support and/or pay the housing element of your UC direct to your landlord. If you have rent arrears of an amount equal to 2 months rent your landlord can ask the DWP to consider if managed payments of UC direct to the landlord are appropriate. They can also request that rent arrears be recovered by deduction from your UC – see para 12.33.

12.15   Your landlord may get managed payments of UC by filling in and submitting a UC47 Rent Arrears Form [www]. To complete this form your landlord needs to know your NI number or your date of birth. They must also provide proof of your rent arrears and a full breakdown of how the amount of rent and the arrears are calculated. The completed form is sent to: Freepost Plus RTEU-LESU-EXTJ, Universal Credit, Post Handling Site B, Wolverhampton, WV99 1AJ. Once the DWP gets the completed form and evidence it decides whether to make managed payments to your landlord. Both you and your landlord are told about this decision in writing. It is not appealable but you may ask the DWP to look at it again.

12.16   The DWP also offers an email address for landlords to use for urgent enquiries if for example you are facing eviction or your landlord needs an urgent response [www].

12.17   The DWP looks again at its decision to pay UC direct to your landlord and other alternative payment arrangements periodically. The DWP sets a review date based on your particular circumstances.

Scotland

12.18   Following the recommendations of the Smith Commission [www] the Scotland Bill 2015 has provisions which, once passed by the UK Parliament, enable Scottish Ministers to provide for alternative UC payment arrangements for claimants in Scotland. In particular it enables Scottish Ministers, in consultation with the DWP, to make regulations on such matters as the frequency of UC payments and the circumstances in which the UC housing element is paid directly to landlords.

12.15   www.gov.uk/government/publications/universal-credit-and-rented-housing
         D&A Regs, sch 3 para 1(n)

12.16   uc.servicecentrehousing@dwp.gsi.gov.uk

12.18   www.smith-commission.scot/wp-content/uploads/2014/11/The_Smith_Commission_Report-1.pdf

Direct payment to your lender for mortgage interest etc

12.19   If your UC award includes support for interest payments on a loan that is secured on the house you occupy, e.g. mortgage interest, and it is payable to a qualifying lender, it should be paid by the DWP direct to the lender in monthly instalments in arrears.

Information that must be provided by your lender

12.20   Your lender should provide the DWP with the following information when asked by the DWP to do so (either when you make a claim for UC or the housing cost element is to be included in your UC at some other point):

   (a)   the loan interest payments for which you meet the payment condition (see para 4.2) and the liability condition (see para 4.3);

   (b)   the amount of the loan;

   (c)   the purpose for which the loan was made;

   (d)   the amount outstanding on the loan;

   (e)   the amount of arrears of loan interest payments due.

12.21   Your lender should also tell the DWP about the following when asked by the DWP to do so:

   (a)   any change in the amount of the loan interest payable; and

   (b)   the amount outstanding on the loan.

12.22   If your lender gets notice that the loan is going to be redeemed they must tell the DWP about this at once.

The lender must put the direct payments against your loan interest liability

12.23   Where the DWP is making a direct payment to your lender, the lender must apply the amount of the payment towards discharging your liability to make loan interest payments, in respect of which the direct payments are made.

Administration of direct payments to lenders

12.24   The DWP Third Party Payments (TPP) team (part of Payment Resolution Service) based at Norcross act as paying agents. They are responsible for all payments to third party creditors (ADM D4031). In return for getting direct payments of mortgage interest, your lender pays a fee of £0.44 (from 1st April 2016) to the DWP for each transaction.

12.25   There is no right of appeal against a decision to pay mortgage interest payments etc direct to a qualifying lender.

12.19   AA s15A, C&P Regs, 59, sch 5 paras 1(1), 2(2)(a), 3(1)-(2), 8

12.20   C&P Regs, sch 5, para 11(1)-(2)

12.21   C&P Regs, sch 5, para 11(3)

12.22   C&P Regs, sch 5, para 11(4)

12.23   C&P Regs, sch 5, para 6

12.24   C&P Regs, sch 5 para 9

12.25   D&A Regs, sch 3 para 1(o)

Payment to third parties for certain priority debts

12.26   The DWP can make deductions from your UC to repay certain priority debts (such as rent, utility bills and fines) you owe to a third party. The debts for which deductions can be made include:

   (a)   housing costs – not covered by the direct payment arrangements (see para 12.19);

   (b)   rent and service charges;

   (c)   council tax; and

   (d)   several other items including fuel debts, water charges and fines.

12.27   The DWP says (ADM D2022) that it is normally in your interests to make third party deductions if you have:

   (a)   a history of persistent mis-spending; or

   (b)   a threat of eviction or repossession; and

   (c)   no other suitable method of dealing with the debt.

12.28   Deductions are not normally made (ADM D2023) if you:

   (a)   show evidence of determination to clear the debt; or

   (b)   agree to clear the debt yourself.

Constraints on third party deductions

12.29   The DM can't deduct an amount from your UC and pay it to a third party if, in any assessment period, that would:

   (a)   reduce the amount payable to you to less than 1p; or

   (b)   result in more than three deductions being made, in relation to that assessment period (though there are certain exceptions to this).

12.30   Your consent is not required for the DWP to make deductions for housing costs, rent or service charges. You should, however, be given the opportunity to dispute the liability and the DWP should only make deductions where there is evidence that you are liable to pay the debt (ADM D2026-8).

Third party deductions for arrears of an owner's housing costs

12.31   The DWP may make deductions equal to 5% of the standard allowance from your UC and pay it direct to the creditor where, in any assessment period, you are in debt for any of the following housing costs that have been included in the calculation of your UC:

   (a)   loan interest payments;

   (b)   alternative finance payments, e.g. a Shariah-compliant arrangement;

   (c)   service charge payments; or

   (d)   payments under a shared ownership scheme.

12.26   C&P Regs, sch 6, para 2(1)

12.29   C&P Regs, sch 6, para 3(1)(a)-(b), 3(2)

12.31   C&P Regs, 60, sch 6, para 6(2)-(3|)

12.32   The DWP says it only does this if it is satisfied that two months' arrears have accrued (ADM D2093). Also a deduction cannot be made under this rule where the item is payable direct to a qualifying lender (see para 12.19).

Third party deductions for arrears of rent and service charges

12.33   If your rent is being met through either UC (or HB because you live in exempt accommodation) the DWP can make deductions of between 10% and 20% from your UC standard allowance (para 9.14) and pay it direct to your landlord to meet arrears of rent, service charges and ineligible service charges. The provision is for a minimum priority deduction of 10%. Whether the deduction can be as high as 20% depends on whether the DWP is making other deductions as the maximum that may normally be deducted from your UC in respect of deductions for arrears, overpayments, repaying advances, child support etc is 40% of your standard allowance. The DWP may, however, exceed this 40% figure to allow it to make a deduction equal to 10% of the standard allowance to pay for rent and service charge arrears.

12.34   In all cases for these deductions to be payable you must be occupying the accommodation to which the debt relates. Because these deductions may be made where your rent is met through HB in exempt accommodation they can be made for example to cover arrears of ineligible service charges in such accommodation.

12.35   The DWP says it only makes these deductions if satisfied that two months' arrears have accrued (ADM D2120). Also these deductions can only be started if your (and any partner's) earned income in relation to the previous assessment period is not greater than the work allowance (para 10.13 and table 10.1). They must stop if, in relation to the three assessment periods immediately before the date on which the next deduction could otherwise be made, your (and any partner's) earned income is equal to or greater than the work allowance.

12.36   Your landlord may apply for these deduction to be made in the same way as they apply for managed payments of the UC housing element and the same form is used (para 12.15).

Deductions to recover arrears of council tax

12.37   If you have arrears of council tax the authority can make an application to the DWP for deductions to be made from your UC if they have got a liability order or have been granted a summary warrant or decree. The DWP may deduct an amount equal to 5% of your UC standard allowance and pay it to the authority. You must be entitled to UC throughout the assessment period for this deduction to be made. Also a deduction can't be made if a deduction arrangement is already in place to recover arrears of council tax or community charges.

12.32   C&P Regs, 60, sch 6, para 6(5)

12.33   C&P Regs, reg. 60, sch 6 para 7(1)-(5)

12.34   C&P Regs, sch 6 para 7(4)

12.35   C&P Regs, sch 6 para 7(6)-(7)

12.37   SI 1993 No. 494, 1(2), 2, 3, 5(1A), 8

Loss of the right to a UC payment if you fail to get it

12.38   If you (or your appointee, attorney, etc) haven't got your UC payment after 12 months from the date on which your right to the payment arose, you lose the right to that payment (CDLA/2609/2002 and CDLA/2807/2003). But this period may be extended if you write to the DWP after the 12 months are up asking for payment and have continuous good cause (R(S)2/63) from a day within the 12 month period for the late request.

What happens to any UC payment if you die

12.39   Any payment that should have been made to you (unless it has been lost because you didn't get it within 12 months) may be paid or distributed by the DWP among people who are your personal representatives, legatees, next of kin or creditors (all over the age of 16). Where the DWP is satisfied that the payment is needed for the well-being of a child (someone under 16), it may pay it to someone aged 16+ who satisfies the DWP that they will use it for the child's well-being. The 12 month rule still applies (see para 12.38) but here is calculated from the date on which the right to payment arose in relation to these other people. A written application for the payment should be made to the DWP within 12 months from the date of your death – though the DWP may extend this period.

Payments on account

Two types

12.40   Two types of payments on account of benefit may possibly be available to you:

   (a) advances of benefit (UC advances); and

   (b) interest free loans – called budgeting advances.

12.41   If the DWP decides to pay you a UC advance or budgeting advance, it also writes to you (and any partner) telling you that:

   (a) the advance payment will be deducted from subsequent payments of benefit; and

   (b) if it is not deducted in this way you will have to repay it.

The detailed rules regarding these payments are set out in the Social Security (Payments on Account of Benefits) Regulations SI 2013 No 383.

12.38   C&P Regs, 55

12.39   C&P Regs, 56(2)-(8)

12.41   POA 8, 17

UC advances

12.42   A UC advance may be available if you are in financial need and:

(a) you have made a claim for UC that has yet to be decided but it appears to the DWP likely that you are entitled; or

(b) you haven't had to claim to become entitled to UC but the award has not yet been made; or

(c) UC has been awarded but the first payment has not yet been made; or

(d) a first UC payment has been made but it was for a shorter period than the normal period and a second payment hasn't been received yet; or

(e) you have had a change of circumstance that increases the amount of UC you are entitled to but the award has not yet been altered or the resulting increased payment has not yet been made; or

(f) delays mean that a UC payment hasn't been made on the date due.

The DWP says that the maximum advance it pays in the case of a new UC claim is 50% of your estimated UC payment; or in the case of a significant change of circumstance, 50% of the expected increase in your UC payment [www].

12.43   Financial need means that there is a serious risk of damage to your health or safety or the health or safety of any partner or child or young person you are responsible for. When you ask for a UC advance you should provide as much information and evidence as possible about the circumstances and financial need. Explain how the delay etc is placing at risk your, or your family's, health or safety.

12.44   If the DWP refuses your request for a UC advance there is no right of appeal but you can ask the DWP to reconsider the decision. You should also look into other sources of help such as a discretionary housing payment from the council to help you pay the rent.

Budgeting advances

12.45   You may be able to get an interest free loan in the form of a budgeting advance to help you with one-off expenses such as furniture or household equipment, or expenses related to starting work. You pay back the advance by having the DWP deduct an amount from your monthly UC payments over a 12 month period (this may be extended to 18 months in exceptional circumstances).

12.46   To qualify for a budgeting advance you must have:

(a) been getting UC or a predecessor benefit (IS, JSA(IB), ESA(IR) or pension credit) for a continuous period of at least six months before making the application (except where the expense necessarily relates to getting or keeping a job);

12.42   POA 4-6
        www.whatdotheyknow.com/request/253340/response/627394/attach/3/Reply 549.pdf

12.43   POA 7

12.44   D&A Regs, sch 3 para 14

12.46   POA 12-14

(b) not have earned more than £2,600 in the previous six months (£3,600 for a couple);

(c) repaid any previous budgeting advance and the DWP must be satisfied that the budgeting advance can reasonably be expected to be recovered.

12.47   The minimum amount of budgeting advance payable is £100. The maximum amount is set out in the following table.

Table 12.1 **Maximum amount of budgeting advance**

Your circumstances	Maximum amount of budgeting advance
Single and not responsible for a child or young person	£348
A couple but not responsible for a child or young person	£464
Responsible for a child or young person	£812

12.48   The amount of any budgeting advance you can get is reduced pound for pound by any assessable capital you have above £1,000. If this would reduce the amount to less than £100, then no budgeting advance is payable.

12.49   You can't appeal against a DWP refusal to make a budgeting advance but you can ask for the decision to be reconsidered.

T12.1   POA 15

12.48   POA 16

12.49   D&A Regs, sch 3 para 14

Chapter 13 **UC overpayments**

- Why overpayments occur: see para 13.1.
- How overpayments are created: see paras 13.2-4.
- Recoverability and the DWP's discretion not to recover: see paras 13.5-6.
- Calculation of the recoverable overpayment: see paras 13.7-18.
- People overpayments of UC housing costs and other UC overpayments are recoverable from: see paras 13.19-26.
- Methods of recovery available to the DWP: see paras 13.27-43.

Why overpayments occur

13.1   An overpayment occurs when you are paid more UC than you are legally entitled to. This can happen for a variety of reasons including:

(a) you give the DWP wrong information, fail to give relevant information or are late in telling the DWP about a change in your circumstances;

(b) your landlord, employer or someone else gives the DWP incorrect information or fails to provide relevant information they are required to provide;

(c) the backdating of an income or benefit that affects your UC; or

(d)   the DWP makes a mistake or is late in acting on information.

The creation of UC overpayments

13.2   Once the DWP has awarded and paid you an amount of UC you are normally entitled to that money until:

(a) it revises or supersedes the awarding decision in accordance with the rules – resulting in you being entitled to less money than you have been paid; or

(b) an appeal decision means that you are entitled to less money than you have been paid.

13.3   The DWP advises decision makers to make sure that the new entitlement decision revises or supersedes all the awarding decisions which operated during the period of the overpayment. They should be able to produce evidence that the necessary revisions or supersessions have taken place (ADM D1032-33). If it is realised after an overpayment decision has been made that there has been no proper alteration of entitlement for all or some part of the overpayment period, the overpayment decision has no force or effect (ADM D1035).

13.1   AA s 71ZB(1)(a), s 71ZB(5)

13.2   AA s 71ZB(3)

Overpayments where there is no requirement for a revision or supersession

13.4   The requirement for a revision or supersession does not apply however where the circumstances of the overpayment do not provide a basis for the awarding decision to be revised or superseded. This is the case, for example, if you have been paid twice by mistake for the same period.

Recoverability

13.5   All UC overpayments that have been properly decided by the DWP are recoverable even if they are caused by the DWP (i.e. are due to official error). Its decision to recover however is a discretionary one.

Discretion not to recover

13.6   The law does not say that the DWP must recover a UC overpayment, only that it may recover such overpayments. The DWP says that it may decide not to recover an overpayment, or part of it, in exceptional circumstances. It says this could be where recovery is likely to cause you, or your immediate family, significant hardship and be a threat to you, or your family's, health or welfare (COP1 [www]). If you think that repaying the overpayment will cause you hardship, you should tell the DWP and ask it not to recover the overpayment. If it still decides to recover you cannot appeal this decision but if you think it is failing to take into account relevant factors or being unreasonable you can complain (para 14.3-4).

Calculating the overpayment

Establishing the overpayment period

13.7   To work out the amount of the overpayment, the DWP must first establish the start date and the end date of the period for which your UC has been overpaid.

Diminution of capital

13.8   The DWP should calculate the amount of the overpayment in a particular way that is 'favourable' to you where:

(a)   it occurred because of an error about your capital; and

(b)   the overpayment period is three months or more.

13.4   AA s 71ZB(3), OP Regs 5

13.5   AA s 71ZB(1)(a), OP Regs 3(1)

13.6   AA s 71ZB(1)(a)
            www.gov.uk/government/uploads/system/uploads/attachment_data/file/
            206533/UC-JSA-ESA-overpayments-customer_guidance-cop1-june13.pdf

13.9   If this applies to you then the DWP, when calculating the recoverable overpayment, should:

(a) at the end of the first three months of the overpayment period – treat your capital as reduced by the amount of UC overpaid during those three months and then use this reduced capital figure to calculate the overpayment after that; and

(b) at the end of each subsequent three month overpayment period – treat your capital as further reduced by the amount of UC overpaid during each three month period and use the resulting reduced capital figures to calculate the overpayments.

This rule reflects the fact that if you had been awarded less UC due to the capital being taken into account you might have used some of it to meet your essential expenditure.

Overpayments of UC housing costs when you move home

13.10   When calculating the recoverable amount of an overpayment caused by you moving home, the DWP has the discretion to subtract an amount equal to your entitlement to UC housing costs on your new home from the amount of the overpayment on your old home. This is done for the same number of assessment periods as you were overpaid UC housing costs on your old home. The DWP can only do this, however, where:

(a) you are not entitled to UC housing costs on your former home because you no longer occupy it; and

(b) the UC housing costs are payable to the same person for both homes.

13.11   Where this rule is used, the DWP treats the same amount as having been paid towards the home you moved into. Again this is for the same number of assessment periods as you were overpaid UC housing costs on your former home.

Additions to the recoverable amount

13.12   In addition to the amount you have been paid above your entitlement, the recoverable sum may be increased by:

(a) recovery of a payment on account (see para 12.41);

(b) recovery of hardship payments;

(c) recovery of penalties imposed as an alternative to prosecution (see para 13.13);

(d) recovery of civil penalties (see para 13.17); and

(e) the costs of court action.

13.9   OP Regs 7

13.10   OP Regs 9(1)-(2)

13.11   OP Regs 9(3)

13.12   OP Regs 3

Administrative penalties

13.13   The DWP may offer you the chance to pay an 'administrative penalty' rather than face prosecution, if:

  (a) a UC overpayment was caused by an 'act or omission' on your part; and

  (b) there are grounds for bringing a prosecution against you for an offence relating to that overpayment.

You do not have to agree to a penalty. You can opt for the possibility of prosecution instead.

13.14   The DWP's offer of a penalty must be in writing, explain that it is a way of avoiding prosecution, and give other information – including the fact that you can change your mind within 14 days (including the date of the agreement), and that the penalty will be repaid if you successfully challenge it by asking for a reconsideration or appeal. The DWP does not normally offer a penalty (but prosecutes instead) if an overpayment is substantial or there are other aggravating factors (such as you being in a position of trust).

13.15   The amount of the penalty is 50% of the recoverable overpayment. This is subject to a minimum of £350 and a maximum of £5,000 where your act or omission causing the overpayment occurred wholly on or after 1st April 2015. The maximum penalty where the relevant act or omission occurred before that date is £2,000.

13.16   The DWP may also make an offer of a penalty where your act or omission could have resulted in an overpayment and it thinks there are grounds for bringing a prosecution for a related offence. In these cases the penalty is the fixed amount of £350.

Civil penalties

13.17   The DWP may impose a civil penalty of £50 on you if you:

  (a) make incorrect statements in a benefit claim without taking reasonable steps to correct them; or

  (b) have been awarded benefit but fail to disclose information or report relevant changes in circumstance without reasonable excuse.

13.18   The amount of the civil penalty is added to the amount of the recoverable overpayment. If you have been successfully prosecuted for fraud or offered an administrative penalty or caution, the DWP cannot issue you with a civil penalty for the same offence.

13.13   AA 115A(1)-(1A)

13.14   AA 115A(5)-(6),

13.15   AA 115A(3)(a)-(b); art 1(3) of SI 2015/202

13.16   AA 115A(3A)

13.17   AA 115C-115D, SI 2012/1990

13.19   AA s 71ZB(2), OP Regs 4

People from whom an overpayment may be recovered

13.19   An overpayment is normally recoverable from the person it was paid to (the 'payee') but in specific circumstances it may be recoverable from someone else, either:

(a) in addition to the person paid; or

(b) instead of the person paid.

Couples

13.20   When an award of UC is made to you jointly with a partner, if an amount is overpaid to one of you it is treated as overpaid to both of you, and so can be recovered from either of you – even the one who didn't get the payment.

Who overpayments of UC housing costs are recovered from

Due to a misrepresentation or a failure to disclose a material fact

13.21   An overpayment of UC housing costs is recoverable from someone who misrepresented or failed to disclose information and not the person who actually got the overpayment where the DWP is satisfied:

(a) that the overpayment occurred because that person misrepresented, or failed to disclose, a material fact (in either case, whether fraudulent or otherwise), and

(b) that person is not the same person who got the overpayment.

13.22   DWP decision makers are advised that where recovery is sought from the landlord under this rule they must be able to show that the landlord has a legal duty to disclose the fact in question (ADM D1170).

On moving home

13.23   If the DWP is satisfied that an overpayment of UC housing costs occurred because you moved home and the overpayment was paid to someone else, e.g. your landlord, the overpayment is recoverable from you as well as that other person.

Other overpayments of UC housing costs

13.24   If the DWP is satisfied that an overpayment of UC housing costs occurred for some other reason than you moving home, or someone misrepresenting or failing to disclose a material fact, then the overpayment is recoverable from you and not the person paid. The exceptions to this rule are where:

(a) the payee was your appointee or someone else such as a landlord getting the payment under an alternative payment arrangement; or

(b) the overpayment occurred because the amount of the payment was greater than the amount of housing costs you are liable for.

13.20   AA s 71ZB(6)

13.21   OP Regs 4(4),(6)

13.23   OP Regs 4(4)-(5)

13.24   OP Regs 4(7)-(8)

Who other UC overpayments may be recovered from

Appointees and payees under alternative payment arrangements

13.25   Where the person who was overpaid is your appointee, or someone such as your landlord who got the overpayment under an alternative payment arrangement (see paras 12.11-14), then the overpayment is recoverable from you in addition to the person who got the overpayment (but also note the above paragraphs regarding the recovery of overpaid UC housing costs).

Third parties

13.26   If the person who got a payment is a third party, such as the landlord in a case of rent arrears direct, then to the extent that the amount overpaid does not exceed the amount payable to that third party an overpayment is recoverable from you instead of that third party.

Methods of recovery

13.27   The DWP may recover a UC overpayment by any lawful method including sending you a bill for payment. The following methods are also available:

(a) deduction from your future UC payments and arrears;

(b) deduction from other DWP benefits;

(c) deduction from a landlord's own UC or other DWP benefits;

(d) adjustment of subsequent payments of benefit;

(e) deduction from earnings (direct earnings attachment – DEA); or

(f) through the courts.

Recovery by deductions from your future UC payments

13.28   Overpaid UC recoverable from you may be recovered by deductions from your (or any partner's) future UC payments. This method is limited as follows:

(a) the amount deducted must not be greater than shown in table 13.1;

(b) no deduction should be made that reduces your UC for the assessment period to less than 1p;

(c) the DWP should consider deducting a lower amount where the maximum rate of deduction would cause hardship to you or your family.

13.29   The 'appropriate UC standard allowance' is the appropriate UC standard allowance included in the award of UC for you, or for you and your partner as joint claimants.

13.25   OP Regs 4(2)

13.26   OP Regs 4(3)

13.27   AA s 71ZB(7)

13.28   OP Regs 10(2)(b), 11(2)-(3), (7)

13.29   OP Regs 11(11)

Table 13.1 **Maximum deduction from UC in the assessment period (2016-17)**

Circumstances	You	Maximum deduction (% of the appropriate UC standard allowance)
You have: (a) been found guilty of an offence in relation to the overpayment; (b) made an admission after caution of deception or fraud for the purpose of obtaining benefit; or (c) agreed to pay a penalty as an alternative to prosecution and the agreement has not been withdrawn Recovery of hardship payments		40%
	Single	
	Under 25	£100.71
	25 or over	£127.13
	Joint claimants	
	Both under 25	£158.08
	One or both	
	25 or over	£199.56
Your earned income is greater than the work allowance in the calculation of your UC		25%
	Single	
	Under 25	£62.94
	25 or over	£79.46
	Joint claimants	
	Both under 25	£98.80
	One or both	
	25 or over	£124.72
Any other case		15%
	Single	
	Under 25	£37.77
	25 or over	£47.67
	Joint claimants	
	Both under 25	£59.28
	One or both	
	25 or over	£74.83

T13.1   OP Regs 11(2)-(4)

13.30   The limits shown in Table 13.1 do not apply where:

(a)   the deduction is from any payment of arrears of UC – except arrears paid following the suspension of payments; or

(b)   the recoverable amount is an overpayment of UC housing costs that are being recovered from someone else, e.g. the landlord.

Deductions from UC paid to the landlord on your behalf

13.31   The DWP can decided to recover an overpayment from you by making a deduction from the UC it pays to a landlord on your behalf. Where this happens this leaves you with more rent to pay, or rent arrears if you don't. These arrears can lead to your eviction if they are not dealt with.

13.32   If the DWP decides to recover the overpayment from your landlord, it may still recover the overpayment from the on-going UC payments it makes to the landlord on your behalf. A special rule applies if the DWP is recovering from these on-going payments of UC because your landlord has:

(a)   been found guilty of an offence relating to the overpayment; or

(b)   agreed to pay a penalty as an alternative to prosecution and the agreement has not been withdrawn.

13.33   In these circumstances your rental obligation to the landlord for the same amount is in law considered to be paid off and your landlord cannot put you into rent arrears for this amount.

13.34   The DWP should tell both you and the landlord

(a)   that the overpayment it has decided to recover is one to which this rule applies; and

(b)   that your landlord has no right in relation to an equivalent sum against you, and that your obligation to the landlord is to be taken as paid off by the amount so recovered.

Deductions from a 'blameless' tenant's UC payments

13.35   If a UC overpayment is recoverable from a landlord the DWP may recover it by deductions from payments to that landlord of another tenant's UC. This is talked about as recovery from a 'blameless' tenant because the tenant had nothing to do with the overpayment. In these cases the blameless tenant's obligation to the landlord is treated by the law as paid off and the landlord cannot in law put the 'blameless' tenant into rent arrears because of this deduction.

13.30   OP Regs 11(8)-(9)

13.31   AA s 71ZC(2)(b)

13.33   AA s 71ZC(3), OP Regs 15(1)-(2)

13.34   OP Regs 15(3)

13.35   AA s 71ZC(2)(c),(4)

Deductions from a landlord's own benefits

13.36   Where UC has been paid to a third party such as your landlord on your behalf, and the DWP decides to recover the overpayment from the landlord, the overpayment may (though this is rare) be recovered from the landlord's personal entitlement to UC or other DWP benefits (table 13.2).

Recovery by deduction from other DWP benefits

13.37   An overpayment of UC may be recovered by deductions from other DWP benefits that you or any partner are getting. Table 13.2 identifies the other DWP benefits from which recovery can be made.

Table 13.2 **DWP benefits from which UC overpayments can be recovered**

(a) UC	(b) incapacity benefit
(c) maternity allowance	(d) widow(er)'s benefits
(e) bereavement benefits	(f) retirement pension
(g) child's special allowance	(h) attendance allowance
(i) invalid care allowance	(j) disability living allowance
(k) industrial injuries benefit	(l) JSA
(m) ESA	(n) state pension
(o) PIP	

Deductions from earnings

13.38   Overpayments may be recovered by the DWP requiring your employer to make deductions from your earnings without the need for court action. The DWP suggests that this method of recovery is useful for people who no longer get benefit and who will not come to a voluntary agreement to repay the debt [www].

13.39   The DWP should send a notice to both you and your employer before deductions are made. The employer should tell the DWP if they are not in fact your employer or if they think they are exempt from the deduction arrangement because they are a new business or a micro-business. This should be done within ten days of the day after the notice was sent.

13.36   AA s 71ZC(2)(a)

13.37   AA s 71ZC(1)

T13.2   AA s 71ZC(1), OP Regs 10

13.38   AA s71ZD, OP Regs 20
             www.legislation.gov.uk/uksi/2013/384/pdfs/uksifia_20130384_en.pdf

13.39   OP Regs 19, 24

13.40   Your employer should tell you the amount of the deductions and pay the amount deducted (excluding that for administrative costs) to the DWP. They must also keep records of the amounts deducted and of people for whom such deductions have been made. You must tell the DWP within seven days if you leave the employment or when you become employed or re-employed. Your employer should also tell the DWP if you are no longer employed by them. It is a criminal offence to fail to make or pay deductions or to provide information. Guides to direct earnings attachments for employers and others are available on the gov.uk website [www].

Recovery through the courts

13.41   UC overpayments are recoverable through the county court in England and Wales and through the sheriff court in Scotland. The DWP tries to recover court costs when there is a court judgment in its favour. It can add these to the recoverable overpayment and recover them by any method by which overpaid UC can be recovered.

Adjustment of benefit

13.42   In certain circumstances the DWP may recover overpayments of UC by adjusting later benefit payments. UC paid but then determined as not payable, can be treated as properly paid and be set against future payments of benefit or against certain payments to third parties.

Time limits on recovery

13.43   In England, Wales and Northern Ireland the DWP/DFC can't use the courts to enforce a recovery (para 13.41) more than six years from the date you were first notified of the decision (para 14.7) but this does not stop the DWP/DFC from recovering the overpayment by other means (such as deductions from your future UC payments: para 13.28). In Scotland the time limit for recovery through the courts is five years from the date you were notified or 20 years by any method.

13.40   OP Regs 21-22, 23, 30
         www.gov.uk/government/publications/direct-earnings-attachments-an-employers-guide

13.41   AA s71ZE(1)-(3)

13.42   AA s71ZF

13.43   Limitation Act 1980 s9, 38(11) (as amended by WRA 108);
         Prescription and Limitation (Scotland) Act 1973 s6, 7 sch 1 para 1(b);
         Limitation (Northern Ireland) Order 1989 art 6, 2(11) (as amended by NIWRO 111)

Chapter 14 **UC appeals**

- An overview of the appeal and complaint procedures: see paras 14.1-4.
- Who can appeal: see paras 14.5-6.
- The DWP's decision and how to get a written explanation of it: see paras 14.7-9.
- Applying for a revision of the disputed decision: see paras 14.10-17.
- Non-appealable decisions: see paras 14.18 and table 14.1.
- Appealing to the First-tier Tribunal, the DWP's response and your submission: see paras 14.19-32.
- The First-tier Tribunal and the appeal hearing: see paras 14.33-50.
- What can be done if the First-tier Tribunal's decision is wrong: see paras 14.51-66.
- Appeals to the Upper Tribunal and beyond: see paras 14.67-75.

Overview

Appeals

14.1   You may be able to get a UC decision changed by asking the DWP to look at it again in the light of any additional information, evidence or explanations you can provide. Legally you are applying for a revision of the decision. The DWP refers to the process it carries out when it gets your request as a 'mandatory reconsideration'. Once the mandatory reconsideration has been carried out, and if you don't get the decision you want, you can appeal to the independent First-tier Tribunal [www]. A further appeal (on a point of law and only if you are given permission) then goes to the Upper Tribunal [www]. The administrative arrangements relating to appeals are the responsibility of Her Majesty's Courts and Tribunals Service (HMCTS) [www]. Not all decisions are appealable (but you can ask for any such non-appealable decisions to be revised).

14.2   You may be dissatisfied not with a decision but with the way you, or your claim, have been dealt with, for example a delay by the DWP in making a decision. Non-appealable decisions and delays in making decisions may in certain instances, and as a last resort, be remedied by (a letter warning of) judicial review (but you should seek advice when considering this action).

Complaints

14.3   If you want to make a complaint, rather than an appeal, you should first contact the DWP office you are dealing with, explain the matter and give them the opportunity to put things right. It is probably best to do this in writing so that you have a record of the action you

---

14.1   SSA s12, D&A 5, 10, 50
        www.gov.uk/social-security-child-support-tribunal
        www.gov.uk/administrative-appeals-tribunal
        www.gov.uk/courts-tribunals/first-tier-tribunal-social-security-and-child-support

have taken. If this is unsuccessful the DWP has a formal complaints procedure that may provide a remedy for your problem [www]. If you remain dissatisfied you can escalate your complaint by asking the Independent Case Examiner to look at it (this is a free and independent complaint resolution and examination service provided by the DWP) [www]. If you're still dissatisfied you can ask your MP [www] to send your complaint to the Parliamentary and Health Service Ombudsman (this is also a free and independent service) [www].

14.4 The DWP says that if it gets something wrong it will act quickly to put it right. This might include any of the following: an apology; an explanation; putting things right, or a special payment if something the DWP has done (or not done) has caused injustice or hardship (see DWP (2012) 'Financial Redress for Maladministration') [www].

Who can appeal

14.5 In addition to the claimant (or the claimants in a joint claim) the following also have a right of appeal. An appeal is accepted where it is made by:

(a) a person appointed by the DWP to act on behalf of someone else;

(b) anyone e.g. a landlord from whom an amount of benefit is recoverable, but only if their rights, duties or obligations are affected by the decision; and

(c) a person appointed by the DWP to proceed with a claim of someone who has claimed benefit and subsequently died.

Representatives

14.6 You can ask a representative to act for you. The DWP's guidance for staff 'Working with Representatives' (August 2015) [www] explains its policy on providing information to representatives. In relation to an appeal you (or your representative if they are a legal representative) must send written notification to HMCTS of the representative's name and address. HMCTS should send a copy of that notice to the DWP and any other party. Anything you are allowed to do or required to do under the First-tier Tribunal procedural rules can be done by your representative (except signing a witness statement). The Tribunal and other parties are able to assume that your representative is authorised to act on your behalf until they receive written notification that this is not the case from either you or the representative.

14.3   www.gov.uk/government/organisations/department-for-work-pensions/about/
         complaints-procedure#complaining-about-our-service
         www.gov.uk/government/organisations/independent-case-examiner
         www.parliament.uk/mps-lords-and-offices/mps/
         www.ombudsman.org.uk/

14.4   www.gov.uk/government/uploads/system/uploads/attachment_data/file/275187/
         financial-redress-for-maladministration-240114.pdf

14.5   SSA, s 12(2), D&A Regs, 49(b), 49(d), 49(a)

14.6   www.gov.uk/government/publications/working-with-representatives-guidance-for-dwp-staff
         FTPR 11(2), 11(5)-(6)

The DWP's decision

14.7　You may get told about decisions relating to your UC entitlement via an online account and the DWP also has the power to tell you in person or through the post. Landlords are likely to be notified of any relevant decision by post. A decision notice is treated as given to you on the date that it becomes available for you to view in your online account or it is given or posted to you. The time limit for disputing a decision begins at the point the decision notice is issued.

14.8　The decision notice from the DWP should tell you about:

(a) its decision;

(b) your right to request a statement of reasons for the decision – if this is not included;

(c) the time limit in which you may make an application for the decision to be revised;

(d) your right of appeal against the decision (and that this can be exercised only if the DWP has considered an application for revision).

Getting a written statement of reasons from the DWP

14.9　The DWP thinks that most UC decision notifications include reasons but if you're dissatisfied with the decision and the DWP haven't explained it you may find it useful to ask for a written statement of reasons. You should do this so that your request gets to the DWP within one calendar month of the date the decision notice was issued. The DWP should provide you with the statement of reasons within 14 days of receipt of your request or as soon as practicable after that.

Example: Calendar month

On 19th November a claimant is notified of the decision on his claim. The one month period is 20th November to 19th December.

Applying for a mandatory revision

14.10　If, having read the decision notice and any explanations offered by the DWP, you remain dissatisfied you can apply for a revision of the decision. There is no application form for this. You can ask for the decision to be revised by telephoning the DWP or by putting your request in writing. The telephone number and contact address should be on your decision notice. It's usually best to apply in writing, keeping a copy of what you send and a note of the date you send it. However you apply, you should make sure that your application gets to the DWP within one calendar month of the date the decision was notified. However, if you asked for a written statement of reasons, and it was provided:

14.7　D&A 3, 4, C&P 3, sch 2

14.8　D&A 7(1), 7(3)

14.9　D&A 3(1), 7(1), 7(3), 7(4)

(a) within the one-month period – you have a month and 14 days to get your request to the DWP;

(b) outside the one-month period – you have 14 days from the date on which the statement was provided to get your request to the DWP.

14.11   While the DWP may allow a late application for revision (see below), if it doesn't you lose your right to a mandatory reconsideration and your right of appeal to the First-tier Tribunal. In these circumstances, the DWP should consider whether an 'any time' revision is appropriate because, for example, of a mistake it made in arriving at the original decision (DM A3047).

Allowing a late application for revision

14.12   If you want to get a late application for revision accepted it must satisfy a number of conditions. It should:

(a) include a request for an extension of time in which to apply;

(b) identify the decision that you want changed; and

(c) explain why the extension of time has been needed and identify the special circumstances that stopped you applying within the normal time limit.

Your application must be made within 13 calendar months of the latest date by which the application for revision should have been received by the DWP.

14.13   If the DWP is to accept your late application it must be satisfied that:

(a) it is reasonable to grant the extension; and

(b) it was not practicable for you to make the application within the normal time limit due to special circumstances.

14.14   The DWP advises that the term 'special circumstances' is not defined in legislation and should be interpreted broadly (ADM A3055). It indicates that the term can include factors such as:

(a) a death or serious illness;

(b) not being in the UK;

(c) normal postal services being adversely affected;

(d) learning or language difficulties;

(e) difficulty getting evidence or information to support the application; and

(f) ignorance or misunderstanding of the law or time limits.

But these are only examples and each application should be considered on its merits.

14.11   D&A 5(1)(b)

14.12   D&A 6(1)-(3)

14.13   D&A 6(4)-(5)

14.15 In deciding whether it is reasonable to grant an extension of time, the DWP must have regard to the principle that the greater the amount of time that has passed between the end of the normal time limit and the actual date of receipt of the application, the more compelling must be your special circumstances for the late application.

DWP's mandatory reconsideration

14.16 The DWP should reconsider the decision you are unhappy with on the basis of the information and evidence it has available and any additional information, evidence and explanations you supply. Make sure you include everything that you want considered because the DWP needn't consider any issue you haven't raised. If the DWP can't change the decision fully in your favour, a decision maker should try to call you and tell you about this. They should also ask you if you have any other information or evidence that relates to the decision. If you do, they should tell you where to send it to and the time limit for doing this. You normally get one calendar month in which to supply any additional information or evidence but this period can be extended by the DWP if it would be appropriate to do so.

14.17 There is no statutory timescale for the completion of a mandatory reconsideration. Once the DWP has completed the process it sends out two mandatory reconsideration notices. One is for you to keep and the other is for you to send to HMCTS if you want to appeal to the First-tier Tribunal. If the decision has been changed in your favour you should get any benefit owed backdated to the effective date of the revised decision.

Decisions you cannot appeal

14.18 You can appeal most decisions and the DWP's decision notice should tell you if a decision is appealable. There are some decisions, however, that are not appealable. Table 14.1 identifies the main decisions you cannot appeal. You can ask for an 'any time' revision or supersession of such decisions, but if the DWP doesn't agree to do this the only legal remedy is judicial review.

Table 14.1 **Main non-appealable decisions**

1. Decisions about the information or evidence required in connection with a claim.

2. Decisions about appointees where the claimant is unable to act.

3. A decision in default of a nomination by a couple of the assessment period when separate claimants become a couple.

4. A decision to nominate a main carer, where more than one person cares for a disabled person and they cannot agree who should be nominated as the main carer.

5. A decision to award a particular amount of UC dependent upon someone's age.

6. A decision which adopts a rent officer's decision.

14.15   D&A 6(6)

14.16   SSA 9(1)-(2), D&A 20(2)-(3)

14.18   D&A 7(1)(b), 10, 50(2), sch 3

7. Suspension of payment of UC.

8. Staying making a decision where decisions/appeals involve issues that arise on appeal in other cases.

9. UC payment arrangements.

10. Making payments by direct credit transfer into a specific bank or other account.

11. Payments of UC to third parties in the claimant's or family's interests including direct payment of housing costs (other than arrears) to a landlord.

12. Payments of mortgage interest direct to lenders.

13. Ending the right to obtain a payment of UC where the claimant has not obtained payment of their benefit after 12 months – except a decision to extend the 12 month period where there is good cause.

14. Arrangements for the payment of UC following the death of the claimant.

15. Deductions for council tax except a decision whether there is an outstanding sum due of the amount to be deducted; whether there is sufficient benefit to make a deduction and on the priority to be given to the deduction.

16. A decision on payments on account, except a decision to offset an advance payment of UC against a future award of benefit.

17. A decision on recovery of overpaid UC except:

    (a) who an overpayment of a housing payment is recoverable from;

    (b) the treatment of capital to be reduced (diminution of capital rule);

    (c) the sums to be deducted in calculating recoverable amounts;

    (d) sums to be deducted where there is a change of dwelling and housing costs are payable to the same person.

    Note however that you can appeal the DWP's decision that led to the overpayment and if successful (or partially successful) establish that there is no overpayment or that it is less than the original amount decided by the DWP.

18. Uprating of the benefit.

Appealing to the First-tier Tribunal

14.19   If you are dissatisfied with an appealable decision you can send an appeal in writing to HMCTS and an independent body called the First-tier Tribunal should consider it. In some guides you may see this process referred to as 'direct lodgement'. If you make an appeal to the tribunal you may see or hear yourself referred to as the 'appellant'. You may also come across the term 'respondent' – this is a reference to the DWP decision-maker (i.e. the maker of the decision you have appealed) and also a reference to anyone else who has a right of appeal (for example the landlord in some overpayment cases). Each of you is a 'party' in the proceedings before the tribunal.

T14.1   D&A sch 3

14.19   FTPR 1(3)

The First-tier Tribunal

14.20 The First-tier Tribunal is an independent tribunal established under the Tribunals, Courts and Enforcement Act 2007. It is divided into a number of chambers. The Social Entitlement Chamber considers UC appeals as well as appeals on other social security benefits and certain other matters. The procedural rules of the Social Entitlement Chamber are set out in The Tribunal Procedure (First-tier Tribunal) (Social Entitlement Chamber) Rules SI 2008 No 2685 (as amended). The rules currently in force can be found on the Gov.uk website [www].

Making an appeal

14.21 Perhaps the easiest way to appeal is for you (or your representative if you have one) to fill in the appeal form SSCS1. If you use the form and complete it properly this should make sure that all the required information is provided. The form can be downloaded from various government websites [www] or a paper version obtained from some advice agencies. The form gives you the option of indicating whether you wish to attend a hearing or have your appeal decided on the papers. A lot of people find attending a face-to-face hearing stressful, but research shows that you are more likely to win your appeal if you do attend. The form also asks you to indicate if there are any times or dates when you will be unavailable to attend a hearing over the next six months and if you have any particular needs such as a requirement for a signer or an interpreter.

14.22 Your appeal should be written in English or Welsh and signed by you or your authorised representative. If you don't use the SSCS1 appeal form you should make sure that your appeal includes:

(a) your name and address;

(b) the name and address of your representative (if you have one);

(c) an address where documents for you can be sent or delivered;

(d) the name and address of anyone else (not the DWP) who has a right to appeal the decision, for example a landlord in relation to certain overpayment decisions; and

(e) the reasons why you disagree with the DWP's decision.

Also it would be useful to indicate whether you wish to attend a hearing and any times or dates when you would be unavailable to attend over the next six months.

14.23 If your appeal is going to get to HMCTS later than one calendar month after the date on which you were sent the mandatory reconsideration notices it should also include a request for an extension of time and include the reason why your appeal is not provided in time.

14.20 Part 1 of the Tribunals, Courts & Enforcement Act 2007, art 6(c) of SI 2010 No 2655, FTPR; www.gov.uk/government/publications/social-entitlement-chamber-tribunal-procedure-rules

14.21 hmctsformfinder.justice.gov.uk/HMCTS/GetForm.do?court_forms_id=3038

14.22 FTPR 22(3), 11(2), 11(5)

14.23 FTPR 22(6)

14.24   You must provide with your appeal:

(a) a copy of the mandatory reconsideration notice;

(b) any statement of reasons for the decision that you have; and

(c) any documents in support of your case which have not already been supplied to the DWP (although additional documents may also be supplied at a later date).

If you have lost your mandatory reconsideration notice you should ask the DWP for a copy before sending in the appeal.

14.25   If you live in England or Wales send your appeal to: HMCTS, SSCS Appeals Centre, PO Box 1203, Bradford BD1 9WP. If you live in Scotland send your appeal to: HMCTS SSCS Appeals Centre, PO Box 27080, Glasgow G2 9HQ. HMCTS should write back to you acknowledging receipt of your appeal and providing you with a contact telephone number and the address of the HMCTS office that is dealing with it.

14.26   HMCTS should send a copy of your appeal and any accompanying documents to the DWP (and any other respondent) as soon as reasonably practicable after it gets it.

Time limits for making an appeal

14.27   You should normally get your appeal to HMCTS within one calendar month after the date on which you were sent the mandatory reconsideration notices. Anything in relation to an appeal that must be done by a particular day should be done by 5pm on that day. If the day on which something must be done is not a working day, it is done in time if it is done by 5pm on the next working day. A 'working day' is any day except a Saturday or Sunday, Christmas Day, Good Friday or a bank holiday.

Allowing a late appeal

14.28   Where your appeal is not made in time it may nevertheless be treated as in time if it is made within 12 calendar months of the time limit and neither the DWP nor any other respondent objects. The time for bringing the appeal can't be extended beyond this 12 month period.

14.29   The DWP has the right to object to a late appeal but decision-makers are advised (ADM A5081) that it might not be appropriate to object where there are special circumstances such as:

(a) a difficulty in getting an appointment with a representative (especially in rural areas);

(b) problems in writing the appeal if you are a blind person living alone;

(c) a difficulty in getting an appeal form;

(d) an allegation that the decision notice was not received;

(e) an inability to read, write or understand English where you live alone;

14.24   FTPR 22(4)

14.26   FTPR 22(7)

14.27   FTPR 22(2)(d), 12

14.28   FTPR 5(3)(a), 22(6) 22(8)

14.29   FTPR 5(2), 5(3)(a)

(f)   a change of address during the one month appeal period;

(g)   an allegation that an earlier appeal was made; or

(h)   an inability to understand the decision notice where you have a mental disability or learning difficulties and live alone.

Where the DWP does object you should be sent a copy of its objections and invited to comment before the matter is referred to a judge. It is the judge who must decide whether or not the late appeal is to be considered.

The DWP's actions on receipt of the appeal and accompanying documentation

14.30   When the DWP gets the appeal from HMCTS it considers (ADM A5100-A5183) whether:

(a)   the appeal is duly made, e.g. whether the person making the appeal has appeal rights;

(b)   the appeal is outside the First-tier Tribunal's jurisdiction, e.g. made about a non-appealable decision;

(c)   the appealed decision should be revised to your advantage – in which case the appeal lapses.

The DWP's response to your appeal

14.31   The DWP must get its response back to HMCTS as soon as reasonably practicable after getting the appeal papers. It should normally do this within 28 calendar days though it may ask HMCTS to extend the time limit in exceptional cases. A tribunal judge decides if an extension to the time limit is agreed to. The DWP's response should provide a comprehensive explanation of the reasons for its decision. It should also normally include copies of all the documents relevant to your case in the DWP's possession. The DWP provides you, and any other party, with a copy of its response at the same time as it is provided to HMCTS. If you have a representative then the DWP should provide your representative with a copy and need not also provide it to you. If you are represented and get a copy of its response from the DWP you should contact your representative as soon as possible to make sure that they have also got a copy.

Your submission

14.32   You, or your representative (if you have one), can make a written submission and supply further documents in reply to the DWP's response. You should normally get these to HMCTS within one calendar month after the date DWP sent out its response, but request more time if you think you will need it. Submissions, etc, are often submitted late. If relevant they may normally be considered by the tribunal but if other parties have not been given adequate time to consider the material this may lead to the adjournment of a hearing. Also note the warning in para 14.39. HMCTS should send a copy of your submission, etc, to the DWP and any other parties.

14.30   SSA s9(6), D&A 52

14.31   FTPR 24(1)(c), 24(4)(b), 24(4)(a), 11(6)

14.32   FTPR 24(6)-(7)

The First-tier Tribunal

Membership

14.33　　The tribunal that considers your case should never consist of more than three people. It normally consists of just one person – a judge who is legally qualified. But if your appeal is about the work capability assessment the judge is joined by a medically qualified member. In rare instances where the appealed decision raises difficult financial questions (e.g. about company accounts) there may be a member with relevant financial qualifications. Another member may also be present to provide experience or to help with the monitoring of standards (Practice Statement of the Senior President of Tribunals, 'Composition of Tribunals in Social Security and Child Support Cases in the Social Entitlement Chamber on or after 1st August 2013') [www].

Venues

14.34　　Your hearing normally takes place at a venue near where you live. HMCTS has 152 venues across England, Wales and Scotland. You can find information on venue locations and the available facilities on the web [www].

The tribunal's functions

14.35　　The tribunal's task is to reconsider the decision you have appealed and either change it or confirm it. It should reconsider the decision in a way that is fair and just. It cannot alter the law but must interpret and apply the law to the facts of your case. It cannot award compensation or costs in relation to a UC appeal. It does not have to consider any issue that has not been raised, but it does have the power to do so. The tribunal should not shut its eyes to things if to do so would cause an injustice. In certain instances, this could mean that you end up with a decision that is even less favourable than the one you have appealed. The tribunal can't take into account any factual matters that didn't exist at the time the original appealed decision relates to but it can consider evidence that was not available to the original decision maker that relates to those facts.

14.36　　The tribunal also has the power to make a decision in the form of a consent order. This ends the proceedings and makes such other provisions as you, the DWP and any other parties have agreed to. This may be done at the request of the parties if the tribunal considers it appropriate. Perhaps unfortunately the DWP's presenting officers are advised not to agree to any suggestion of a consent order (ADM A5422).

14.37　　The tribunal may also give directions (i.e. instructions on how the appeal should be dealt with). You and the DWP can both ask the tribunal to do this or the tribunal can do it on its own initiative (para14.48).

14.33　　www.judiciary.gov.uk/wp-content/uploads/JCO/Documents/Practice+Directions/Tribunals/sec-composition-sscs-cases-01082013.pdf

14.34　　www.appeals-service.gov.uk/Venues/venues.htm

14.35　　SSAct s12(8)(a)-(b)

14.36　　FTPR 32

14.37　　FTPR 5(2)-(3), 6

The appeal hearing

Notice

14.38   HMCTS should give you notice of the time and place of the (oral) hearing. This should be given at least 14 days before the hearing (beginning with the day on which the notice is given and ending on the day before the hearing takes place). If notice has not been given to you, or to someone else it should have been given to, the hearing may go ahead only with everyone's consent or in urgent or exceptional circumstances.

14.39   Where you, the DWP and any other party have all chosen not to have a hearing, and the tribunal also thinks that it is able to decide the matter without a hearing, you won't be notified of the date on which the appeal is considered on the papers. You need to make sure that all relevant submissions and documents are with the tribunal before this happens.

Postponement

14.40   The tribunal may postpone the hearing at any time before it starts but need not do this. If you want a postponement, write to the HMCTS clerk giving the reasons for your request. If it is too late to ask for a postponement you may request an adjournment at the hearing. The tribunal may grant or refuse this request as it thinks fit.

Public or private hearings

14.41   Hearings are normally in public but usually only the people involved are present. There is no pre-publication of the cases listed before the First-tier Tribunal (Social Entitlement Chamber) and in practice administrative and security arrangements at tribunal venues mean that obtaining public access to a hearing is tortuous. The Upper Tribunal has nevertheless held that as hearings take place within reasonable office hours and at a publicly recognised court or tribunal hearing centre they meet the minimum requirement of a public hearing ([2015] UKUT 143 (AAC) at [25]). The tribunal may decide that the hearing (or part of it) should be in private if, for example, sensitive or family matters are to be considered. Certain people such as trainee members or clerks may be present (whether or not the hearing is in private), but they must not take part in the proceedings.

Deciding to go ahead in someone's absence

14.42   If you or someone else who has a right to be present fails to attend the hearing, the tribunal may, having regard to all the circumstances including any explanations offered, go ahead with the hearing if:

    (a)   it is in the interest of justice to do so; and

    (b)   it is satisfied that the absent person was told about the hearing or that reasonable steps were taken to do this.

14.38   FTPR 27-29

14.40   FTPR 5(3)(h), 6

14.41   FTPR 30(1), 30(3)

14.42   FTPR 31

Your rights at the hearing

14.43   The tribunal sets the procedure at the hearing, but you and the other parties have the right to be present, to be heard and to be represented.

14.44   You may be able to attend a hearing by telephone or via a live link, e.g. a video conference facility, but only where the judge gives permission. You should contact HMCTS about this.

14.45   You may be accompanied to the hearing, for example by a friend or relative. With the tribunal's permission they can help you present your case or act as your representative. This is true even if their name has not been previously notified to HMCTS or the DWP.

Order and conduct of the hearing

14.46   The procedure for the hearing is set by the tribunal within the appropriate legal framework, e.g. the need to ensure that you and the other parties have the opportunity to put your case. Failure to observe proper procedures or each party's rights may leave the tribunal's decision open to appeal on grounds of natural justice or the right to a fair hearing (CJSA/5100/2001).

14.47   The way the tribunal conducts itself varies according to the issues it has to decide. You should expect to have those present introduced and their role explained at the start. The tribunal should also tell you about the procedure it wishes to follow and seek your, and any other parties', agreement to going ahead in this way. You may be asked to start by explaining why you think the decision is wrong. If the DWP's presenting officer is present (they are not always), they may be asked to explain the basis of the decision. At some point the tribunal is likely to question you. This questioning may be assertive and inquisitorial. You may be offered the opportunity to have the final word before the tribunal goes on to consider its decision.

Directions – including directions to postpone or adjourn a hearing

14.48   The tribunal may at any stage of the proceedings:

(a) give the directions it thinks necessary or desirable for the just, effective and efficient conduct of the proceedings; and

(b) direct you, or any other party, to provide items or documents as may be reasonably required.

The judge may, for example, direct the postponement of a hearing or the adjournment of a hearing to allow new evidence to be obtained or considered. The tribunal can decide to do this itself, or you or any other party may make a written application giving reasons for a direction to the clerk before a hearing or by an oral request during the hearing.

14.43   FTPR 2, 5, 11, 28

14.44   FTPR 1(3) definition: 'hearing'

14.45   FTPR 11(7)-(8)

14.46   FTPR 5, 6

14.47   FTPR 2, 5, 6, 8

14.48   FTPR 5(2)-(3), 6

14.49 If you are dissatisfied with a direction you may apply for it to be amended, suspended or set aside. But if you fail to comply with one that is in force there is a possibility that your appeal may be struck out (if you have been warned about this). If the DWP fails to comply there is a possibility that it may be barred from the proceedings and may have all issues decided against it.

Withdrawing your appeal

14.50 You can withdraw (end) your appeal application any time before the hearing by writing to HMCTS telling it that you are withdrawing your appeal. You may also withdraw your appeal at the hearing itself if the judge agrees. If this happens the clerk sends a written notice to any party who is not present, telling them that the appeal has been withdrawn. If you, or a respondent (a term which includes your landlord in relation to certain decisions) subsequently decide that you or they want to have your appeal considered after all (reinstated), a written application should be made to HMCTS within one calendar month after the date of the hearing requesting this.

The First-tier Tribunal's decision

14.51 The tribunal reaches a decision once it has considered all the evidence. In reaching its decision the tribunal should:

(a) consider the relevant law including any applicable case law;

(b) identify the relevant facts on the basis of the available evidence; and

(c) where the facts are in doubt or dispute, establish them (if necessary on the balance of probability); and

(d) apply the law to the relevant facts to arrive at a reasoned decision.

Duty to follow precedent

14.52 In its consideration of the legal issues the tribunal must follow the legal points held in past decisions of the Upper Tribunal, the Commissioners and the courts unless the case before the tribunal is distinguishable (R(U)23/59). Northern Ireland decisions are not binding in England, Wales or Scotland but are of persuasive authority (R(I)14/63). Decisions of the First-tier Tribunal itself do not set any precedent and so cannot be cited as authority in subsequent cases.

14.53 There is an order of precedence to Upper Tribunal decisions (including the former Commissioners' decisions) (R(I)12/75(T) and [2009] UKUT 4 (AAC) para 37), as follows:

(a) decisions of the Upper Tribunal where a Three Judge Panel (formerly a Tribunal of Commissioners) heard the case are the most authoritative – whether reported or unreported;

(b) reported decisions come next. For many years these were given serial numbers by the year and identified by having the prefix 'R', e.g. R(H)1/02. However, since 1st January 2010 these are known as the Administrative Appeals Chamber Reports and are indicated (after a reference to the parties) by the year of reporting, e.g. [2010], the abbreviation AACR, and the consecutive reporting number within that year's series, e.g. [2010] AACR 40: this is the 'neutral citation';

(c)   then come other decisions. These are identified by the file number, e.g. CH/1502/2004, or since 1st January 2010 by a reference to the parties and a neutral citation e.g. JD v Leeds City Council [2009] UKUT 70 (AAC).

14.54   If there is conflict between two or more decisions the above hierarchy should be applied. If the conflicting decisions are of equal rank, the tribunal is free to choose between them. More recent decisions should be preferred to older decisions. If a more recent unreported decision has fully considered all the earlier authorities, and given reasons for disapproving one or more earlier reported decisions, the tribunal should generally follow the more recent unreported decision (R(IS) 13/01).

14.55   Most Upper Tribunal decisions are available online [www]. By February 2016 only one UC specific judgment was available (([2015] UKUT 696 (AAC)). If you want to use an unreported decision in support of your case, a copy should, where possible, be sent in advance to HMCTS, otherwise an adjournment may be necessary.

The First-tier Tribunal's decision notice

14.56   If you attend the hearing you may be given the decision on the day. The judge should confirm the decision in writing as soon as practicable after the hearing. You should also be sent information on:

(a)   how to apply for a written statement of reasons for the tribunal's decision; and

(b)   what you need to do if you want to appeal the decision and the time limits within which this should be done.

Implementing the decision

14.57   The decision notice is the legal document that enables the DWP to correct and pay (or recover) UC in line with the tribunal's decision. The DWP should action the tribunal's decision as soon as practicable. Exceptions to this are where:

(a)   an appeal is pending against the decision, in which case the DWP has the discretion to suspend payment in whole or in part; or

(b)   the First-tier Tribunal suspends the effect of its own decision pending an application for permission to appeal, and any appeal of the decision.

Getting a 'statement of reasons' for the tribunal's decision

14.58   A statement of reasons sets out the judge's findings of fact and reasons for the decision. If you think you may want to appeal to the Upper Tribunal against the First-tier Tribunal's decision you should ask for a statement of reasons.

14.55   www.osscsc.gov.uk/aspx/default.aspx

14.56   FTPR 33(1)-(2)

14.57   D&A 44(1), 44(2)(b), 44(3), 44(4), FTPR 5(3)(l)

Time limit for application for statement of reasons

14.59   You may apply to the clerk at the hearing for a statement of the reasons for the decision. Otherwise your application to HMCTS should be received within one calendar month of the date the First-tier Tribunal's decision notice was given or sent to you. This tribunal may extend this time limit where it is fair and just to do so but if your application is not made in time the chance of appeal may be lost.

Requirement to supply written statement of reasons

14.60   The tribunal must send a copy of its written statement of reasons to you and every other party within one month of the date the application is received or as soon as practicable after that.

The record of the proceedings

14.61   The judge makes a record of the tribunal's proceedings. The record should indicate the evidence received and submissions made as well as any procedural applications. (Practice Statement, 30th October 2008 [www].) This record, together with the decision notice, and any statement of the reasons for the decision, should be preserved for six months from the latest date of: the tribunal's decision, the production of written reasons, any correction, refusal to set aside or determination of an application for permission to appeal the decision. If there is a delay, for example in providing a statement of reasons, this places a duty on the tribunal to keep the record of proceedings for a minimum of six months after the statement of reasons is actually provided ([2015] UKUT 509 (AAC) at [37]). The record may be evidence to support an appeal to the Upper Tribunal. You can apply in writing to HMCTS for a copy within that six month period. It should be supplied on request.

If the First-tier Tribunal's decision is wrong

14.62   Once the First-tier Tribunal has made and communicated its decision, the decision may be:

(a) altered if the DWP supersedes it;

(b) corrected, where there is an accidental error;

(c) set aside on certain limited grounds;

(d) appealed on a point of law to the Upper Tribunal.

14.59   FTPR 34(3)-(4)

14.60   FTPR 34(5)

14.61   www.judiciary.gov.uk/wp-content/uploads/JCO/Documents/Practice+Directions/Tribunals/
RecordofproceedingsinSocialSecurityandChildSupportcasesintheSocialEntitlementChamber.pdf

When may the DWP supersede the decision?

14.63   The decision may be superseded, either following an application from you or on the DWP's own initiative, where:

(a) the decision was made in ignorance of a material fact; or

(b) the decision was based on a mistake as to a material fact; or

(c) there has been a relevant change of circumstances since it had effect.

When may the decision be corrected?

14.64   The tribunal may correct clerical mistakes, accidental errors such as a typing mistake, miscalculations or omissions at any time. A correction made to a decision or to a record of it is treated as part of the decision or record. Any of the parties to the appeal can ask for a correction to be made. A written notice of the correction should be given to every party as soon as practicable. You do not have a right of appeal against the decision to make a correction or a refusal to make a correction.

When may the decision be set aside?

14.65   If the tribunal decision is 'set aside' this means that it is cancelled and a new tribunal hearing may need to be arranged. You, or any other party, can apply for a decision to be set aside. The tribunal may set aside a decision if it considers that it is in the interests of justice to do so; and

(a) a document relating to the proceedings was not sent to, or was not received at an appropriate time by, a party or a party's representative;

(b) a document relating to the proceedings was not sent to the tribunal at an appropriate time;

(c) a party, or a party's representative, was not present at a hearing; or

(d) there has been some other procedural irregularity.

14.66   If you want to apply for a decision to be set aside you must make a written application to the tribunal so that it is received within one calendar month of the date on which the decision was sent out to you. This time limit may be extended where it is fair and just to do so. Other parties to the appeal should be notified of the application and given the right to make representations. There is a right of appeal against a decision to set aside: [2013] UKUT 170 (AAC).

14.63   D&A 31(a), 23(1)

14.64   FTPR 36

14.65   FTPR 37(1)-(2), 5(3)(a)

14.66   FTPR 37(3)

Appeals to the Upper Tribunal

14.67   You can appeal against a First-tier Tribunal's decision but only if it made an error of law. If the tribunal's decision was in your favour you should be aware that the DWP and any other party to the proceedings can also apply for permission to appeal.

The Upper Tribunal

14.68   The Upper Tribunal is an independent tribunal established under the Tribunals, Courts and Enforcement Act 2007. The Upper Tribunal is divided into a number of chambers. The Upper Tribunal (Administrative Appeals Chamber) (UT(AAC)) considers appeals against a First-tier Tribunal's decisions on UC. All cases in the Upper Tribunal (AAC) are decided by judges, supported by registrars who deal with procedural matters. The Upper Tribunal is a superior court of record. This means that it gives interpretations of the law which are binding on all decision makers and tribunals. Its judges are barristers, solicitors or advocates of not less than ten years' standing who are specialists in social security law, and have a legal status comparable to that of a High Court judge in their specialised area. The procedural rules of the Upper Tribunal are set out in the Tribunal Procedure (Upper Tribunal) Rules SI 2008 No 2698 (as amended). The procedural rules currently in force together with detailed advice regarding appeals to the Upper Tribunal may be found on the Ministry of Justice and gov.uk websites [www].

Getting permission to appeal and the appeal itself

14.69   If, having considered the First-tier Tribunal's statement of reasons, you think that its decision contains an error of law you may apply to it for permission to appeal. Your application should identify the decision in question and the errors of law in it. The application should normally be received by HMCTS within one calendar month from the date the statement of reasons was sent to you. This time limit may be extended by the First-tier Tribunal but you cannot rely on this. If you are making a late application you should include a request for an extension of time and the reason why the application is late.

14.70   The First-tier Tribunal may:

(a) decide to review the decision without the need to refer the case onwards – if it is satisfied that there was an error of law in the decision. The case may be re-decided or heard again by a different tribunal;

(b) give permission for the appeal – in which case you will be able to send it on to the Upper Tribunal;

(c) refuse permission together with a statement of reasons for refusal – in this case you may then apply (normally within one calendar month) directly to the Upper Tribunal for permission to appeal.

14.67   FTPR 38, 39, UTPR 21

14.68   TCEA s3, UTPR
www.gov.uk/government/publications/upper-tribunal-procedure-rules
www.gov.uk/administrative-appeals-tribunal/how-to-appeal

14.69   FTPR 38(2)-(3), 38(5)

14.70   TCEA s.9; FTPR 38-40

14.71 If the First-tier Tribunal has refused you permission to appeal you can apply directly to the Upper Tribunal for permission. This should be done on form UT1 [www] and should normally be made within one month of receipt of a refusal from the First-tier Tribunal – this period may be extended by the Upper Tribunal but you cannot rely on this. If permission is given then your appeal can go ahead.

14.72 You make your appeal in writing – form UT1 can also be used for this. If you have been given permission to appeal by the First-tier Tribunal your appeal to the Upper Tribunal should normally be received within one calendar month of the date of the letter which came with the decision of the First-tier Tribunal on your application for permission to appeal. The Upper Tribunal may extend (or shorten) this period but you can't rely on this happening. Most appeals to the Upper Tribunal are decided on the papers without a hearing. You may, however, ask for a hearing.

What is an error of law?

14.73 An appeal to the Upper Tribunal can only be made on an error of law. An error of law is where the First-tier Tribunal did one or more of the following:

   (a) failed to apply the correct law;

   (b) wrongly interpreted the relevant Acts or Regulations;

   (c) followed a procedure that breached the rules of natural justice;

   (d) took irrelevant matters into account, or did not consider relevant matters, or did both of these things;

   (e) did not give adequate reasons in the full statement of reasons;

   (f) gave a decision which was not supported by the evidence;

   (g) decided the facts in such a way that no tribunal properly instructed as to the law, and acting judicially, could have reached that decision.

These are examples, not an exhaustive list (R(IS) 11/99).

Appeals against the Upper Tribunal's decision

14.74 There is a right to appeal against a decision of the Upper Tribunal to the Court of Appeal or the Court of Session in Scotland (but you should seek advice on this). An appeal can only be made on a point of law. Permission to appeal must be obtained from the Upper Tribunal or, if refused, from the relevant court. The time limit for applying for permission to appeal is three months, but it may be extended. If permission is refused the application may be renewed in the relevant court within six weeks.

14.75 Separately from the above, cases involving European Union law can be referred by the Upper Tribunal direct to the European Court of Justice.

14.71   UTPR 21, 5(3)(a)
             hmctsformfinder.justice.gov.uk/courtfinder/forms/ut001-eng.doc

14.72   UTPR 23, 5(3)(a)

14.73   TCEA s11(2)

14.74   TCEA s.13(1)

Chapter 15 **Liability for council tax**

- An overview of the council tax – including valuation and banding: see paras 15.1-7.
- Who is liable for the council tax: see paras 15.8-13.
- Exemptions, disability reductions and discounts: see paras 15.14-23.
- Discretionary reductions: see paras 15.24-25.

Council tax overview

15.1   This chapter applies only in Great Britain (England, Wales and Scotland), where council tax is the form of local taxation. It describes how the gross liability for council tax (i.e. before any rebate) is determined and who is responsible for paying it. The footnotes to this chapter give the law in England; for Scotland and Wales see appendix 4 table A.

15.2   The council tax is the means by which local people help meet the cost of local public services in Great Britain. It is a tax on residential properties, known as dwellings. In England, Scotland and Wales the same authorities that are responsible for the billing and collection of the tax (para 15.5) are also responsible for administering CTR. Table 15.1 lists the key considerations that arise when considering council tax liability, etc. Fuller details of the council tax are in CPAG's regularly revised *Council Tax Handbook* (11th edition), which covers matters not included in this guide (such as billing, payment, penalties, and so on).

Table 15.1 **Council tax liability: key considerations**

(a)   Which dwelling is being considered?

(b)   What valuation band does it fall into?

(c)   How much is the council tax for that band?

(d)   Who is liable to pay the council tax there?

(e)   Is the dwelling exempt from council tax altogether?

(f)   Do you qualify for a disability reduction?

(g)   Do you qualify for a discount?

How your liability is calculated

15.3   Liability for the council tax normally falls on the occupier rather than the owner – although there are exceptions. Your liability is calculated on a daily basis, starting from the day you first occupy the dwelling as your 'sole or main residence' and ending on the day that ceases to be the case. If your dwelling is exempt or if you are entitled to a disability reduction, discount or discretionary reduction these are also calculated on a daily basis.

15.3   LGFA 1,2,6

Dwellings and valuation bands

15.4 One council tax bill is issued per dwelling unless the dwelling is exempt (para 15.15). A dwelling means a house or a flat, etc, whether lived in or not; but also includes houseboats and mobile homes.

15.5 The amount of tax depends first on which valuation band a dwelling has been allocated to, and this is shown on the bill. The lower the valuation band, the lower the tax. An amount for each band is fixed each year by the billing or local authority, and often includes amounts for other bodies (such as a county council, a parish council, the police, etc).

15.6 In England and Scotland, dwellings are valued as at 1st April 1991 and there are eight valuation bands – band A to band H. In Wales, dwellings are valued as at 1st April 2003 and there are nine valuation bands – band A to band I. In each case, band A is the lowest. The valuation list holds details of which band each dwelling is in and it can be viewed online [www].

Increased council tax: unoccupied dwellings

15.7 In England and Wales, council tax liability can be increased for dwellings which have been unoccupied and substantially unfurnished for two years or more. The increase (depending on the individual authority) can be up to 50%.

Who is liable to pay council tax?

The general rule: liability of occupiers

15.8 If you are aged 18 or over, you are normally responsible for paying the council tax for the dwelling where you live as your 'sole or main residence', but there are also exceptions described in the next paragraph. If there are other people who live in the dwelling with you the liability falls on the occupier with the greatest legal interest in the dwelling. So, for example, if you are a home-owner with a lodger, you are liable, not the lodger. Likewise, if you are a tenant (council, housing association or private) with a lodger, you are liable, not the lodger.

Exception: when owners are liable

15.9 For certain types of dwelling, council tax liability falls on the owner rather than on the occupier. In other words, the residents are not liable (but the owner may pass on the cost of paying the council tax when fixing the rent). Liability for council tax falls on the owner if the dwelling is:

(a) unoccupied (unless the dwelling is exempt: para 15.15);

(b) a 'house in multiple occupation' (para 15.10);

(c) in England and Wales, a 'hostel' (para 15.11) that is not a residential care home;

(d) a bail or probation hostel;

15.4   LGFA 3,7; SI 1992/550

15.6   LGFA 5(1),(2)
        http://cti.voa.gov.uk/cti/inits.asp

15.7   LGFA 11A

15.8   LGFA 6(1),(2)

(e) a residential care home including local authority residential home;

(f) occupied by residents who are members of a religious community;

(g) occupied by a minister of religion; or

(h) provided as accommodation for asylum seekers by the Home Office under the asylum support provisions.

15.10   A 'house in multiple occupation' is:

(a) a building that has been purpose built or adapted for people who are not all part of the same household;

(b) inhabited by two or more residents who have a licence or tenancy to occupy only part of it; or

(c) inhabited by two or more residents who have licence to occupy but who are only liable to pay rent for their share.

15.11   A hostel is a building or part of a building used solely or mainly for residential accommodation that is provided in non-self-contained units, together with personal care for people who are elderly, disabled, have a past or present alcohol or drug dependence or a past or present mental disorder.

Joint liability of residents

15.12   Except where the owner is liable (para 15.9) you can be jointly liable for the council tax with one or more other occupiers. If you are jointly liable (or 'jointly and severally liable') it means you can be held responsible for paying the full bill (rather than just your 'share'). There are two ways in which you can be jointly liable:

(a) if other people live with you, then all of the residents who possess the same greatest legal interest in the dwelling (para 15.8) are jointly liable for the council tax. For example, if you are a joint owner occupier with your sister, or you jointly rent your home with two friends, they are jointly liable with you;

(b) if (by (a) above) you are liable as the occupier then your partner (provided you live together) is jointly liable with you, even if their legal interest is inferior to yours.

For exceptions see the next paragraph. There are further rules (not in this guide) about joint liability for unoccupied properties.

15.9   LGFA 8; SI 1992/551

15.10   SI 1992/551 reg 2 Class C; SI 1993/151; SI 1995/620

15.11   SI 1992/548 art 6

15.12   LGFA 6,9; SI 1992/558

Students and people with severe mental impairment

15.13   The rule about joint liability (para 15.12) does not apply if;

(a)   you are a student or severely mentally impaired (in either case as defined in table 15.2); and

(b)   there is at least one other resident in the dwelling with the same legal interest in the dwelling as you who does not fall into either of these two categories.

If all of you have the same legal interest in the dwelling and you all fall into either of these two categories, see paragraph 15.15.

Exemptions, disability reductions and discounts

15.14   This section describes how your council tax bill can be reduced before any claim for CTR is applied. In some cases (if your dwelling is exempt) your liability can be reduced to zero. Except in the case of a discretionary reduction, these exemptions, reductions and discounts depend only on your status and not your income or capital.

Exempt dwellings

15.15   Only dwellings, rather than people, can be exempt from the council tax. If your dwelling is exempt it means your liability (i.e. your council tax bill) is reduced to zero for each day the exemption applies. Your dwelling is exempt from council tax if:

(a)   all the residents are students or education leavers aged under 20 (table 15.2);

(b)   in England and Wales only, all the occupants are students (though their normal residence is elsewhere);

(c)   it is a hall of residence mainly occupied by students;

(d)   except where the owner is liable (para 15.9), all the occupiers are severely mentally impaired, including if the only other occupiers are students;

(e)   all the residents are aged under 18;

(f)   it is armed forces accommodation;

(g)   in England and Wales only, it is an annex or other similar self-contained part of the property which is occupied by an elderly or disabled relative of a resident living in the rest of it; or

(h)   in Scotland only, it is a dwelling owned by a registered housing association which uses it as a trial flat for a pensioner or a disabled person.

15.16   In addition, various unoccupied dwellings are also exempt. For example, an unoccupied dwelling which is substantially unfurnished is exempt for six months (but see para 15.7) – and there are many other categories.

15.13   LGFA 9(2)

15.15-16   LGFA 4(1),(2); SI 1992/558

Disability reductions

15.17   Your council tax bill is reduced if your home qualifies for a disability reduction. The effect of the reduction is to reduce your bill to the amount that would be payable if your home was in the next lowest valuation band, or if your home is in band A, your bill is reduced by one sixth.

15.18   Your home qualifies for a disability reduction if there is at least one disabled resident living there and the property provides:

(a) an additional bathroom or kitchen for use by the disabled person;

(b) an additional room, other than a bathroom, kitchen or toilet, used predominantly to meet the disabled person's special needs (for example, a downstairs room used as a bedroom); or

(c) sufficient floor space to enable the use of a wheelchair required by the disabled person within the dwelling.

15.19   In each case the authority must be satisfied that the facility provided is either essential, or of major importance, for the disabled person (who may be an adult or a child) in view of the nature and extent of the disability. Disability reductions are not limited to specially adapted properties.

Discounts

15.20   Your council tax bill is reduced if:

(a) there is only one 'resident' in your home or only one resident who is not a disregarded person. In this case the discount is always 25%; or

(b) the dwelling is unoccupied or the only residents are all disregarded persons (para 15.21). In this case, the discount can be up to 50% depending on the policy of the local billing authority (but see below).

A 'resident' means anyone aged 18 or over. Note in the case of (b) if the dwelling is actually unoccupied (rather than occupied by disregarded persons) it could be exempt (para 15.16) or liable for increased council tax (para 15.7) depending on the policy of the billing authority.

15.21   For the purpose of deciding the level of discount, certain residents are disregarded (a 'disregarded person'). The categories of residents who are disregarded include students, apprentices, carers, severely mentally impaired people. The full details are found in table 15.2. Note that disregarded status does not affect your liability to pay council tax.

15.17   LGFA 13(1),(4),(6),(7); SI 1999/1004

15.18   SI 1992/554; SI 1993/195

15.20   LGFA 11

15.21   LGFA 11(5), sch 1

Table 15.2 **Who is a disregarded person**

Regardless of whether you are liable (or jointly liable) for the council tax, you or anyone else who lives in your home (also referred to as 'you' in this table) is a disregarded person if you are:

(a) **a young person for whom child benefit is payable:** You qualify if you are a young person (para 16.64) for whom child benefit could be paid (i.e. during the child benefit extension period) even if it is not in payment.

(b) **an education leaver aged under 20:** You qualify if you are a former student (as defined in the next category) after your course ends during the period 1st May to 31st October or until you reach age 20 if that occurs earlier.

(c) **a student:** You are a student if you are:

- on a course of further or higher education in the UK or EU (paras 2.20-22) which lasts for at least one academic or calendar year, and in which you are expected to study at least 21 hours per week for at least 24 weeks per year; or

- aged under 20 on a course of further education in the UK or EU which lasts at least three months', during which you are expected to study at least 12 hours per week during term times; or

- a student nurse studying for the first time to be included in parts one to six or eight in the nursing register;

- a foreign language assistant who is registered with the British Council.

(d) **a youth trainee:** You are a youth trainee if you are aged under 25 and undertaking youth training funded by the Skills Funding Agency in England (or equivalent body in Scotland and Wales).

(e) **an apprentice:** You are an apprentice if you are:

- in employment for the purpose of learning a trade, profession, vocation or similar; and

- studying for an accredited qualification; and

- paid no more than £195 per week.

T15.2(a)-(m) For amendments to DDO & DDR and for Scotland and Wales see appendix 4 table A

T15.2(a) LGFA sch 1 para 3

T15.2(b) LGFA sch 1 para 11; DDR 3, Class C

T15.2(c) LGFA sch 1 paras 4,5; DDO art 4, sch paras 2-7

T15.2(d) LGFA sch 1 para 4; DDO art 4; sch 1 para 8

T15.2(e) LGFA sch 1 para 4; DDO art 4, sch 1 para 1; SI 2006/3396

(f) **a care worker:** You are a care worker if you live with the person you care for so that you can better perform your duties and you:

- are employed by that person to provide care or support for at least 24 hours a week; and

- are paid no more than £44 per week; and

- were introduced to them by a local authority, government department or charity.

(g) **a carer of a severely disabled person:** You qualify as a carer if you :

- live with the person you care for; and

- provide care for at least 35 hours a week; and

- you are not the spouse or partner of the person you care for, or their parent if you care for a child aged under 18; and

- the person you care for is entitled to (para 17.73) either the middle or higher rate of the care component of disability living allowance (only the higher rate in Scotland), the daily living component of personal independence payment at any rate (only the enhanced rate in Scotland), attendance allowance at any rate (only the higher rate in Scotland), armed forces independence payment or the highest rate of constant attendance allowance.

(h) **are 'severely mentally impaired':** You qualify as severely mentally impaired if you have a medical certificate confirming your intelligence and social functioning (however caused) is severely impaired; and receive at least one of the following benefits (or would do but for the fact that you have reached pension age):

- the highest or middle rate of the care component of disability living allowance; or

- attendance allowance or equivalent addition to industrial injury disablement benefit; or

- incapacity benefit, or severe disablement allowance; or

- income support or JSA(IB) (or your partner is) – but only if it includes a disability premium on the grounds of incapacity for work; or

- in Scotland universal credit, or in England and Wales the LCW or LCWRA element of universal credit; or

- the daily living component of personal independence payment; or

- armed forces independence payment; or

- in Scotland only, employment and support allowance.

T15.2(f)   LGFA sch 1 para 9; DDR reg 2, sch paras 1,2; SI 2006/3395 reg 4

T15.2(g)   LGFA sch 1 para 9; DDR reg 2, sch paras 3,4; SI 2013/388 sch para 3; SI 2013/591 sch para 6

T15.2(h)   LGFA sch 1 para 2; DDO art 3; SI 2013/388 sch para 12; SI 2013/591 sch para 5; SI 2013/630 reg 55

(i) **a member of a religious community:** You qualify if you are a member of a religious community whose principal occupation includes prayer, contemplation, education or the relief of suffering; and you

- have no income (other than an occupational pension) or capital; and

- are dependent on the community for your material needs.

(j) **a diplomat or member of an international body or visiting forces:** You qualify if you are a member of the international headquarters of certain defence organisations or visiting forces (or in some cases you are the dependant of a person who is).

(k) **a non-British spouse or civil partner:** You qualify if you are the husband, wife or civil partner of an education leaver, a student, or member of an international body (as defined in categories (b), (c) and (j)) who is not permitted to work or claim benefits.

(l) **a long-term hospital patient:** You are a long-term patient if you have been in a care home or NHS hospital for more than 52 weeks (adding together periods where the break between them is four weeks or less) or if your sole or main residence is in a care home or independent hospital.

(m) **a prisoner or detainee:** You are a prisoner or detainee if you are in any kind of detention (whether on bail, on remand or serving a sentence, including members of armed forces under military authority).

How to apply for an exemption, disability reduction or discount

15.22   Your authority is expected to take reasonable steps to find out whether any dwellings in its area qualify for an exemption, disability reduction or discount. It can award these on the basis of information available to it, or you can request it in writing. There is no time limit to obtain an exemption, disability reduction or discount, but your authority can ask you to provide appropriate evidence. Appeals about all these things go first to the authority and then to a Valuation Tribunal: the procedures are the same as for CTR appeals in England (chapter 21).

Other reasons why liability may be lower

15.23   In addition to the disability reductions and discounts mentioned above, your authority can offer a discount for prompt payment or if you agree to pay your bill by one of its preferred payment methods.

T15.2(i)   LFGA sch 1 para 11; DDR 3, Class B

T15.2(j)   LGFA sch 1 para 11; DDR 3, Class A, Class D; Class F

T15.2(k)   LGFA sch 1 para 11; DDR 3, Class A, Class E; SI 1995/620 reg 4

T15.2(l)   LGFA sch 1 paras 6,7; DDO art 6

T15.2(m)   LGFA sch 1 para 1; DDO art 2

Examples: Council tax liability, exemptions and discounts

Unless stated below, none of the following are students, severely mentally impaired, or under 18.

A couple with a lodger

A couple live in a house which the man owns in his name only. They have children in their 20s living at home, and a lodger who rents a room and shares facilities. The couple are jointly liable for the council tax, because the man is the resident with the greatest legal interest in the dwelling and the woman is jointly liable with him by being his partner. There is no reason to suppose they qualify for exemption, or a disability reduction or a discount.

A lone parent

A lone parent owns her home and lives there with her three children, all under 18. The lone parent is solely liable for the council tax, because she is the resident with the greatest legal interest in the dwelling. She is the only (adult) resident so she qualifies for a 25% discount.

Three sharers

Three friends jointly rent a house (in other words all their names are on the tenancy agreement). No-one else lives with them. They are all jointly liable for the council tax, because they are all residents with the greatest legal interest in the dwelling. There is no reason to suppose they qualify for exemption, or a disability reduction or a discount.

The sharers' circumstances change

One of the sharers leaves and is not replaced. One of the others becomes a full-time university student. The remaining non-student resident is now the only liable person (para 15.13), and qualifies for a 25% discount because the student is disregarded when counting the residents (para 15.21).

Discretionary council tax reductions

15.24   In England and Wales only, your council can reduce your liability for council tax (whether or not you qualify for CTR). This is a wide discretion, which permits the authority to reduce liability 'to such extent as it thinks fit' and 'includes power to reduce an amount to nil'. Your council can award discretionary CTR based on your individual circumstances or by determining that a particular class of case qualifies for reduced liability. Your council must publish its rules for discretionary CTR and how to apply, along with its rules for ordinary CTR (para 16.8).

15.25   A claim for discretionary reduction may be made in writing or, if the authority permits it, by telephone or online. If your authority provides reductions for a particular class of case it can treat your application for CTR also as an application for a discretionary reduction.

15.24   LGFA 13A(1)(c),(6),(7), sch 1A para 2(7)

15.25   CTP sch 7 para 9; CTR sch 1 para 11

Chapter 16 **Eligibility for CTR**

- Council tax rebate schemes (England, Scotland, Wales): see paras 16.1-15.
- Basic conditions for council tax rebate: see paras 16.16-21.
- Absence from the home and Great Britain: see paras 16.22-30.
- Eligibility: migrants and recent arrivals: see paras 16.31-44.
- Eligibility: students: see paras 16.45-50.
- Who is included in your claim: see paras 16.51-83.

Council tax rebate schemes (England, Scotland, Wales)

16.1　Council tax rebate (CTR) helps you pay your council tax if you are on a low income. In the law CTR is called a 'council tax reduction'. Like the council tax benefit scheme (CTB) it replaced there are many rules that mirror the rules for housing benefit (HB).

16.2　The rules for CTR schemes vary:

(a) between England, Wales and Scotland;

(b) in England and (to a lesser extent) in Wales from one authority to another; and

(c) between pension age and working age claims (para 16.13).

These variations are described below (paras 16.3-12) and table 16.1 summarises the main differences, the main similarities with the HB scheme and other key points.

16.3　CTR rules about procedure are the same across Great Britain including, for example, most of the rules about how to claim (chapter 19).

Table 16.1 **CTR national variations (2016-17)**

	England	Wales	Scotland
Eligibility for CTR (paras 16.16-21)	P: Eligible W: Varies locally – usually eligible	Eligible	Eligible (extra rules for two homes and absences: paras 16.26, 16.28)
Upper capital limit (para 16.20)	P: £16,000 W: Varies locally up to £16,000	£16,000	£16,000

Maximum CTR (paras 17.2-4)	P: 100% of council tax W: Varies locally up to 100%	100% of council tax	100% of council tax
Excess income taper (paras 17.8-13)	P: 20% W: Varies locally	20%	20%
Second adult rebate (paras 17.29-38)	P: Included in CTR W: Varies locally	Not included in CTR	Included in CTR
Minimum CTR (para 17.14)	P: No minimum W: Varies locally	No minimum	No minimum
Start date of CTR (paras 19.45-48)	Monday following date of claim	Exact date of claim	Monday following date of claim
Backdating limit (para 19.42)	P: 3 months W: Varies locally up to 6 months	P: 3 months W: 3 months – can be improved locally	P: 3 months W: 6 months
Extended payments (para 20.27)	P: Included in CTR W: Varies locally	Included in CTR – can be improved locally	Included in CTR
Overpayments (para 20.39)	Recoverable via council tax account	Recoverable via council tax account	Recoverable via council tax account
Appeals (chapter 21)	To authority then Valuation Tribunal	To authority then Valuation Tribunal	To authority then CTR Review Panel
Migrant eligibility (table 16.4)	Excluded as for HB	Excluded as for HB	Excluded as for HB
Student eligibility (paras 16.5 and 16.45)	P: Included W: Excluded as for HB. Financial criteria vary locally	P: Excluded W: Excluded as for HB	P: Included W: Excluded as for HB

Entries are simplified. 'P' refers to pension age and 'W' to working age claims (para 16.13). Other entries refer to both groups.

CTR in England

16.4   In England your local council (your district or borough council in two-tier counties) may make and run its own local CTR scheme. But these local scheme rules must obey certain 'prescribed requirements' set by the government (in effect certain minimum standards). The main requirement is that for pension age claimants (para 16.13) CTR (including second adult rebate) must be calculated as described in chapters 16-18.

16.5   However, there is no similar requirement for working age claimants (para 16.13), so your local council CTR scheme can vary substantially from other council areas. For example, some councils have:

(a) set limits on the amount of eligible council tax (para 17.4);

(b) set a minimum award (para 17.14);

(c) reduced the upper capital limit to below £16,000;

(d) increased non-dependant deductions;

(e) varied the assessment of some types of income;

(f) increased the excess income taper above 20%;

(g) limited or removed entitlement to backdated CTR;

(h) limited or removed entitlement to second adult rebate;

(i) set their own rates for some or all of the allowances and premiums in the calculation of the applicable amount (table 17.4);

or done several of those things (see table 16.1). Other councils have formally adopted the 'default' scheme (para 16.6). Your council can only vary the financial conditions for CTR such as (a)-(i) above (chapters 17 and 18). It cannot alter the other basic conditions of eligibility (para 16.17) by, for example, adding in further conditions such as a local residency qualification: R (Winder) v Sandwell MBC.

16.6   The rules described in this guide are the rules set out in the 2013-14 default scheme. In practice, nearly every council operates the default scheme at least in part (and sometimes in whole). Even those councils that diverge from the default scheme adopt the vast majority of its rules and simply modify (in whole or in part) the default scheme rules as appropriate in accordance with the scheme it has adopted locally.

16.7   Most councils in England make no variation to the default scheme except to reduce the maximum eligible rebate from 100% of the council tax to some lower percentage (typically 80% to 90%).

16.8   Your local council must consult its residents about any proposed CTR scheme and that consultation must be meaningful: R (Moseley) v Haringey LBC. The council must also publish its local scheme rules. You can find your local scheme rules on your council's website. The published rules are often expressed as variations to the default scheme.

CTR in Scotland

16.9   In Scotland, the CTR scheme is the same for all authorities, with no local variations, and is almost identical to CTB (and therefore very similar to the rules for HB). However, the Scottish Ministers have added rules relating to CTR on two homes and to absences from Great Britain (paras 16.26 and 16.28).

16.4   LGFA 13A sch 1A para 2; CTP 11(1), 14

16.5   LGFA 13A, sch 1A para 2; R (Winder) v Sandwell MBC 30/07/14 EWHC (Admin) [2014] EWHC (Admin) 2617 www.bailii.org/ew/cases/EWHC/Admin/2014/2617.html

16.8   LGFA sch 1A paras 3(3),5; R (Moseley) v Haringey LBC 27/10/14 UKSC [2014] UKSC 56 www.bailii.org.uk/cases/uksc/2014/56.html

16.9   LGFA 1992 s80; CTS 12-20; CTS60+ 12-19

CTR in Wales

16.10   In Wales your local council may make and run its own local CTR scheme, which must obey certain 'prescribed requirements' set by the Welsh Ministers. Welsh authorities can choose to adopt in whole or in part the 'default' CTR scheme set by the Welsh Ministers and many do this. For 2015-16 the prescribed requirements and the default scheme are substantially the same (para 16.11).

16.11   In Wales in 2015-16, all claimants (of working or pension age) are eligible for CTR – but with the following main differences (see also table 16.1):

(a)   backdating claims need not exceed three months, though individual authorities may choose to extend this;

(b)   there is no provision for second adult rebate.

16.12   The rules in this guide describe the default scheme in Wales. Before making a local scheme your council must publish its draft scheme rules and consult 'any person it considers is likely to have an interest in its operation'. Your council must publish its local scheme rules once they are made, and often it will do this on its website.

Pension age vs working age claims

16.13   The distinction between 'pension age' and 'working age' claims is usually clear-cut and in the case of a couple it refers to the age of the member that makes the claim/application (para 16.14). But if you are receiving JSA(IB), ESA(IR), IS or UC, your claim is always treated as working age (table 16.2). If you (or your partner) are pension age and on one of those benefits and/or if you are in a couple where only one member is pension age, you should consider who makes the claim and/or whether you should claim guarantee credit instead in order to achieve the most favourable outcome (para 16.14).

16.14   Some CTR rules are different between pension age and working age claims, for example in relation to backdating (paras 19.37-42) and the assessment of income and capital (para 18.10).

16.15   The main dividing line is the qualifying age for state pension credit (SPC). The law refers to people below that age as being 'working age', people above it as 'pension age'. The qualifying age for SPC is increasing from 60 (before April 2010) to 66 (from April 2020). During the 2016-17 financial year it rises from (approximately) 63 to 63¾. A complete list of qualifying ages is given in appendix 3.

16.10   LGFA sch 1B paras 2-7; CTPW 12,13

16.11   CTPW 14,15, sch 13 paras 3,4; CTR 109,110

16.12   CTPW 17,18

16.13   CTP 3; CTR 3

16.15   CTP 2(1) definition: 'qualifying age for state pension credit', 3; CTR 2(1),3

Table 16.2 **Pension age or working age claim?**

Single claimant/lone parent

- under SPC age   Working age
- at or over SPC age:
  - not on JSA(IB)/ESA(IR)/IS/UC   Pension age
  - on JSA(IB)/ESA(IR)/IS/UC   Working age

Couple/polygamous marriage

- both/all under SPC age   Working age
- at least one at or over SPC age:
  - neither on JSA(IB)/ESA(IR)/IS/UC   Pension age
  - one on JSA(IB)/ESA(IR)/IS/UC   Working age

Appendix 3 gives a complete list of the qualifying ages for state pension credit ('SPC age').

Basic conditions for council tax rebate

16.16 To get CTR you must satisfy all the conditions in paragraph 16.17. Once an award is made, it continues until such time as you no longer satisfy all these conditions, at which point it ends (para 20.24).

16.17 The basic conditions for CTR (both versions) are:

(a) you are liable to pay council tax in respect of a dwelling (chapter 15);

(b) you must be resident in the dwelling for each day that you are claiming a rebate (para 15.8) – and in Scotland only you must also be present in Great Britain (para 16.28);

(c) you have made a valid claim and have provided the relevant information and evidence to support it (chapter 19);

(d) you are not excluded as either
- a migrant or recent arrival to the UK (paras 16.31-44);
- a student (paras 16.45-50);

(e) in the case of second adult rebate only, there is no-one else in your home who pays you rent as a lodger or sub-tenant (this does not include any payments made to you by a non-dependant);

(f) your capital does not exceed £16,000 (but this does not apply if you are on guarantee credit and, in most cases, if you are claiming a second adult rebate: paragraph 16.20);

16.17   England: LGFA sch 1A para 2(2),(9); CTP sch 1 paras 1-4; CTR 12-18;
       Scotland: CTS 14; CTS60+ 14;
       Wales: LGFA sch 1B para 3(1),(7); CTPW 21-25; CTRW 12-17

(g) any non-dependant deductions (para 17.15) are less than your eligible council tax; and

(h) your income is not too high (para 16.21) – but this does not apply to second adult rebate (because it is calculated on the income of the second adult).

However, in England (and to a lesser extent in Wales) the details of the CTR scheme in your area can be varied by the local council that administers it (para 16.6) – for example, the £16,000 capital limit is lower in some English local authority areas.

16.18   If you are excluded from CTR you may still be able to get your council tax bill reduced if your home is exempt from the council tax, or if you are entitled to a disability reduction or discount (chapter 15). In particular if you are a student or from outside the EEA, you may be a 'disregarded person' and qualify for a discount (table 15.2).

Couples and claims for CTR

16.19   Only one person is the claimant for CTR and this applies to couples even if both members sign the claim form. One member is the claimant and the other member is their partner – but you can choose who makes the claim and, if necessary, swap. In most cases it does not matter which member makes the claim but in certain circumstances it can affect your entitlement, in particular if only one of you has reached state pension credit age, qualifies for the disability premium or is an excluded migrant or student. Where any of these arise you can swap the claimant role and this is sufficient to get round the exclusion or reduced award.

Income and capital: maximum amounts

16.20   If your capital exceeds £16,000 you are excluded from the main CTR unless you are receiving guarantee credit. If your capital exceeds the £16,000 limit you are also excluded from second adult rebate:

(a) in England only, if you are pension age and your income is greater than your applicable amount (in every other case all your capital is disregarded);

(b)   in Scotland, in every case except where you receive IS/JSA(IB)/ESA(IR) or guarantee credit.

16.21   Your income is low enough to qualify for CTR if any of the following apply:

(a) you are receiving JSA(IB), ESA(IR), income support or guarantee credit, or treated as being in receipt of one of those benefits (para 17.5);

(b) you have no income (para 17.10);

(c) your income is less than or equal to your applicable amount (para 17.10); or

(d) your income is greater than your applicable amount but the 'taper' calculation (para 17.11) still leaves an entitlement to CTR.

In addition, in some local councils in England, if you are working age there is a minimum CTR award (table 16.1 and para 17.14) which has the effect of reducing your maximum income figure to a lower amount.

16.19   CTP 2(1) definition: 'applicant', sch 8 para 4(1); CTR 2(1), 109

16.20   CTP 11(2), sch 6 para 27; CTR 20,23 sch 9 para 27, sch 10 para 49

16.21   CTP sch 1 paras 1-3; CTR 13,14,16,17

Absence from the home and Great Britain

16.22   To be entitled to CTR you must be resident in your home for each day you are claiming a rebate (para 16.17(b)), and in Scotland it must be your sole or main residence and you must also be present in Great Britain. This section describes when you can get CTR during a temporary absence from your home and, in Scotland, temporary absence from Great Britain.

16.23   Except where you have sub-let your home, you are treated as being resident during a period of absence:

(a) for up to 13 weeks during a trial period in a care home (or immediately following that: R(H) 4/06) – so long as you intend to return home if the care home is unsuitable (but the total length of your absence must not exceed 52 weeks); or

(b) for up to 52 weeks, but only if you are absent for one of the reasons in table 16.3 – and you intend to return home within 52 weeks or, in exceptional circumstances, not substantially later; or

(c) for up to 13 weeks during an absence for any other reason, but only if you intend to return to your normal home within 13 weeks.

Except in Scotland where different rules apply (paras 16.28-30), a period of absence under (b) or (c) above can include an absence outside Great Britain.

16.24   To satisfy 16.23(a)-(c) above you must have an 'intention to return'. It is your own intention and not, say, the intention of a relative or official that counts. However, your hope or wish is not on its own sufficient to amount to an intention: it must be capable of being realised. So if it appears (to an impartial observer) that it is impossible for you to return then you cannot be said to have an intention (CSHB/405/2005).

Counting the length of the absence

16.25   The 13-week and 52-week time limits refer to absences which are continuous: R v Penwith DC HBRB ex parte Burt. So, except if you are a prisoner on temporary release, if you return to and occupy the home, even for a short time, the time is reset to zero and starts to run again.

16.26   Your authority must judge whether your absence is likely to exceed the 13/52 week limit by reference to the date you left the home and then subsequently on a week by week basis. If at any later date it seems likely that the limit will be exceeded, then your entitlement to CTR can be revised and ended from that later date (CH/1237/2004). In Scotland only, you may be entitled to a further four weeks CTR at the end of your claim if you move; are liable for council tax on both your old and new home and you could not have reasonably avoided dual liability.

16.22   CTP sch 1 paras 2-4; CTR 13-18

16.23   CTP sch 1 para 5; CTR 19

16.25   R v Penwith DC HBRB ex p Burt 26/02/90 QBD 22 HLR 292

16.26   CTS 5(6)(d); CTS 60+ 5(6)(d)

Table 16.3 **Who can get CTR for an absence of up to 52 weeks**

For rule 16.23(b) above you can get CTR up to 52 weeks if you are:

  (a) in prison and have not yet been sentenced (para 16.27);

  (b) in a probation hostel, or a bail hostel, or bailed to live away from your normal home;

  (c) in a care home or independent hospital other than during a trial period (e.g. during a period of respite care);

  (d) a patient in hospital, or receiving medically approved care;

  (e) undergoing medical treatment or medically approved convalescence;

  (f) absent because your or your partner's child is undergoing medical treatment or medically approved convalescence;

  (g) undertaking medically approved care of someone else;

  (h) caring for a child whose parent is absent from home in order to receive medical treatment or medically approved care;

  (i) following a training course;

  (j) a student who is eligible for CTR (e.g. if you have to study away from home for part of your course);

  (k) absent from your normal home because of fear of violence from someone who is living there.

Note: 'medically approved' means approved in writing by a GP, nurse or similar.

Absences in prison

16.27   If you are in prison but have not been sentenced (for example if you are on remand) you can get CTR for up to 52 weeks. If you are later sentenced this counts as a change of circumstances and your authority must then consider whether you return home within 13 weeks from the date you first left the home. You can only continue to be entitled if it looks like you will return within 13 weeks from your first day in custody: this time limit is rigid (CH/499/2006 and CH/1986/2009). However, most sentences qualify for remission, so if your sentence is six months or less (ten if you are eligible for Home Detention Curfew) you are likely to be entitled.

Absence from Great Britain: CTR in Scotland

16.28   In Scotland, to qualify for CTR you must be present in Great Britain (as well as being resident in your home). The following paragraphs describe how you can be treated as being

---

T16.3   CTP sch 1 para 5(3),(6); CTR 19(3),(6)
        Scotland: definition: 'medically approved'

16.28   CTS 16(1); CTS60+ 16(1)

present even if you are absent from Great Britain. You are treated as being present in Great Britain for a limited period if the circumstances in the next paragraph apply, or without time limit if the reason for your absence is due to you working in one of the occupations in paragraph 16.30.

16.29   You are treated as being present in Great Britain:

(a)   during your first month of absence, whatever the reason, so long as you were not absent on more than two occasions during the 52 weeks before it began;

(b)   during your second month of absence but only if it is in connection with the death of a family member or a close relative of your family and your authority is satisfied that it would be unreasonable to expect you to return;

(c)   for up to six months if it is solely in connection with:

- you or a member of your family being treated for an illness or physical or mental disability, by a person qualified to provide medical treatment, physiotherapy, or similar or related treatment; or

- you undergoing convalescence or care, which results from treatment for an illness or physical or mental disability you had before you left and which is medically approved (see note to table 16.3).

And in each case ((a)-(c) above) your absence must be 'temporary' so you must have an intention to return; and if you later decide not to return your CTR ends from the date you make that decision.

16.30   You are treated as being present in Great Britain (and so is your partner if the only reason they are outside Great Britain is because they are living with you) during an absence of any length if it is due to your employment as:

(a)   a member of HM forces;

(b)   an aircraft worker or mariner with a UK contract of employment;

(c)   a continental shelf worker in EU or Norwegian waters; or

(d)   a Crown servant.

Eligibility: migrants and recent arrivals

16.31   If you are a migrant or have recently arrived in the UK you are excluded from CTR except as described in table 16.4. If you are a member of a couple 'you' here refers to the member that makes the claim for CTR – if only one of you is a migrant/recent arrival see paragraph 16.19. The rules that exclude you are mainly based on your immigration status and your rights to live and work in the UK and these, in turn, depend on your nationality. In broad terms your right to CTR is greater if you are citizen of an EEA member state (table 16.4) (or a family member of an EEA national).

16.29   CTS 18; CTS60+ 18

16.30   CTS 17; CTS60+ 17

16.31   CTP 12(1)-(3), 13; CTR 21(1)-(3), 22(1),(2)

Table 16.4 **Migrants and recent arrivals eligible for CTR**

The following rules describe when you are entitled to CTR as a migrant or recent arrival in the UK:

(a) You are entitled to CTR if you have been granted refugee status, humanitarian protection or discretionary leave by the Home Office following your application for asylum or leave granted by the Home Office under the 'destitution domestic violence concession' (see note 2).

(b) If you are a national from a country outside the EEA, Macedonia or Turkey you are not entitled to CTR unless:

- you have a 'right of abode', 'settled status', or visa from the Home Office in one of the appropriate visa categories that allows you access to UK benefits (paras 16.32-35); and

- you are habitually resident in the UK or Ireland.

(c) You are entitled to CTR if you are national of Macedonia or Turkey, and

- you have any kind of visa (including one with a no public funds condition or a maintenance undertaking); and

- you are habitually resident in the UK or Ireland.

(d) If you are an EEA national (other than a citizen of UK, Ireland or Croatia) you are entitled to CTR if you:

- are in work, temporarily unable to work or retired ('worker or former worker');

- are 'habitually resident' and have lived in the UK continuously for at least five years (para 16.38);

- are 'habitually resident' and are a migrant worker whose child is in education here (para 16.39);

- are 'habitually resident' and are not engaged in the labour market (including if you are a student) but you have sufficient resources not to be a burden on the UK benefits system.

(e) If you are a Croatian national you are entitled to CTR if you:

- are self employed (including temporarily unable to work due to sickness);

- are in 'authorised work' or in work and exempt from Home Office authorisation;

- have completed one year's continuous employment in authorised work (para 16.41) and satisfy any of the conditions in (d) above.

(f) If you are a 'family member' of an EEA national (para 16.40) you are entitled to CTR if either of the first two items in (d) apply (workers and long-term residents).

(g) If you are a British or Irish citizen you are entitled to CTR if you are 'habitually resident' in the UK or Ireland.

T16.4   CTP 12(5),(6), 13(1),(1A); CTR 21(5),(6)

Notes:

1. You are an EEA national if you are a citizen of one the following states: Austria; Belgium; Bulgaria; Croatia; Cyprus; Czech Republic; Denmark; Estonia; France; Finland; Germany; Greece; Hungary; Iceland; Italy; Latvia; Liechtenstein; Lithuania; Luxembourg; Malta; Netherlands; Norway; Poland; Portugal; Romania; Slovakia; Slovenia; Spain; Sweden; Switzerland. (British and Irish citizens: see para 16.32.)

2. You are granted the destitution domestic violence concession if you have a UK partner visa and you want to claim welfare benefits while you apply to settle in your own right because of domestic violence. For other definitions see paragraphs 16.32-40.

16.32   'Right of abode' is an immigration law term which means you are entirely free of any immigration control. It applies to British citizens (but not necessarily other forms of British nationality), citizens of the Irish Republic and certain citizens of Commonwealth countries who are long-term residents. Non-British citizens with a right of abode can apply for a sticker in their passport to confirm their status.

16.33   You have 'settled status' (in immigration law 'indefinite leave to remain') if you have legal permission to be in the UK without time limit or conditions.

16.34   'Visa' means you have legal permission from the immigration authorities (in immigration law 'leave') to be in the UK . The visa is the document or endorsement in your passport confirming this. Your visa can be for a set period or open ended ('indefinite') and/or with or without conditions, such as that you cannot receive welfare benefits.

16.35   You have an 'appropriate visa' (table 16.4(b)) if it was granted otherwise than as a result of a 'maintenance undertaking' and/or it does not include a 'no recourse to public funds' condition. 'Temporary admission' is not a visa: it is merely the period of grace granted by the Home Office while it considers your application to stay in the UK (often on humanitarian grounds, such as if you are seeking asylum here).

16.36   A 'maintenance undertaking' means that a relative or friend (your 'sponsor') has signed a written agreement with the Home Office to support and house you. However, you are not excluded from CTR if you have been resident in the UK for at least five years, or your sponsor (or all your sponsors if there was more than one) has since died.

16.37   If you are an EEA national you are a 'worker or former worker' if you:

(a)   are self-employed (in the UK);

(b)   are in paid employment and pay national insurance (but if you are a Croatian national you will normally require authorisation by the Home Office before you can start work);

(c)   you were previously working (employed or self employed) in the UK but are temporarily unable to work due to sickness;

(d)   you were in paid employment in the UK, are seeking work and have a genuine prospect of being engaged, and you have been seeking work for no longer than six months;

16.37   Great Britain: EEA 6(1)-(4), 14(1)

(e) you have worked in the UK for at least one year and have taken retirement or have
     finished working due to incapacity (further conditions apply: see *Guide to Housing
     Benefit,* chapter 21).

16.38   You qualify as an EEA long-term resident only if you accumulated your five years
continuous residence while exercising one of your EU free movement rights (i.e. to live and
work in the UK). It does not apply if you are a British or Irish citizen (because you have a right
to reside in the UK without exercising an EU free movement right). Your qualifying period of
continuous residence can include absences of up to one year for certain specified reasons (for
military service, pregnancy, child birth, serious illness): see *Guide to Housing Benefit,* chapter
21 for further details.

16.39   You qualify as an EEA migrant worker with a child in education here if:

(a) you are the primary carer of a child in education here;

(b) either you or the child's other parent must have been at some time an EEA worker.

Note that it does not matter that the parent who was the EEA worker has since stopped
working, or if you are not an EEA national yourself.

16.40   You qualify as an EEA 'family member' if you are related to an EEA national in one of
the following ways:

(a) as their spouse, civil partner or partner;

(b) as their dependent child or grandchild;

(c) as their child or grandchild who is not dependent but under age 21;

(d) as their dependent parent or grandparent; or

(e) in any other case, if you are a member of their household who is dependent on them.

16.41   If you are a Croatian you can only take up work that has been authorised by the
Home Office. Authorised work is limited to certain specified occupations and in most cases
you must also meet other conditions. Each category of work is limited to strict quotas.
Restrictions on your employment last until you have completed 12 months continuous
(authorised) work.

Habitual residence

16.42   If you have recently arrived in the UK you may have to show that you are habitually
resident in the UK or Ireland to qualify for CTR (table 16.4). You do not have to satisfy this
requirement if you:

(a) have been granted refugee status, humanitarian protection or discretionary leave
     following your application for asylum in the UK, or the destitution domestic violence
     concession;

16.38   Great Britain: EEA 3,5,15(1)(a)

16.39   Great Britain: EEA 15A

16.40   Great Britain: EEA 5, 7(1)(a)-(c)

16.41   Great Britain: SI 2013 No. 1460 Regs 2,5; England: CTP 12(3); CTR 12(3);
         Scotland: CTS 16(3); CTS60+ 16(3); Wales: CTPW 28(3); CTRW 19(3)

16.42   CTP 12(5),(6); CTR 21(5),(6)

(b)   are an EEA national who is a worker or former worker (para 16.37) including if you are a Croatian in authorised work;

(c)   are a British citizen or a person with a right of abode or settled status who has been deported to the UK from another country;

(d)   you are a member of HM armed forces or employed by the Crown and you are performing your duties overseas, provided that you were habitually resident immediately prior to your posting.

In any other case, including if you are a British, Irish or EEA citizen who is not engaged in the UK labour market, you must show you are habitually resident to qualify for CTR.

16.43   If you recently left another country with the intention to settle in the UK you cannot become habitually resident immediately on arrival. You must be resident for an 'appreciable period of time' and have an intention to settle (R(IS) 6/96). There is no fixed period that amounts to an appreciable period of time but in general it will normally lie between one and three months depending on the particular 'length, continuity and nature' of the residence (R(IS) 6/96, CIS 2326/1995, CIS 4474/2003).

16.44   Your intention to settle can often be implied from such things as: whether you have close relatives here; your decisions about the location of your and your family's personal possessions; substantial purchases, such as furnishings, which indicate a long term commitment; and the membership of any clubs or organisations in connection with your hobbies or recreations.

Eligibility: students

16.45   This section describes how and when you are excluded from CTR as a student. Many students are excluded from CTR, but see paragraphs 16.46-47 and table 16.5 for exceptions and paragraph 16.19 if you are a member of a couple. In any other case (i.e. you are excluded) see paragraphs 15.22 and 16.18 for other ways that your council tax bill can be reduced.

Pension age vs working age students

16.46   In England and Scotland, if you are a student and pension age you are eligible for CTR in the normal way (and any income from student loans and grants is disregarded). In Wales, you are not entitled to CTR: there are no exceptions.

16.47   In England, Scotland and Wales, if you are a working age 'full-time student' (paras 16.48 and 16.50) you are excluded from CTR unless you fall into one of the 'eligible groups' in table 16.5.

Definition of 'student' and 'full time student'

16.48   You are a student if you are:

(a)   'attending or undertaking a course of study at an educational establishment'; or

(b)   if you are claiming JSA and attending an employment-related qualifying course (but this does not apply if you are receiving a training allowance).

16.46   CTP 3,11(1),sch 1 para 1; CTR 74

16.47   CTR 24,74,75(1)

The definition in (a) above is broad enough to cover sandwich courses, those where no grant or loan is available and institutions that provide training and instruction as well as education.

Table 16.5 **Students eligible for CTR**

If you are a student you are eligible for CTR (and not excluded) if you are:

  (a) state pension credit age (or your partner is);

  (b) on JSA(IB), ESA(IR) or income support;

  (c) on a part-time course (para 16.50);

  (d) aged under 20, in approved training and you were enrolled or accepted on that course before your 19th birthday;

  (e) aged under 21 and your course is at a level up to and including GCSE A Level or BTEC/SCOTVEC National Diploma or National Certificate up to level 3 [www] or you are aged 21 and continuing on such a course;

  (f) a lone parent or single person responsible for a foster child placed with you by a local authority or voluntary organisation;

  (g) a member of a couple who are responsible for a child or young person (para 16.63);

  (h) entitled to a disability premium[1] or a severe disability premium;

  (i) assessed by the DWP as having limited work capability for ESA[2] purposes for a period of at least 28 weeks;

  (j) assessed in your grant award as entitled to an allowance for deafness;

  (k) unable to get a grant or student loan following an approved absence from your studies due to illness or providing care. This applies only for the period starting when your illness or caring responsibility ends until the day before you resume your course – and only up to a maximum of one year.

Notes:

  1. Including where you would be entitled to the disability premium but for the fact that you have been disqualified from incapacity benefit as being capable of work.

  2. Or you are incapable of work for incapacity benefit purposes.

16.49   Once your course has started, you continue to be counted as a student until your course finishes or you abandon it. So you are counted as a student during any vacation, periods of work experience or sickness absence that occur within the course. But you do not count as a student at the end of the course or between courses.

16.48–50   CTR 73 definitions: 'course of study', 'full-time course of study', 'full-time student', 'modular course', 'student'

T16.5   CTR 75(2); www.gov.uk/what-different-qualification-levels-mean

16.50   There is no all-embracing definition of 'full-time' (or 'part-time') but your course always counts as full-time if:

(a) it is a sandwich course (i.e. has a period of work experience);

(b) in England and Wales, it is funded by the Department for Education, Welsh Ministers or Skills Funding and requires more than 16 hours guided learning each week (see the students learning agreement or similar document);

(c) in Scotland, you are studying at a college of further education for a course up to and including Scottish Higher or SCOTVEC level 3 that involves more than 16 hours a week in the classroom or workshop based programmed learning or 21 hours a week of either type of tuition or other structured learning supported by teaching staff (as defined in the document signed by the college).

In any other case your council must decide whether a course is full-time by considering factors such as the nature of the course, including the number of hours you are required to attend, how the institution itself describes it and the amount and nature of any grant or loan you receive. But if you are studying on a modular course you will only count as full-time during the parts of the course that you are registered on as full-time.

Who is included in your claim

16.51   This section describes how other people who live with you are categorised (e.g. dependent child, lodger, etc) when assessing your CTR claim. This is important because each category affects your CTR assessment in different ways. It describes:

(a) who counts as a member of your family (partners and dependent children);

(b) who counts as your partner;

(c) how and when a child is treated as part of your family;

(d) how fostered and adopted children are treated in your claim;

(e) what happens when your partner or child is absent from the home;

(f) who counts as a non-dependant; and

(g) other occupiers who live with you.

Who is a member of your household

16.52   The members of your household include:

(a) family members:

- you (para 16.55),
- your partner(s) (para 16.58),
- dependent children or young persons (para 16.63);

(b) foster children (para 16.68);

(c) non-dependants (para 16.70).

Other people who live with you

16.53   Other people who live in your home that affect your CTR award may include:

(a) lodgers (with or without board) (para 16.74);

(b) joint tenants or joint owners (para 16.78);

(c) certain carers (para 16.80).

In each case the effect on your CTR award is as described in the appropriate paragraph.

Straightforward cases vs complex households

16.54   In most cases assessing your CTR is fairly straightforward if the only people who live with you are the members of your family (i.e. you, your partner and dependent children). But where your circumstances are more complex such as: responsibility for children is shared; your child has reached age 16; a member of your family lives elsewhere; or other people live with you (e.g. a lodger); there are rules to deal with these situations and how they affect your CTR (see example for a complex household).

Example: People who live with you

The following people live with you in your (large) home.

(a) Your partner and dependent children. They are your (CTR) 'family' (para 16.56).

(b) Your foster child. This child is ignored when assessing your CTR (para 16.68), and so is the income from any fostering allowance you receive (para 18.51).

(c) Your parents and your sister. They are your non-dependants (para 16.70).

(d) Your sister has a partner who lives abroad. Because her partner does not live with you, they are ignored when assessing your CTR.

(e) Your sister's baby. Her baby is ignored in assessing CTR (para 16.73).

(f) A lodger who rents a room from you. Part of the income from the lodger is counted (para 18.53).

Claimant and family

16.55   To assess your CTR claim the law will consider you to be in one of three basic household types:

(a) a single claimant – i.e. if you do not have a partner and are not responsible for a child/young person;

(b) a lone parent – i.e. if you do not have a partner and you are responsible for a child or young person; or

(c) you are a member of a couple or polygamous marriage – whether or not responsible for a child or young person. Only one member of a couple or polygamous marriage can claim (the other member is the claimant's partner).

16.55   CTP 2(1) definitions: 'couple', 'lone parent', 'single applicant', 4; CTR 2(1), 4;

16.56   A person is a member of your 'family' if they are:

(a)   your partner; or

(b)   a child or young person you are responsible for (they need not be your son or daughter);

and, in each case, they are also a member of your household (para 16.57).

16.57   The term 'household' is not defined in the law but broadly it means anyone who lives in the same dwelling as part of a larger interdependent unit that is self-sufficient as a whole and independent from other occupiers. For example, a landlady and her family would be one household and her lodger another.

Your partner

16.58   If you are in a couple your partner simply means the other member unless they are absent and not treated as part of your household (para 16.57). Partner includes any member of a polygamous marriage, provided the union took place in a country that allows polygamy; in any other case any second or subsequent partner is a non-dependant.

16.59   The term 'couple' refers to married couples and civil partners, and also to two people living together as though they were married or in a civil partnership.

16.60   In deciding whether you live together as though you are married, the first consideration is your intention (for example, if your relationship is one of lodger and landlord you will not normally be considered a couple). If this is unclear, it is decided by looking at your relationship and living arrangements (e.g. stability of your relationship, financial arrangements, how others see you). No single factor is conclusive: what matters is the relationship as a whole (R(SB)17/81).

16.61   If your partner is temporarily living away from your home they will continue to be included as a member of your household, but what temporary absence means is not defined in CTR law.

16.62   If your partner does not count as a member of the household, their needs, income and capital should not be taken into account when calculating your CTR. Any money you receive from them should be treated as maintenance (paras 18.54-55).

Children and young persons

16.63   Any child or young person you are responsible for and who is part of your household counts as a member of your family. A 'child' means someone under the age of 16.

16.56   CTP 6; CTS 2(1) definition: 'family'; CTS60+ 2(1) definition: 'family'; CTR 6; CTPW 6; CTRW 6

16.58   CTP 2(1) definition: 'partner'; CTR 2(1)

16.59   CTP 4; CTR 4; CTS 2(1) definition: 'couple'; CTS60+ 2(1) definition: 'couple'; CTPW 4; CTRW 4

16.61   CTP 8(1); CTR 8(1)

16.62   CTP 4(1); CTR 4(1); CTS 2(1) definition: 'couple'; CTS60+ 2(1) definition: 'couple'; CTPW 4(1); CTRW 4(1)

16.63   CTP 8(1); CTR 8(1)

16.64   A 'young person' means someone aged 16-19 who you are getting (or could get) child benefit for because they are in secondary education or their 'child benefit extension period'. Broadly this means any child who is: still at school or sixth form college studying a course up A Level, Scottish Higher or NVQ level 3 and not claiming JSA/IS/ESA in their own right. It also includes some 16-17 year olds who have recently left education or training for up to 20 weeks after they left the course.

16.65   You are treated as being responsible for any child or young person who normally lives with you. This is usually straightforward; and when it is, whether you receive child benefit (or not) is irrelevant. But if the child spends an equal amount of time in another household (such as when you share responsibility with your ex-partner), or if there is doubt over which household they are living in, they are treated as living with the person who gets the child benefit.

16.66   If a child or young person you are responsible for is temporarily living elsewhere, they continue to be included in your household. CTR law does not define what is meant by temporary absence in this case, so it must be decided according to the facts in each case (but it may be reasonable to take an approach similar to the rules for an absent partner).

16.67   If you are not responsible for a child or young person (because of the rules above) they are ignored when calculating your applicable amount (chapter 17).

Fostering, adoption, etc

16.68   A child or young person is not counted as a member of your household if they are living with you as your foster child or placed with you for adoption (but once adopted they become part of your household).

16.69   A child is not counted as part of your household if they are absent because they are looked after, or in the care of a local authority. But if that child is still living with you while under supervision they do count as part of your household.

Non-dependants

16.70   In broad terms, a non-dependant is someone who normally lives with you on a non-commercial basis. Typical examples are adult daughters, sons, other relatives and friends.

16.71   Anyone who 'normally resides' with you is a non-dependant, unless they are:

   (a)   a member of your family (para 16.56);

   (b)   a foster child or other child who is not counted as part of your household (paras 16.68 and 16.73);

16.64   CTP 2(1) definition: 'young person', 6(2),(3); CTR 2(1) definition: 'young person', 6(2),(3); CTS 2(1) definition: 'family', 4; CTS60+ 2(1) definition: 'family', 4; CTPW 2(1) definition: 'young person', 6(2),(3); CTRW 2(1) definition: 'young person', 6(2),(3)

16.65   CTP 7; C TR 7

16.66   CTP 8(1); CTR 8(1)

16.67   CTP sch 1 para 6; CTR 25,26

16.68   CTP 8(2),(3); CTR 8(2),(3)

16.69   CTP 8(4); CTR 8(4)

16.71   CTP 9(1),(2); CTR 9(1),(2)

(c)   a lodger (para 16.74) and any member of their household;

(d)   a joint occupier (para 16.78);

(e)   a paid carer in certain circumstances (para 16.80).

'Normally resides' is not defined, so each case must be considered on its own facts.

16.72   A person who is staying with you but who normally lives elsewhere (such as a visitor or friend on holiday) is not normally residing and so is not a non-dependant. But a temporary arrangement could eventually become permanent and so at some point (for example a homeless friend after six months) the council may decide a change of circumstances has occurred and they have become a non-dependant (CH/4004/2004 and CH/3935/2007).

16.73   The partner of a non-dependant is also a non-dependant (but there is only one non-dependant deduction, if any: para 17.26). If your non-dependant has a child, there is normally no deduction made (table 17.1).

Lodgers

16.74   A lodger is someone who lives with you as a commercial arrangement and pays you (or your partner) 'rent'. CTR rules distinguish between two different types:

(a)   a lodger who pays you an inclusive charge for meals as well as their accommodation (sometimes called a 'boarder');

(b)   any other lodger (i.e. no meals included), sometimes called a 'sub-tenant'.

16.75   In the first case above (para 16.74(a)), at least one 'meal' must be provided – for example, breakfast every day is enough. The meal must be cooked or prepared, and consumed on the premises; and the cooking or preparation must be done by someone other than the boarder themselves.

16.76   Income from a lodger is taken into account in the assessment of your CTR (para 18.53). The method is more favourable if you provide your lodger with meals.

Lodger vs non-dependant

16.77   Both lodgers and non-dependants may make payments to the claimant and have exclusive occupation of, say, a bedroom. But there are 'many examples... of family arrangements and acts of friendship or generosity not... giving rise to a tenancy even where exclusive occupation is given' ([2012] UKUT 114 (AAC)). The distinction between a lodger and a non-dependant therefore hinges more on whether there is a tenancy or similar commercial arrangement between the parties.

Joint occupiers

16.78   If you have joint liability for the council tax with someone other than your partner then they are a joint occupier for CTR purposes (para 15.12). It includes both joint owners and joint tenants who are not part of your household, for example they might be your friend, brother, sister, or parent as house-sharers or flat-sharers.

16.74   CTP 9(2)(e); CTR 9(2)(e)

16.77   CTP 9(3); CTR 9(3)

16.78   CTP 9(2)(d),(3); CTR 9(2)(d),(3)

16.79   Each joint occupier is eligible for CTR in their own right (so long as they meet the conditions in the ordinary way). But in calculating your CTR your eligible council tax is apportioned between you by dividing your council tax bill by the number of occupiers that are jointly liable. For example, if you are a joint owner with your sister and your council tax bill is £1,000, then your eligible council tax for calculating CTR is £500 (and so is your sister's if she claims CTR). But in the case of second adult rebate your CTR is worked out in the normal way (as if you were not a joint occupier) and before any discount you may be entitled to. The resulting second adult rebate award is then apportioned between you (in other words, the apportionment is done at end of the calculation instead of at the beginning).

Carers

16.80   If you receive care from a member of your family, a non-dependant, a lodger or a joint occupier, then they are taken into account in that category. For example, if your nephew comes to care for you, he is taken into account as a non-dependant and there are no further rules.

16.81   Any other resident carer who lives with you will count as a non-dependant unless:

(a) they live with you to look after you or your partner; and

(b) the carer is engaged by a charity or voluntary organisation (not a public or local authority); and

(c) that organisation makes a charge to the claimant or partner for the services provided.

If the carer meets all of the conditions (a)-(c) then they cannot be a non-dependant and so no non-dependant charge can be made. Note that certain other paid carers are a disregarded person in terms of council tax liability (table 15.2) and these two categories may sometimes overlap.

Employees

16.82   If you employ someone who lives in your home (e.g. a nanny or au pair) they are not a non-dependant and have no effect on your CTR.

Second adults

16.83   A second adult is any non-dependant who lives with you who is not a disregarded person for council tax liability (table 15.2). It also probably includes carers and domestic staff.

16.81   CTP 9(2)(d),(3); CTR 9(2)(d),(3)

16.82   CTP 9(2)(e); CTR 9(2)(e)

16.83   CTP sch 1 para 4(3); CTR 15(3),18(3)

Chapter 17 **Calculating CTR**

- ■ Calculating CTR: see paras 17.1-14.
- ■ Non-dependant deductions: see paras 17.15-28.
- ■ Second adult rebate: see paras 17.29-38.
- ■ Converting figures to weekly amounts: see paras 17.39-41.
- ■ Applicable amounts: see paras 17.42-81.

Calculating CTR

17.1   The CTR rules in this chapter vary across Great Britain (paras 17.4, 17.7, 17.12, 17.14, 17.16 and 17.30). There are also differences between 'working age' and 'pension age' claims (as defined in paras 16.13-15). The following steps (paras 17.2-14) give the calculation of CTR.

Maximum rebate

17.2   The starting point for all CTR calculations is your weekly 'maximum rebate' (in the law this is called your 'maximum reduction'. This is either:

(a) your weekly eligible council tax minus any non-dependant deductions which apply; or

(b) in England and Scotland only, a second adult rebate (in law this is called 'alternative maximum council tax reduction').

But if you qualify for both types (a) and (b) you are awarded the higher figure of the two (this is sometimes referred to as the better buy).

17.3   Paragraphs 16.78-79 explain how your CTR maximum rebate is calculated if there is more than one household in your dwelling (e.g. if you are a joint tenant).

17.4   In England if you are working age, your maximum CTR can be lower (para 16.5); for example, it can be limited to a percentage of council tax (usually between 70% and 90%) or to a particular band. If you are pension age or if (regardless of your age) you live in Scotland or Wales, your weekly eligible CTR is always 100% of eligible council tax.

On a passport benefit

17.5   If you or your partner receive a passport benefit you qualify for maximum rebate (para 17.2). A passport benefit means:

(a) guarantee credit (element of state pension credit);

(b) income support – (IS);

(c) income-based jobseeker's allowance – JSA(IB);

(d) income-related employment and support allowance – ESA(IR).

17.2   CTP sch 1 para 7(1); CTR 29(1)

17.5   CTP sch 1 paras 2, 10(2); CTR 13, 16, 32(2)

In each case you are entitled to maximum rebate because the law says your income is treated as being zero (and therefore your income is less than your applicable amount). If you are on universal credit or savings credit see para 17.9.

Capital

17.6   If you have capital over £16,000 (assessed as in chapter 18) you do not qualify for CTR. (But being on a passport benefit over-rides this; and in England and Scotland see paras 16.20 and 17.35 for whether you qualify for a second adult rebate.)

17.7   In England if you are working age, the capital limit can be lower (para 16.5): in some areas it is as low as £6,000. But it is always £16,000 if you are pension age (in England), and (regardless of your age) if you live Scotland or Wales.

Income and excess income

17.8   In any other case (not on passport benefit, capital within the £16,000 limit) weekly income (chapter 18) is compared with your applicable amount (para 17.42 onwards). But special rules apply as to how these are calculated if you are on savings credit or UC (see next paragraph).

17.9   If you are on savings credit (without guarantee credit) or universal credit your income and capital are calculated as follows:

(a) if you are only on savings credit your income and capital are based on the DWP's figures (para 18.6) but your applicable amount is calculated in the normal way (paras 17.42-81);

(b) if you are on universal credit your income is based on the DWP's figures (para 18.6) and your applicable amount on the DWP's figure for your maximum UC (para 17.48).

17.10   If you have no income, or your income is less than (or equal to) your applicable amount, you qualify for maximum benefit (para 17.2).

17.11   If your income is more than your applicable amount, the difference between the two is called 'excess income'. You qualify for maximum benefit (para 17.2) minus 20% of this excess income.

17.12   In England if you are working age, the percentage deduction from your maximum benefit can be a higher figure (para 16.5): in some authorities it is as high as 35%.

17.13   For pension age claims in England, and all claims (regardless of your age) in Scotland and Wales it is always 20%.

Minimum award

17.14   In England for pension age and all claims (regardless of your age) in Scotland and Wales there is no minimum award figure. For working age claims in England, there can be a minimum CTR award figure (para 16.5): it is usually between 50p and £5 per week.

17.6   CTP 11(2); CTR 23

17.8   CTR 14(f),17(f)

17.11   CTP sch 1 paras 3, 10(3); CTR 14, 17, 32(3)

> **Examples: Calculating CTR**
>
> (For variations which can apply in CTR, see paras 17.4 and 17.12.)
>
> **Claimant on a passport benefit**
>
> A claimant has no non-dependants: she lives alone. The council tax is £20.00 per week but she qualifies for a 25% weekly discount, reducing her liability to £15.00 per week.
>
> Claimants on JSA(IB), ESA(IR), IS or guarantee credit get maximum CTR – which equals their eligible council tax. So in this case her weekly CTR is £15.00.
>
> **Claimant not on a passport benefit**
>
> A couple have no non-dependants. They are not on JSA(IB), ESA(IR), IS or guarantee credit. Their joint weekly income exceeds their applicable amount by £20.00. Their eligible council tax liability is £22.56 per week.
>
> Claimants with excess income get maximum CTR minus 20% of their excess income.
>
> | | |
> |---|---:|
> | Eligible council tax | £22.56 |
> | Minus 20% of excess income (20% x £20.00) | £4.00 |
> | Equals weekly CTR | £18.56 |

Non-dependant deductions

17.15   A non-dependant is, usually, a grown-up son, daughter, friend or relative who lives with you in your home (para 16.70). The CTR calculation assumes they will contribute to your council tax. This contribution is called a 'non-dependant deduction' – because it is deducted from the eligible council tax in the calculation of maximum benefit (para 17.2(a)). It is sometimes also called a non-dependant 'charge' or 'contribution'. This section explains when non-dependant deductions apply, and how much they are.

17.16   If you are working age and claiming CTR in England, the rules in this section can vary (para 16.5): in particular, the rates of deduction in table 17.1 can be higher and/or the rules about when a deduction applies may differ. The rules cannot be varied if you are pension age (in England), nor for any claim (regardless of your age) if you live in Scotland or Wales.

When no deduction is made

17.17   There is no deduction for any non-dependant at all (regardless of how many there are or what their income is), if you or your partner:

    (a)   are severely sight impaired or blind or have recently regained your sight (para 17.78);

    (b)   receive the care component of disability living allowance;

    (c)   receive the daily living component of personal independence payment;

    (d)   receive attendance allowance (or any of the related benefits in para 17.77); or

    (e)   in England and Wales only, receive an armed forces independence payment.

Cases (b)-(e) continue to apply if the only reason the qualifying benefit ceases is that the person is in hospital for four weeks or more.

17.15   CTP 9; CTR 9

17.17   CTP sch 1 para 8(6),(11),(12); CTR 2(1),30(6)

17.18   Table 17.1 shows the non-dependants for whom no deduction is made and the amount of the deduction for any other case. In addition there is no non-dependant deduction for any member of your 'family' (para 16.56), or lodger (because the law says they are not non-dependants).

When a deduction is made

17.19   In all cases not mentioned above (paras 17.17-18) there is one non-dependant deduction per non-dependant (or per non-dependant couple: para 17.26), as follows:

(a) if the non-dependant is in full-time work (para 17.21), the amount of the deduction depends on the level of their gross income (para 17.22);

(b) if the non-dependant is not in full-time work, the amount of the deduction is always the lowest amount (in the case of a non-dependant couple both members must not be in full-time work).

The details and the figures are in table 17.1. (For local variations in England, see para 17.16.)

Table 17.1 **Non-dependant deductions**

No non-dependant deduction

There is no non-dependant deduction for any person in your household who is:

- a member of your family or other occupier who is not a non-dependant (para 16.71)

- a temporary resident or visitor or any other person whose normal home is elsewhere

- aged under 18

- on a passport benefit or on savings credit

- in England and Wales only, on universal credit on the basis that they do not have any earned income

- a youth trainee receiving a training allowance

- a full-time student

- a patient who has been in hospital for 52 weeks or more

- in Scotland only, a member of the armed forces away on operations

- a 'disregarded person', other than a student, youth trainee or apprentice (table 15.2 categories (a), (b) and (f)-(m)).

17.18   CTP 9(2), sch 1 para 8(1),(2),(7),(8); CTR 9(2),30(1),(2),(7),(8)

17.20   CTP sch 1 para 8(1)(a); CTR 30(1)(a)

Lower rate non-dependant deduction

The lower rate non-dependant deduction applies for any non dependant who:

- is not in work (but not on a passport benefit or savings credit)
- works less than 16 hours per week
- is on maternity, paternity, adoption or sick leave.

For each non-dependant to whom this applies the weekly rate of deduction is:

- in England £3.77
- in Scotland £3.90
- in Wales £4.05

Higher rate deductions

For all other non-dependants working at least 16 hours per week a non-dependant deduction applies at the appropriate rate depending on their gross income (para 17.22) according to the following scale (for England see 17.47):

Gross income	Weekly deduction	
	England	**Scotland**
£420.00 or more per week	£11.45	£11.80
£338.00 to £419.99 per week	£9.56	£9.85
£195.00 to £337.99 per week	£7.58	£7.75
under £195.00 per week	£3.77	£3.90

Gross income	Weekly deduction Wales
£420.00 or more per week	£12.25
£338.00 to £419.99 per week	£10.25
£194.00 to £337.99 per week	£8.10
under £194.00 per week	£4.05

Assuming the amount of a non-dependant deduction

17.20   It is common practice for local councils to assume the highest rate deduction until they know what the non-dependant's actual circumstances are; and the law allows this if they are in full-time work (para 17.21) but not if this is unlikely to reflect their circumstances: CH/48/2006 (e.g. evidence of employment without earnings details but in an occupation where they are likely to be paid the minimum wage). In all such cases, once your authority has evidence showing what the true deduction should be, it should award any arrears of CTR that are due.

T17.1   CTP 10, sch 1 para 8(1),(2),(7),(8)
England: SI 2015/2041 reg 2(3)(a)
Scotland: CTS 6,67(1),(2),(7),(8); CTS60+ 6,48(1),(2),(7),(8); SSI 2016/81 regs 13,23
Wales: CTPW 10, sch 1 para 3(1),(2),(7),(8) sch 6 para 5(1),(2),(7),(8); CTRW 10,28(1),(2),(7),(8); SI 2016/50 regs 5(a),9(a),18

Full-time work

17.21   Full time work (the law calls this 'remunerative work') is any paid work which averages 16 hours or more per week. Once a person is in full-time work, it includes holidays, and other periods of absence without good cause. But it does not include:

(a) maternity, paternity or adoption leave (with the right to return to work under a contract or under employment law);

(b) absences due to illness (whether or not wages or sick pay are being paid);

(c) periods the person is laid off;

(d) voluntary work;

(e) work where the person's only income is from a Sports Council Award; or

(f) any benefit week in which the non-dependant receives a passport benefit (para 17.5) for four days or more.

Gross income

17.22   It is gross income, not net income, which is used to determine the level of the higher rate charges (para 17.19), but in England this could be varied: para 17.16. Gross income means all sources (except those in para 17.25) before the deduction of tax and national insurance. The law does not say what should be included but your council is likely to include all the kinds of income in chapter 18, such as earnings before deductions (tax etc) and without disregards, other unearned income such as benefits (without disregards), plus any actual income from capital (e.g. interest earned on the non-dependant's savings).

17.23   The non-dependant's gross full-time earnings are calculated from the average of any recognisable work cycle. But if there is none, your council should base it on the average for the five week period before the claim, unless some other period would give a more accurate estimate.

17.24   If the recognisable cycle of work is one year (e.g. in a school), weekly hours are averaged only during the periods the non-dependant works (e.g. term-times). The average weekly hours is then applied for the whole year but any changes in pay between the working and non-working periods are taken into account so different levels of deduction may apply in term-times and holidays.

17.25   If a non-dependant receives any of the following it is disregarded in calculating their gross income:

(a) personal independence payment;

(b) disability living allowance (both components);

(c) attendance allowance (or any of the related benefits in para 17.77);

17.21   CTP 10(1),(5)-(8); CTR 10(1),(5)-(8)

17.22   CTP sch 1 para 8(1),(2); CTR 30(1),(2)

17.23   CTP 10(4),(5); CTR 10(4),(5)

17.24   CTP 10(3); CTR 10(3)

17.25   CTP sch 1 para 8(9),(10),(13); CTR 2(1),30(9)

(d) in England and Wales only, an armed forces independence payment;

(e) any payment from (or originally derived from) the government trusts identified in para 18.59 (Macfarlane Trust, Skipton Fund, etc).

Examples: Calculating CTR with non-dependants

Claimant on ESA(IR) with working non-dependant

A claimant living in England is on ESA(IR). Her eligible council tax liability is £19.00 per week. Her 26-year-old son lives with her. He earns £450 per week gross for a 35-hour week.

Claimants on ESA(IR) get maximum benefit, which in this case involves a non-dependant deduction. The son is in remunerative work and the level of his gross income means the highest level of deduction applies (table 17.1).

Eligible council tax	£19.00
minus non-dependant deduction	£11.45
Equals weekly CTR	£7.55

Claimant on ESA(IR) with non-dependant on JSA(C)

The son in the previous example loses his job and starts receiving JSA(C).

The lower rate non-dependant deduction applies because they are not in work and receive JSA(C) (which unlike JSA(IB) is not a passport benefit).

Eligible council tax	£19.00
the lower non-dependant deduction applies	£3.77
Equals weekly CTR	£15.23

Both examples are based on the CTR 'prescribed' scheme in England. Local variations may apply to working age claims (para 17.16).

Non-dependant couples

17.26   In the case of a non-dependant couple, only one deduction applies, being the higher (or highest) of any that would have applied to the individuals if they were single claimants. In appropriate cases, there is no deduction (e.g. if they are both under 18). In calculating the gross income for the higher rate charges the gross income of both members is added together. (For CTR variations, see para 17.16.)

Non-dependants of joint occupiers

17.27   If you are jointly liable for the council tax with someone else (other than your partner) and a non-dependant also lives in the same dwelling as you and your joint occupier then the deduction (if it applies) is apportioned as follows:

17.26   CTP sch 1 para 8(3),(4); CTR 30(3),(4)

17.27   CTP sch 1 para 8(5); CTR 30(5)

(a) If the non-dependant is part of just one household (para 16.52, for example if they are your son/daughter), then the full deduction is made solely from that claim (and any claim for benefit by the other occupiers is entirely unaffected).

(b) If the non-dependant is a household member of more than one joint occupier, then the full deduction is shared equally between each joint occupier.

(But see para 17.16 for CTR variations in England.)

Delayed non-dependant deductions for people aged 65+

17.28   In England and Scotland only, if you or your partner are aged 65 or over and there is a change in your non-dependant's circumstances that results in an increase in the deduction rate, the resulting change in your CTR award is delayed until the day 26 weeks after the change actually occurred.

Second adult rebate

17.29   This section applies only in England and Scotland. It explains the alternative form of CTR known as second adult rebate (SAR) (in the law it is called 'alternative maximum CTR'). SAR is awarded to the claimant (the council tax payer) but based on the circumstances of a 'second adult' (para 17.31). Because of the 'better buy' comparison (para 17.38), it is awarded only if it results in an award that is greater than under the normal rules (paras 17.2-28).

17.30   In England if you are working age, the rules in this section can vary (para 16.5): some councils do not award SAR, and in others the award is reduced (or confined to certain types of case). The rules cannot be varied for pension age claims in England, nor for any claims in Scotland.

Who is a 'second adult'?

17.31   A second adult is a non-dependant who is not a 'disregarded person' (para 17.32). But it also includes others who live with you who do not pay you rent on a commercial basis (e.g. a live-in carer or employee), provided they are not a disregarded person.

Who are 'disregarded persons'?

17.32   A disregarded person is anyone who is disregarded for council tax discount purposes. Typical examples are young people, people who are severely mentally impaired, and certain students, youth trainees, apprentices and carers. Table 15.2 gives the full rules.

Entitlement to SAR (basic conditions)

17.33   You are entitled to SAR if:

(a) all, or all but one, of the occupiers jointly liable for council tax on your home (e.g. you, your partner and other joint tenants: para 15.12) are disregarded persons;

(b) there is at least one second adult that lives with you in your home;

17.28   CTP sch 1 para 46(10)-(13); CTR 107(10)-(13)

17.31   CTP sch 1 para 4(3), sch 3 para 1(1); CTR 15(3),18(3), sch 4 para 1(1)

17.32   CTP sch 1 para 4(3)(a); CTR 15(3)(a),18(3)(a)

   (c)   you do not receive rent from anyone aged 18+ in your home; and

   (d)   the additional condition (in para 17.34 or 17.35 as appropriate) is met.

The student type of SAR

17.34   The additional condition for this type of SAR is that everyone in your home is either:

   (a)   a student who is not in the 'eligible student groups' listed in table 16.5; or

   (b)   a second adult on JSA(IB), ESA(IR), IS or pension credit.

In this case, the amount of your SAR equals 100% of your liability for council tax (but for variations see para 17.30).

The general type of SAR

17.35   The additional condition for this type of SAR is that the gross income of the second adult(s) who live with you is low enough. The amount of SAR can be up to 25% of your liability for council tax. The details are in table 17.2 (but for variations see para 17.30). Because general SAR is based on the income and capital of the second adults and not your income and capital it is often awarded if your income is too high to qualify for CTR (para 17.11) or your capital exceeds the capital limit (para 17.6).

Table 17.2 **Amount of second adult rebate**

Student type of SAR

All cases	100%

General type of SAR

Second adult is on JSA(IB)/ESA(IR)/IS/pension credit (or, if there are two or more second adults, all of them are)	25%
Second adult is not on JSA(IB)/ESA(IR)/IS/pension credit (or, if there are two or more second adults, at least one is not):	
in England (see also para 17.47) with gross income:	
under £193.00 pw	15%
£193.00-£249.99 pw	7½%
£250.00 or more pw	nil
in Scotland with gross income:	
under £191.00 pw	15%
£191.00-£248.99 pw	7½%
£249.00 or more pw	nil

Gross income includes the income of a partner. If there are two or more second adults it means the combined gross income of all of them (and their partners).

17.33-35   CTP sch 1 paras 4(1),(2),9(1),10(4), sch 3 para 1; CTR 15(1),(2),18(1),(2),31(1),32(4), sch 4 para 1

T17.2   SI 2015/2041 reg 2(5); CTP sch 3 para 1(2); SSI 2016/81 regs 15,27; CTS sch 2 para 1; CTS60+ sch 5 para 1

Second adults' gross income

17.36   In calculating the appropriate rate of SAR, the gross income of the second adult is used in precisely the same way as the gross income of a non-dependant (paras 17.22-25). If there is more than one second adult that lives with you, your council uses the combined income of all of them (and of their partners) to assess second adult rebate. Table 17.2 gives the figures.

SAR for joint occupiers

17.37   If there are any people who live with you who are jointly liable for the council tax (other than your partner) then each one who claims CTR qualifies for an equal share of the total SAR. (The share will always be equal between all the joint occupiers.)

The 'better buy'

17.38   You cannot be paid the main type of CTR (para 17.2) and SAR at the same time. If you qualify for both, you are awarded whichever of the two is higher (or, if the two are the same, the main type of CTR). This is called a 'better buy' comparison. If you are jointly liable for the council tax, the comparison is carried out separately for yourself and each other joint occupier who claims.

Example: Better buy

Lone parent with one non-dependant/second adult

A lone parent living in Scotland is liable for council tax of £16 per week on her home. She has excess income of £25. The only people living with her are her daughter of 15 and her son of 21. The son's gross income is £200 per week. Only the daughter (because of being under 18) is a 'disregarded person'.

Main CTR calculation

Weekly eligible council tax	£16.00
minus non-dependant deduction for son (he works under 16 hours a week, so the lowest deduction applies: table 17.1)	£3.90
minus 20% of excess income (20% x £25.00)	£5.00
equals CTR	£7.10

SAR calculation

The level of the son's gross income means that the claimant qualifies for a 7½% second adult rebate:

weekly second adult rebate (7½% x £16.00)	£1.20

Better buy comparison

The claimant's main CTR is the higher of the two amounts, which is £7.10.

(For variations which could affect this example, see paras 17.4, 17.12, 17.16 and 17.30.)

17.36   CTP sch 3 paras 2,3; CTR sch 4 paras 2,3

17.37   CTP sch 1 para 9(2),(3); CTR 31 (2),(3)

17.38   CTP sch 1 para 10(5)-(6); CTR 32 (5),(6)

Conversion to weekly amounts, etc

Council tax

17.39 Whenever a weekly figure is needed for council tax liability, the following rules apply:

(a) for annual figures, divide the council tax by the number of days in the financial year (365 or 366) to find the daily figure, and then multiply the daily figure by seven;

(b) for figures which do not relate to a whole year, divide the council tax by the number of days it covers to find the daily figure, and then multiply the daily figure by seven.

Income

17.40 Whenever a weekly income figure is needed, the following rules apply:

(a) for an amount relating to a whole multiple of weeks, divide the amount by the number of weeks it covers;

(b) for an amount relating to a calendar month, multiply the amount by 12 to find the annual figure, then divide the annual figure by 52;

(c) for an amount relating to a year, there are two rules. For working age claims, divide the annual amount by 365 or 366 as appropriate to find the daily figure, and then multiply the daily figure by seven. For pension age claims, simply divide the annual amount by 52;

(d) for an amount relating to any other period longer than a week, divide the amount by the number of days it covers to find the daily figure, then multiply the daily figure by seven;

(e) for an amount relating to a period less than a week:

- if the period to which the payment relates straddles two rebate weeks (i.e. includes a Sunday and Monday) the whole amount is taken as income in the second week (i.e. the week starting on the Monday);

- if the period is wholly within the same rebate week, the whole amount is included in the following rebate week (although the law is not entirely clear on this point).

Rounding

17.41 There is no rule about rounding your (weekly) CTR award to the nearest penny: in fact in many council areas the practice is to calculate entitlement to at least six decimal places as this avoids reconciliation errors at the end of the financial year. However, your council can round any figures to the nearest penny in the decision notice it sends you about your award.

17.39   CTP sch 1 para 7(1)(b); CTR 29(1)(b)

17.40   CTP sch 1 para 17(1); CTR 40(1),50(1)

Applicable amounts

17.42 This section describes how your council calculates your applicable amount when assessing your CTR. It covers:

(a) the basic rules;

(b) the detailed conditions for personal allowances, premiums and components; and

(c) further rules and special cases.

17.43 The terms 'family', 'single claimant', 'lone parent', 'couple', 'partner', 'child' and 'young person' are defined in paras 16.52-66. For 'pension age' and 'working age' see para 16.13.

What is an applicable amount?

17.44 Your applicable amount is a standardised assessment of the minimum income required to meet the basic living needs of you and your family. It is compared with your income (chapter 18) when calculating how much CTR you are entitled to (paras 17.8-12).

How much is the applicable amount?

17.45 Your applicable amount is the total of:

(a) a personal allowance for yourself (and any partner);

(b) a personal allowance for each child or young person in your family; and

(c) any additional amounts (known as premiums and components) you qualify for.

Your applicable amount always includes a personal allowance but any additional amounts depend on your circumstances. Except as described below, there are no limitations on how many premiums and components can be awarded.

17.46 The figures for 2016-17 are given in tables 17.3 and 17.4. Detailed conditions are in the rest of this chapter. In England your council has the power to vary applicable amounts for working age CTR claims (para 16.5). In practice councils do not do this (para 17.47).

17.47 In England the rates for the applicable amount are only prescribed by law for pension age claims (paras 16.4, 16.6 and 16.13). For all working age claims your council can set its own rates even though most adopt the 2013-14 default scheme as a model. The weekly rates in the 2013-14 default scheme have not been up-rated although the 'prescribed requirements' (para 16.4) effectively set the 2016-17 rates for pensioners (table 17.3). If your council uses the default scheme it must vary it each year to effect an up-rating for working age claims. However, in practice this is not a problem because for reasons of efficiency most councils use the same rates that they use for HB (appendix 2) (and which apply in Scotland and Wales: table 17.4).

17.46   SI 2015/2041 reg 2(4); SSI 2016/81 reg 24; SI 2016/50 regs 6(a),25(a)

17.47   CTP 6, sch 2 para 4; CTR 25-27, sch 2 para 4, sch 3 paras 5-7

If you are on universal credit

17.48 If you or your partner are on UC, your council uses the DWP's figure to calculate your applicable amount instead of the figures in tables 17.3 and 17.4 (but in England your council may use a different method (para 16.4)). The DWP's figure is based on their assessment of your maximum UC award. This is a monthly figure, and your council converts it to a weekly one by multiplying by 12 and dividing the result by 52.

Table 17.3 **Weekly applicable amounts: England**

Personal allowances: pensioners

Single claimant	over pension age but under 65	£155.60
	aged 65+	£168.70
Lone parent	over pension age but under 65	£155.60
	aged 65+	£168.70
Couple	at least one pension age, both under 65	£237.55
	at least one aged 65+	£252.30
Plus for each dependent child		£66.90

Additional amounts: pensioners

Family premium	at least one dependent child	£17.45
	From 1st May 2016	Nil
Disabled child premium	each dependent child	£60.06
Enhanced disability premium	each dependent child	£24.43
Carer premium	claimant or partner or each	£34.60
Severe disability premium	single rate	£61.85
	double rate	£123.70

Note:

For working age claims see para 17.47.

17.48   CTR 28

T17.3   CTP sch 2 paras 1-3, part 4; SI 2014/3312 reg 2(6); SI 2015/2041 reg 2(4)

Table 17.4 **Weekly applicable amounts: Scotland and Wales**

Personal allowances

Single claimant	aged under 25 – on main phase ESA	£73.10
	aged under 25 – other	£57.90
	aged 25+ but under pension age	£73.10
	over pension age but under 65	£155.60
	aged 65+ in Scotland	£168.70
	aged 65+ in Wales	£170.45
Lone parent	aged 18+ but under pension age	£73.10
	over pension age but under 65	£155.60
	aged 65+ in Scotland	£168.70
	aged 65+ in Wales	£170.45
Couple	at least one aged 18+ both under pension age	£114.85
	at least one pension age, both under 65	£237.55
	at least one aged 65+ in Scotland	£252.30
	at least one aged 65+ in Wales	£255.50
Plus for each dependent child		£66.90

Additional amounts

Family premium	at least one dependent child (Wales)	£17.45	
	at least one dependent child (Scotland)	£17.45	
	From 1st May 2016 (Scotland)	nil	
Disability premium	single claimant/lone parent	£32.25	*
	couple (one/both qualifying)	£45.95	*
Disabled child premium	each dependent child	£60.06	
Enhanced disability premium	single claimant/lone parent	£15.75	*
	couple (one/both qualifying)	£22.60	*
	each dependent child	£24.43	
Work related activity component	single claimant/lone parent/couple	£29.05	*
Support component	single claimant/lone parent/couple	£36.20	*
Carer premium	claimant or partner or each	£34.60	
Severe disability premium	single rate	£61.85	
	double rate	£123.70	

Only awarded with working age claims (para 16.13).

T17.4   Scotland: SSI 2016/81 reg 24
         Wales: CTPW sch 2 paras 1-3,12,sch 7 paras 1-3,17; CTRW sch 2 paras 1-3,12,sch 3 paras 1-3,17; SI 2016/50 regs 6(a),25

Examples: Applicable amounts

Except for the lone parent in the fourth example, none of the following qualifies for any of the premiums for disability or for carers.

Single claimant in Scotland aged 23

Personal allowance:

Single claimant aged under 25	£57.90
No additional amounts apply	
Applicable amount	£57.90

Couple with two children in Wales aged 13 and 17

The older child is still at school so still counts as a dependant of the couple.

Personal allowances:

Couple, at least one over 18, both under pension age	£114.85
Child aged 13	£66.90
Child aged 17	£66.90
Additional amount: family premium	£17.45
Applicable amount	£266.10

Couple in England aged 38 and 65

Personal allowance:

Couple at least one aged 65	£252.30
Applicable amount	£252.30

Disabled lone parent in Scotland with a child aged 6

The lone parent is in receipt of the highest rate of the care component of disability living allowance and so qualifies for a disability premium and enhanced disability premium. She has one child aged 17 but is applying for CTR in Scotland so there is no family premium. Her mother (who lives elsewhere) receives carer's allowance to care for her. So she does not qualify for the severe disability premium.

Personal allowances:

Lone parent aged over 18 (and under pension age)	£73.10
Child	£66.90
Additional amounts:	
Disability premium (single rate)	£32.25
Enhanced disability premium (single rate)	£15.75
Applicable amount	£188.00

Better off problems: couples on ESA

17.49   If you are part of a couple and either (or both) of you receive ESA, the amount of your CTR award can depend on which one of you makes the claim. This dilemma is sometimes called the better off problem and it can arise in relation to:

   (a) the disability premium (para 17.55 and the example there); and

   (b) the enhanced disability premium (para 17.66).

Your council is not obliged to notify you if you would be better off if you swapped who makes the claim, but it is good practice to do so.

Example: A 'better off' problem for couples

Information

A working age couple meet the additional condition for a disability premium because one of them receives personal independence payment, but the other partner is on ESA(C).

Entitlement to additions in the applicable amount

This depends on which partner is the CTR claimant.

   (a) If the claimant is on ESA(C):

      their applicable amount does not include a disability premium (at any point), but it does include a work-related activity or support component from the claimant's 14th week on ESA(C).

   (b) If the partner is on ESA(C):

      their applicable amount includes a couple-rate disability premium (from the beginning), but it never includes a work-related activity or support component.

Conclusion

So they are better off if (b) applies to them – by over £5 per week in CTR, during the first 13 weeks on ESA(C) (and by a lower amount after that).

Personal allowances

17.50   Your applicable amount always includes a personal allowance for yourself (if you are single or a lone parent), or for both of you if you are a member of a couple. (For polygamous marriages see para 17.80.)

17.51   A personal allowance is awarded for each child or young person in your family (paras 16.63-69).

17.49   CTR 25,26, sch 3 paras 10(8),18-20

17.51   CTP sch 2 para 2; CTR sch 2 para 2, sch 3 para 3

Family premium

17.52 You are awarded a family premium if:

(a) in England and Scotland

- at least one member of your family (para 16.52) is a child or young person in respect of any period of your award that falls between 1st April 2016 and 30th April 2016 (both dates included), or

- for any period after that provided the premium was included in your award on 30th April 2016 and there has been no break in your award since;

(b) in Wales for any period of your award in which at least one member of your family (para 16.52) is a child or young person.

Work-related activity component and support component

17.53 If you are working age you are entitled to a work-related activity component or support component if you (or your partner) receive the equivalent component in your CTR applicable amount as you receive in your ESA award as follows:

(a) if you are a single claimant or a lone parent you get the same component;

(b) if you are in a couple and only one member receives ESA you get (one lot of) that component;

(c) if you are in a couple and you both qualify for the same component in your ESA, you get (one lot of) that component;

(d) if you are in a couple and you receive a different component from your partner in your ESA, you get (one lot of) the ESA component received by whichever of you makes the claim.

In the last case, you are better off (para 17.49) if the member who receives the support component makes the claim. See para 17.76 if you receive national insurance credits in lieu of ESA.

17.54 If your ESA assessment is delayed so that you receive arrears of your ESA component, your CTR component is also awarded retrospectively for the same period.

Disability premium

17.55 If you are working age you meet both of the following conditions:

(a) you (or if you are in a couple, the member who claims CTR) must not be on ESA (including during a period of ESA disqualification); and

(b) you (or if you are in a couple, you or your partner) meet the additional condition in the next paragraph.

In the case of a couple, the couple rate is awarded even if only one partner fulfils the conditions, so if only one member is on ESA you are better off (para 17.49) if the one who is not on ESA makes the claim for CTR (see example).

17.52   England: SI 2015/2041 regs 2(4)(b),3; Scotland: SSI 2016/81 regs 2,5,18; Wales: CTPW sch 2 para 3, sch 7 para 4; CTRW sch 2 para 3, sch 3 para 4

17.53-54   CTR sch 3 paras 18-22

17.55   CTR sch 3 para 9

17.56   You will meet the additional condition for the disability premium if:

(a) you or your partner are severely sight impaired or blind or have recently regained your sight (para 17.78);

(b) you or your partner receive any of the following benefits;

   ▪ personal independence payment; or

   ▪ disability living allowance; or

   ▪ any benefit which is treated as attendance allowance (para 17.77); or

   ▪ in England and Wales only, an armed forces independence payment; or

   ▪ war pensioner's mobility supplement; or

   ▪ the disability element or severe disability element of working tax credit;

(c) you, or your partner, were receiving long-term incapacity benefit and CTR immediately before you moved onto retirement pension and you have continued to receive CTR ever since;

(d) you, or if you are a part of a couple the member who makes the claim for CTR, are treated as long-term sick in one of the ways described in paragraph 17.58; or

(e) you or your partner have an invalid vehicle supplied by the NHS or get DWP payments for car running costs.

17.57   If you were receiving one of the first four benefits in 17.56(b) (PIP/DLA/AA) but payment has been suspended solely because you have been in hospital for four weeks you continue to be entitled to the premium.

Who counts as 'long-term sick'?

17.58   You are awarded a disability premium in your HB if you count as long-term sick under the 'old' fitness for work test. This only applies to you if your period of sickness started before 27th October 2008 and you:

(a) get long-term incapacity benefit (IB);

(b) get severe disablement allowance (SDA); or

(c) are getting national insurance credits (instead of IB or SDA) and you have been incapable of work for one year or more. This one year period need not be continuous: two or more periods of sickness are added together if the gap between them is eight weeks or less.

17.59   The rules are more complex if you are a couple. You get a disability premium at the couple rate in your CTR if:

(a) either of you is on long-term IB or SDA, even if the other one is on ESA; or

(b) you (the CTR claimant) are getting national insurance credits and have been incapable of work for one year or more, even if your partner is on ESA.

This means you can be better off depending on which one of you claims HB (see para 17.49).

17.56-60   CTR sch 3 para 10

17.60 You do not count as long-term sick under the old fitness for work test if you have transferred from IB or SDA to ESA, or from receiving national insurance credits under the 'old' test to receiving them under the ESA fitness for work test. Once you have transferred you can't go back, but you may qualify for a transitional addition in your CTR (see paras 17.61-63).

Transitional addition after transferring to ESA

17.61 You qualify for a transitional addition in your HB if your disability premium stops because you transfer:

(a) from long-term IB, SDA, or national insurance credits instead of these (see paras 17.58-59);

(b) to contributory ESA, or national insurance credits instead of this (see para 17.76).

The transitional addition prevents you from being worse off as a result of transferring.

17.62 But you do not qualify for a transitional addition if:

(a) you transfer to income-related ESA; or

(b) you are a couple and you qualify for a disability premium under the rules in para 17.56.

In each case, this is because you can't be worse off (but if (b) applies to you, see para 17.49 to ensure this).

17.63 A transitional addition restores your applicable amount to the value it had immediately before you transferred to contributory ESA or national insurance credits. After that:

(a) any subsequent increase in your applicable amount due to a change in your circumstances or the annual up-rating is deducted from your transitional addition until it is eroded to nil;

(b) you transitional addition ends before it is eroded to nil if your contributory ESA ends or your HB ends;

(c) but if you start back on HB within 12 weeks of your previous award, your transitional addition is restored.

Disabled child premium

17.64 The condition for this premium is that a child or young person in your family:

(a) is severely sight impaired or blind or has recently regained their sight (para 17.78);

(b) receives personal independence payment; or

(c) receives disability living allowance.

One premium is awarded for each child or young person who qualifies. If the child/young person dies the premium continues for eight weeks following the death. The premium continues while your child is in hospital (even though PIP/DLA is lost after 12 weeks).

17.61-63   CTR sch 3 paras 25-29

17.64   CTP sch 2 para 8; CTR sch 2 para 8, sch 3 para 13

Enhanced disability premium

17.65 This premium can be awarded in respect of any member of your family if you are working age; or in respect of a child or young person if you are pension age. One premium is awarded for each child who qualifies plus one per claim whether you are single or a couple. If your qualifying family member is in hospital and as a result loses their PIP or DLA, the premium continues to be awarded.

17.66 If you are working age you (or you and your partner) qualify if:

(a) you (or, in the case of a couple, either you or your partner) receive the daily living component (at either rate) of personal independence payment;

(b) you (or, in the case of a couple, either you or your partner) receive the highest rate of the care component of disability living allowance; or

(c) you (or, in the case of a couple, the member that claims CTR) qualify for an ESA support component.

And if you are in a couple you are always awarded the couple rate (regardless of whether one or both of you qualify). So if only one of you gets a support component in their ESA(C), you are better off if that member makes the claim for CTR (para 17.49).

17.67 The condition for a child or young person is that they receive the daily living component of personal independence payment (at either rate) or the highest rate of the care component of disability living allowance. The premium continues for eight weeks following the child's death.

Severe disability premium

17.68 You qualify for this premium only if you meet all three conditions:

(a) you receive one of the following qualifying benefits:

- the daily living component of personal independence payment; or
- the middle or highest rate of the care component of disability living allowance; or
- attendance allowance at either rate; or
- a benefit which is treated as attendance allowance (para 17.77); and

(b) you must have no non-dependants (but see paragraph 17.70 below for exceptions); and

(c) no-one must be receiving carer's allowance in respect of you (but see paragraph 17.69 if you are in a couple, and paragraph 17.76 for exceptions).

If you are single or a lone parent and satisfy all three conditions you get the single rate of the severe disability premium. If you are in a couple see the next paragraph.

17.65-67   CTP sch 2 para 7; CTR sch 2 para 7, sch 3 para 12

17.69   If you are a member of a couple, a severe disability premium is awarded as follows:

(a) if both of you satisfy all three conditions, you get the double rate;

(b) if both of you satisfy the first two conditions but only one satisfies the third condition, you get the single rate;

(c) if only one of you receives a qualifying benefit but the other member is blind you qualify for the single rate provided you meet the other two conditions. But in this case the member who receives the qualifying benefit must make the claim for CTR;

(d) if you have been getting the double rate but one member then loses their qualifying benefit because they have been in hospital for four weeks, you get the single rate from that point.

17.70   In deciding whether you meet condition 17.68(b) the following occupiers do not prevent you from being awarded a severe disability premium:

(a) any person aged under 18 or who is excluded from the definition of a non-dependant (para 16.71);

(b) a non-dependant who is severely sight impaired or blind or who has recently regained their sight (para 17.78);

(c) a non-dependant who receives:

■ the daily living component of personal independence payment;

■ the middle or highest rate of the care component of disability living allowance; or

■ attendance allowance; or

■ a benefit which is treated as attendance allowance (para 17.77).

17.71   In deciding whether you meet condition 17.68(c):

(a) your carer is not receiving carer's allowance if it is fully overlapped by other benefits (para 17.76);

(b) a backdated award of carer's allowance is ignored in respect of any period before the first payment is made: in other words the backdated part does not cause an overpayment;

(c) if you are in a couple getting the single rate and the member with the carer has been in hospital for four weeks or more, that carer is treated as receiving carer's allowance. This ensures that you continue to receive the premium at the same rate;

(d) your carer is treated as receiving carer's allowance if they have lost it as a result of a benefit fraud conviction.

17.68-71   CTP sch 2 para 6, sch 3 para 11

Example: Severe disability premium, etc

A husband and wife are both under pension age and both receive the standard rate of the daily living component of personal independence payment. Neither of them is blind. Their daughter of 17 is in full-time employment and lives with them. Their son lives elsewhere and receives carer's allowance for caring for the husband. No-one receives carer's allowance for the wife.

Disability premium: Because of receiving personal independence payment, they are awarded the couple rate of disability premium.

Enhanced disability premium: Because they get the standard rate of the daily living component of personal independence payment, this cannot be awarded.

Severe disability premium:

- Both receive the appropriate type of personal independence payment.
- Although their daughter is a non-dependant, she is under 18.
- Someone receives carer's allowance for caring for only one of them.

So they are awarded the single rate of severe disability premium (for the second reason in para 17.69).

Carer premium

17.72 The condition for this premium is that you or your partner is 'entitled to' (para 17.73) carer's allowance or you were entitled to it within the past eight weeks. If you are a couple you get one premium if one of you satisfies the condition, two if both of you do.

17.73 You need only to be 'entitled' and not 'in receipt' of carer's allowance. So you still qualify if your carer's allowance is overlapped by another benefit (see examples): but you must make a claim for carer's allowance to be entitled to it. Once a claim for carer's allowance has been made and entitlement established, it continues indefinitely and it does not matter if the original claim was made before you claimed CTR.

17.74 You are treated as still receiving carer's allowance if you lose it as a result of taking part in a government training scheme (para 17.79).

Interaction of carer and severe disability premium

17.75 Although an award of carer's allowance qualifies you for a carer premium, the person you care for may lose their severe disability premium. However, if your carer's allowance is overlapped any severe disability premium in your own claim or the person you care for is unaffected (see second example). It you are a couple who care for each other it is therefore possible to qualify for a severe disability premium (at the single or double rate) and one or two carer premiums at the same time.

17.72   CTP sch 2 paras 5(2),9; CTR sch 2 paras 5(2),9, sch 3 paras 8(2),14

17.75   CTP sch 2 para 11; CTR sch 2 para 11, sch 3 para 16

Examples: Carer premium and overlapping benefits

Claimant over 65

A claimant and her partner are both aged over 80 and in receipt of retirement pension. She looks after her partner who has been in receipt of attendance allowance since 29th January 2016. On 5th February 2016 she made a claim for carer's allowance and was notified by the DWP that she was entitled to carer's allowance but it could not be paid because it was overlapped by her retirement pension (in other words, payment of the latter prevents payment of the former).

On 2nd May 2016 she makes a claim for CTR for the first time and is awarded it from 8th February 2016 (para 19.40). The award includes the carer premium. If her partner subsequently dies, she would no longer be entitled to carer's allowance, but the premium would continue for a further eight weeks.

Claimant under 65

A claimant aged 50 is in receipt of bereavement allowance. He cares for his severely disabled sister who receives the daily living component of personal independence payment. He lives alone in his own flat. He claims carer's allowance and is entitled to it but it cannot be paid because it is overlapped by his bereavement allowance but he is awarded a carer premium in his CTR. Once he has claimed carer's allowance he remains 'entitled' to it until such time as he no longer meets the conditions for it (e.g. he starts work, or his sister no longer qualifies for PIP) and until that time his entitlement to it continues without the need for a further claim even if there are breaks in his CTR award. Note that his sister would also be entitled to the severe disability premium, because although he is 'entitled' to carer's allowance he is not 'in receipt' of it (para 17.76).

Being 'in receipt' of a benefit including 'main phase ESA'

17.76   Many of the qualifying conditions for a premium or component in this section depend on being in 'receipt of' a social security benefit. The general rule means the benefit in question must be in payment and it is not sufficient if you are entitled to it but it cannot be paid because it is overlapped by another benefit. The only exceptions to this rule are:

(a)   if you receive a DWP concessionary payment in lieu of a qualifying benefit for any premium (but not the work-related or support component) you are treated as receiving that benefit;

(b)   if you were awarded any premium before your qualifying benefit was overlapped by another payment you continue to be entitled to that premium (this avoids a sudden drop in your award);

(c)   if you receive national insurance credits in lieu of main phase ESA you are treated as receiving ESA for the purpose of the work-related or support component;

(d)   if your qualifying benefit is only partially overlapped (in other words the overlapping benefit is less than your qualifying benefit) you are still in receipt of it;

(e)   if your carer's allowance is overlapped you still get the carer premium.

17.76   CTP sch 2 paras 5,10,11; CTR sch 2 paras 5,10,11, sch 3 paras 8,15,16

Benefits treated as attendance allowance

17.77   You are treated as receiving attendance allowance if you receive any type of increase for attendance paid with an industrial injury benefit or war disablement pension. Qualifying payments include constant attendance allowance, 'old cases' attendance payments, severe disablement occupational allowance and exceptionally severe disablement allowance.

Meaning of severely sight impaired, blind or recently regained sight

17.78   In deciding whether a non-dependant deduction applies (para 17.17) or entitlement to certain premiums in this section (paras 17.56, 17.64, 17.68-69) a member of your household is 'severely sight impaired' or 'blind' if they registered as blind with your council social services department; or in either case for a further 28 weeks from the date they were removed from the register due to them having regained their sight.

People on training courses or in receipt of a training allowance

17.79   If you qualify for the disability premium through being long-term sick (paras 17.58-59) or the carer premium, your disability/carer premium continues while you are on a government training scheme or receive a training allowance.

Polygamous marriages

17.80   If you are in a polygamous marriage (para 16.55) you get the appropriate amount in table 17.3 or table 17.4 for a couple according to the age of the oldest member in the marriage plus the appropriate amount below for each additional spouse:

(a)   where all of the partners in the marriage are under pension age (para 16.13): £41.75 (but in England the council may use a different figure: paras 16.5 and 17.47);

(b)   where at least one of the partners is pension age or over but none of them are aged 65 or over: £81.95;

(c)   where at least one of the members of the marriage is aged 65 or over: £83.60 (in Wales, £84.55).

Except for the severe disability premium (para 17.81), all premiums and components are awarded in a similar way as for the first partner in a couple.

17.81   In the case of a severe disability premium you receive the double rate if all members in the marriage satisfy all three conditions in para 17.68. You get the single rate if all members of the marriage satisfy the first two conditions but one member has a carer who gets carer's allowance; or if the member who claims CTR satisfies all three conditions and all the other members of the marriage are blind.

17.77   CTP 2(1); CTR 2(1)

17.78   CTP sch 2 para 6(4),(5); CTR sch 2 para 6(4),(5) sch 3 para 10(1)(a)(vii),(2)

17.79   CTP 2(1), sch 2 para 5(1); CTR 2(1), sch 2 para 5(1), sch 3 para 8(1)

17.80   CTP sch 2 para 1; CTR 27 sch 2 para 1
         England: SI 2015/2041 reg 2(4)(a)(vi),(viii); Scotland: SSI 2016/81 reg 24; Wales: SI 2016/50 reg 6(a)(iii),(iv), 25(a)(iii),(iv)

17.81   CTP sch 2 para 6(1)(b); CTR sch 2 para 6(1)(b), sch 3 para 11(1)(b)

Chapter 18 **Income and capital for CTR**

- General rules: see paras 18.1-15.
- Social security benefits, tax credits and war pensions: see paras 18.16-23.
- Income from employment and self employment: see paras 18.24-49.
- Other kinds of income: see paras 18.50-62.
- Capital: see paras 18.63-76.

General rules

18.1   This chapter explains how income and capital are calculated for CTR. It provides a summary of the most common types of income and capital that are likely to be encountered and how they are generally treated in the calculation of CTR. For less common items of income and capital and for less common exceptions to the general rules outlined in this chapter, see para 18.15.

Finding the law

18.2   The law on how income and capital is treated for CTR can be difficult to identify because of differences between England, Scotland and Wales and how the law is constructed in each of these countries (para 16.2). In addition:

(a) in all three countries, the rules about how your income and capital is treated depend on whether you are a pension age or a working age claimant;

(b) in England (and to a lesser extent in Wales) your local council is free to set its own rules about how your income and capital are treated for working age claims, but in practice most have adopted the 'default scheme' either in full or in part (paras 18.3-4); and

(c) in England and Wales your local council's scheme rules must comply with the 'prescribed requirements' (para 16.4).

The law in England

18.3   The footnote references in this chapter are to the 'prescribed requirements' and the 'default scheme' for England that operated during the first year of CTR (2013-14). While the default scheme ended on 1st April 2014, most councils have either adopted it entirely or express their own scheme rules in terms of how they comply with, or vary from, the equivalent rule in the default scheme. (And in practice councils only vary a very small number of the default scheme rules.) Your local council must publish its local scheme rules (para 16.8).

The law in Scotland and Wales

18.4   In Scotland, all councils must comply with Scottish Government CTR scheme and cannot vary the rules locally. In Wales, local CTR schemes must comply with the Welsh Government 'prescribed requirements'. The Welsh Government issued a revised default scheme in 2014-15 which most councils comply with (in effect it is a model scheme) and which is updated each year to reflect any changes to the prescribed requirements and the annual up-rating. In this chapter equivalent footnote references (for reasons of space and elegance) for Scotland and Wales are in Appendix 4.

Assessing cases on passport benefits

18.5   CTR is calculated by comparing your income with your requirements ('applicable amount'). If you are on a passport benefit your income is taken to be zero, so calculating your requirements is unnecessary and all the other detailed rules in this chapter are irrelevant: you get the maximum award. The passport benefits are:

(a)   income-based jobseeker's allowance;

(b)   income-related employment and support allowance;

(c)   income support; and

(d)   guarantee credit.

Assessing cases for universal credit and savings credit

18.6   If you receive universal credit or savings credit only (i.e. without guarantee credit) your council must use the income and capital figures supplied to it by the DWP and none of the other rules about income in this chapter apply. Your council must adjust the DWP figures according to the following rules:

(a)   if you receive savings credit, the amount of the savings credit itself is added to the DWP's income figure. This is the income figure used to calculate your CTR (plus any income derived from the DWP's figure for your capital). The only uncommon exceptions are if you have earnings from work, maintenance from a partner/former partner or a war pension: the rules are the same as for HB (see *Guide to Housing Benefit* table 13.3 for details);

(b)   if you receive universal credit, the amount of the universal credit itself is added to the DWP's income figure. The total is then multiplied by 12 and divided by 52 (to convert to a weekly figure). This is the income figure used to calculate your CTR (plus any income derived from the DWP's figure for your capital).

Assessing income and capital: all other cases

18.7   CTR is calculated by comparing your requirements ('applicable amount') with your income only. If you possess capital (e.g. savings) its value is converted into a hypothetical income figure ('tariff income': para 18.65) and this is then added to your other sources of income – unless its value exceeds the upper capital limit (para 18.8).

The upper capital limit

18.8   The upper capital limit is £16,000 (the same figure for pension age and working age) but in England if you are working age your council can set its own upper capital limit as part

---

18.6   CTP sch 1 para 14; CTR 36, 37

18.7   CTP sch 1 para 24(1)(b); CTR 57(1)(b)

of its own local scheme rules (para 16.5). If your capital is above the upper capital limit then you are not entitled to CTR (even if your income is zero). The only exception is if you are on guarantee credit (para 18.9).

18.9 If you are on guarantee credit the whole of your capital is disregarded even if it is more than £16,000. Unlike working age passport benefits (where the upper capital limit is the same as for CTR) there is no upper capital limit for guarantee credit.

Differences in treatment: working age and pension age

18.10 CTR law treats your income differently depending on whether you are a working age or pension age claimant (para 16.13). The approach taken by the law in either case is quite different:

(a) if you are working age every source of income you possess is included in your assessment, unless it is an item that is specifically listed in the law as being disregarded;

(b) if you are pension age nothing counts as income unless the law says it does. Some types of income (as the law acknowledges) are then also disregarded (for example, social security benefits count as income, but disability living allowance is disregarded).

18.11 In broad terms the law treats your capital in the same way whether you are pension age or working age: all of your capital counts unless the law specifically lists it as being disregarded; although there are some differences in the list of items that are disregarded between pension age and working age claims (identified as they arise).

Differences in treatment: earned income and unearned income

18.12 CTR law makes the distinction between:

(a) earned income (i.e. from work as an employee or from self-employment);

(b) unearned income: anything else which is not from work. The list is almost endless but typically it includes social security benefits and pensions, tax credits (and universal credit), private pensions (such as from a former employer), rental income (i.e. if you are a landlord) and maintenance (including maintenance received for a child who lives with you).

As a general rule earned income is treated more generously than unearned income because it is always subject to a disregard (i.e. only part of it is taken into account). Certain less common items of unearned income that qualify for a disregard (war pensions, student income and widows/widowers) are subject to an overall (maximum) limit on the amount disregarded of £20: these are identified as they arise.

18.8   CTP 11(2); CTR 20,23

18.9   CTP sch 1 para 13; CTR 35

18.10   CTP sch 1 paras 16,17,18,24; CTR 38,39,40,52,54,57

18.11   CTP sch 1 para 31(1); CTR 63(1)

18.12   CTP sch 5 para 12(3); CTR sch 6 para 12(3), sch 8 para 40

Distinguishing income from capital

18.13   In most cases distinguishing between income and capital is fairly straightforward. Capital can usually be distinguished from income because it is made without being tied to a past period and is not intended to form part of a series of payments. Further details about distinguishing income from capital can be found in the *Guide to Housing Benefit,* paras 15.10-11.

Deprivation of income and capital

18.14   As a general rule only income and capital you currently hold count in your assessment. However, there are special rules that can treat you as possessing income or capital you have given away, spent, or in some cases money you would be entitled to but have failed to apply for, if your purpose in depriving yourself of that resource was to increase your CTR award. The rules are the same as for HB: for further details see the *Guide to Housing Benefit,* paragraphs 13.46-57 and 15.56-69.

Less common items of income and capital

18.15   This chapter covers only the most common kinds of income and capital; for less common items and other types of case where special rules apply (in particular, students) see the *Guide to Housing Benefit*. The CTR (default scheme) rules for these less common items and special cases are as described for HB.

Social security benefits, tax credits and war pensions

What counts as social security

18.16   In this section 'social security' means those benefits and pensions you receive from the DWP. It also includes any housing benefit (HB) paid by your local authority. It does not include:

(a)   tax credits paid by HMRC (para 18.21);

(b)   war pensions for disability or surviving partners (para 18.23);

(c)   social benefits paid by your employer (such as statutory sick pay or statutory maternity pay) which are usually treated as earned income (para 18.30);

(d)   other social benefits (whether in cash or in kind) paid by your local authority (e.g. discretionary housing payments, 'supporting people' payments and fostering allowances (paras 18.51);

(e)   private pensions and cash benefits (such as a company pension or insurance scheme).

Social security benefits: the general rule

18.17   The general rule is that any social security benefits and pensions you receive are counted in full as your income for the period they cover (including any arrears). The more common benefits covered by this rule include retirement pension; contribution-based JSA or ESA; incapacity benefit and carer's allowance; but it includes other less common benefits as well. The exceptions to this are in the next paragraph.

18.14   CTP sch 1 paras 22(9),34(1); CTR 45(9),56(1),67(1)

18.17   CTP sch 1 paras 16(1),17(7); CTR 39(1),40(7), 49(2)

Social security benefits: exceptions to the general rule

18.18   The exceptions to the general rule that social security benefits and pensions count in full as income are:

(a) the 'passport benefits' IS, JSA(IB), ESA(IR) and guarantee credit;

(b) savings credit and universal credit;

(c) housing benefit;

(d) disability living allowance and personal independence payments;

(e) attendance allowance;

(f) constant attendance allowance (for industrial injury);

(g) child benefit and guardian's allowance;

(h) winter fuel, cold weather, funeral and maternity payments (all paid by the social fund);

(i) a Christmas bonus paid with any DWP benefit;

(j) widowed parent's allowance; and

(k) bereavement payment.

For other local authority administered cash benefits (e.g. discretionary housing payments and social services payments) see para 18.51.

18.19   The rules for the benefits and pensions (a)-(k) above are:

(a) if you receive any of the 'passport benefits' your total income and capital (no matter what other sources of income or capital you have) is treated as being zero;

(b) if you receive savings credit or universal credit your total income and capital is based on the DWP's figures for these (no matter what other sources of income or capital you have), adjusted only as described in paragraph 18.6;

(c) all of the benefits (c)-(i) are disregarded in full as income (but you must still declare them in your claim);

(d) the first £15 of widowed parent's allowance is disregarded (but see para 18.12);

(e) bereavement payment is a single lump sum and counts (in full) as capital not income.

18.20   The amount of your social security benefit that counts as income is the gross figure before any deductions are made to recover an overpayment or to pay someone else (typically to pay off a priority debt such as rent, water or fuel arrears). This applies to any benefit covered by the general rule or any of the exceptions above.

18.19(a) CTP sch 1 para 13; CTR 35, sch 7 para 14, sch 8 paras 8,9, sch 10 paras 8,9

18.19(b) CTP sch 1 para 14; CTR 36, 37

18.19(c) CTP sch 1 para 16(1)(j); CTR 39(1)(j), sch 8 paras 11,14,37,38,42,52,66

18.19(d) CTP 16(1)(j), sch 5 paras 7,8; CTR sch 6 paras 7,8, sch 8 para 21

18.19(e) CTP 16(1)(j)(xiii); CTR 39(1)(j)(xiii)

18.20   CTP sch 1 para 16(2); CTR 39(2), 54(3)

Working tax credit (WTC) and child tax credit (CTC)

18.21 Any income you receive from tax credits only counts from the date it is paid. Arrears of tax credits count as capital, but are disregarded for 52 weeks from the date they are paid. If your tax credit award has been reduced to recover an overpayment from the previous year, it is the reduced award that is counted. Once in payment, each instalment counts as income for the period it covers as described in the next paragraph.

18.22 Your tax credit instalment is counted as income for CTR:

(a) any child tax credit counts in full as income if you are working age but is disregarded in full if you are pension age;

(b) except where (c) applies, the whole of your working tax credit is counted as income whether you are pension age or working age;

(c) if your earnings from work are insufficient for you to use up the whole of any child care disregard and/or additional earnings disregard you are entitled to, any balance can be deducted from your working tax credit (see *Guide to Housing Benefit* for details).

War pensions for disablement and surviving partners

18.23 If you have a war pension paid for disablement or as a war widow or widower:

(a) in England and Wales, the first £10 is disregarded as income (but see para 18.12), plus any additional amount allowed by your local authority under a local scheme (which most local authorities have);

(b) in Scotland, the whole of your war pension is disregarded; and

(c) in England, Scotland and Wales the whole of any constant attendance allowance or mobility supplement paid with your war pension is disregarded.

For further details about which types of war pension are included, see the *Guide to Housing Benefit*.

Income from employment and self-employment

18.24 Income from employment or self-employment is generally treated slightly more generously than unearned income (para 18.41).

18.25 Your earnings are always converted into a weekly figure regardless of your cycle of payment. If you are an employee in regular paid employment with a fixed salary or wage (i.e. if your hours of work and/or your earnings do not fluctuate) then calculating your earnings for CTR is straightforward: your weekly gross earnings are calculated using the period immediately before the claim, adjustments are made for tax, etc, and then the appropriate earnings disregard is applied.

18.21 CTP sch 1 paras 16(3),27,31(3), sch 6 paras 18,21; CTR 39(3), 54(5), 59, 63(3), 64(10), sch 9 paras 18,21, sch 10 para 12

18.22 CTP sch 1 paras 16(1)(b), 24(1)(c),(2), sch 5 para 21; CTR 39(1)(b), 57(1)(c),(2), sch 6 para 21, sch 8 para 58

18.23 CTP sch 1 paras 16(1)(e)-(h),(l), sch 5 paras 1-6; CTR 39(1)(e)-(h),(l), sch 6 paras 1-6, sch 8 paras 13-14,20,53-56

18.26   However, if your hours of work or earnings are variable, or are irregular for some other reason (e.g. absence due to sickness, or your pay contains a bonus or overtime), or you are in self-employment, then special rules apply (para 18.28).

Assessment period: employees with regular earnings

18.27   This is the first stage in assessing income from employment. The aim is to select a period which gives the most accurate reflection of your income. If you have been in regular employment for at least two months at the time when you claim, your hours follow a regular pattern, and your earnings are constant, then your assessment period is:

(a) if you are working age and paid weekly, the five weeks before your claim;

(b) if you are pension age and are paid at intervals less than a month apart (e.g. weekly, fortnightly) the last four payments before your claim;

(c) in any other case (e.g. paid monthly) the last two payment months immediately before the claim; or

(d) some other period if this would produce a fairer result.

Assessment period: employees with fluctuating earnings and self-employed

18.28   In any other case (i.e. if hours or earnings fluctuate or you are self-employed) the guiding principle is that the length of the assessment period is the one that produces the most accurate result according to the following guidelines:

(a) if you have only just started work then the assessment period is based on what you have already been paid, so long as this is representative;

(b) if your hours vary over a recognisable cycle, then the period selected is one complete cycle (including periods where no work is done);

(c) if it would be fairer to do so, or there is as yet no evidence of earnings, the gross earnings are estimated from a certificate of actual or estimated earnings;

(d) if you are self-employed and have been for some time, the assessment period is normally the last year's trading accounts;

(e) if you have been self-employed for less than a year, the assessment period is the period that will produce the most accurate assessment;

(f) if you are just setting up a business, DWP guidance for HB recommends that gross income (and expenses) should be estimated. Awards based on an estimate usually only last a short period (say three months) after which a new assessment is made.

Employee gross earnings

18.29   If you are an employee (i.e. not self-employed) the next stage is always to calculate your gross earnings. Your gross earnings are simply your total earnings (para 18.30) less any work expenses.

18.27   CTP sch 1 paras 17(2)-(4), 20; CTR 40(2)-(4),43,47(1)(a)

18.28   CTP sch 1 paras 17(2)-(3),20; CTR 40(2),(3), 43,47(1)(b),(2),(3)

Employee earnings: elements included in your pay

18.30   Your total earnings comprise all the following elements of your pay:

(a) regular pay;

(b) arrears of pay or earnings paid as a lump sum;

(c) pay for overtime;

(d) bonus, tips or commission;

(e) holiday pay;

(f) a retainer;

(g) statutory sick pay;

(h) statutory maternity, paternity, or adoption pay.

Items (e)-(h) only count as your earnings while you are still employed (i.e. you will return to work); different rules apply if your employment has already ended (see *Guide to Housing Benefit,* chapter 14). Any earnings paid that relate to a period that ended before your CTR award starts are disregarded.

Employee expenses and tax refunds

18.31   The following items are not part of your gross earnings:

(a) expenses that are 'wholly, exclusively and necessarily' incurred as a result of your work (except any travel to work or child care costs, which must be included in your pay);

(b) if you are working age, any tax refund on your earnings (this counts as your capital).

If any items in (a) and (b) above have been included in your pay packet along with the rest of your pay then they must be deducted to arrive at your gross earnings.

Self-employment: gross income (business income)

18.32   Income derived from the business counts as your gross income from self-employment. It is calculated over your assessment period (paras 18.27-28). The following items do not count as income:

(a) grants to the business (they count as unearned income or capital, typically voluntary or charitable);

(b) any payment made under the Access to Work scheme (i.e. setting up work if you are disabled);

(c) a payment to the business, including a loan, such as an investment by a relative, entrepreneur or bank. This is capital and it is disregarded as a business asset (para 18.72);

(d) payments from the New Enterprise Allowance (they count as unearned income but are disregarded).

18.30   CTP sch 1 para 18(1), sch 4 para 9; CTR 41(1), 51(1), sch 5 para 9, sch 7 paras 1(b),2

18.31   CTP sch 1 para 18(2); CTR 41(2), 51(2)

18.32   CTP sch 1 para 21(1); CTR 44(1), 53(1)

Self-employment: allowable business expenses

18.33   Next calculate your business expenses over the same assessment period as your business income (para 18.28). The general rule is that a business expense is allowable (and so deducted from the gross income) if:

(a)   it is wholly and exclusively incurred for the purpose of the business; and

(b)   the authority is satisfied that the amount incurred is reasonable.

A special rule applies for calculating your business expenses if you work as a child minder: two thirds of your earnings are disregarded instead of your actual business expenses.

18.34   Allowable expenditure includes items used in your business that also relate to your private use. In such cases the expenditure is apportioned and so long as the apportionment is reasonable it is allowed. For example, loan repayments (capital and interest) for a family car and expenses for its use (e.g. insurance, VED and fuel). Likewise, if you work from home a proportion of your rent and utility bills are eligible. Any wages you pay your partner out of the business are also allowable (although it will count as their earned income): a different rule applies if you both work in a business partnership (See *Guide to Housing Benefit* for details).

Self-employment: pre-tax profit

18.35   Once you have calculated your business income (para 18.32) and allowable expenses the next stage is to calculate your pre-tax profit. This is simply your business income less allowable business expenses (para 18.33).

Employees and self-employed: net income

18.36   To calculate your net income (called your 'net profit' if you are self-employed) start with your gross earnings if you are an employee (para 18.29), or your pre-tax profit if you are self-employed (para 18.35), and deduct:

(a)   income tax (para 18.37);

(b)   national insurance contributions (para 18.37); and

(c)   half of any contributions you pay into a pension scheme (para 18.39).

In each case the amount deducted is based on the amount paid (or estimated) over the same period used to calculate your gross income (i.e. the assessment period).

Income tax and national insurance

18.37   The amount of income tax and national insurance deducted from your gross earnings/pre-tax profit is:

(a)   if you are an employee and your actual gross earnings have been used (i.e. not estimated) then the amount deducted is the actual amount of tax and national insurance paid over that period;

18.33   CTP sch 1 para 29(2)(a),(3),(6),(8); CTR 61(3)(a),(4),(7),(9)

18.34   CTP sch 1 para 29(2)(a),(3),(6); CTR 61(3)(a),(4),(7)

18.36   CTP sch 1 paras 19(1),(2), 29(1),(2); CTR 42(1),(2), 52(1),(3), 61(1),(3)

18.37   CTP sch 1 paras 19(2),(5), 30; CTR 42(2),(5), 52(3),(6),62

(b) if your earnings have been estimated or you are self-employed a notional amount is deducted for income tax based only on your basic personal allowance and the basic rate of tax (see next paragraph) on a pro-rata basis;

(c) if your earnings have been estimated your national insurance is calculated on those earnings on a pro rata basis;

(d) if you are self-employed the amount of national insurance deducted is based on the class 2 (nil or a flat rate amount) and class 4 contributions calculated on a pro rata basis. In both cases, these are notional amounts based on the method set out in the regulations and so may be different from the actual amount paid.

18.38   If you are self-employed, the notional amounts of tax and national insurance deducted (for the tax year 2016-17) are calculated as follows:

(a) for tax, start with annual pre-tax profit and subtract the basic personal allowance (£11,000 for anyone born after 5th April 1948). If there is any remainder, multiply it by 20%. The result is your notional income tax;

(b) for class 2 national insurance, if the annual pre-tax profit is £5,965 or more, the amount of notional class 2 contributions is £145.60;

(c) for class 4 national insurance, start with the pre-tax profit (or £43,000 if the pre-tax profit is greater) and subtract £8,060. If there is any remainder multiply it by 9%. The result is your notional class 2 contributions.

Pension contributions

18.39   Half of any pension contributions paid over the assessment period are also deducted from your gross earnings (even if your earnings are estimated). It includes payments into a company pension or a personal pension. If you are self-employed it only applies to any regular contributions you make (not to a lump sum).

Net weekly earned income

18.40   Your net earned income over your assessment period (i.e. gross income less tax, etc) is converted into a weekly figure: see paragraph 17.40.

Earned income taken into account

18.41   The amount of your earned income that is taken into account for CTR is your net weekly earned income less any earned income disregard that applies. The earnings disregards applied are as follows (in this order):

(a) if your earnings are paid in a foreign currency – any banking charge or commission paid to convert that sum into GB pounds;

(b) the appropriate standard earnings disregard (para 18.42 and table 18.1);

(c) if it applies, the child care disregard; and

(d) if it applies, the additional earnings disregard.

These are all weekly amounts.

18.39   CTP sch 1 paras 19(2),(4), 29(1),(2),(8),(10); CTR 42(2),(4), 52(3),(5),61(1),(3),(9),(11)

18.41   CTP sch 1 paras 19(1), 24(1),(c), sch 4; CTR 42(1), 52(2),57(1)(c), sch 5, sch 7

The standard earnings disregard

18.42   The standard earnings disregard is always deducted from the net weekly earnings – whether or not any or all of the other disregards apply. The deduction is made once only from the total earned income – regardless of how many sources. For example, if you have a partner and you both work, it is deducted only once from your combined earnings.

18.43   The appropriate earnings disregard is the highest amount that applies in your case of the amounts in table 18.1. Table 18.1 gives the rules for the most common circumstances for each level of disregard. The rules are the same as for HB; for less common circumstances that apply for the £20 standard disregard, see *Guide to Housing Benefit.*

Table 18.1 **Standard earned income disregards**

Your standard earned income disregard is the highest of the following that applies. The qualifying criteria in each case are:

£115.50 per week (disabled – permitted work)

You or your partner receive contribution-based ESA (or national insurance credits in lieu of ESA) and the DWP has allowed you to earn up to the amount of this disregard without it affecting your ESA.

£25 per week (lone parent)

You are a lone parent and qualify for the family premium.

£20 per week (disabled, carers, special occupations)

(a)   you are working age and entitled to at least one of the following in the calculation of your applicable amount: disability premium, severe disability premium, work-related activity component, or support component;

(b)   you are pension age and in receipt of attendance allowance, or main phase ESA, or you would be entitled to a disability premium but for the fact you are pension age;

(c)   you are single or a lone parent and in receipt of carer's allowance;

(d)   you are a member of a couple and receive carer's allowance, but only from the earnings of the member who receives the carer's allowance;

(e)   you or your partner are employed as either a part-time firefighter, auxiliary coast guard, part-time lifeboat worker or as a member of the Territorial Army.

£10 or £5 per week (any other)

In any other case not mentioned above the disregard is

(a)   £10 if you are a member of a couple;

(b)   £5 if you are single.

18.43   CTP sch 1 para 19(1), sch 4 paras 1-8; CTR 42(1), 52(2), sch 5 paras 1-8, sch 7 paras 4-12

T18.1   CTP sch 1 para 19(1), sch 4 paras 1-8; CTR 42(1), 52(2), sch 5 paras 1-8, sch 7 paras 4-12

The child care disregard

18.44   The child care disregard is made to any net earnings that remain after the standard disregard has been applied. As far as possible it is made to your earnings, but if the amount is greater than you and your partner's earnings any balance is deducted from your working tax credit. The amount of the disregard is the total of weekly child care costs you pay up to a maximum of:

(a)   £175.00 if you have child care costs for one child; or

(b)   £300.00 if you have child care costs for two or more children.

You are entitled to the child care disregard if you meet the first and second condition (paras 18.45-46).

18.45   The first condition is that you or your partner pay child care costs to a qualifying child care provider for a child who is:

(a)   aged 14 or under;

(b)   aged 15 until the first Monday in September after their 15th birthday;

(c)   aged 16 until the first Monday in September after their 16th birthday provided they qualify for a disabled child premium.

18.46   The second condition is:

(a)   you are a lone parent and you work 16 hours or more each week;

(b)   you are part of a couple and you both work at least 16 hours each week;

(c)   you are part of a couple and one of you works at least 16 hours and the other is too sick or disabled to work (para 18.47);

(d)   you are part of a couple and one of you works at least 16 hours a week and the other is aged 80 or over;

(e)   you are part of a couple and one of you works at least 16 hours a week and the other is unable to work because they are in prison.

Working 16 hours a week includes periods when you are on statutory sick pay or, in certain circumstances, statutory maternity pay or certain other benefits paid for sickness or maternity. The full conditions are in the *Guide to Housing Benefit*.

18.47   To satisfy 18.46(c) you or your partner count as too sick or disabled to work if you/they:

(a)   receive main phase ESA (i.e. with a work-related or support component);

(b)   receive disability living allowance, personal independence payment, or attendance allowance (or would but for the fact they are currently in hospital);

(c)   receive incapacity benefit at the short-term higher rate or the long-term rate;

(d)   receive severe disablement allowance;

18.44   CTP sch 1 para 24; CTR 57

18.45   CTP sch 1 para 25(5),(6); CTR 58(5),(6)

18.46   CTP sch 1 para 25(1),(2); CTR 58(1),(2)

18.47   CTP sch 1 para 25(1)(c),(10); CTR 58(1)(c),(11)

(e) have been accepted by the DWP as being unfit for, or having limited capacity for work for a period of at least 28 weeks (i.e. get national insurance credits); or

(f) have an NHS invalid vehicle (i.e. in lieu of DLA/PIP).

The additional earnings disregard

18.48 In addition to the standard earned income disregard and child care disregard (if it applies) you are entitled to the additional earnings disregard if you meet the conditions in the next paragraph. The rate of the disregard is £17.10 per week. It is deducted from your/your partner's earnings (after the standard and child care disregard) unless the result would be to produce a negative earnings figure, in which case it is deducted from your working tax credit instead.

18.49 You are entitled to the additional earnings disregard if:

(a) you receive the 30 hour element in your working tax credit award;

(b) you work at least 16 hours per week and are responsible for a child (i.e. receive the family premium);

(c) you are working age, work at least 16 hours per week and your applicable amount includes a disability premium, work-related activity component or support component;

(d) you are aged at least 25 and you work for an average of at least 30 hours per week;

(e) you are pension age, and work at least 16 hours per week and meet the conditions for £20 standard earnings disregard.

'You' here also refers to your partner – but they must meet the condition in full themselves (not part by you and part by your partner). For items (b)-(e) whether you work 16 or 30 hours each week is decided in the same way as for a non-dependant.

Other sources of income

Other unearned income

18.50 Almost any other regular payment that is not earnings, a social security benefit, tax credit, war pension or local authority benefit counts as unearned income. It includes private pensions (e.g. a personal pension or company pension); rental income from property or a lodger; maintenance received for your child or from a partner/former partner; regular payments from charities or from a trust or any regular source of income including student income (grant, loan, etc). But it does not include any income generated from any savings or investments you own: they count as your capital (para 18.67).

18.48 CTP sch 1 para 19(1), sch 4 para 10(1),(3), sch 5 para 21; CTR 42(1),52(2), sch 5 para 10(1),(3), sch 6 para 21, sch 7 para 18(1),(3), sch 8 para 58

18.49 CTP sch 4 para 10(2); CTR sch 5 para 10(2), sch 7 para 18(2)

Local authority cash benefits

18.51   Most local authority cash benefits are disregarded as income including:

(a) discretionary housing payments and the (Scottish) welfare fund;

(b) payments for housing-related support to help you maintain your tenancy ('Supporting People' payments);

(c) 'local welfare provision' or 'occasional assistance' paid to help you

- meet a crisis and avoid harm; or

- avoid entering institutional care (e.g. prison, residential care, hospital) or becoming homeless; or

- to set up home after leaving institutional care;

(d) social services payments made to help avoid your child going into care;

(e) community care payments (including personal budgets and direct payments);

(f) payments for fostering/kinship, adoption or guardianship.

(If you are pension age they are disregarded because they do not count as income.)

Private pensions and annuities etc

18.52   Private pensions count in full as your income for the period it covers (but remember to convert it into a weekly amount). Private pensions include: public sector pensions (e.g. local government); company pensions; payments from the Pension Protection Fund; personal pensions (including NEST for those automatically enrolled) and regular payments from any annuity.

Income from lodgers or renting other property

18.53   Income from lodgers or renting out property that is not your home is treated as follows:

(a) disregard any rent received from a family member or non-dependant;

(b) income from lodgers (people living in your home):

- disregard the first £20.00 for each letting or, if meals are provided, each occupier (e.g. including any child);

- then count only half the remainder as income if you provide meals, or all of the remainder in any other case;

(c) if you are pension age any income from property other than your home is disregarded in full;

(d) If you are working age any income from property other than your home:

- if the property is disregarded as capital (table 18.2) deduct from the gross rent any

---

18.51   CTP sch 1 para 16(1), sch 6 paras 21, 29, 29B
            CTR sch 1 para 16(1), sch 8 paras 30-34, 37,59,64,65, sch 9 paras 21,29 sch 10 paras 12,23-25,61-64

18.52   CTP sch 1 para 16(1)(c),(d),(x); CTR 39(1)(c),(d),(x), 54(1),(2)

18.53   CTP sch 1 para 16(1)(p),(v), sch 5 paras 9,10; CTR 39(1)(p),(v), 54(1),(2), sch 6 paras 9,10, sch 8 paras 26,27

mortgage payments (interest and capital), council tax and water charges (but nothing else) – the result is your income;

■ in any other case, including where the capital value is nil, take the rental income for an appropriate period (e.g. six months, a year) deduct any letting expenses (e.g. agents' fees, repairs, cleaning, council tax, water charges and mortgage repayments, etc). The remainder counts as capital, not as income.

Maintenance received

18.54 If you receive maintenance payments (such as from a former partner) it is counted as follows:

(a) If it is made to support a child the whole amount is disregarded if:

■ you are pension age; or

■ you are working age and the payment is made by a 'liable relative'.

(b) If it is for an adult then the first £15 from all such payments (whether from one or two or more payments) is disregarded but only if there is a child or young person in your family and either:

■ you are working age and the payment is made by your former partner or your partner's former partner; or

■ you are pension age and the payment is made by your former spouse/civil partner or your partner's former spouse or civil partner.

18.55 'Liable relative' means:

(a) you or your partner's spouse or civil partner from whom you/they are separated or divorced;

(b) the parent or step-parent of a child/young person in your family (i.e. a child you or your partner get child benefit for);

(c) a person who is making maintenance payments and who for that reason can reasonably be treated as the father (whether or not this has been settled by the court).

Payments from charities and friends etc

18.56 If you receive a regular income from a charity or on a voluntary basis (e.g. from a relative or friend) these are completely disregarded (a different rule applies to a lump sum, i.e. capital).

Payments from a trust

18.57 Regular payments from a private trust (i.e. one where you are named as a beneficiary) count in full as your income unless the payments are for a personal injury (see next paragraph) or, if you are pension age, the trust is discretionary (see *Guide to Housing Benefit* for details).

18.54   CTP sch 1 para 16(1)(o), sch 5 para 20; CTR 39(1)(o), sch 6 para 20, sch 8 paras 49,50

18.55   CTR sch 8 para 50(2)

18.56   CTP sch 1 para 16(1); CTR 39(1),64(7), sch 8 para 19

Personal injury payments

18.58　　Payments of income for a personal injury, including payments from a trust, are disregarded in full. For lump sum awards see paragraph 18.75.

Government supported special trust funds

18.59　　Payments from certain government-created trusts to compensate you if you have contracted certain diseases are disregarded in full as income and capital (para 18.76) as follows:

(a) if you have contracted Variant Creutzfeldt-Jacob Disease (the Variant Creutzfeldt-Jacob Disease Trust);

(b) if you have been infected through NHS blood products with HIV, haemophilia or hepatitis C (Caxton Fund, Eileen Trust, Macfarlane Trust, MFET Ltd, Skipton Fund, and their successor trusts). In certain circumstances these payments may also be disregarded if you have received the payment from a relative as a gift or inheritance (see the *Guide to Housing Benefit*).

18.60　　Payments from the independent living fund and London Bombings Charitable Relief Fund are also disregarded as income and capital.

Expenses for voluntary work

18.61　　Expenses for unpaid work (whether for a charity, voluntary organisation or friend, etc) are disregarded as are expenses paid to you as a member of a service user group (e.g. a health authority or social landlord).

Student income

18.62　　If you are a student there are special rules about how your income from grants, loans and other sources is treated (e.g. elements that are disregarded and the period over which these are calculated). These rules are same as for HB (*Guide to Housing Benefit,* chapters 13 and 22) but most students are in any case excluded from CTR (para 16.45).

Capital

18.63　　This section describes how your capital is taken into account in the calculation of your CTR. Paragraphs 18.64-69 describe general rules about how your capital is taken into account and valued. Paragraphs 18.70 onwards describe the rules for specific items of capital where the whole or part of its value is disregarded – only the most common items have been included. For less common items see the *Guide to Housing Benefit*.

18.58　　CTP sch 5 paras 14,15; CTR sch 6 paras 14,15, sch 8 para 19

18.59　　CTP sch 1 para 16(1); CTR 39(1),64(7), sch 8 para 41

18.61　　CTP sch 1 para 18(2)(f); CTR 41(2)(f), 51(2)(d), sch 8 paras 5,6

18.62　　CTR 24, 75-86

18.64   Your capital is assessed to determine whether you are entitled to CTR. If your capital is above the 'upper capital limit' then you are not entitled to CTR (para 16.20). If your capital is assessed as being below the 'lower capital limit' then your tariff income is zero and the amount of CTR you receive is unaffected (i.e. it is calculated using your actual income only). The lower capital limit is:

(a)   £6,000 if you are working age;

(b)   £10,000 if you are pension age.

18.65   If you have capital that is valued between 'the lower capital limit' and 'the upper capital limit' then your capital is converted into a hypothetical income figure (the 'tariff income') and added to any other income in your assessment. Your tariff income is calculated as follows:

(a)   If you are working age deduct £6,000 from the total and divide the remainder by 250.

(b)   If you are pension age deduct £10,000 and divide the remainder by 500.

(c)   Then, in either case, if the result is not an exact multiple of £1, round the result up to the next whole £1. This is your weekly tariff income.

18.66   Any capital held wholly by you or your partner or both of you together is described in the next two paragraphs. However, if your capital is jointly owned with someone else, you must first work out your share (or deemed share) and then value that share in the same way.

Valuing capital: straightforward cases (savings and cash etc)

18.67   In many cases valuing capital is straightforward. The value of the capital is simply the current cash value. This applies to the following:

(a)   any savings (in UK sterling) held in a bank or savings account;

(b)   National Savings Certificates. These are valued at their current value rather than the face value purchase price (which can be calculated online [www]);

(c)   Premium Bonds (at face value);

(d)   any other item held in cash, whether or not in an account.

Valuing items: other than savings

18.68   In any other case, any capital that you own that is not in cash or UK sterling (e.g. property, stocks and shares, foreign currency) is valued as follows:

(a)   take the current market value or surrender value of the item;

(b)   deduct 10% if selling the item or converting into UK sterling would involve costs;

(c)   then disregard any debt or charge secured against it (e.g. a mortgage if the item is property) (but not any other debts you may have such as rent arrears).

18.64   CTP sch 1 paras 24(1)(b),37; CTR 57(1)(b),71,72

18.65   CTP sch 1 paras 24(1)(b),37; CTR 57(1)(b),71,72

18.67   CTP sch 1 para 32; CTR 65
         www.nsandi.com/savings-index-linked-savings-certificates-calculator

18.68   CTP sch 1 para 32; CTR 65

Table 18.2 **Capital: the value of your home and former home**

The value of your home or former home can be disregarded as capital. The circumstances are described below.

(a) **The home you occupy.** The value of the dwelling you normally occupy as your home is disregarded in full without any time limit.

(b) **Your partner's home if you are living apart but still a couple.** If you and your partner are currently living as separate households but are still committed to each other (i.e. not divorced, separated or estranged, etc) then the value of their home is disregarded.

(c) **Your home or former home following a relationship breakdown.** if you have divorced your partner or become estranged the value of your former home is disregarded if:

- your ex-partner is now a lone parent and continues to live in the property; or

- in any other case, for up to 26 weeks from the date it ceased to be occupied.

(d) **The home of a disabled or elderly relative.** The value your partner's home or any relative of a family member is disregarded provided they are pension age or incapacitated.

(e) **A home you have recently purchased.** The value of any property you intend to occupy is disregarded for up to 26 weeks or such longer period as is reasonable.

(f) **A home you are taking steps to obtain possession of.** The value of any home you are taking steps to obtain possession of (e.g. from squatters or an abusive ex-partner) is disregarded for up to 26 weeks or such longer period as is reasonable.

(g) **A home that requires repairs etc, to make it fit to live in.** If your home requires essential repairs or alterations to make it fit to live in, it is disregarded for up to 26 weeks from the date you first take steps to make it habitable, or such longer period as is reasonable.

(h) **Money from selling your home (working age).** If you are working age any money from selling your home is disregarded for up to 26 weeks (or longer if it is reasonable) but only if you intend to use it to buy a new home. Money from selling includes money received as compensation for compulsory purchase for the home's market value together with any home loss payment intended to be used for the same purpose.

T18.2(a) CTP sch 6 para 26; CTR sch 9 para 26, sch 10 para 4

T18.2(b) CTP sch 6 para 4(b); CTR sch 9 para 4(b), sch 10 para 7(b)

T18.2(c) CTP sch 6 para 6; CTR sch 9 para 6, sch 10 para 30

T18.2(d) CTP sch 6 para 4(a); CTR sch 9 para 4(a), sch 10 para 7(a)

T18.2(e) CTP sch 6 para 1; CTR sch 9 para 1, sch 10 para 5

T18.2(f) CTP sch 6 para 2; CTR sch 9 para 2, sch 10 para 32

T18.2(g) CTP sch 6 para 3; CTR sch 9 para 3, sch 10 para 33

(i) **Money deposited with a housing association (working age).** If you are working age any money deposited with a housing association to obtain a home is disregarded for as long as it remains deposited, or if that money is refunded for up to 26 weeks or longer if reasonable, but only if it is intended to be used to buy another home.

(j) **Money received for buying a home (pension age).** If you are pension age any payments received for the sole purpose of buying a home are disregarded for one year. This is wider than the rule for working age claims (h). For example, it can include the proceeds from a sale but also money gifted or loaned by a relative for that purpose.

(k) **A property you have rented out.** The value of any home you have rented out counts as capital except:

  ■ if it forms part of a business it is disregarded as a business asset; or

  ■ in any other case, the fact that it is occupied may mean its market value is reduced (i.e. its sale value with a sitting tenant) CH/1953/2003.

Note: These conditions may apply simultaneously – or one after another – so long as the relevant conditions are met.

Valuing capital jointly held

18.69   If you own an item of capital jointly with someone other than your partner, you must first determine your share before valuing it as above. If the item owned is held in distinct known shares (e.g. one person holds a one third share and the other two thirds) then it is your actual share that is valued. It is the market value of your share itself (i.e. what would someone be prepared to pay – knowing the remainder is held by someone else) that is valued, not the whole item pro rata. This may mean that the actual share itself has very little value. In any other case (i.e. if the shares are not known) it is assumed that you and all the other owners each hold an equal share.

Arrears of social security benefits and tax credits

18.70   Arrears of social security benefits count as capital if they are still unspent at the end of the period they were paid for, but arrears of tax credits count as capital from the date the payment is received. However, any capital from tax credits arrears or any of the social security benefits (a)-(f) in paragraph 18.18 are disregarded for 52 weeks, or longer if they are large arrears of a passport benefit that was paid late due to official error. 'Large arrears' in this case means £5,000 or more.

T18.2(h) CTR sch 10 para 6

T18.2(i)   CTR sch 10 para 14

T18.2(j)   CTP sch 6 para 18; CTR sch 9 paras 18,20(a)

T18.2(k) CTP sch 6 paras 5,9,10; CTR sch 9 paras 5,9,10, sch 10 paras 10,11

18.69   CTP sch 1 para 36; CTR 70

18.70   CTP sch 1 para 31(3), sch 6 paras 18,21,22; CTR 63(3),64(10), sch 9 paras 18,21,22, sch 10 para 12

Personal possessions

18.71   The value of any personal possessions (e.g. jewellery, art) you hold is ignored. However, if you are working age and you purchased those items in order to dispose of your capital and increase your CTR award, then they can be taken into account.

Business assets

18.72   The value of the assets of a business that is wholly or partly owned by you are disregarded so long as you are engaged in self-employment in that business – including for up 26 weeks or longer if reasonable if you are unable to work due to sickness. If you have stopped working, the business assets are also disregarded for as long as is reasonably needed for their disposal.

Life insurance and annuities etc

18.73   The surrender value of any life insurance policy you hold is ignored. But any money you receive from the policy counts as your capital. The capital value of any money invested in an annuity is also disregarded (although any income it generates is counted as your income).

Compulsory purchase compensation

18.74   Compensation for the market value of your home is disregarded for up to 26 weeks. Home loss payments count in full as part of your capital unless you intend to use the payment to purchase a new home. (See rules in table 18.2 for both items.)

Compensation for personal injury and special trusts

18.75   If you receive a lump sum payment for a personal injury, including from a trust, the payment is disregarded for up to 52 weeks, or without any time limit if you are pension age. If more than one payment is made, the 52 week time limit runs from the date of the first payment. Any lump sum payments you receive for a personal injury that are held in a trust are disregarded in full without time limit (whether you are pension age or working age).

18.76   If you receive a lump sum from any of the special trusts in paragraph 18.59, it is disregarded in full, including in certain circumstances if it has been passed on to you as a gift or an inheritance from a relative (see the *Guide to Housing Benefit* for further details).

18.71   CTP sch 6 para 8; CTR sch 9 para 8, sch 10 para 15

18.72   CTP sch 6 paras 9,10; CTR sch 9 paras 9,10 sch 10 para 11

18.73   CTP sch 6 paras 11,24,32; CTR sch 9 paras 11,24,32

18.75   CTP sch 6 para 17; CTR sch 9 para 17

18.76   CTP sch 6 para 16; CTR sch 9 para 16, sch 10 para 29

Chapter 19 **Applying for council tax rebate**

- Who can apply for council tax rebate and how to apply: see paras 19.1- 9.
- The information and evidence needed: see paras 19.10-15.
- How complete and incomplete applications are dealt with: see paras 19.16-21.
- Date of application: see paras 19.22-36.
- Backdating: see paras 19.37-44.
- When 'awards' start: see paras 19.45-51.

Who can apply

19.1 Normally you only get council tax rebate if you apply for it. This is your responsibility. In CTR law you are called the 'applicant'. You can ask anyone you like to help you fill in the application form.

People who were on CTB or a Welsh CTR scheme adopted under the 2012 rules

19.2 If you were on CTB on 31st March 2013, or made a CTB claim which was not decided by that date, you should have been treated as having applied for CTR from 1st April 2013. Also in Wales transitional rules enable an award (or application) to be transferred from a council's CTR scheme adopted under the 2012 rules (a 2013 scheme) to the new scheme (2014 onwards) adopted by the council.

Couples

19.3 If you have a partner or are in a polygamous marriage you or a partner can make the application. In practice both you and any partner may be asked to sign the form. You can choose between you who is going to apply but if you can't agree, the council must choose. In some circumstance you are better off if one of you rather than the other is the applicant. These circumstances are identified in this guide as they arise (e.g. paras 16.31, 17.59).

Unable to act

19.4 Someone else can apply for CTR on your behalf if you are unable, for the time being, to act. This other person takes over all rights and responsibilities in relation to the CTR application and any award. (The rules in paras 19.5-6 apply to CTR in England and Wales. Though they are not contained in the CTR law in Scotland, similar principles apply.)

19.1   LGFA sch 1A para 2(5); CTP 15, sch 7 paras 1-7, 10-16, sch 8 para 4; CTR 11, 109, sch 1 paras 1-7, 12-18

19.2   LGFA sch 1A para 9; SI 2013 No 215, 2; CTPW 37-40

19.3   CTP sch 8 para 4(1); CTR 109(1)

19.4   CTP sch 8 para 4(2)-(7); CTR 109(2)-(6)

19.5   Where one of the following has been appointed to act for you, the council must accept an application from them:

(a) a receiver or deputy appointed by the Court of Protection;

(b) an attorney;

(c) in Scotland, a judicial factor or any guardian acting or appointed under the Adults with Incapacity (Scotland) Act 2000; or

(d) a person appointed by the DWP to act on your behalf in connection with some other benefit.

19.6   In any other case, the council may accept a written request from someone over 18, or a firm or organisation, to be your 'appointee' – for example, a friend or relative, a social worker or solicitor. In doing this the council should take account of any conflict of interests. Once appointed, your appointee has all the rights and responsibilities that normally belong to you. Either the council or the appointee can end the appointment by giving four weeks' written notice.

How to apply

Applications made to the council

19.7   You, or someone acting on your behalf (para 19.4), should make your application for CTR to the council that issues your council tax bill (para 15.2). Many councils accept CTR applications by telephone or online; and can require you to approve a written statement of a telephone application, or keep written or electronic records of an online application. In all other cases, CTR applications must be in writing to a 'designated office'. This is the address of the office(s) the council has identified on the form for the receipt of applications. Application forms must be provided free of charge and give the address of every designated office and optionally an online address.

19.8   If you make a claim to the DWP for JSA, ESA, IS, UC or pension credit (or IB when it is linked to a former claim) you may be asked if you want to apply for CTR. If you do the DWP may send relevant information to the council. But this is not an application for CTR. Your application for CTR should be made direct to the council (DCLG – *Localising council tax support administrative matters – guidance note* (March 2013 paras 10-12)) [www].

Amending or withdrawing your application

19.9   Before a decision is made on your application, you may:

(a) amend it: the change is treated as having been made from the outset;

(b) withdraw it: the council is then under no duty to decide it.

You can amend or withdraw a telephone application on the phone or in writing. If you phone the council you may be asked to confirm matters in writing. You must amend or withdraw other applications by writing to the council's designated office.

19.5   CTP sch 8 para 4(2)-(7); CTR 109(2)-(6)

19.6   CTP sch 8 para 4(3),(5)-(6); CTR 109(3), (5)-(6)

19.7   CTP 2(1) 'designated office', sch 7 paras 2-3, 11-13; CTR 2(1), sch 1 paras 2-3,13-14

19.8   https://www.gov.uk/government/publications/localising-support-for-council-tax-guidance-note-on-administrative-matters

Information and evidence

19.10   You are responsible for providing 'certificates, documents, information and evidence' which are 'reasonably required by the council in order to determine… entitlement' to CTR. This applies when you make an application, and also during the course of an award. The council should only get evidence direct from someone else with your written agreement but you usually give this in the declaration you make when you apply.

19.11   The law does not specify (except as described in paras 19.12-14) what information and evidence is required in relation to particular matters. In practice authorities require evidence about your household members and their status, income and capital (if you are not on a passport benefit), and other matters; and expect you to provide original documents rather than copies. In written applications, your signature is a reasonable requirement, and many authorities also require a partner's signature.

Information you need not tell the council about

19.12   The council cannot require any information or evidence whatsoever about the following types of payment, whether they are made to you, your partner, a non-dependant or a second adult:

(a)   payments from the Macfarlane Trusts, the Eileen Trust, MFET Ltd, the Skipton Fund, the Caxton Fund, the Fund or the London Bombing Charitable Relief Fund, and in certain cases payments derived from these sources;

(b)   payments in kind of capital from a charity or from the above sources;

(c)   payments in kind of income from any source.

National Insurance numbers

19.13   You must either:

(a)   provide your National Insurance (NI) number and the NI number of your partner, along with information or evidence establishing this; or

(b)   provide information or evidence enabling the council to ascertain it; or

(c)   make an application for an NI number and give information or evidence to assist with this – even if it is highly improbable that one will be granted: CH/4085/2007.

19.14   There are two exceptions:

(a)   the rule does not apply in certain cases where your partner is a foreign national and has not previously been allocated an NI number;

(b)   in Scotland the rule is not included in CTR law.

Matters relating to the provision of an NI number are appealable, including the evidence needed to ascertain one: CH/1231/2004; and the consequences in a CTR decision of a refusal to allocate one: 2009 UKUT 74 (ACC).

19.9   CTP sch 8 para 8; CTR 114

19.10   CTP sch 8 para 7(1),(4),(6); CTR 113(1),(4),(6)

19.12   CTP sch 8 para 7(5),(7); CTR 113(5),(7)

19.13   CTP sch 8 para 7(2),(3); CTR 113(2),(3)

19.15   If you have been lawfully awarded a passport benefit by the DWP, this is binding on the council as proof that (at the relevant dates) you meet the income-related conditions for getting maximum CTR: R v Penwith District Council ex parte Menear and R v South Ribble Council Housing Benefit Review Board. If you have been lawfully awarded savings credit or UC, certain figures are also binding on the council (paras 17.9 and 18.6).

Complete and incomplete applications

A complete application

19.16   Your application is complete if it is made:

(a) in writing or online and is on an application form approved by the council and completed in accordance with the instructions on the form – including any instructions to provide information and evidence;

(b) in some other written form which the council accepts as sufficient in the circumstances of a particular case or class of cases, having regard to whether the information and evidence provided with it is sufficient;

(c) by telephone and you provide the information and evidence needed to decide it.

Dealing with complete applications

19.17   A complete application (also sometimes called an 'effective' or 'valid' application) must be decided by the council.

Dealing with incomplete applications

19.18   An incomplete application (sometimes called a 'defective' application) is one which the council gets but which does not meet the conditions in para 19.16. The council should give you the opportunity of doing whatever is needed to make it complete. Depending on the circumstances, this could mean the council:

(a) sending you an application form;

(b) returning a form to you for completion; or

(c) asking you for information and evidence (or further information and evidence).

In all cases, the council must also inform you of your duty to tell it about relevant changes of circumstances which occur, and say what these are likely to be.

19.19   The council must allow you at least one month to provide what is required (para 19.23), and you must be allowed longer if it is reasonable to do so. In the case of telephone applications, the law specifically permits more than one reminder, and the month is counted from the last such reminder. In the case of written and online applications, some authorities send a reminder, allowing a further period for the reply. In all these cases, if you do what is required within the time limit, your application is treated as having been complete from the outset.

19.15   R v Penwith DC ex p Menear 11/10/91 QBD 24 HLR 115;
         R v South Ribble HBRB ex p Hamilton 24/01/00 CA [2000] EWCA Civ 518 www.bailii.org/cases/EWCA/Civ/2000/518.html

19.16   CTP sch 7 paras 2-4,11; CTR sch 1 paras 2-4,13

19.18   CTP sch 7 paras 4-7, sch 8 paras 5(3)-(5),7(4),(6); CTR 110(3)-(5), 113(4),(6), sch 1 paras 4-7

Deciding incomplete applications

19.20　　Even if your application remains incomplete it must be decided by the council. In such cases, the council may:

(a) decide that you are not entitled to CTR because you do not satisfy the conditions of entitlement, as you have not provided the necessary information or evidence; or

(b) make a negative inference (which means it 'assumes the worst') in order to make its decision. For example, if your bank statement shows that you withdrew £20,000 three weeks ago, and you refuse to explain this, it might be reasonable to decide that your capital remains at £20,000. In each case, you may appeal.

Applications not received

19.21　　The council can't decide an application that it hasn't received – for example an application form which is lost in the post. An (attempted) telephone application in which you do not answer all the questions, or fail to approve a written statement if asked to do so, is treated as 'not received' – but in this case the council may nonetheless decide it. An (attempted) online application which the council's computer does not accept or which is not in the form approved (para 19.7) is treated as 'not received'. In all these cases, if you apply for CTR again, the council should consider whether the conditions for backdating are met (para 19.37).

Date of application

19.22　　When your CTR starts depends on your date of application. The rules about what counts as your 'date of application' are summarised in table 19.1. Further details follow.

Definition of 'month'

19.23　　Many of the rules in this guide refer to allowing you a 'month' to do something in connection with an application, etc. This means a calendar month, and the month is counted as follows (R(IB) 4/02):

(a) if the council sends out a letter on 26th June asking you to provide something, you have provided it within a month if you get it to the council by the end of 26th July;

(b) if the council sends out a letter on 31st January asking you to provide something, you have provided it within a month if you get it to the council by the end of 28th (or 29th) February.

Things sent out by the council (such as requests for information or evidence, decision letters) are counted in the law as being sent out on the date of posting. Things received by the council (such as CTR application forms, information and evidence) are counted in the law as received on the date of receipt. In the case of online communications, this is the date recorded by the computer as the date of sending or receipt unless the council reasonably directs otherwise.

19.21　　CTP sch 7 paras 3,11(7); CTR sch 1 paras 3,13(7)

19.22　　CTP sch 8 para 5; CTR 110

19.23　　CTP sch 7 para 13; CTR sch 1 para 15

Table 19.1 **Date of CTR application: summary**

Situation	Date of application
You asked for a form (or told the council about your an intention to apply) and return it, properly completed, within one month of when it was sent out (or longer if reasonable).	The date you asked for the form or told the council about your intention to apply.
Within the last month your partner has died or you have separated and they were on CTR at the time.	The date of death or separation.
You or your partner were awarded JSA(IB), ESA(IR), IS, guarantee credit or UC and the council gets your CTR application within one month from when the claim for that benefit was received.	The date you or your partner were first entitled to JSA(IB), ESA(IR), IS, guarantee credit or UC.
You or a partner are on JSA(IB), ESA(IR), IS or guarantee credit and the CTR application is received within a month of you or your partner first becoming liable for council tax.	The date of liability for council tax.
In any other case.	The date the CTR application is received by the council.

Definition of 'reduction week'

19.24   Many of the rules in this guide refer to a 'reduction week' as it is known in CTR law. This begins on a Monday and ends on the following Sunday.

Telling the council about an intention to apply

19.25   This rule applies if:

(a) you told the council about your intention to apply for CTR;

(b) it sent you an application form; and

(c) you returned the form within one month of when it was sent out (or longer if the council considers this reasonable).

19.26   In this case, the date of application is the date you told the office in question about your intention to apply for CTR. You can do this 'by any means' (which includes telephoning, emailing, writing, texting, visiting or sending a friend: CIS/2726/2005).

T19.1   CTP sch 8 para 5; CTR 110

19.24   CTP 2(1) definition: 'reduction week'; CTR 2(1)

19.25   CTP sch 8 para 5(1)(f); CTR 110(1)(f)

Application following your partner's death or separation

19.27   This rule applies if:

(a) you apply for CTR within one month of your partner's death or of your separation; and

(b) your partner was on CTR at the date of death or separation.

19.28   In this case, the date of application is the date of the separation or death in question, the intention being that there should be no gap in entitlement to CTR. The one month time limit cannot be extended, but in some cases backdating should be considered (para 19.42).

On a passport benefit or UC

19.29   This rule applies if:

(a) you, or a partner, claim and are awarded a passport benefit (JSA(IB), ESA(IR), IS or guarantee credit) or UC; and

(b) your CTR application gets to the council no more than one month after the passport benefit or universal credit claim was received by the DWP.

19.30   In this case, the date of application for CTR is the date of first entitlement to the passport benefit (and in the case of JSA(IB) and ESA(IR) this means the first 'waiting day') or to UC. The one month time limit cannot be extended.

On a passport benefit and now liable for council tax

19.31   This rule applies if:

(a) you or your partner are getting a passport benefit (para 19.29); and

(b) you become liable for council tax for the first time; and

(c) your CTR application gets to the council no more than one month after the new liability begins.

19.32   In this case the date of application for CTR is the first day of your new liability for council tax. The one month time limit cannot be extended.

Other applications

19.33   This rule applies if none of the earlier rules applies (but see also para 19.37). In this case, the date of application is the day the application is received at the designated office.

Advance applications

19.34   The following rule (para 19.35) operates if you apply for:

(a) CTR up to 17 weeks before you reach pension credit age (para 16.13); or

(b) CTR up to 17 weeks before an event which makes you entitled to CTR (pension age applicants); or

---

19.27   CTP sch 8 para 5(1)(e); CTR 110(1)(e)

19.29   CTP sch 8 para 5(1)(a),(c),(2),(8); CTR 110(1)(a),(c),(2),(8)

19.31   CTP sch 8 para 5(1)(b),(d); CTR 110(1),(b),(d)

19.33   CTP sch 8 para 5(1)(g); CTR 110(1)(g)

19.34   CTP sch 8 para 5(6),(7); CTR 110(6),(7)

(c) CTR up to 13 weeks before an event which makes you entitled to CTR (working age applicants); or

(d) CTR up to eight weeks before you become liable for council tax.

Rules (c) and (d) do not, however, apply to you if you are a migrant or new arrival (para 16.31).

19.35   The date of application, in cases (a)-(c) above, is any date in the week before the reduction week (para 19.24) containing the birthday or event in question: in case (d) above, the date of first liability for council tax.

Delays in setting council taxes in Scotland

19.36   This rule applies, in Scotland only, when:

(a) a council delays setting its council tax until after 31st March; and

(b) your CTR application is made within four weeks after the council tax is set.

In this case, the date of application for CTR is set so that entitlement begins on 1st April in that year (or the reduction week in which your entitlement begins if this falls between 1st April and the date the application is received).

Backdating

19.37   Your CTR can be backdated to cover periods in the past. The main rules are as follows:

(a) for pension age CTR applications backdating for up to three months is automatic (para 19.40);

(b) for working age CTR applications, backdating rules vary across Great Britain (para 19.42).

'Pension age' vs 'working age' applicants

19.38   Pension age and working age applicants are defined in paragraphs 16.13-15 and table 16.2. In CTR only, some couples meet both definitions, so whether (or for how long) they qualify for backdated CTR can depend on which of them is the applicant (para 16.13).

19.39   The following points apply to both age groups:

(a) It is the date of application which is backdated. So even if you are not currently entitled to CTR a backdated award can still be made.

(b) When CTR is backdated it is calculated using the rules which applied at the relevant times. Entitlement during the backdated period need not have been continuous or at the same address (or even, arguably, in the same council's area).

(c) Basing an application for CTR on a form which was (on the balance of probability) received by the council, but then mislaid or not acted on, is not backdating (because in fact an application was made).

19.36   CTS 85(4); CTS60+ 65(4)

Backdating CTR for pension age applicants

19.40 If you are of pension age an application for CTR covers any period in the three months before the day the council actually gets it (or the day you notified your intention to apply, so long as you followed that up within the relevant time limits: paras 19.25-26) – but only back to the day you reached pension credit age, or the day you became liable for council tax, if this is later.

19.41 You do not have to ask for this rule to apply, and you do not have to have 'good cause' (or any reason whatsoever): the rule applies automatically.

Example: Backdating for a pension age applicant

An applicant aged 73 sends in his first ever application for CTR. It reaches the council on Friday 9th September 2016. He would have qualified for several years for a small amount of CTR had he applied.

His date of application is Friday 10th June 2016, which is three months earlier, and (unless the week-one-yes rule applies: para 19.49) the first day of his entitlement to CTR is the following Monday, 13th June 2016 (but see para 19.48 for Wales).

Backdating CTR for working age applicants

19.42 For working age CTR applicants (para19.38), the rules about backdating vary:

(a) In Scotland CTR must be backdated for up to one month (from 1st April 2016 – before this date the period had been six months) if you ask for this in writing (whether on the council's application form or separately later); and 'had continuous good cause for your failure to make an application' (as described in paras 19.43-44).

(b) In Wales, the CTR backdating rules are usually the same as for Scotland but with a time limit of three months. However authorities may extend (or reduce) this time limit and vary the backdating rules in other ways (para 16.11).

(c) In England, it is up to each council to decide what provisions, if any, to make about backdating CTR (para 16.5). For example, some authorities allow backdating for 'good cause' for up to six months, and some have no backdating (but may consider making a discretionary council tax reduction instead: para 15.22).

'Good cause'

19.43 Good cause has been explained by tribunals and courts right back to the late 1940s, and this case law is binding: CH/5221/2001. The following are the main principles.

19.44 Good cause includes 'any fact that would probably have caused a reasonable person to act as the claimant did', but they are expected to take reasonable steps to ascertain what their rights may be. However, 'claimants cannot always be assumed to have an understanding of public administration' (CS/371/1949, quoted with approval in CH/450/2004). However, this

---

19.40   CTP sch 8 para 6; CTR 111

19.42   CTS 85(7),(8), CTRW 110, CTPW 4, CTR 112

'traditional formulation' has more recently been criticised ([2010] UKUT 64 (ACC)) because:

(a) it does not reflect the language of the regulations;

(b) it introduces subjective elements while what is 'reasonable' is objective;

(c) though ignorance of itself is not good cause, it may be a factor to be taken into account. The law does not 'require a person to be acquainted with the "rules and regulations".'

When CTR starts

Overview

19.45   CTR starts on the Monday following your 'date of application' (or for CTR in Wales only, on the date of application). But if the 'week-one-yes rule' applies, it can start earlier. The details follow. The main rules are:

(a) the 'date of application' usually means the date you first told the council about your intention to apply for CTR – but it can be earlier (paras 19.25-32);

(b) the 'week-one-yes rule' applies if you become liable for council tax on your new home (para 19.49).

Duration of award

19.46   There is no fixed limit to your award of CTR. Your entitlement may change if there is a change in circumstances (para 20.10). Otherwise it simply continues until you stop being entitled – for example, gain too much capital or income, die or become an ineligible student (para 20.24).

First day of entitlement: the general rule

19.47   The general rule is that your first day of entitlement to CTR is the Monday following your 'date of application' (paras 19.22-36). Even if your date of application is a Monday, your first day of entitlement is the following Monday. The exceptions follow.

CTR in Wales

19.48   For CTR in Wales only, the general rule is that your first day of entitlement to CTR is your 'date of application' (paras 19.22-34), whichever day of the week it falls on; and the 'week-one-yes rule' (see below) does not apply.

The week-one-yes rule

19.49   The week-one-yes rule applies only if you or your partner become liable for council tax in the reduction week (para 19.24) containing your 'date of application'. In such cases, your entitlement begins on the day your liability for council tax begins, whichever day of the week that falls on. (It does not apply to CTR in Wales: para 19.48.)

19.45   CTP 45(1),(2); CTR 106(1),(2)

19.47   CTP 45(1); CTR 106(1)

19.48   CTPW sch 1 para 39; CTRW 104

19.49   CTP 45(2); CTR 106(2)

Examples: First day of entitlement

The general rule

A man applies for CTR because his income has reduced. His date of application is Thursday 14th July 2016.

His first day of entitlement to CTR is the Monday following his date of application, which is Monday 18th July 2016.

The week-one-yes rule: whole weeks

A woman moves into her flat on Monday 4th July 2016, and is liable for council tax from that very day. Her date of application is Thursday 7th July 2016.

Her first day of entitlement to CTR is the day her liability for council tax begins, which is Monday 4th July 2016.

The week-one-yes rule: part weeks

A woman moves into her flat on Saturday 4th June 2016, and is liable for council tax from that very day. Her date of application is Friday 3rd June 2016.

Her first day of entitlement to CTR is the day her liability for council tax begins, which is Saturday 4th June 2016. In her first week she gets two-sevenths of a week's CTR (for the Saturday and the Sunday).

The week-one-yes rule: applicant does not move in immediately

A man has been living with relatives (and not liable for council tax there). He obtains a tenancy which starts on Monday 30th May 2016. He does not fully move in until Wednesday 1st June 2016, and that is the night he starts sleeping there. His date of application for CTR is Thursday 2nd June 2016.

His first day of entitlement to CTR depends on when he is regarded for council tax purposes as becoming liable for council tax. Practice varies, but it is likely to be Monday 30th May 2016 or Wednesday 1st June 2016.

Note: The examples differ for CTR in Wales (para 19.48).

Payments of CTR

19.50 Payment of CTR is normally in the form of a rebate (credit) to your council tax account. This reduces your overall liability for the tax. Any resulting credit on your council tax account may be refundable. The DCLG advises this can be done 'where, for example, [the applicant] is no longer liable for council tax' (*Localising council tax support,* November 2012, para 23).

19.51 However, in England and Wales only, the council may pay CTR directly to you if:

(a) you are jointly liable for council tax; and

(b) awarding CTR as a rebate 'would be inappropriate'.

If you are unable to act, this payment can be made to an appointee, etc.

19.50   LGFA 10(1),13A; CTPW sch 13 para 10(1); CTRW 116(1)

19.51   CTP sch 8 para 14; CTR 118

Chapter 20 **CTR changes to entitlement**

- Duty to tell the council about changes of circumstances: see paras 20.2-6.
- How changes are dealt with: see paras 20.7-8.
- When changes take effect: see paras 20.9-26.
- Extended reductions and continuing reductions: see paras 20.27-36.
- Reviewing awards of CTR: see paras 20.37-41.
- Fraud and penalties: see paras 20.42-46.

20.1   Your entitlement to CTR can change or end. Decisions change when there is a relevant change in your circumstances, or the circumstances of someone else relevant to your CTR entitlement such as a household member, or in the law itself (paras 20.9-36). They can also change when the council reviews entitlement (paras 20.37-38) or as a result of the disputes and appeals procedures.

Duty to tell the council about relevant changes

20.2   You must tell the council about any 'relevant' change of circumstances. The same duty applies to anyone acting for you (paras 19.4-6). This means any change that you (or the other person) could reasonably be expected to know might affect:

(a) your entitlement to CTR; or

(b) the amount of CTR you get.

This duty to notify begins on the date your application is made, and continues for as long as you are getting CTR. (For time limits etc, see paras 20.5-6.)

20.3   The law lists changes that you must tell the council about and changes that you don't have to notify (summarised in tables 20.1 and 20.2). These are not exhaustive. For example, you should also tell the council of changes in your:

(a) personal details (name, address, etc);

(b) family and household details (which could affect the applicable amount or non-dependant deductions); and

(c) capital and income.

20.2   CTP sch 8 para 9(1),(6); CTR 115(1),(6)

Table 20.1 **Changes you must tell the council about**

The following is a list of the items specifically mentioned in the law. Your duty is wider (paras 20.2-3).

If you are a working age applicant

(a) The end of your (or your partner's) entitlement to JSA(IB), ESA(IR), IS or UC.

(b) Your child or young person stops being a member of the family: e.g. when child benefit stops or they leave your household.

If you are a pension age applicant

(a) A non-dependant moves in or out or their income changes.

(b) Absences exceeding or likely to exceed 13 weeks.

Additional matters if you are on savings credit

(a) Changes affecting any child living with you (other than age) which might affect the amount of CTR.

(b) Changes to your capital which take it (or may take it) above £16,000.

(c) Changes to a non-dependant if their income and capital was treated as being yours.

(d) Changes to a partner who was ignored in assessing savings credit but is taken into account for CTR.

Additional matters if you are on second adult rebate

(a) Changes in the number of adults in your home.

(b) Changes in the total gross incomes of the adults in your home.

(c) The date any adult in your home stops getting JSA(IB), ESA(IR) or IS.

How to tell the council about changes

20.4   You must notify a change to the council – or to someone acting on its behalf. Some councils accept notification by telephone or online, though they can require written rather than telephone notifications, or require written or electronic records to be kept if you make online notifications. In Scotland, authorities can specify an address which you can attend to notify births and deaths. In all other cases, changes must be notified in writing to a 'designated office' (para19.7).

CTR time limits, etc

20.5   For CTR in England and Wales you should tell the council about relevant changes within 21 days beginning with the day on which the change occurs or as soon as reasonably practicable thereafter. There is no equivalent time limit for CTR in Scotland.

T20.1   CTP sch 8 para 9; CTR 115

20.4   CTP sch 7 para 11, sch 8 para 9(2); CTR 115(2), sch 1 para 11

20.5   CTP sch 8 para 9(2); CTR 115(2)

Table 20.2 **Changes you don't have to tell the council about**

(a) Beginnings or ends of awards of pension credit (either kind) or changes in the amount – because it is the DWP's duty to tell the council.

(b) Changes which affect JSA(IB), ESA(IR), UC or IS but do not affect CTR.

(c) Changes in council tax.

(d) Changes in the age of any member of your family or non-dependant.

(e) Changes in the CTR regulations.

20.6   CTR law does not say what happens if you fail to tell the council about a relevant change or (in England and Wales) within the above time limits. In practice, if the change would:

(a) reduce or end your entitlement to CTR – councils are likely to regard an overpayment as having occurred and recover it;

(b) increase your entitlement to CTR – it is arguable that councils should award the arrears (since council tax law does not generally contain time limits for adjusting liability), but you should not rely on this and it is likely to be a matter for tribunals and the courts to decide.

Dealing with changes

Decisions, information and evidence

20.7   The council must decide whether to alter (or end) your entitlement to CTR as a result of the change. It may ask you to provide information and evidence it requires in connection with this. You are responsible for providing this in the same way as when you made your application (para 19.10).

Notifications

20.8   When the council alters (or ends) entitlement to CTR, it must tell you about this within 14 days or as soon as reasonably practicable after that. The notification must include:

(a) its new decision; and

(b) your right to obtain a written statement of reasons and to appeal, etc.

The exception to the above is that in Scotland CTR law contains no duty to notify.

T20.2   CTP sch 8 para 9(3)-(4),(7)-(9): CTR 115(3)-(4),(7)-(9)

20.7   CTP sch 8 para 7(4); CTR 113(4)

20.8   CTP sch 8 para 12(1)(b),(2),(4); CTR 117(1)(b),(2)-(4)

When changes take effect

20.9 This section describes when a change affects your entitlement to CTR. There are two steps involved for the council:

(a) determining the date the change actually occurred; and

(b) working out (from that) what date it takes effect in CTR.

The date a change occurs: the general rule

20.10 The starting point is that the date a change actually occurs is the date something new happens (for example, a new baby arrives, a birthday, a change in pay). This is a question of fact.

The date a change takes effect: the general rule

20.11 The date a change takes effect is:

(a) in CTR in Wales, the exact date the change occurs (whatever day of the week this is);

(b) in CTR in England and Scotland, the Monday after the date the change occurs. Even if the change occurs on a Monday, CTR changes on the following Monday.

20.12 There are different rules for changes in pension credit. These and other special cases are described below (paras 20.13-36).

Moves and changes in council tax liability

20.13 This rule applies when:

(a) you move home; or

(b) your liability for council tax changes.

20.14 The date your council tax goes up (or down) is usually clear. The date a move occurs can be less straightforward. However, it is the date you change your normal home, rather than a date on a letting agreement, etc (R(H) 9/05 para 3.4). All moves and all changes in council tax take effect in CTR on the exact day.

Changes to pension credit

20.15 If a change in either your guarantee credit or savings credit, whether due to a change in your circumstances or due to official error, affects your entitlement to CTR, this takes effect from the date shown in table 20.3.

Changes to UC

20.16 When your entitlement to UC starts, changes or ends, the general rules apply (paras 20.10-12).

20.11   CTP sch 1 para 46(1); CTR 107(1)

20.14   CTP sch 1 para 46(3),(4); CTR 107(3),(4)

20.15   CTP sch 1 para 47; CTR 108

Examples: Moves and changes in liability

Moving within the council's area

A woman moves from one address to another within the council's area on Friday 28th October 2016. She is liable for council tax at her old address up to and including Thursday 27th October 2016 and at her new address from Friday 28th October.

Her CTR changes on and from Friday 28th October (on a daily basis) to take account of her new eligible council tax.

Moving out of the council's area

A man moves out of the council's area on Saturday 14th May 2016. He is liable for council tax at his old address up to and including Friday 13th May.

His CTR ends on the last day of his liability for council tax. In other words, his last day of CTR is Friday 13th May.

Table 20.3 **CTR – When pension credit starts, changes or ends**

The change	When it takes effect in CTR
Pension credit starts, increasing your entitlement to CTR	The Monday following the first day of entitlement to pension credit
Pension credit starts, reducing your entitlement to CTR	The Monday following the date the council gets notification from the DWP about this (or, if later, the Monday following the first day of entitlement to pension credit)
Pension credit changes or ends, increasing your entitlement to CTR	The Monday of the benefit week in which pension credit changes or ends
Pension credit changes or ends, reducing your entitlement to CTR due to a delay by you in notifying a change of circumstances to the DWP	The Monday of the benefit week in which pension credit changes or ends
Pension credit changes or ends, reducing your entitlement to CTR in any other case	The Monday following the date the council got notification from the DWP about this (or, if later, the Monday following the pension credit change or end)

If any of the above would take effect during your 'continuing reduction' period (para 20.35), the change is deferred until afterwards.

T20.3   CTP sch 1 para 47; CTR 108

Changes to tax credits

20.17 When your entitlement to working tax credit or child tax credit starts, changes or ends, the general rule applies (paras 20.10-12). But because of the way tax credits are paid it can involve counting backwards or forwards from the pay date to work out when the change actually occurs. Table 20.4 explains this and includes examples.

Table 20.4 **CTR – When a tax credit starts, changes or ends**

Four-weekly instalments

The pay date is the last day of the 28 days covered by the tax credit instalment. So if a four-weekly instalment is due on the 30th of the month, it covers the period from 3rd to 30th of that month (both dates included).

For example:

   (a) if that is the first instalment ever of your tax credit, your CTR changes on the Monday following the 3rd of the month;

   (b) if that is the first instalment of a new rate of your tax credit, your CTR changes on the Monday following the 3rd of the month;

   (c) if that is the last instalment of your tax credit, the date the change occurs is the 31st of the month, and your CTR changes on the Monday following the 31st of the month.

Weekly instalments

The pay date is the last day of the 7 days covered by the tax credit instalment.

So if a weekly instalment is due on the 15th of the month, it covers the period from 9th to 15th of that month (both dates included).

For example:

   (a) if that is the first instalment ever of your tax credit, your CTR changes on the Monday following the 9th of the month;

   (b) if that is the first instalment of a new rate of your tax credit, your CTR changes on the Monday following the 9th of the month;

   (c) if that is the last instalment of your tax credit, the date the change occurs is the 16th of the month, and your CTR changes on the Monday following the 16th of the month.

Different rules apply for CTR in Wales: para 20.11.

Changes relating to social security benefits

20.18 The following rules apply when entitlement to a social security benefit starts, changes, ends or is reinstated. They apply to all social security benefits (apart from the credits described in paras 20.15-17) received by you, your partner, or a child or young person.

20.19 The date such a change actually occurs is the first day of your new, different, nil or re-instated entitlement. The date the change takes effect in CTR follows the general rules in para 20.11.

20.18   CTP sch 1 para 46(1),(2); CTR 107(1),(2)

20.20 When a social security benefit is found to have been awarded from a date in the past, any resulting increase in CTR is awarded for the past period (so you get your arrears: see the second example). This is the effect of the general rules (para 20.11).

Changes in income, capital, household membership, etc

20.21 The general rules (paras 20.10-12) apply to all other changes – including changes in income, capital, membership of your family or household, and so on. But see also para 17.28 for when non-dependant deductions may be delayed, and para 18.17 for when arrears of income are (or are not) taken into account.

20.22 Authorities also have a discretion to disregard, for up to 30 weeks, changes in the rates of income tax and any personal tax relief, national insurance, the amount of tax payable as a result of an increase in the weekly rate of Category A, B, C or D retirement pension, additional graduated pension or state pension and the maximum rate of tax credits when these result from a change in the law (e.g. the Budget). This discretion does not apply to CTR in Scotland (and is in any case rarely used).

Starting work

20.23 The general rules (paras 20.10-12) apply when you start work. Their effect is that if you start work on a Monday you get a whole week of CTR (except in Wales) as though you had not started work. You may – after that – also qualify for an extended reduction (para 20.27).

Changes ending CTR

20.24 The general rules (paras 20.10-12) apply to any change of circumstances which means that you no longer satisfy all the basic conditions for benefit – for example if your capital now exceeds the upper limit or your income is now too high to qualify.

Changes in the law: regulations and up-ratings

20.25 When regulations relevant to CTR are amended, the council alters your entitlement to CTR from the date on which the amendment takes effect (unless entitlement reduces to nil, in which case para 20.24 applies).

More than one change

20.26 If more than one change occurs in a case, each is dealt with in turn. But in England and Scotland the following rules apply when changes which actually occur in the same reduction week would have an effect (under the earlier rules in this chapter) in different reduction weeks. In all CTR cases, work out the various days on which the changes have an effect (under the earlier rules): all the changes instead apply from the earliest of these dates.

20.22   CTP sch 1 para 28; CTR 60

20.26   CTP sch 1 para 46(7); CTR 107(7)

Extended reductions

20.27 Extended reductions (ERs) help you if you are long-term unemployed and looking for work, by giving you four weeks' extra CTR. They are like the extended payments some people get in HB, JSA or ESA (and people often get them at the same time).

Entitlement

20.28 You are entitled to an ER if you meet the conditions in table 20.5. Authorities in England and Wales can vary those conditions for CTR ERs, and in Wales the law specifies that this can include making ERs more generous.

20.29 No application is required for an ER. All the matters referred to in table 20.5 are for the council to determine (not the DWP). You must be notified about your entitlement to an ER (or not).

Table 20.5 **Entitlement to an ER**

Applicants who have been on a 'qualifying income-related benefit'

You are entitled to an ER if:

(a) you or any partner start employment or self-employment, or increase hours or earnings;

(b) this is expected to last for at least five weeks;

(c) you or any partner have been entitled to ESA(IR), JSA(IB), JSA(C) or IS continuously for at least 26 weeks (or any combination of those benefits in that period);

(d) immediately before starting the job, etc, you or your partner were on ESA(IR), JSA(IB) or IS. At this point being on JSA(C) is not enough; and

(e) entitlement to ESA(IR), JSA(IB) or IS ceases as a result of starting the job, etc.

Applicants who have been on a 'qualifying contributory benefit'

You are entitled to an ER if:

(a) you or any partner start employment or self-employment, or increase hours or earnings;

(b) this is expected to last for at least five weeks;

(c) you or any partner have been entitled to ESA(C), IB or SDA continuously for at least 26 weeks (or any combination of those benefits in that period);

(d) immediately before starting the job, etc, you or any partner were on ESA(C), IB or SDA. And neither of you must be on ESA(IR), JSA(IB) or IS; and

(e) entitlement to ESA(C), IB or SDA ceases as a result of starting the job, etc.

20.27   CTP 2(1), definition: 'extended reduction'; sch 1 para 38; CTR 2(1), 87,88,94,95,100

20.28   CTPW 32(3), 33(3)

T20.5   CTP 2(1), definitions: 'qualifying contributory benefit', 'qualifying income-related benefit', sch 1 para 38; CTR 2(1), 87, 88, 94, 95, 100

Period and amount

20.30 An ER is awarded from the date the change (getting a job, etc) takes effect, and it lasts for four weeks (as illustrated in the example). In each of those four weeks, the amount of the ER is the greater of:

(a) the amount awarded in the last full benefit week before the ER started;

(b) the amount which would be your entitlement in that particular week if there were no such thing as ERs. For example, if your non-dependant left home you might qualify for more CTR this way.

20.31 Throughout the ER, all changes in your circumstances are ignored. And no ER is awarded for council tax during any period during which you are not liable for council tax.

20.32 In Scotland only, if you or your partner reach pension age during the ER, the figure used for 20.30 (b) throughout the ER is whichever would have been higher using your entitlement before and after that age.

CTR after an ER

20.33 If you qualify for CTR based on your new income after the end of the ER, this is awarded in the normal way – and there is no requirement for you to make a fresh application for this.

Variations for movers

20.34 If you are are entitled to an ER you are entitled to it even if you move home during the ER. In Great Britain, if the move is to another council's area, the determination, notification and award of the ER is done by the council whose area you are moving out of. That council may liaise with the council whose area you are moving into; and may pay the ER to them or to you.

Example: ERs

An applicant who meets all the conditions for an ER starts work on Monday 4th July 2016.

His award of CTR continues up to and including Sunday 10th July 2016. His ER covers the period from Monday 11th July 2013 to Sunday 7th August 2013. If he then continues to qualify for CTR after that, the new amount of CTR is awarded from Monday 8th August 2016.

20.30   CTP sch 1 paras 39,40; CTR 89,90,96,97,101,102

20.32   CTS60+ 54

20.33   CTP sch 1 para 42; CTR 92, 99, 104

20.34   CTP sch 1 paras 41,44, sch 6 paras 1,2; CTR 91,98,103,105

Continuing reductions

Entitlement

20.35   Continuing reductions are awarded in CTR whenever the DWP tells the council that:

(a) you are on JSA(IB), ESA(IR) or income support and have now reached pension credit age (para 16.13) (or 65 if you stayed on JSA(IB) beyond that age); or

(b) you have a partner who has claimed pension credit.

Continuing reductions enable the award of CTR to continue without a break while the new entitlement to pension credit (if any) is determined.

Period and amount

20.36   The continuing reduction starts immediately after the last day of entitlement to JSA(IB)/ESA(IR)/IS, and lasts for four weeks plus any extra days to make it end on a Sunday. The amount during that period is calculated by treating you as having no income or capital. And if you move home, your eligible council tax is the higher of the amounts at the old and new addresses; and any non-dependant deductions are based on the circumstances at the new address.

Reviewing awards of CTR

20.37   The council may reconsider any decision it has made about your CTR, and in doing so may ask you to provide information and evidence it reasonably requires (para 19.10).

20.38   A review may show that:

(a) there has been an unreported change of circumstances, in which case the earlier rules apply (paras 20.6-36);

(b) a decision was wrong from the outset. CTR does not have special rules for this but in practice the considerations in paragraph 20.6 are also likely to apply here.

In both the above situations the council must tell you what it has done.

Excess CTR

20.39   If following a review your award is reduced for any period in the past this will result in an overpayment of your CTR. In the law overpaid CTR is called 'excess CTR'.

20.40   There are no nationally set rules about excess CTR. The DCLG has reframed excess CTR as an underpayment of council tax (*Localising council tax support: administrative matters – guidance note,* paras 29-36 [www]). Where you have paid too little council tax because of excess CTR the council can recover the excess as unpaid council tax (in the absence of limitations in its local scheme). The council tax billing, collection and enforcement rules have been amended to allow these 'adjustments' to CTR.

20.35   CTP sch 1 para 43; CTR 93

20.37   CTP sch 8 para 7(4),(6); CTR 113(4),(6)

20.40   http://tinyurl.com/DCLGNote
           Council Tax (Administration and Enforcement) Regulations 1992 (SI 1992/613)
           Council Tax (Administration and Enforcement) (Scotland) Regulations 1992 (SI 1992/1332)

20.41   Rules for dealing with excess CTR (as opposed to the billing for, or enforcement of, unpaid council tax) may be found in the council's local scheme. There is significant variation between authorities ranging from 'an overpayment is rectified by the amount being clawed back by an adjustment to the council tax bill' to 'the treatment of overpayments of council tax support reflects the former CTB regulations'. The power to devise local schemes has also allowed authorities to make more subtle changes to the considerations previously applicable to excess CTB, e.g. 'no underlying entitlement for periods of overpayment is to be calculated'.

Fraud and penalties

20.42   Authorities have powers to investigate and prosecute CTR fraud. Regulations made under those powers provide English and Welsh authorities with investigatory powers, and create offences, administrative and civil penalties in relation to local CTR schemes.

Administrative penalties

20.43   The council may offer you the chance to pay an 'administrative penalty' rather than face prosecution, if:

(a)   an 'act or omission' on your part caused excess CTR; and

(b)   there are grounds for bringing a prosecution against you for an offence relating to that excess CTR.

You do not have to agree to a penalty. You can choose the possibility of prosecution instead.

20.44   The offer of a penalty must be in writing, explain that it is a way of avoiding prosecution, and give other information – including the fact that you can change your mind within 14 days (including the date of the agreement), and that the penalty will be repaid if you successfully challenge it by asking for a reconsideration or appeal. Authorities do not normally offer a penalty (but prosecute instead) if an overpayment is substantial or there are other aggravating factors (such as being in a position of trust). For excess CTR the penalty is 50% of the excess (subject to a minimum of £100 and a maximum of £1,000). In these circumstances the council should calculate the amount of the excess CTR on a daily basis beginning with the first day in respect of which the excess is awarded and ending with the day on which the council knew or ought reasonably to have known that an excess had been awarded.

20.45   An offer of a penalty may also be made where your act or omission could have resulted in excess CTR and there are grounds for bringing a prosecution for a related offence. In these cases the penalty is the fixed amount of £100.

20.42   LGFA ss 14A-14C

20.43   LGFA s.14C, SI 2013/501, 11; SI 2013/588, 13, 1

20.45   SI 2013/501 11(2), (6); SI 2013/588 14(1)-(2)

Civil penalties

20.46   The council can impose a £70 penalty on you if you negligently make an incorrect statement in connection with an application for CTR without taking reasonable steps to correct it, or have been awarded CTR but didn't disclose information or report changes in your circumstances without reasonable excuse. In each case, the action or inaction has to result in excess CTR before a civil penalty can be considered. If you are successfully prosecuted for fraud or offered an administrative penalty or caution, you cannot be issued with a civil penalty for the same offence. The amount of the civil penalties is added to the amount of the excess CTR.

20.46   SI 2013/501, 12, 13; SI 2013/588 16-17

Chapter 21 **CTR appeals and further reviews**

- The different independent appeal bodies in England, Wales and Scotland: see para 21.1.

- Obtaining a written explanation for a CTR decision in England and Wales: see paras 21.2-3.

- Appealing to the council in England or Wales: see paras 21.4-5.

- Appealing to the independent Valuation Tribunals in England or Wales: see paras 21.6-11.

- How appeals are dealt with by the Valuation Tribunal and what happen afterwards: see paras 21.12-15.

- Applying for an internal review of a CTR decision made by a Scottish council: see paras 21.16-17.

- Applying to the independent Council Tax Reduction Review Panel for a further review of a CTR decision made by a Scottish council, how further reviews are dealt with and what happens afterwards: see paras 21.18-31.

The CTR appeals process in England, Wales and Scotland

21.1   Different administrative processes in England, Wales and Scotland apply for appealing CTR decisions after a review by the council (paras 20.37-38). In England CTR appeals are considered by the Valuation Tribunal for England [www]. Administrative arrangements are the responsibility of the Valuation Tribunal Service. In Wales appeals are considered by, and administered by, the Valuation Tribunal Service for Wales [www]. In England and Wales further appeals (on a point of law and if given permission) may be considered by the High Court. In Scotland independent further reviews of CTR decisions are carried out by the CTR Review Panel [www]. Administrative arrangements are the responsibility of the Scottish Courts and Tribunals Service.

21.1   www.valuationtribunal.gov.uk/
        www.valuation-tribunals-wales.org.uk/
        http://counciltaxreductionreview.scotland.gov.uk/

CTR appeals in England and Wales

Decision notices should include appeal rights

21.2 The CTR decision letter you get from the council should tell you how to appeal and point you to the provisions in the council's scheme about appeals. CTR law refers to someone who has a right of appeal as the 'person aggrieved'. This terminology reflects the fact that CTR appeals in England and Wales are dealt with in a similar way to appeals about council tax generally.

Getting a written explanation of the council's CTR decision

21.3 You can write to the council to ask for a written statement that sets out the reasons for any decision in its decision letter. Your request should be made within one month of the date of the council's decision letter. The council should send you its written statement of reasons within 14 days – or as soon as reasonably practicable after that.

Appealing to the council

21.4 Appealable CTR decisions are those which affect:

(a) your entitlement to a reduction under the scheme; or

(b) the amount of any reduction that you are entitled to.

If you want to appeal you should write to the council identifying the matter in dispute. You should also say why you are appealing, e.g. the council has established the wrong facts, considered the wrong law (including the rules in its own local scheme), has misapplied the law to the facts, etc. For the avoidance of doubt your appeal should identify itself as a 'notice of appeal under section 16 of the Local Government Finance Act 1992'. Neither the English default scheme nor the prescribed requirements place time limits within which appeals should be made, but some local schemes do include such limits. In Wales your appeal should reach the council within one month of the date its decision was issued or, where you requested a statement of reasons, within one month of the date the statement of reasons was issued.

The council's response to your appeal

21.5 The council must consider the matters raised in your appeal. It should then write to you describing the steps it has taken to deal with the grievance. But if it thinks that the grounds for the grievance are not well founded, it should give you its reasons for thinking this.

Appealing to the Valuation Tribunal

21.6 If you are still dissatisfied once you've got the council's written response you can appeal directly to the valuation tribunal. You can also do this if the council fails to respond to your appeal within the two months following the date the council got it.

21.2   CTP sch 8 para 12(4), (7)-(8); CTR 117(4), (7)-(8); CTPW sch 14, para 3, sch 13 para 9(7)-(8); CTRW sch 10, para 3, 115(7)-(8)

21.3   CTP sch 8 para 12(5)-(6); CTR 117(5)-(6); CTPW sch 13 para 9(5)-(6); CTRW 115(5)-(6)

21.4   CTP sch 7 para 8(1); CTR sch 1 para 8; CTPW sch 12 para 8; CTRW sch 1 para 8; s16 of the Local Government Finance Act 1992

21.5   CTP sch 7 para 8(2); CTR sch 1 para 9; CTPW sch 12 para 9; CTRW sch 1 para 9

21.6   CTP sch 7 para 8(3); CTR sch 1 para 10; CTPW sch 12 para 10 ; CTRW sch 1 para 10

The Valuation Tribunal for England and the Valuation Tribunal for Wales

21.7   In England further appeals are considered by the Valuation Tribunal for England and administered by the Valuation Tribunal Service [www]. In Wales further appeals are considered and administered by the Valuation Tribunal for Wales [www]. The tribunal provides a free service and cannot award costs against the parties. Members of the valuation tribunal are volunteers. They are not required to have any relevant qualifications but should have received training. Normally two or three members sit on a hearing. A clerk who is a paid official advises on points of law and procedure. In England the power exists for members of the First-tier Tribunal to act as members of the valuation tribunal in a CTR related appeal. A First-tier Tribunal member sits with a senior member of the tribunal to consider CTR appeals on issues relating to the assessment of income, capital or right of residence and sometimes on other cases involving difficult points of law. Most other CTR appeals in England are normally considered by two valuation tribunal members.

Procedural rules and practice statements/protocols

21.8   The tribunal's procedural rules are set out in regulations and supplemented by practice statements or protocols. In England the procedural rules are in the Valuation Tribunal for England (Council Tax and Rating Appeals) (Procedure) Regulations SI 2009 No 2269 as amended. SI 2013 No 465 amends these rules to deal with CTR appeals. Relevant practice statements are on the website [www]. In particular, Practice Statement VTE/PS/A11 (effective from 17th June 2014) contains important information and standard directions on CTR appeals for both you and the council. In Wales the procedural rules are in the Valuation Tribunal for Wales Regulations SI 2010 No 713 as amended. SI 2013 No 547 amends these regulations to take account of CTR appeals. Relevant practice protocols are on the website [www].

The time limits in which to make your further appeal to the tribunal

21.9   You should normally make your appeal to the tribunal within:

(a) the two months following the date the council responded to your initial appeal; or

(b) the four months following the date your initial representation is made if the council fails to respond to it.

You may be allowed to make an out of time appeal if you fail to initiate the appeal within the time limits due to circumstances beyond your control such as illness, absence from home or bereavement. A practice statement and protocol sets out how your application should be made and the relevant considerations [www].

21.7   www.valuationtribunal.gov.uk/
          www.valuation-tribunals-wales.org.uk
          s136, sch 11 para A18A of the Local Government Finance Act 1988

21.8   www.valuationtribunal.gov.uk/Attending_A_Hearing/PracticeStatements.aspx
          www.valuation-tribunals-wales.org.uk/best-practice-protocols.html

21.9   21(2)-(3), (6) of SI 2009/2269; 29(1)-(2),(5) of SI 2010/713
          www.valuationtribunal.gov.uk/Libraries/Publications/ Practice_Statement_-_A1_Extension_of_times.sflb.ashx
          www.valuation-tribunals-wales.org.uk/best-practice-protocols.html

Making an appeal

21.10   You appeal to the tribunal by writing directly to it. An appeal form is available on the relevant website [www]. For England this can be filled in and submitted online or downloaded, filled in and posted to: Valuation Tribunal CTR Team, Hepworth House, 2 Trafford Court, Doncaster, DN1 1PN or emailed to: appeals@vts.gsi.gov.uk. The phone number for any queries is 0300 123 1033. For Wales you can use the council tax reduction appeal form that can be filled in and submitted online or downloaded from the website [www] and returned to the regional office of the tribunal that covers your council. The contact details for the four regional offices and the areas they cover are identified in the Guidance Notes.

21.11   Your appeal needs to include the following information:

(a)   your full name and address;

(b)   the address of the relevant chargeable dwelling – if different from your address;

(c)   the relevant council's name – and the date on which your initial appeal was served on it;

(d)   the date, (if any) that you were notified of the council's response;

(e)   the grounds on which you are aggrieved;

(f)   brief reasons why you think that the decision or calculation made by the council is incorrect.

If you have made an equivalent HB appeal on the same matter to the First-tier Tribunal, you should also say this in the appeal to the valuation tribunal. In Wales the HB appeal letter should also be included with the CTR appeal application. The clerk should acknowledge receipt of your appeal within two weeks and send a copy of it to the council.

How appeals are dealt with

21.12   Appeals are normally heard but if you and the council agree and the tribunal considers it appropriate they can be dealt with on the written representations. In England, if a hearing is to be held you should normally be given at least 14 days notice of the time and place. In Wales, the equivalent period is four weeks. In England shorter notice than the 14 days may be given in urgent or exceptional circumstances. Hearings are normally held in public so it is possible for you to attend a hearing as an observer to see a tribunal in action. You may be accompanied to your own hearing by someone else. That other person may act as your representative or otherwise assist you in presenting your case. The tribunal itself decides what form the hearing should take (subject to the rules of natural justice). It may give a decision orally at a hearing.

21.10   www.valuationtribunal.gov.uk/CTReduction/CTRForm.aspx
www.valuation-tribunals-wales.org.uk/council-tax-reduction.html

21.11   20A, 28(2) of SI 2009/2269; 30(1),(2), (5) of SI 2010/713

21.12   2, 29, 30, 31, 36(1) of SI 2009/2269; 33(1),(6); 34(1); 36, 37, 40(2) of SI 2010/713

Decision notice and statement of reasons

21.13   The tribunal should provide you with a notice of its decision as soon as reasonably practicable. It should also explain your right to request a written statement of reasons (if not given with the decision) and any right of appeal. In Wales the decision notice should be accompanied by a statement of reasons.

21.14   In England, if you want to ask for a statement of reasons (and it has not been supplied with the decision notice) your request should normally be received by the tribunal within two weeks of the date of the decision notice (though the tribunal does have the power to extend this period). The statement of reasons should be sent to you (and the council) within two weeks of the request being made or as soon as reasonably practicable thereafter.

After the decision

21.15   The procedural rules enable the tribunal to correct clerical mistakes, accidental slips and omissions and also to review its decision in specific circumstances. A further appeal to the High Court may only be made on a point of law (para 14.73). It should normally be made within four weeks of the decision notice being issued or in England within two weeks of the statement of reasons being issued if later. You should get legal advice before embarking on this course of action.

Scotland: CTR reviews and further reviews

Asking the council to review its decision

21.16   If you are dissatisfied with a Scottish council's decision on your CTR application you can write to it asking it to review the decision. Your request should get to the council within two months of the date its decision was sent to you. You should set out what you are dissatisfied with and why.

The council's actions on receipt of your review request

21.17   On receipt of your review request the council should:

   (a)   consider the issue(s) identified in your request,

   (b)   decide if it is going to change the decision you are dissatisfied with (this should be done within two months of getting the request from you);

   (c)   tell you in writing about its decision; and

   (d)   tell you that if you remain dissatisfied you can request a further review, the address to which this should be sent, and the time period in which this must be done (42 days from the date of the council's letter).

21.13   36(2) of SI 2009/2269; 40(3) of SI 2010/713

21.14   37(3)-(7) of SI 2009/2269

21.15   39, 40, 43(1)-(2), of SI 2009/2269; 42, 44(1)-(2) of SI 2010/713

21.16   CTS 90A(2)-(3); CTS60+ 70A(2)-(3)

21.17   CTS 90A(4); CTS60+ 70A(4)

Requesting a further review by the CTR Review Panel

21.18   If you are dissatisfied with the council's decision following its internal review you, or your representative, can request a further review by writing directly to the CTR Review Panel, Europa Building, 450 Argyle Street, Glasgow, G2 8LH. Further information, including further review request application forms, are available on its website [www], by telephoning 0141 242 0223 or emailing ctrrpadmin@scotland.gsi.gov.uk. The Review Panel strongly recommends that you use the provided application form to make the further review request. Your application for a further review should be received by the Review Panel within six weeks (42 days) from the date of the council's written response to your internal review request.

21.19   You can also ask for a further review if the council fails to respond to your initial review request and more than two months have passed since they got it. In these circumstances, the written request for a further review should be sent to the council. The council is prevented from writing to you about any decision on your initial review request and must pass on your request for a further review to the CTR Review Panel as soon as possible.

21.20   Your request for a further review should set out the matter(s) you are dissatisfied with, the reasons why and include a copy of the authority's CTR internal review decision notice (if there is one).

The CTR Review Panel

21.21   The Review Panel is appointed by the Scottish Cabinet Secretary for Finance, Employment and Sustainable Growth. One of the panel must also be appointed as senior reviewer. To be appointed, members of the panel have to be solicitors or advocates with at least five years' experience. A further review is normally carried out by one member of the Review Panel, though in particular circumstances three members of the Review Panel may undertake a further review.

The council's response to your further review application

21.22   If the Review Panel decides that your further review application is complete and valid, it writes to the council, informing it of your request. The council's response should normally be submitted within six weeks (42 days). It should contain all the material it wishes the Review Panel to consider. The council should also forward a copy of its submission to you at this time. If the Review Panel does not get a response from the council within the six weeks, it has the power to exclude the council from any further participation in the proceedings and allow your application [www].

21.18   http://counciltaxreductionreview.scotland.gov.uk/index.htm
         CTS 90B(1); CTS60+ 70B(1)

21.19   CTS 90B(2)-(3) (5); CTS60+ 70B(2)-(3) (5)

21.20   CTS 90B(4); CTS60+ 70B(4)

21.21   CTS 90C(1)-(2), 90D(1), 90D(8) ; CTS60+ 70C(1), 70C(8)

21.22   CTS 90D(4); CTS60+ 70C(4)
         http://counciltaxreductionreview.scotland.gov.uk/documents/LA%20Guidance%20Note.pdf

How further reviews are dealt with

21.23 The responsible panel member:

(a) decides the procedure to be adopted for the further review (having regard to any guidance issued by the senior reviewer);

(b) can hold any oral hearing in public or private;

(c) can ask for, but has no power to require, the production of documents or the attendance of anyone as a witness;

(d) can refuse to allow a particular person to represent you at an oral hearing if there are good and sufficient reasons for doing so.

21.24 The further review should be by way of an oral hearing unless you, the council and the panel member agree that it is to be dealt with on the papers. If asked, you and the council must tell the panel member whether you both agree (or not) to it being dealt with in this way. You should also tell the panel member if you have disputed the equivalent housing benefit decision and if it has already been decided on appeal.

21.25 If you or the council are asked by the panel member to provide documents or information and fail to respond within the time limits set, the panel member may draw any inference from this failure they see fit. This can include allowing or refusing the further review.

Withdrawing your request for further review

21.26 You can withdraw your request for further review only with the permission of the senior reviewer.

The decision

21.27 The panel member reaches a decision in private after the hearing. The decision can be to uphold or reject your request, in full or in part. It is either given on the day or sent out in the post, depending on the circumstances of the case. Any re-calculation of your CTR entitlement is carried out by the authority.

21.28 If you had an oral hearing, a letter setting out the panel member's decision is given or posted to you and to the authority on the day of the hearing. If your case has been decided on the papers, you should get a letter through the post a day or two after the decision has been made. A copy of the decision is also sent to the council.

21.29 Both you and the council are entitled to a full statement of reasons for the decision. You can request this by writing to the Review Panel, at the address above, within 14 days of the date on which the decision was given. You should quote your CTR RP reference number [www]. You or the council may also request a set-aside of the decision in the interests of

---

21.23   CTS 90D(6); CTS60+ 70C(6)

21.24   CTS 90D(2)-(3); CTS60+ 70C(2)-(3)

21.25   CTS 90D(4); CTS60+ 70C(4)

21.26   CTS 90D(5); CTS60+ 70C(5)

21.27   CTS 90D(6)(e); CTS60+ 70C(6)(e)

justice. This should be done within 14 days of the date the decision was made. You should give reasons for the request. Where a panel member decides to set aside the decision the further review must be carried out again.

After the Review Panel's further review

21.30   The council should carry out any necessary re-calculation of the amount of your CTR entitlement and put into effect the Review Panel's decision as soon as reasonably practicable. Any queries you have about how the decision is implemented should be addressed to the council [www].

21.31   There is no right of appeal against the Review Panel's decision [www] but it would presumably be susceptible to judicial review. You should get legal advice about this.

21.29   CTS 90D(6)(f),(6A)-(6C); CTS60+ 70C(6)(f),(6A)-(6C)
         counciltaxreductionreview.scotland.gov.uk/documents/LA%20Guidance%20Note.pdf

21.30   CTS 90D(7); CTS60+ 70(C)(7)
         http://counciltaxreductionreview.scotland.gov.uk/documents/CTRRP%20FAQ%20-%20Public.pdf

21.31   http://counciltaxreductionreview.scotland.gov.uk/documents/CTRRP%20FAQ%20-%20Public.pdf

Chapter 22 **Rate rebates for UC**

- Rates and rate rebates in Northern Ireland: see paras 22.1-2.
- HB-related vs UC-related rate rebates: see paras 22.3-8.
- Rate rebates for UC claimants: see paras 22.9-12.
- Calculating rate rebate for UC: see paras 22.13-21.
- Claims, awards and changes: see paras 22.22-27.

Rate rebates for UC claimants in Northern Ireland

22.1   This chapter applies only in Northern Ireland. It describes the new rate rebate scheme if you claim UC. It does not apply if you get HB: in which case help with your rates continues to be paid as part of your HB claim: see chapter 11, *Help with Housing Costs Volume 2*.

Dwellings and liability for rates

22.2   An overview of domestic rates in Northern Ireland including who is responsible for paying them, how your rates liability (before any rebate) is calculated; and other matters such as exemptions, disability reductions and arrangements for billing can be found in chapter 11 of *Help with Housing Costs Volume 2*.

HB-related versus UC-related rate rebates

UC pilots and the roll out of UC live

22.3   At the time of writing UC (and the new rate rebate scheme for UC claimants) has not yet been introduced in Northern Ireland. It is expected that UC is to be piloted in some parts of Northern Ireland possibly as early as September 2016 with the extension of 'UC live' (para 1.14) to other jobcentre plus offices for new claims in early 2017.

22.4   You can only claim a rate rebate under the rules in this chapter in a UC pilot area and the 'UC live' areas if you are working age and do not have an existing HB award. If you or your partner are state pension credit age see paras 22.7-8.

22.5   If you claim UC (whether or not you receive an award: para 22.6) you can only claim help with your rates through the new rate rebate scheme. You cannot get help with your rates through HB, rate relief or lone pensioner allowance.

22.6   If you live in a UC pilot/UC live area and make a claim for UC you can only get a rate rebate if UC is awarded. So for example, if your income is too high to qualify for UC then you cannot get a rebate (or claim a HB-related rate rebate).

Rate rebates if you are state pension credit age

22.7   If you are single and state pension credit age you claim HB to get a rent rebate (whether or not you get SPC or live in a UC pilot or 'UC live' area).

22.8　　　If you have a partner and at least one of you is state pension credit age (para 2.10) you claim HB if:

(a)　you or your partner already get SPC;

(b)　both of you have reached state pension credit age (whether or not you get SPC);

(c)　only one of you is state pension credit age and you do not get SPC and either

- you already get HB, or

- you do not live in a UC pilot area or 'UC live' area.

In any other case if only one of you is state pension credit age you claim a rate rebate as described in this chapter.

Rate rebates for UC claimants

22.9　　　The remainder of this chapter describes the rate rebate scheme for UC claimants. It is based on the best available information at the time of writing but cannot be relied on as to the state of the law (because the regulations had not yet been published).

What is a rate rebate

22.10　　A rate rebate reduces the amount of rates you pay. The amount you receive depends on your UC award: the higher your UC award the higher your rate rebate. It is funded partly by a UK government grant paid to Land and Property Services and from money raised through the rates themselves.

How do you claim a rate rebate

22.11　　If you claim UC you must make a separate claim for a rate rebate directly from Land and Property Services (LPS). You cannot claim rate rebate as part of, or via your UC claim (unlike HB if you get help with your rent or if you claim a legacy passport benefit (IS/JSA(IB)/ESA(IR)). You can find out more about how to claim online [www].

22.12　　The claim form only requires your name and address and declaration that you agree to the information held by the Department for Communities (DFC) on your UC claim being used to calculate your entitlement to rate rebate. The information about your UC claim that you agree can be passed to LPS to calculate your rebate is:

(a)　date of your entitlement to UC;

(b)　your UC maximum award;

(c)　your UC work allowance (if you are in work);

(d)　your income as assessed by UC;

(e)　the amount of your UC award.

22.9　　　　https://www.nidirect.gov.uk/articles/rate-rebate-scheme

22.10-27　Art 30A(3)(a) of Rates (Northern Ireland) Order 1977 (SI 1977 No. 2157) as amended by art 134 NIWRO

Calculating rate rebate for UC

Eligible rates

22.13   Your eligible rates is the figure used in calculating your entitlement to rate rebate. It is calculated by working through the following steps:

  (a) start with the annual rates due on your home after any capping that may apply;

  (b) if you are entitled to a disability reduction, use the figure after it has been made;

  (c) if you are a joint occupier or part of your home is used for business apportion the result (para 22.14);

  (d) convert it to a monthly figure by dividing it by 12.

You can find out how your annual rates and any disability reduction (if it applies) is calculated in chapter 11 of *Help with Housing Costs Volume 2*.

Apportionment of eligible rates

22.14   Your eligible rates figure is apportioned if:

  (a) you occupy only part of a rateable unit (for example, if you are a lodger or live with others in a multi-occupied property). In this case only the proportion of the rates payable for your accommodation is eligible for a rebate;

  (b) if you are jointly liable to pay rates with one or more other occupiers – for example if you have a joint tenancy (paras 5.13-14);

  (c) part of the rateable unit is for business use – such as a shop with a flat above. This is done in the same way as for eligible rent for HB (see *Help with Housing Costs Volume 2*).

How your rate rebate is calculated if a non-dependant lives with you

22.15   Unlike HB for rates, no deduction is made from your eligible rates for any non-dependant who lives with you but this may affect the way your eligible rates are apportioned. But see also para 22.9.

How your UC award affects your rate rebate

22.16   If you claim UC (including if you claim UC but do not qualify for any award) your rate rebate is calculated as follows:

  (a) if you are not entitled to UC you are not entitled to a rate rebate;

  (b) if you receive the maximum UC award (para 9.4) your rate rebate is your full eligible rates figure (para 22.13);

  (c) if your UC award is less than the maximum UC then your rate rebate is reduced: see para 22.21.

The UC claimant commitment and your rate rebate

22.17   Because entitlement to UC depends on you accepting a claimant commitment (paras 2.40-44) you cannot get a rate rebate if you do not agree to sign one (for example, if you decide not to because you have retired early or because your partner has reached state pension credit age).

How your capital affects your rate rebate

22.18   Your capital is assessed by the DFC and any figures are passed to the LPS. You cannot get a rate rebate if your capital exceeds the capital limit for UC (para 9.6). If your capital is less than £6,000 then it does not affect your UC or your rate rebate (para 10.55). If your capital is more than £6,000 but not more than £16,000 then the assumed income from capital used in your UC award (para 10.56) is taken account of in the income figure the DFC passes to the LPS to calculate your rate rebate (para 22.19).

Income and excess income

22.19   The income figure used to calculate your rate rebate is:

(a)   your UC award; plus

(b)   your unearned income (para 10.31); plus

(c)   your earned income (para 10.7) less

   ▪   half your work allowance

All of these figures are those supplied by the DFC to calculate your UC award and are monthly. If your UC award is reduced due to a sanction or a deduction for an overpayment or third party payment the DFC uses the award figure before the deduction.

22.20   Your excess income is:

(a)   your income for rate rebate (para 22.19); less

(b)   your maximum UC as calculated by DFC (para 9.4).

If (a) is greater than (b) then your rebate is calculated as in the next paragraph. In any other case your excess income is zero and you get the maximum rebate (para 22.16). Any transitional addition that is payable because your previous HB/IS/JSA(IB)/ESA(IR) award was converted to UC is not counted as part of your UC award.

22.21   If you have an excess income (para 22.20) your monthly rate rebate is:

(a)   your eligible rates (para 22.13); less

(b)   10% of your excess income.

See examples for calculation. If (b) is equal to or more than (a) then you do not qualify for a rate rebate.

Examples: rate rebate calculation

Claimant on maximum UC

A single claimant aged over 25 is unemployed. His rates liability is £45 per month. His only income is his UC award which he receives at the maximum rate.

Maximum UC (para 9.4 and table 9.2)	£317.82
Income: UC	£317.82

His income (£317.82) does not exceed his maximum UC therefore he is awarded the full rate rebate of £45 per month.

Claimant with unearned and earned income

A lone parent aged 34 cares for her child aged 7. Her monthly earnings are £499.20 (16 hours per week at minimum wage). She does not pay for any child care. She receives maintenance from her former partner of £130.00 per month. Her UC award is £544.81. She pays rent of £325 per month. Her rates liability is £45.00 per month.

Maximum UC (single 25+, child, housing costs: para 9.4)	£874.49
Universal credit	£544.81
Unearned income (maintenance: para 10.38)	£130.00
Earned income less half of work allowance (£499.20 – ½ of £192.00)	£403.20
Total income	£1,078.01
Excess income (total income less maximum UC)	£203.52
Eligible rates	£45.00
Less 10% of excess income	– £20.35
Monthly rate rebate	£24.65

Awards, payments and changes

Start date, time limits and backdating

22.22   The start of your award is the date you first become entitled (usually the date you first become entitled to UC or your income is low enough).

22.23   The time limit for claiming a rate rebate for UC is three months. If you claim within three months of you becoming entitled your arrears are paid in full (subject to proof of income). There is no requirement to show good cause for a late claim but you cannot get any arrears for any period that is more than three months before you claim.

How your rate rebate is paid

22.24   Your rate rebate is awarded as a credit to your rates account.

Reviews and changes of circumstance

22.25   Your rate rebate is reviewed annually, the only exception being changes that affect the amount of your rates liability (para 22.13) such as a change of address or death of the claimant. Other changes occurring within the year (such as changes in income) do not affect your award.

Overpayments

22.26   All overpayments are recoverable. Your rate rebate is treated as if it is part your UC award so if, for example, your UC is recovered because the wrong information was used to calculate it your rate rebate is also recovered. However, if your UC is changed because of a change in your circumstances occuring mid-year this will not result in an overpayment (para 22.25).

Appeals

22.27   Most matters about your rate rebate cannot be appealed because your award is based on decisions about your UC (e.g. income and capital) and because most changes are only taken into account annually (para 22.25). However, if a UC decision on which your rate rebate is based is changed on appeal then your rate rebate is also recalculated.

Appendix 1 **UC/CTR legislation**

UC: England, Scotland and Wales

Main primary legislation (Acts)

The Social Security Administration Act 1992

The Welfare Reform Act 2012

The Welfare Reform and Work Act 2016

Main secondary legislation (regulations and orders)

SI 2013/376	The Universal Credit Regulations
SI 2013/380	The Universal Credit, Personal independence Payment, Jobseeker's Allowance and Employment and Support Allowance (Claims and Payments) Regulations 2013
SI 2013/381	The Universal Credit, Personal Independence Payment, Jobseeker's Allowance and Employment and Support Allowance (Decisions and Appeals) Regulations 2013
SI 2013/382	The Rent Officers (Universal Credit Functions) Order 2013
SI 2013/383	The Social Security (Payments on Account of Benefit) Regulations 2013
SI 2013/384	The Social Security (Overpayments and Recovery) Regulations 2013
SI 2013/386	The Universal Credit (Transitional Provisions) Order 2013
SI 2014/1230	The Universal Credit (Transitional Provisions) Regulations 2014
SI 2012/1483	Social Security (Information-sharing in relation to Welfare Services etc) Regulations 2012

Recent amending regulations and orders

The following is a list of regulations and orders amending the main secondary legislation since 1st April 2015. This list is up to date as at 1st April 2016.

SI 2015/457	The Social Security Benefits Up-rating Order 2015
SI 2015/478	The Social Security (Miscellaneous Amendments No. 2) Regulations 2015
SI 2015/546	The Universal Credit (EEA Jobseekers) Amendment Regulations 2015
SI 2015/1362	The Universal Credit (Waiting Days)(Amendment) Regulations 2015
SI 2015/1647	The Social Security (Housing Costs Amendments) Regulations 2015
SI 2015/1649	The Universal Credit (Work Allowance) (Amendment) Regulations 2015
SI 2015/1753	The Rent Officers (Housing Benefit and Universal Credit Functions) (Local Housing Allowance Amendments) Order 2015
SI 2015/1754	The Universal Credit and Miscellaneous Amendments Regulations 2015
SI 2015/1780	The Universal Credit (Transitional Provisions) (Amendment) Regulations 2015

SI 2016/215   The Universal Credit (Surpluses and Self-employed Losses)
                 (Change of coming into force) Regulations 2016

SI 2016/232   The Universal Credit (Transitional Provisions)
                 (Amendment) Regulations 2016

SI 2016/543   The Universal Credit (Care Leavers and Looked After Children)
                 Amendment Regulations 2016

Recent commencement orders

The following is a list of orders bringing UC provisions into force since April 2015. This list is
up to date as at 1st April 2016.

SI 2015/32   The Welfare Reform Act 2012 (Commencement No. 9, 11, 13, 14, 16, 17 and
                 19 and Transitional and Transitory Provisions (Amendment)) Order 2015

SI 2015/33   The Welfare Reform Act 2012 (Commencement No. 21 and Transitional and
                 Transitory Provisions) Order 201

SI 2015/101   The Welfare Reform Act 2012 (Commencement No. 22 and Transitional and
                 Transitory Provisions) Order 2015

SI 2015/634   The Welfare Reform Act 2012 (Commencement No. 23 and Transitional and
                 Transitory Provisions) Order 2015

SI 2015/740   The Welfare Reform Act 2012 (Commencement No. 23 and Transitional and
                 Transitory Provisions) (Amendment) Order 2015

CTR: England, Scotland and Wales

Main primary legislation (Acts)

The Local Government Finance Act 1992

The Local Government Finance Act 2012

Main secondary legislation England

SI 2012/2885   The Council Tax Reduction Schemes (Prescribed Requirements) (England)
                 Regulations 2012

SI 2012/2886   The Council Tax Reduction Schemes (Default Scheme) (England) Regulations
                 2012

SI 2013/215   Council Tax Reduction Schemes (Transitional Provision) (England)
                 Regulations 2013

SI 2013/501   Council Tax Reduction Schemes (Detection of Fraud and Enforcement)
                 (England) Regulations 2013

SI 1996/1880   Local Authorities (Contracting Out of Tax Billing, Collection and Enforcement
                 Functions) Order 1996

SI 2013/502   Local Authorities (Contracting Out of Tax Billing, Collection and Enforcement
                 Functions) (Amendment) (England) Order 2013

SI 2009/2269   Valuation Tribunal for England (Council Tax and Rating Appeals) (Procedure) Regulations 2009

SI 2013/465   The Valuation Tribunal for England (Council Tax and Rating Appeals) (Procedure) (Amendment) Regulations 2013

Recent amending secondary legislation England

SI 2015/2041   The Council Tax Reduction Schemes (Prescribed Requirements) (England) (Amendment) Regulations 2015

Main secondary legislation Scotland

SSI 2012/303   The Council Tax Reduction (Scotland) Regulations 2012

SSI 2012/319   The Council Tax Reduction (State Pension Credit) (Scotland) Regulations 2012

SSI 2013/87   Council Tax (Information-sharing in relation to Council Tax Reduction) (Scotland) Regulations 2013

Recent amending secondary legislation Scotland

SSI 2016/81   The Council Tax Reduction (Scotland) Amendment Regulations 2016

Main secondary legislation Wales

SI 2013/3029   The Council Tax Reduction Schemes and Prescribed Requirements (Wales) Regulations 2013

SI 2013/3035   The Council Tax Reduction Schemes (Default Scheme) (Wales) Regulations 2013

SI 1993/255   Council Tax (Demand Notices) (Wales) Regulations 1993

SI 2013/63   Council Tax (Demand Notices) (Wales) (Amendment) Regulations 2013

SI 1996/1880   Local Authorities (Contracting Out of Tax Billing, Collection and Enforcement Functions) Order 1996

SI 2013/695   Local Authorities (Contracting Out of Tax Billing, Collection and Enforcement Functions) (Amendment) (Wales) Order 2013

SI 2013/588   Council Tax Reduction Schemes (Detection of Fraud and Enforcement) (Wales) Regulations 2013

SI 2013/111   Council Tax Reduction Schemes (Transitional Provisions) (Wales) Regulations 2013

SI 2010/713   The Valuation Tribunal for Wales Regulations 2010

SI 2013/547   The Valuation Tribunal for Wales (Wales) (Amendment) Regulations 2013

Recent amending secondary legislation Wales

SI 2016/50   The Council Tax Reduction Schemes (Prescribed Requirements and Default Scheme) (Wales) (Amendment) Regulations 2016

UC: Northern Ireland

Main primary legislation (Acts and Orders)

Northern Ireland (Welfare Reform) Act 2015

The Welfare Reform (Northern Ireland) Order 2015 SI 2015 No. 2006 (N.I. 1)

Main secondary legislation (statutory rules)

NISR 2016/216   The Universal Credit Regulations (Northern Ireland) 2016

NISR 2016/220   The Universal Credit, Personal Independence Payment, Jobseeker's Allowance and Employment and Support Allowance (Claims and Payments) Regulations (Northern Ireland) 2016

NISR 2016/221   The Universal Credit, Personal Independence Payment, Jobseeker's Allowance and Employment and Support Allowance (Decisions and Appeals) Regulations (Northern Ireland) 2016

NISR 2016/222   The Universal Credit Housing Costs (Executive Determinations) Regulations (Northern Ireland) 2016

NISR 2016/226   The Universal Credit (Transitional Provisions) Regulations (Northern Ireland) 2016

NISR 2016/178   The Welfare Supplementary Payments Regulations (Northern Ireland) 2016

NISR 2016/56   The Social Security (Information-sharing in relation to Welfare Services etc) Regulations (Northern Ireland) 2016

Recent amending regulations and orders

NISR 2016/46   The Welfare Reform (Northern Ireland) Order 2015 (Commencement No. 1) Order 2016

NISR 2016/166   The Welfare Reform (Northern Ireland) Order 2015 (Commencement No. 2) Order 2016

NISR 2016/215   The Welfare Reform (Northern Ireland) Order 2015 (Commencement No. 3) Order 2016

Appendix 2 **Selected weekly benefit rates from April 2016**

Attendance allowance

Higher rate	£82.30
Lower rate	£55.10

Bereavement benefits

Widowed parents allowance (standard rate)	£112.55
Bereavement allowance (standard rate)	£112.55
Reduction in standard rate for each year aged under 55 (approx)	£7.88

Child benefit

Only or older/oldest child	£20.70
Each other child	£13.70

Carer's allowance

Claimant	£62.10

Disability living allowance

Care component

Highest rate	£82.30
Middle rate	£55.10
Lowest rate	£21.80

Mobility component

Higher rate	£57.45
Lower rate	£21.80

Employment and support allowance (contributory)

Personal allowances

Under 25/lone parent under 18	£57.90
18 or over/under 25 (main phase)	£73.10
Couple both under 18 with child	£87.50
Couple both over 18	£114.85

Components

Work-related activity	£29.05
Support	£36.20

Guardian's allowance   £16.55

Housing benefit applicable amounts

Personal allowances

Single claimant	aged under 25 – on main phase ESA	£73.10
	aged under 25 – other	£57.90
	aged 25+ but under pension age	£73.10
	over pension age but under 65	£155.60
	aged 65+	£168.70
Lone parent	aged under 18 – on main phase ESA	£73.10
	aged under 18 – other	£57.90
	aged 18+ but under pension age	£73.10
	over pension age but under 65	£155.60
	aged 65+	£168.70
Couple	both under 18 – claimant on main phase ESA	£114.85
	both under 18 – other	£87.50
	at least one aged 18+ both under pension age	£114.85
	at least one pension age, both under 65	£237.55
	at least one aged 65+	£252.30
Plus for each child/ young person		£66.90

Additional amounts

Family premium	at least one child/young person	£17.45	
Disability premium	single claimant/lone parent	£32.25	*
	couple (one/both qualifying)	£45.95	*
Disabled child premium	each child/young person	£60.06	
Enhanced disability premium	single claimant/lone parent	£15.75	*
	couple (one/both qualifying)	£22.60	*
	each child/young person	£24.43	
Work related activity component	single claimant/lone parent/couple	£29.05	*
Support component	single claimant/lone parent/couple	£36.20	*
Carer premium	claimant or partner or each	£34.60	
Severe disability premium	single rate	£61.85	
	double rate	£123.70	

Only awarded with working age claims

Incapacity benefit

Short-term lower rate (under pension age)	£79.45
Short-term higher rate (under pension age)	£94.05
Long-term rate	£105.35
Spouse or adult dependant (where appropriate)	£61.20
Increase for age higher rate (under 35)	£11.15
Increase for age lower rate (35-44)	£6.20

Industrial disablement pension

20% disabled	£33.60
For each further 10% disability up to 100%	£16.80
100% disabled	£168.00

Jobseekers allowance (contribution-based)

Aged under 18 to 24	£57.90
Aged 25 or more	£73.10

Maternity and paternity pay and allowance

Statutory maternity, paternity and adoption pay	£139.58
Maternity allowance	£139.58

Personal independence payment

Daily living

Enhanced	£82.30
Standard	£55.10

Mobility component

Enhanced	£57.45
Standard	£21.80

Retirement pension

Single person (basic rate)	£119.30
Couple (basic rate)	£190.80

Severe disablement allowance

Basic rate	£74.65
Age-related addition	
Higher rate	£11.15
Middle rate	£6.20
Lower rate	£6.20

Statutory sick pay

Standard rate	£88.45

Appendix 3 **Qualifying age for state pension credit**

Date of birth	Date qualifying age for state pension credit is reached
Before 6th April 1950	On reaching age 60
6th April 1950 to 5th May 1950	6th May 2010
6th May 1950 to 5th June 1950	6th July 2010
6th June 1950 to 5th July 1950	6th September 2010
6th July 1950 to 5th August 1950	6th November 2010
6th August 1950 to 5th September 1950	6th January 2011
6th September 1950 to 5th October 1950	6th March 2011
6th October 1950 to 5th November 1950	6th May 2011
6th November 1950 to 5th December 1950	6th July 2011
6th December 1950 to 5th January 1951	6th September 2011
6th January 1951 to 5th February 1951	6th November 2011
6th February 1951 to 5th March 1951	6th January 2012
6th March 1951 to 5th April 1951	6th March 2012
6th April 1951 to 5th May 1951	6th May 2012
6th May 1951 to 5th June 1951	6th July 2012
6th June 1951 to 5th July 1951	6th September 2012
6th July 1951 to 5th August 1951	6th November 2012
6th August 1951 to 5th September 1951	6th January 2013
6th September 1951 to 5th October 1951	6th March 2013
6th October 1951 to 5th November 1951	6th May 2013
6th November 1951 to 5th December 1951	6th July 2013
6th December 1951 to 5th January 1952	6th September 2013
6th January 1952 to 5th February 1952	6th November 2013
6th February 1952 to 5th March 1952	6th January 2014
6th March 1952 to 5th April 1952	6th March 2014
6th April 1952 to 5th May 1952	6th May 2014
6th May 1952 to 5th June 1952	6th July 2014
6th June 1952 to 5th July 1952	6th September 2014

App 3   Pensions Act 1995 schedule 4; Pensions Act 2011 s1; SI 1995 No 3213 sch 2; Pensions Act (Northern Ireland) 2012 sl

6th July 1952 to 5th August 1952	6th November 2014
6th August 1952 to 5th September 1952	6th January 2015
6th September 1952 to 5th October 1952	6th March 2015
6th October 1952 to 5th November 1952	6th May 2015
6th November 1952 to 5th December 1952	6th July 2015
6th December 1952 to 5th January 1953	6th September 2015
6th January 1953 to 5th February 1953	6th November 2015
6th February 1953 to 5th March 1953	6th January 2016
6th March 1953 to 5th April 1953	6th March 2016
6th April 1953 to 5th May 1953	6th July 2016
6th May 1953 to 5th June 1953	6th November 2016
6th June 1953 to 5th July 1953	6th March 2017
6th July 1953 to 5th August 1953	6th July 2017
6th August 1953 to 5th September 1953	6th November 2017
6th September 1953 to 5th October 1953	6th March 2018
6th October 1953 to 5th November 1953	6th July 2018
6th November 1953 to 5th December 1953	6th November 2018
6th December 1953 to 5th January 1954	6th March 2019
6th January 1954 to 5th February 1954	6th May 2019
6th February 1954 to 5th March 1954	6th July 2019
6th March 1954 to 5th April 1954	6th September 2019
6th April 1954 to 5th May 1954	6th November 2019
6th May 1954 to 5th June 1954	6th January 2020
6th June 1954 to 5th July 1954	6th March 2020
6th July 1954 to 5th August 1954	6th May 2020
6th August 1954 to 5th September 1954	6th July 2020
6th September 1954 to 5th October 1954	6th September 2020
6th October 1954 or after	On reaching age 66

Appendix 4 **Equivalent footnote references for Scotland and Wales**

Table A **Chapter 15: Council tax liability**

This table shows the equivalent footnote references in chapter 15 for the law on council tax liability in Scotland and Wales. 'Not Scotland' means there is no equivalent law in Scotland. For abbreviations see the key to footnotes at the front of this guide.

	Scotland	Wales
15.3	LGFA 70,71,75	LGFA 1,2,6
15.4	LGFA 72	LGFA 3,7; SI 1992/550
15.6	LGFA 74(1),(2); http://www.saa.gov.uk/	LGFA 5(1A),(3); https://www.gov.uk/council-tax-bands
15.7	Not Scotland	LGFA 12
15.8	LGFA 75	LGFA 6(1),(2)
15.9	LGFA 76; SI 1992/1331	LGFA 8; SI 1992/551
15.10	SI 1992/1331 sch para 3	SI 1992/551
15.11	Not Scotland	SI 1992/548 art 6
15.12	LGFA 75,77,77A	LGFA 6,9; SI 1992/558
15.13	LGFA 77(2)	LGFA 9(2)
15.15-16	LGFA 72(1),(6); SI 1992/728	LGFA 4(1),(2); SI 1992/558
15.17	LGFA 80(1),(4),(6),(7); SI 1992/1335	LGFA 13(1),(4),(6),(7); SI 1999/1335
15.18	SI 1992/1335 reg 3	SI 1992/554; SI 1993/195
15.20	LGFA 79	LGFA 11
15.21	LGFA 79(5), sch 1	LGFA 11(5), sch 1
T15.2(a)	LGFA sch 1 para 3	LGFA sch 1 para 3
T15.2(b)	LGFA sch 1 para 11; SI 1992/1409 reg 3, sch para 3	LGFA sch 1 para 11; DDR 3 class C
T15.2(c)	LGFA sch 1 paras 4,5; SSI 2003/176 art 6,7; SSI 2011/5; SSI 2014/7	LGFA sch 1 paras 4,5; DDO art 4, sch 1 paras 2-7
T15.2(d)	LGFA sch 1 para 4; SSI 2003/176 art 8	LGFA sch 1 para 4, DDO art 4, sch 1 para 8
T15.2(e)	LGFA sch 1 para 4; SSI 2003/176 art 5; SSI 2007/214	LGFA sch 1 para 4, DDO art 4, sch 1 para 1; SI 2007/580
T15.2(f)	LGFA sch 1 para 9; SI 1992/1409 reg 2(2); SSI 2007/213 reg 2	LGFA sch 1 para 9, DDR reg 2, sch paras 1,2; SI 2007/581

	Scotland	Wales
T15.2(g)	LGFA sch 1 para 9; SI 1992/1409 reg 2(3); SSI 2013/65; SSI 2013/142 reg 2	LGFA sch 1 para 9, DDR reg 2, sch paras 3,4; SI 2013/639; SI 2013/1049
T15.2(h)	LGFA sch 1 para 2; SSI 2003/176 art 4; SSI 2008/1879 reg 39; SSI 2013/65; SSI 2013/137 reg 14, SSI 2013/142 reg 8	LGFA sch 1 para 2, DDO art 3; SI 2013/638; SI 2013/1048
T15.2(i)	LGFA sch 1 para 11; SI 1992/1409 reg 3, sch para 2	LGFA sch 1 para 11; DDR reg 3, Class B
T15.2(j)	LGFA sch 1 para 11; SI 1992/1409 reg 3, sch para 1	LGFA sch 1 para 11; DDR reg 3, Class A,D,F
T15.2(k)	LGFA sch 1 para 11; SI 1992/1409 reg 3, sch para 1	LGFA sch 1 para 11; DDR reg 3, Class A,E
T15.2(l)	LGFA sch 1 para 8	LGFA sch 1 paras 6,7; DDO art 6
T15.2(m)	LGFA sch 1 para 1; SSI 2003/176 art 3	LGFA sch 1 para 1; DDO art 2
15.24	Not Scotland	LGFA 13A(1)(c),(6),(7), sch 1B para 5(1)(c),(2)
15.25	Not Scotland	CTPW sch 12 para 11; CTRW sch 1 para 11

Table B **Chapters 16-21: CTR legislation**

This table shows the equivalent footnote references in chapters 16-21 for CTR law in Scotland and Wales. 'Not Scotland'/ 'Not Wales' means that there is no equivalent law in that country. N/A means not applicable, usually because the law applies to working age or pension age claims only. 'See text' means the equivalent reference is in the footnote for that paragraph (usually because the law is unique to that country). For abbreviations see the key to footnotes at the front of this guide.

Para	Scotland CTS	CTS60+	Wales CTPW	CTRW
16.3	81-91	59-71	sch 12, sch 13	107-115, sch 1
16.4	Not Scotland	Not Scotland	Not Wales	Not Wales
16.5	Not Scotland	Not Scotland	Not Wales	Not Wales
16.8	Not Scotland	Not Scotland	Not Wales	Not Wales
16.9	See text	See text	Not Wales	Not Wales
16.10	Not Scotland	Not Scotland	See text	See text
16.11	Not Scotland	Not Scotland	See text	See text
16.12	Not Scotland	Not Scotland	See text	See text
16.13	12	12	3	3
16.15	2(1),12	2(1),12	2(1),3	2(1),3
16.17	See text	See text	See text	See text
16.19	2(1),7	2(1),7	2(1),sch 13 para 1(1)	2(1),107
16.20	14, 42, sch 5 paras 7,8,49	14,24,40 sch 4 para 27	27,30	18,21
16,21	14(5)	14(5)	22-25	13-16
16.22	15(1),18	15(1),18	22-25	13-16
16.23	15(3),18	15(3),18	26	17
T16.3	2(1),15(4)	2(1),15(4)	26(3),(6)	17(3),(6)
16.28	See text	See text	Not Wales	Not Wales
16.29	See text	See text	Not Wales	Not Wales
16.30	See text	See text	Not Wales	Not Wales
16.31	16(1)-(3), 19	16(1)-(3), 19	28(1)-(3), 29(1),(3)	19(1)-(3), 20(1),(3)
T16.4	16(5), 19(1),(2)	16(5), 19(1),(2)	28(5),(6), 29(1),(2)	19(5),(6), 20(1),(2)
16.37	See text	See text	See text	See text
16.38	See text	See text	See text	See text
16.39	See text	See text	See text	See text
16.40	See text	See text	See text	See text
16.41	See text	See text	See text	See text
16.42	16(5)	16(5)	28(5),(6)	19(5),(6)
16.46	N/A	14(1),(3)	27,31,sch 11 para 3(1)(a)	18,22,72(1)(a)
16.47	14(3)(b), 20(1),(2)	N/A	sch 11 para 3(1)(b)	22, 72(1)(b)

Para	Scotland CTS	CTS60+	Wales CTPW	CTRW
16.48-50	2(1),(2),(4)	Not Scotland	sch 1 para 1	70
T16.5	20(3)	Not Scotland	sch 1 para 3(2)	72(3)
16.55	2(1)	2(1)	2(1),4	2(1),4
16.56	See text	See text	See text	See text
16.58	2(1)	2(1)	2(1)	2(1)
16.59	See text	See text	See text	See text
16.61	11(1)	11(1)	8(1)	8(1)
16.62	See text	See text	See text	See text
16.63	11(1)	11(1)	8(1)	8(1)
16.64	See text	See text	See text	See text
16.65	10	10	7	7
16.66	11(1)	11(1)	8(1)	8(1)
16.67	21	20	sch 1 para 6	25,26
16.68	11(2),(3)	11(2),(3)	8(2),(3)	8(2),(3)
16.69	11(4)	11(4)	8(4)	8(4)
16.71	3(1),(2)	3(1),(2)	9(1),(2)	9(1),(2)
16.74	3(2)(e)	3(2)(e)	9(2)(e)	9(2)(e)
16.77	3(3)	3(3)	9(3)	9(3)
16.78	3(2)(d),(3)	3(2)(d),(3)	9(2)(d),(3)	9(2)(d),(3)
16.81	3(2)(f),(3)	3(2)(f),(3)	9(2)(d),(3)	9(2)(d),(3)
16.83	79	57	Not Wales	Not Wales
17.2	66(1), 78(1)	47(1), 56(1)	sch 1 para 2(1), sch 6 para 4(1)	27(1)
17.5	14(5)(a),(8)(a), sch 3 para 14, sch 4 paras 7,8, sch 5 paras 7,8	14(5)(a),(8)(a), 24	sch 1 paras 2(1),7, sch 6 para 4(1), sch 8 para 14, sch 9 paras 8,9,sch 10 paras 8,9	13,15, 27(1), 29(2), 32, sch para 14, sch 7 paras 8,9, sch 9 paras 8,9
17.6	42	40	21,30	21
17.8	14(5)	14(5)	22-25	14,16
17.11	14(5)(b),(8)(b)	14(5)(b),(8)(b)	23(f),25(f), sch 1 para 4, sch 6 para 6	14(f), 16(f), 29(3)
17.15	3	3	9	9
17.17	67(6)	48(6)	sch 1 para 3(6), sch 6 para 5(6)	28(6)
17.18	67(1),(2),(7),(8)	48(1),(2),(7)	sch 1 para 3(1),(2), (7),(8), sch 6 para 5(1),(2),(7),(8)	28(1),(2),(7),(8)
17.20	67(1)(a)	48(1)(a)	sch 1 para 3(1)(a), sch 6 para 5(1)(a)	28(1)(a)
T17.1	See text	See text	See text	See text
17.21	6(1),(5)-(8)	6(1),(5)-(8)	10(1),(5)-(8)	10(1),(5)-(8)
17.22	67(1),(2)	48(1),(2)	sch 1 para 3(1),(2), sch 6 para 5(1),(2)	28(1),(2)

17.23	6(4),(5)	6(4),(5)	10(4),(5)	10(4),(5)
17.24	6(3)	6(3)	10(3)	10(3)
17.25	67(9)	48(9)	sch 1 para 3(9), sch 6 para 5(9)	28(9)
17.26	67(3),(4)	48(3),(4)	sch 1 para 3(3),(4), sch 6 para 5(3),(4)	28(3),(4)
17.27	67(5)	48(5)	sch 1 para 3(5), ch 6 para 5(5)	28(5)
17.28	N/A	59(10)-(13)	Not Wales	Not Wales
17.31	14(6),(7), 79, sch 2 para 1	14(6),(7), 57, sch 5 para 1	Not Wales	Not Wales
17.32	79(7)	57(7)	Not Wales	Not Wales
17.33-35	14(6),(7), 79, sch 2 para 1	14(6),(7), sch 5 para 1	Not Wales	Not Wales
T17.2	See text	See text	Not Wales	Not Wales
17.36	sch 2 paras 2,3	sch 5 paras 2,3	Not Wales	Not Wales
17.37	78(2)	56(2)	Not Wales	Not Wales
17.38	14(9)	14(9)	Not Wales	Not Wales
17.39	66(1)(b)	47(1)(b)	sch 1 para 2(1)(b), sch 6 para 4(1)(b)	27(1)(b)
17.40	33(1)	31(1)	sch 1 para 11(1), sch 6 para 13(1)	37(1), 47(1)
17.45	21,22	20	sch 1 para 1(1), sch 6 paras 1,2	23-25, sch 2, para 4, sch 3 paras 5-7
T17.3	See text	See text	See text	See text
T17.4	Not Scotland	Not Scotland	Not Wales	Not Wales
17.47	23	Not Scotland	sch 6 para 3	26
17.49	sch 1 para 1	sch 1 para 2	sch 2 para 1, sch 7 para 1	23,24, sch 2 para 1, sch 3 para 1
17.51	sch 1 para 3	sch 1 para 3	sch 2 para 2, sch 7 para 3	sch 2 para 2, sch 3 para 3
17.52	sch 1 para 4	sch 1 para 4	sch 2 para 3, sch 7 para 4	sch 2 para 3, sch 3 para 4
17.53-54	sch 1 paras 18-22	Not Scotland	sch 7 paras 18-22	sch 3 paras 18-22
17.55	sch 1 paras 9,10(9)	Not Scotland	sch 7 paras 9,10(8)	sch 3 paras 9,10(8)
17.56-60	sch 1 para 10	Not Scotland	sch 7 para 10	sch 3 para 10
17.61-63	sch 1 paras 25-29	Not Scotland	sch 7 paras 25-29	sch 3 paras 25-29
17.64	sch 1 para 13	sch 1 para 9	sch 2 para 8, sch 7 para 13	sch 2 para 8, sch 3 para 13
17.65-67	sch 1 para 12	sch 1 para 8	sch 2 para 7, sch 7 para 12	sch 2 para 7, sch 3 para 12
17.68-71	sch 1 para 11	sch 1 para 7	sch 7 para 11	sch 3 para 11
17.72	sch 1 para 14	sch 1 para 10	sch 2 paras 5(2), 9, sch 7 paras 8(2), 14	sch 2 paras 5(2), 9,sch sch 3 paras 8(2), 14
17.75	sch 1 para 16	sch 1 para 12	sch 2 para 11, sch 7 para 16	sch 2 para 11, sch 3 para 16

Para	Scotland CTS	CTS60+	Wales CTPW	CTRW
17.76	sch 1 paras 8,15,16	sch 1 paras 6,11,12	sch 2 para 5,10,11, sch 7 paras 8,15,16	sch 2 para 5,10,11, sch 3 paras 8,15,16
17.77	See text	See text	See text	See text
17.78	sch 1 para 10(1)(a)(v),(2)	sch 1 para 7(4),(5)	sch 2 para 6(4),(5), sch 7 para 10(1) (a)(vii),(2)	sch 2 para 6(4),(5), sch 3 para 10(1)(a) (vii),(2)
17.79	sch 1 paras 8(1)(b), 10(6)	sch 1 para 6(1)(b)	sch 2 para 5(1)(b), sch 7 para 8(1)(b)	sch 2 para 5(1)(b), sch 3 para 8(1)(b)
17.80	27	sch 1 para 2	sch 6 para 2, sch 7 para 1	25, sch 2 para 1
17.81	sch 1 para 11(2)(b)	sch 1 para 7(2)(b)	sch 1 para 1(1), sch 2 para 6(2)(b), sch 6 para 2(2), sch 7 para 11(2)(b)	sch 2 para 6(2)(b), sch 3 para 11(2)(b)
18.6	23(2A), 26	25	sch 1 para 8, sch 6 para 9	33, 34
18.7	27(1)(b)	28(1)(b)	sch 1 para 18(1)(b), ch 6 paras 20(1)(b)	54(1)(b)
18.8	42	40	27,30	18,21
18.9	N/A	24	sch 1 para 7	32
18.10	27,35,39	26,27,31	sch 1 paras 10,11,12,18, sch 6 paras 15,17	35,36,37,49,51,54
18.11	43(1)	41(1)	sch 1 para 25(1), sch 6 para 26(1)	60(1)
18.12	sch 4 para 40	sch 3 para 11(3)	sch 4 para 12(3), sch 9 para 40	sch 5 para 12(3), sch 7 para 40
18.14	41(1), 48(1)	38(8), 44(1)	sch 1 paras 16(9),25(1), 31, sch 6 paras 19(1),30(1)	42(9),53(1),64(1)
18.17	31(2)	27(1), 31(6)	sch 1 paras 10(1),11(7), sch 6 para 12(2)	36(1),37(7), 46(2)
18.19(a)	sch 3 para 14, sch 4 paras 7,8, sch 5 paras 7,8	24	sch 1 para 7, sch 8 para 14,sch 9 paras 8,9, sch 10 paras 8,9	32, sch 6 para 14, sch 7 paras 8,9, sch 9 paras 8,9
18.19(b)	26	25	sch 1 para 8, sch 6 para 9	33, 34
18.19(c)	sch 4 paras 10,13, 36,42,51,64	27(1)(j)	sch 1 para 10(1)(j), sch 9 paras 11,14,37,38, 42,52,66	36(1)(j), sch 7 paras 11,14,37,38,42,52,66
18.19(d)	sch 4 para 20	sch 3 paras 6,7	sch 4 paras 7,8, sch 9 para 21	sch 5 paras 7,8, sch 7 para 21
18.19(e)	N/A	27(1)(j)(xv)	sch 1 para 10(1)(j)(xiii)	36(1)(j)(xiii)
18.20	39(3)	27(3)	sch 1 para 10(2), sch 6 para 17(3)	36(2), 51(3)
18.21	39(5), 32,45(9), sch 5 para 11	27(4), 30,41(3), sch 4 para 18	sch 1 para 10(3),21,25(3), sch 5 para 18,21(2)(j),(n), sch 6 paras 17(5),27(10), sch 10 para 12	36(3), 51(5), 56, 60(3), 61(10), sch 8 paras 18,21, sch 9 para 12

18.22	27(1)(c),(2), sch 4 para 56	27(1)(b), 28(1)(c),(2), sch 3 para 20	sch 1 para 10(1)(b), 18(1)(c),(2), sch 4 para 21, sch 9 para 58	36(1)(b), 54(1)(c),(2), sch 5 para 21, sch 7 para 58
18.23	sch 4 paras 12-13, 19,52-55	27(1)(e)-(h),(l), sch3 paras 1-5	sch 1 para 10(1)(e)-(h),(l), sch 4 paras 1-6, sch 9 paras 13-14,20,53-56	36(1)(e)-(h),(l), sch 5 paras 1-6, sch 7 paras 13-14,20,53-56
18.27	29(1)(a)	31(2),(3)	sch 1 para 11(2)-(4), sch 6 para 10(1)(a)	37(2)-(4),40,44(1)(a)
18.28	29(1)(b),(2),(3), 30(1)	31(2), 34	sch 1 paras 11(2),(3),14, sch 6 paras 10(1)(b), (2),(3),11(1)	37(2),(3), 40,44(1)(b), (2),(3)
18.30	34	32	sch 1 para 12(1), sch 3 para 9, sch 6 para 14(1), sch 8 paras 1(b),2	38(1), 48(1), sch 4 para 9, sch 6 paras 1(b),2
18.31	34(2)	32(2)	sch 1 para 12(2), sch 6 para 14(2)	38(2), 48(2)
18.32	34(1)	32(1)	sch 1 para 15(1), sch 6 para 16(1)	41(1), 50(1)
18.33	37(3)(a),(4),(7),(9)	36(2)(a), (3),(6),(8)	sch 1 para 23(2)(a), (3),(6),(8)	58(3)(a),(4),(7),(9)
18.34	37(3)(a),(4),(7)	36(2)(a),(3),(6)	sch 1 para 23(2)(a),(3),(6)	58(3)(a),(4),(7)
18.36	37(1),(3),(4), 35(1),(3)	36(1),(2),(3)	sch 1 paras 13(1),(2), 23(1),(2), sch 6 para 15(1),(3)	39(1),(2), 49(1),(3), 58(1),(3)
18.37	35(3),(6), 38	33(2),(4), 37	sch 1 paras 13(2),(5),24, sch 6 para 15(3),(6)	39(2),(5), 49(3),(6),59
18.39	35(3),(5), 37(1),(3),(11)	33(2),(5), 36(1),(2),(10)	sch 1 paras 13(2),(4),23(1), (2),(8),(10), sch 6 para 15(3),(5)	39(2),(4), 49(3),(5), 58(1),(3),(9),(11)
18.41	27(1),(c), 35(2), sch 3	28(1)(c), 33(1), sch 2	sch 1 paras 13(1),18(1)(c), sch 3, sch 6 para 15(2), sch 8	39(1), 49(2),54(1)(c), sch 4, sch 6
18.43	35(2), sch 3 paras 4-12	33(1), sch 2 paras 1-8	sch 1 paras 13(1), sch 3 paras 1-8, sch 6 para 15(2), sch 8 paras 4-12	39(1), 49(2), sch 4 paras 1-8, sch 6 paras 4-12
T18.1	35(2), sch 3 paras 4-12	33(1), sch 2 paras 1-8	sch 1 para 13(1), sch 3 paras 1-8, sch 6 para 15(2), sch 8 paras 4-12	39(1), 49(2), sch 4 paras 1-8, sch 6 paras 4-12
18.44	27	28	sch 1 para 18	54
18.45	28(5),(6)	29(5),(6)	sch 1 para 19(5),(6)	55(5),(6)
18.46	28(1),(2)	29(1),(2)	sch 1 para 19(1),(2)	55(1),(2)
18.47	28(1)(c),(11)	29(1)(c),(11)	sch 1 para 19(1)(c),(11)	55(1)(c),(11)
18.48	35(2), sch 3 para 18(1),(3), sch 4 para 56	33(1), sch 2 para 10(1),(3), sch 3 para 20	sch 1 para 13(1), sch 3 para 10(1),(3), sch 4 para 21, sch 6 para 15(2), sch 8 paras 18(1),(3), sch 9 para 58	39(1),49(2), sch 4 para 10(1),(3), sch 5 para 21, sch 6 para 18(1),(3), sch 7 para 58
18.49	sch 3 para 18(2)	sch 2 para 10(2)	sch 3 para 10(2), sch 8 paras 18(2)	sch 4 para 10(2), sch 6 para 18(2)

Para	Scotland CTS	CTS60+	Wales CTPW	CTRW
18.51	sch 4 paras 29-33, 37,57,62-63, sch 5 paras 11,22-23, 25,61-64	27(1), sch 4 paras 21,29	sch 1 para 10(1), sch 5 paras 21,28,sch 9 paras , 30-34,37,59,64-65, sch 10 paras 12,23-24,25,59-62	36(1), sch 7 paras 30-34, 37,59,64,65, sch 8 paras 21,29 sch 9 paras 12,23-25,61-64
18.52	39(1),(2)	27(1),(c),(d),(x)	sch 1 para 10(1)(c),(d),(x), sch 6 para 17(1),(2)	36(1)(c),(d),(x), 51(1),(2)
18.53	39(1),(2), sch 4 paras 25,26	27(1)(p),(v), sch 3 paras 8,9	sch 1 para 10(1)(p),(v), sch 4 paras 9,10, sch 6 para 17(1),(2), sch 9 paras 26,27	36(1)(p),(v), 51(1),(2), sch 5 paras 9,10, sch 7 paras 26,27
18.54	sch 4 paras 48,49	27(1)(o), sch 3 para 19	sch 1 para 10(1)(o), sch 4 para 20, sch 9 paras 49,50	36(1)(o), sch 5 para 20, sch 7 paras 49,50
18.55	49(2)	N/A	sch 9 paras 50(2)	sch 7 para 50(2)
18.56	45(6), sch 4 para 18	27(1)	sch 1 para 10(1), sch 6 para 27(7), sch 9 para 19	36(1),61(7), sch 7 para 19
18.58	sch 4 para 18	sch3 paras 13,14	sch 4 paras 14,15, sch 9 para 19	sch 5 paras 14,15, sch 7 para 19
18.59	45(6), sch 4 para 41	27(1)	sch 1 para 10(1), sch 6 para 27(7), sch 9 para 41	36(1),61(7), sch 7 para 41
18.61	34(2)(d), sch4 paras 4,5	32(2)(f)	sch 1 para 12(2),(f), sch 6 para 14(2)(d), sch 9 paras 5,6	38(2)(f), 48(2)(d), sch 7 paras 5,6
18.62	20, 53-65	N/A	sch 11 paras 3-15	22, 72-84
18.64	27(1)(b), 51	27(2), 28(1)(b)	sch 1 paras 18(1),(b),31, sch 6 para 33	54(1)(b),68,69
18.65	27(1)(b), 51	27(2), 28(1)(b)	sch 1 paras 18(1),(b),31, sch 6 para 33	54(1)(b),68,69
18.67	46	42	sch 1 para 26, sch 6 para 28	62
18.68	46	42	sch 1 para 26, sch 6 para 28	62
18.69	50	46	sch 1 para 30, sch 6 para 32	67
T18.2(a)	sch 5 para 3	sch 4 para 26	sch 5 para 26, sch 10 para 4	sch 8 para 26, sch 9 para 4
T18.2(b)	sch 5 para 6(b)	sch 4 para 4(b)	sch 5 para 4(b), sch 10 para 7(b)	sch 8 para 4(b), sch 9 para 7(b)
T18.2(c)	sch 5 para 30	sch 4 para 6	sch 5 para 6, sch 10 para 30	sch 8 para 6, sch 9 para 30
T18.2(d)	sch 5 para 6(a)	sch 4 para 4(a)	sch 5 para 4(a), sch 10 para 7(a)	sch 8 para 4(a), sch 9 para 7(a)
T18.2(e)	sch 5 para 4	sch 4 para 1	sch 5 para 1, sch 10 para 5	sch 8 para 1, sch 9 para 5
T18.2(f)	sch 5 para 32	sch 4 para 2	sch 5 para 2, sch 10 para 32	sch 8 para 2, sch 9 para 32
T18.2(g)	sch 5 para 33	sch 4 para 3	sch 5 para 3, sch 10 para 33	sch 8 para 3, sch 9 para 33
T18.2(h)	sch 5 para 5	N/A	sch 10 para 6	sch 9 para 6
T18.2(i)	sch 5 para 13	N/A	sch 10 para 14	sch 9 para 14
T18.2(j)	N/A	sch 4 paras 18,20(a)	sch 5 paras 18,20(a)	sch 8 paras 18,20(a)

T18.2(k)	sch 5 paras 9,10	sch 4 paras 5,9,10	sch 5 paras 5,9,10, sch 10 paras 10,11	sch 8 paras 5,9,10, sch 9 paras 10,11
18.70	45(9)	41(3)	sch 1 para 25(3), sch 5 paras 18,21,22, sch 6 para 27(10), sch 10 para 12	60(3),61(10), sch 8 paras 18,21,22, sch 9 para 12
18.71	sch 5 para 14	sch 4 para 8	sch 5 para 8, sch 10 para 15	sch 8 para 8, sch 9 para 15
18.72	sch 5 para 10	sch 4 paras 9,10	sch 5 paras 9,10, sch 10 para 11	sch 8 paras 9,10 sch 9 para 11
18.73	N/A	sch 4 paras 11,24,33	sch 5 paras 11,24,31	sch 8 paras 11,24,32
18.75	N/A	sch 4 para 17	sch 5 para 17	sch 8 para 17
18.76	sch 5 para 29	sch 4 para 16	sch 5 para 16, sch 10 para 29	sch 8 para 16, sch 9 para 29
19.1	82,83,91	61,63,71	sch 12 paras 1-7,12-18, sch 13 para 1	11,107, sch 1 paras 1-7,12-18
19.2	Not Scotland	Not Scotland	See text	See text
19.3	82	61	sch 13 para 1(1)	107(1)
19.4	See text	See text	sch 13 para 1(2)-(6)	107(2)-(6)
19.5	See 19.4	See 19.4	sch 13 para 1(2)-(6)	107(2)-(6)
19.6	See 19.4	See 19.4	sch 13 para 1(3),(5),(6)	107(3),(5),(6)
19.7	83(1)-(6)	2(1), 63(1)-(6), 64(1),(2)	sch 12 paras 2,3,13,14	2(1), sch 1 paras 2,3
19.8	See text	See text	See text	See text
19.9	87,88	67,68	sch 13 para 6	112
19.10	86(1),(4)	66(1),(4)	sch 13 para 5(1),(4),(6)	111(4),(6)
19.12	86(2),(3)	66(2),(3)	sch 13 para 5(5),(7)	111(5),(7)
19.13	Not Scotland	Not Scotland	sch 13 para 5(2),(3)	111(2),(3)
19.15	See text	See text	See text	See text
19.16	83(1),(6), 84(1)-(3)	63(1)-(6), 64(1)-(3)	sch 12 paras 2-4,13	sch 1 paras 2-4,13
19.18	83(3),(5), 84(3)-(5)	63(3),(5), 64(1)-(3)	sch 12 paras 4-7, sch 13 paras 2(3)-(5), 5(4),(6)	111(4),(6) sch 1 paras 4-7
19.21	83(1),(2), 84(6)	63(1),(2), 64(6)	sch 12 paras 3,13(7)	sch 1 paras 3,13(7)
19.22	85	65	sch 13 para 2	108
19.23	Not Scotland	Not Scotland	sch 11 para 13	sch 1 para 15
T19.1	85	65	sch 13 para 2	108
19.24	2(1)	2(1)	2(1)	2(1)
19.25	85(1)(d)	65(1)(d)	sch 13 para 2(1)(f)	108(1)(f)
19.27	85(1)(c)	65(1)(c)	sch 13 para 2(1)(e)	108(1)(e)
19.29	85(1)(a)	65(1)(a)	sch 13 para 2(1)(a),(c),(2),(8)	108(1)(a),(c),(2),(8)
19.31	85(1)(b)	65(1)(b)	sch 13 para 2(1)(b),(d)	108(1)(b),(d)
19.33	85(1)(e)	65(1)(e)	sch 13 para 2(1)(g)	108(1)(g)
19.34	85(3),(5),(6)	65(2),(3)	sch 13 para 2(6),(7)	108(6),(7)
19.36	See text	See text	Not Wales	Not Wales
19.40	Not Scotland	62	sch 13 para 3	109

Para	Scotland CTS	CTS60+	Wales CTPW	CTRW
19.42	85(7),(8)	No equiv	See text	See text
19.45	80(1),(2)	58(1),(2)	Not Wales	Not Wales
19.47	80(1)	58(1)	Not Wales	Not Wales
19.48	Not Scotland	Not Scotland	See text	See text
19.49	80(2)	58(2)	Not Wales	Not Wales
19.50	Not Scotland	Not Scotland	See text	See text
19.51	Not Scotland	Not Scotland	sch 13 para 10(2),(3),(4)	116(2),(3),(4)
20.2	89(1),(4)	69(1),(4)	sch 13 para 7(1)	113(1)
T20.1	89	69	sch 13 para 7	113
20.4	89(1)	69(1)	sch 12 para 11, sch 13 para 7(2)	113(2), sch 1 para 11
20.5	89(1)	69(1)	sch 13 para 7(2)	113(2)
20.7	Not Scotland	Not Scotland	sch 13 para 5(1)	111(1)
20.8	Not Scotland	Not Scotland	sch 13 para 9(1)(b),(2)-(4)	115(1)(b),(2)-(4)
20.11	81(1)	59(1)	sch 1 para 40(1),(2), sch 6 para 46(1),(2)	115(1),(5),(6)
20.14	81(2),(3)	59(2),(3)	sch 1 para 40(3),(4), sch 6 para 46(3),(4)	105(3),(4)
T20.3	Not Scotland	60	sch 1 para 41	106
20.15	Not Scotland	60	sch 1 para 41	106
20.18	81(1)	59(1)	sch 1 para 40(1),(2), sch 6 para 46(1),(2)	105(1),(2)
20.22	Not Scotland	Not Scotland	sch 1 para 22, sch 6 para 23	57
20.26	81(7)	59(7)	Not Wales	Not Wales
20.27	68,73	49	sch 1 para 32, sch 6 paras 34,39	2(1), 85,86,92,93,98
20.28	Not Scotland	Not Scotland	See text	See text
20.30	74,75	50,51	sch 1 paras 33,34, sch 6 paras 35,36,40,41	87,88,94,95,99,100
T20.5	2(1), 68,73	2(1), 68	sch 1 para 32, sch 6 paras 34,39	85,86,92,93,98
20.32	Not Scotland	See text	Not Wales	Not Wales
20.33	72,77	53	sch 1 para 36, sch 6 paras 38,43	90,97,102
20.34	71,76	52	sch 1 paras 35,38, sch 6 paras 37,42,44	89,96,101,103
20.35	Not Scotland	55	sch 1 para 37	91
20.37	86(1),(4)	66(1),(4)	sch 13 para 5(4),(6)	111(4),(6)
20.41	Not Scotland	Not Scotland	See text	See text
20.42	Not Scotland	Not Scotland	See text	See text
20.43	Not Scotland	Not Scotland	See text	See text
20.46	Not Scotland	Not Scotland	See text	See text
Ch 21	See text	See text	See text	See text

Index

References in the index are to paragraph numbers (not page numbers), except that 'A' refers to appendices, 'T' refers to tables in the text and 'Ch' refers to a chapter.